Browne-Brown

Descendants of England, West Indies Maryland, New England, and the American Frontier

James W. Brown

HERITAGE BOOKS
2020

HERITAGE BOOKS
AN IMPRINT OF HERITAGE BOOKS, INC.

Books, CDs, and more—Worldwide

For our listing of thousands of titles see our website
at
www.HeritageBooks.com

Published 2020 by
HERITAGE BOOKS, INC.
Publishing Division
5810 Ruatan Street
Berwyn Heights, Md. 20740

Copyright © 2006 James W. Brown

All rights reserved. No part of this book may be reproduced or transmitted in any form or by any means, electronic or mechanical, including photocopying, recording or by any information storage and retrieval system without written permission from the author, except for the inclusion of brief quotations in a review.

International Standard Book Number
Paperbound: 978-0-7884-4096-0

To Phyllis

TABLE OF CONTENTS

Foreword	vii
Introduction	ix
First Generation	1
Second Generation	3
Third Generation	5
Fourth Generation	7
Fifth Generation	13
Sixth Generation	15
Seventh Generation	19
Eighth Generation	23
Ninth Generation	31
Tenth Generation	45
Eleventh Generation	69
Twelfth Generation	87
Thirteenth Generation	117
Fourteenth Generation	157
Fifteenth Generation	199
Sources	227
Index	231

FOREWORD

"IN THE BEGINNING . . ." a favorite uncle would proclaim, *"everybody's name was Brown. But as mankind began to sin, those who left that straight and narrow path just had to go off and take other names."*

It was a family joke, because we all knew better.

The present study traces a very human family for fifteen generations, from Central England to the establishment of England's first colonies in the New World, to the forging of a new country, and then overland and into the American West. It is a saga encompassing some five centuries and much history. The family is Browne – later Brown – and those connected with it.

Genealogies are bittersweet things. While they offer names, places, dates, facts found in wills, land sales or court actions, they often give us too little about the lives our forebears led, the hows or the whys that filled their days. The present study doesn't satisfactorily fill that void but it may shed some light within. Bluebloods may boast that their family "goes way back." All families do. The more notable might have left copious records and praiseful histories, while others, not less deserving, passed through their life spans like a plough through the sea. We have both, and they all deserve our attention. Whether there is fame and legend, or only a scrap of information here and there, those forebears all merit our honor and respect. It is the family historian's hope to find whatever trace that can be found and make some sense of it, to assemble the few shards and imagine a larger shape. A life, a family, a story.

I'd like to puff about the years I devoted to this study, but the credit should rather go to those who helped and those who preceded. They are cited and listed. Some are friends, relatives, fellow searchers whom I have pestered without mercy. Others I only know through their written works and who may have passed this way years, decades, centuries ago. My deepest gratitude goes to all.

Special thanks go to my wife Phyllis who has given her advice, always unerring, and to Charles Ford and Debbie Riley, expert readers.

There are errors here, and omissions. For them I apologize. There are also disagreements and discrepancies which I have tried to bring to light and if possible, sort out. If I have failed to please or satisfy, remember Bacchylides who simply said of complaints: "The road is broad."

INTRODUCTION

Few dramas play well without some sort of backdrop or scenery. Following are some brief views of the times and places that framed our forbears' lives.

THE DERBYSHIRE YEARS

England's County Derbyshire (pronounced "Darbysher") or later Derby ("Darby") lies in the East Midlands, near the forests once occupied, says legend, by Robin Hood. Its northern hills were known for mining since prehistory. Brownes and before that the de Buruns (Rudolph and Roger), knights, were found in the area at the time of William's Norman invasion of 1066, and the name was connected with the landed gentry for many years, descendants of the triumphant Norman French conquerors who slowly took on the English language. The historian John Pym Yeatman's *Feudal History of the County of Derby* noted that since movement of individuals and families was practically unknown during the Middle Ages, the idea that the later Derbyshire Brownes dated back to those Norman days in an unbroken line is not unreasonable. Snelston, seat of our Browne family, lies less than three miles southwest of Ashbourne. It is now, as it was then, a small rural village. The Brownes had an estate and considerable tracts of land there and in the near countryside.

Sixteenth Century England's Jacobean Period of the House of Tudor was punctuated by the reigns of Henry VIII and Elizabeth I, although Henry VII, Edward VI and Mary I had their time on stage as well. Henry VIII broke with the Catholic Church and established the Church of England, less on theological grounds (as the Lutheran and Calvinist movements) than on lust and pique. In fact, Henry's Anglicanism remained Catholic in much of its form except for its defiance of the Pope, and only became somewhat Protestant with the passage of time. A long cold war with France and Spain heated every few years into battle and costly campaigns. England controlled portions of France, and Spain controlled much of the Low Country provinces. England was forever strapped for cash to maintain her troops and outposts. Spain's attempted invasion in 1588 meant panic, then triumph as the *Gran Armada* floundered and burned. Henry's daughter Elizabeth sent an expeditionary force to establish a foothold in the Low Countries under the generalship of the Earl of Leicester (pronounced "Lester"). His Lieutenant Governor there was Sir William Browne. Sir William's was a turbulent life. At one point he became embroiled in the vicious Elizabethan court politics and briefly feared for his head.

During the ensuing two centuries successive English rulers imposed their own religion, now Anglican, now Catholic. Under Elizabeth's rule Anglicanism was the official church but Catholic uprisings were feared. Elizabeth cracked down on "recusants" or persons who would not adhere to Anglican dogma. Those so accused were imprisoned, their lands and incomes confiscated (for the Crown's use of course; Elizabeth needed the excuse to grab money). Many nobles and gentry were ruined and fled into exile. One historian believed that such was the case of our Brownes, but another believed not. It is clear, however, that the family later sold off its Derbyshire holdings and moved to London where Sir William's son Percy apparently lived as an arms merchant, for at one point he sold cannon to the ocean colony at Providence.

THE BERMUDA YEARS

One Robert Rich and some other voyagers, bound for Virginia on the "Sea Venture," were shipwrecked in 1609 on an uninhabited Atlantic island. The castaways remained there for forty-two weeks, where they constructed two vessels of the local cedar, and with them returned to England. Their account served as inspiration for Shakespeare's "Tempest."

That island, Bermuda, first took its name from an early Spanish explorer named Juan Bermúdez. It later took the name of an English explorer, Somers, and was known as the Somers Islands. Somehow Bermuda stuck. The site in mention is a cluster of islands (thus it is often and more properly referred to as "the Bermudas") some twenty-two miles in length, far from anything else, and surrounded by treacherous shoals. For some time it was believed haunted because of sounds heard on its shores, probably strange birds, or pigs left by pirates and shipwrecks. It was finally established as a colony by England, although the Spanish and French often threatened. During the 1600s Bermuda became a way-station for ships bound for "Virginia" (a loose term for anything on the mainland), or the island colonies including Barbados, and briefly, "Providence" near the Spanish-held isthmian coast.

The Bermuda Company was founded in 1615, financed in England by investors who wanted a good return on their money in the form of tobacco, fruit, lumber, or whatever the place could produce. Soon after its founding, Bermuda was divided into eight townships or "tribes" (after the tribes of Israel), all named after notables in England. Each tribe was held by fifty shares, owned by "adventurers" or investors in England. Sir Nathaniel Rich of London, the shipwrecked Robert's brother, owned twenty-two shares in Southampton Tribe on the southeast coast and was the largest investor of the Bermuda Company. The Rich family invested heavily in the project; their cousin Robert Rich, later second Earl of Warwick, was yet another heavy investor. Robert Browne of Bermuda, Percy's son, received one Bermuda share from his uncle Nathaniel Rich's 1635 will, and another share from his aunt Elizabeth, a Rich sister who had married Robert's father, Percy Browne. Of the above, only the old soldier Robert Rich and young Robert Browne went to live on the island.

It was a small group of wealthy and aristocratic London-based Puritans who made up the several overseas colonies' absentee ownership, managing their companies in what would today be called interlocking directorships, with charters awarded by the King. (James I was happy to have the bothersome Puritans' attentions directed elsewhere.) Those "adventurers" desired not only profit, but also a spreading of their faith. As for religion, the Puritan Massachusetts Governor John Winthrop noted in his journal of 1634 concerning a report that "there was a verye great change in Bermuda [. . .]: diverse lewde persons beinge become good Christians; they have 3 ministers, (one a Scotche man) who take great paynes amonge them. & had lately (by prayer & fastinge) dispossessed one possessd with a devill." This pious miracle had been wrought before the Puritan minister Reverend Robert Browne stepped into a Bermuda pulpit, but it sheds a light on the thought of the times. There were cases of sorcery and witchcraft that were tried in court, together with other offenses. Ministers (called by the honorific title "Mister" usually reserved for the well-born) were powerful public figures, hired in London by the Company and often fiery and arrogant in their dealings with the flocks. They sat on the governing council, and held "glebe" property, land with tenants which brought in income over and above their contractual stipends. Even before the Puritan uprisings in England, several Bermudan ministers, to the horror of the Council, sought to establish an Independent (Puritan) church. When the Cromwellian dictatorship prevailed, churches and churchmen adhered to Puritan dogma. So did, necessarily, the Island. Robert Browne, although a Puritan, appeared to be a moderate voice and was a well received figure among the Bermudans; shortly before his death at about forty, the Council offered him a stipend to stay on in his post. The Puritan dictatorship ended in England soon after Reverend Browne died, and his survivors may have suffered under the abrupt return to mainstream Anglicanism.

It might be fairly stated that early Bermuda did not thrive. In England Sir Nathaniel Rich was surely the ablest of the managing Company, and did what he could while he lived, but many in that well-bred London group sat through meetings in solemn confusion if they attended at all. The Company governed by means of an unending stream of detailed, often contradictory, letters. They instituted a curious hybrid of feudalism and at the same time a largely bungled attempt at a planned, i.e., socialist, economy. Unlike the New England ventures which were populated by yeoman farmers and families, Bermuda's population was made up mostly of tenants, servants, and slaves. On the island there was also a small cadre of well-born "misters," who held managerial or overseeing posts, or did little. European style crops failed, rats devoured the grain, officials were often paid sporadically, tenants and settlers brought there under indenture complained of the hard work, scrapped among themselves, and mutinied against the governor. Despite a strong church authority, drink flowed freely. When "assizes" day rolled around, court was held and some were whipped, others mutilated or tortured, a few were hanged. Sugar and tobacco thrived, and became the economic mainstay of the settlement, but Bermudan tobacco was often inferior in quality and the market was soon overtaken by competition elsewhere, and prices plunged. In order to protect the investors' expectations, trade was restricted to Bermuda Company ships, but that directive (among others) was often disregarded. As late as the mid-1600s Bermudan houses were mostly of palm thatched roofs without glass windows, and only a few houses such as the Governor's, the Sheriff's and the Minister's were of sound construction. Food was usually plentiful but there was little surplus in the way of fruits or vegetables to export. Clothing, all imported from England, was in great scarcity and the poor went about in tatters. Company supply ships known as "magazines" arrived amid joy or consternation, depending on what the Company saw fit to send. The governing Somers Company dwindled and died by the 1680s, when Bermuda became a crown colony at about the same time as also occurred (for other reasons) in New England.

THE CONNECTICUT YEARS

Reasons were varied for the "Great Migration" to New England, the Chesapeake Bay area and the West Indies. England embarked on a new and ruinous European war in 1618. Wool was more profitable than crops and the English gentry expelled tenant farmers from the land to make room for sheep, leaving a homeless horde to wander the roads and infest the cities. The Stuart monarchs (James I, 1603-1625, and Charles I, 1625-1649) firmly believed in absolute rule, suppressed Parliament and levied fees to pay for their wars. The Puritans saw in the New World an opportunity to escape the Church of England's lingering "Papist" practices and to form their own version of England's Church in purified form. Those of Plymouth and Massachusetts Bay are best known today, but at the time the West Indies seemed a better choice to many for their climate and fertility, and particularly for the golden harvests of the day, tobacco, sugar and fruit. Some, however, chose the northern coast, including an area at the Connecticut River where they founded the towns of Windsor, Wethersfield and Hartford. They were soon joined by more settlers from the northern colonies who had been ejected or who could not tolerate the Massachusetts weather, government, neighbors or theology. Puritans were a quarrelsome lot.

As in the case of the other colonies, real ownership lay in the hands of wealthy London stockholders, many of those same English "grandees" (as one historian called them) who held shares in Virginia or the islands as well, and who expected a profit from raw materials imported to England as well as their monopoly on finished goods sent out. Since profit was involved and the colonies might prove a thorn in Spain's, France's, and Holland's side, the Crown gave royal approval to the colonies' charters and establishment. The colonies also afforded a welcome outlet for the growing ranks of troublesome Puritans. Robert Rich, second Earl of Warwick, was a moving force, as was his cousin Sir Nathaniel Rich. If the Puritans could not have their godlike "City on the Hill" in England or the Netherlands, they hoped it would take root in the New World. Cambridge University's Thomas Hooker, a Puritan firebrand, led the formation of the Connecticut Colony's thoroughly theocratic government. In England, so dangerous had the Church of England's Archbishop Laud considered Hooker, that Hooker barely missed arrest twice before sailing to America. It was Hooker who sponsored Nathaniel Browne's move from England to Connecticut where Browne founded a city and a prolific line of descendants. Nathaniel Browne was Percy Browne's son and Robert Browne's brother.

This study centers on the Maryland branch of the family and somewhat slights that of New England. Others, notably D. L. Jacobus in *The American Genealogist* have dealt with that line to the degree that what appears here is almost wholly derivative but well supported in evidence. I could not reliably check data from some other Connecticut and New England sources that came to my attention.

THE MARYLAND YEARS

Maryland's birth and early years closely reflected England's ongoing turmoil, but its early history differed from other colonies in important ways. As if to add to the longstanding religious conflict, King Charles I, a Protestant, abruptly cut away a handsome slice of northeastern Virginia, including the fish- and oyster-rich waters of upper Chesapeake Bay, and gave it to his converted Catholic friend Sir George Calvert, or Lord Baltimore as he had been dubbed in Ireland. The King made Calvert and his heirs "proprietors," or virtual feudal owners, of the new colony that was named Maryland to honor Queen Henrietta Maria (although some claimed it was named for the Virgin Mary). Neither George Calvert nor his son Cecil Calvert, the second Lord Baltimore, ever visited that faraway land, but they set it on its wobbly course. Both Lords Calvert hoped that the much-persecuted Catholics in England might find a refuge there, and that members of the several other Christian sects which were not welcome in New England or Virginia might find a home in the colony. Indeed, although Catholics were a minority of those who came to Maryland, among those Catholics who did emigrate were the leaders and richest of the colonists, many of whom were given large tracts of choice land. Maryland still reflects that in its old prominent Catholic families. From the first years, the Proprietor and his government sought to include all Christian sects, and through an "Act of Toleration" prohibited the execution, imprisonment or whipping on religious grounds of "dissenting" Christians, meaning Baptist, Presbyterians, Puritans, Quakers, provided that they did not blaspheme against the Holy Trinity, the Virgin Mary, or Jesus. A noble impulse, but in practice the "dissenters" did not get along much better than they did in England.

To populate the colony, the Lord Proprietor granted large holdings, called manors, to influential Englishmen as well as Catholics; other lands were awarded to those who would come and also pay for passage of still more immigrants. Under this "head-right" system, those transported would then be beholden as indentured servants for about four or five years to the landowner who had paid their passage, after which time that person could in turn be granted about fifty acres, often a suit of clothes, an axe, two hoes, and three barrels of corn. Notwithstanding the relative tolerance, with the large land holdings of a few and a servant class of the many, the social system implanted was close to the old feudalism that England at that time had begun to outgrow. All landowners, large and small, paid annual quit-rents to Lord Baltimore, a handsome income for His Lordship in England.

In addition to those coming for, or with, land, there were many indentured servants, tradesmen, persons transported for political or religious trouble, and petty criminals. (The serious criminals were of course hung in England.) Slaves in Maryland were few until after 1700, when the tobacco trade grew and added labor was required. During the Puritan dictatorship in England, partisans of the English King's exiled son made battle, lost, and many of those captured and not hanged were transported to the colonies, including Maryland.

Tobacco: the English, for a time, called it "sot weed," but the old Caribbean Indian name for it eventually won over. Early Maryland's history is entwined with the story of that foul herb, to which Europe was soon addicted. Tobacco was hauled by the ton from plantations to the docks in large barrels called hogsheads, rolled and pushed by men or pulled by horses over the "rolling roads," for export to England. Not only did Maryland's economy depend on tobacco; it was the only official currency for purchases large and small, even after 1683 when crown currency was introduced. Fines in court were often expressed in pounds of tobacco. (Selling strong liquor on the Sabbath was punishable by a fine of 2,000 pounds of tobacco "except in cases of absolute necessity," which judging by the brisk trade in rum, was benignly enforced.) In 1675 Abell Browne purchased the plantation "Harwood" for 7,000 pounds of tobacco.

Rumors often spread among Protestants that the Catholics were plotting to inspire Indians to massacre them. Catholics worried when the Proprietary faltered or was suspended (which was often), that their properties would be lost in a change of government. There were revolts and counter-revolts, and during England's years of revolution, there was conflict between "Roundheads" who supported the British Parliament and Puritan Cromwell, and "Cavaliers," supporters of the Crown. The successive Lords Baltimore controlled Maryland through a series of governors and councils of leading citizens except in 1645-1647, 1654-1657 and 1689-1691 when Puritans gained control. In 1691, with England's monarchy reinstalled, the colony reverted to the Crown, and when in 1715 the current Lord Baltimore converted to Anglicanism, the proprietary was returned to him, where it remained until the American Revolution.

Maryland's first capital was out on a lonely point where the Potomac River and Chesapeake Bay empty into the sea. It was named St. Mary's and was Catholic dominated. In 1649 a group of Puritans who had been banished from Virginia founded a new town northward on the Chesapeake's coast, and gave it its first, typically Puritan, name, Providence.

The area surrounding Providence was made into a county in 1650, and took on the second Lord Baltimore's wife's maiden name, Anne Arundel (it was later divided into numerous smaller entities, including Baltimore County formed in 1659). St. Mary's, as a provincial capital, never prospered, having no good port waters. So in 1692 Providence or Anne Arundel Town, later known as Annapolis as it was incorporated in 1708, became Maryland's capital and all the colony's records, wrapped in hides and under guard, were delivered to the sheriff of Anne Arundel County. Providence was a natural port, the best in Chesapeake Bay; roads to Frederick and Baltimore had existed since 1660 and so the town was soon the principal port of exit for the region's burgeoning commerce in tobacco and of entry for the growing numbers of immigrants. In 1697 a brick state house went up and in 1704 promptly burned, with its precious early records. Some claims to land and property had to be re-recorded by testimony, but other vital records were lost forever.

By this time the Lord Proprietor's government was walking a fine line. In 1692 Sir Lionel Copley was appointed governor, and declared the Church of England to be the Established Church of Maryland. This meant that the Church and its clergy would be supported by the government through taxes and that only members of that church could hold public office, even though non-Anglicans were not to be prosecuted if they professed some Christian belief. Thus encouraged, Quakers and others began to arrive in increasing numbers, and population grew. Abell Browne lived and died in Anne Arundel. He was appointed High Sheriff under Copley, so his status as an Anglican is unquestionable. Both he and his son Robert were not only upstanding members of the Church of England (the nettlesome Puritan experiment of their forebears having run its course); they were, additionally, numbered among the elite landholding class.

THE AMERICAN FRONTIER YEARS

Maryland's many border disputes with Virginia were resolved in 1732, at which time some of its land was returned to Virginia. In the mid-1700s Abell Browne's grandson Abel Brown and his family took up property and settled in that portion of west Baltimore County which became Carroll County. Having abandoned the comparatively cosmopolitan coastal region at the colony's capital Annapolis, they plunged into the backland where a loaded weapon was always at hand. The French and Indian War brought fresh threats of Indian attack and many settlers retreated to coastal cities from fear of attack. Bachelors were subject to a yearly tax to pay for the government's expenses of defense, and all able-bodied males served in the colonial militia. Roads were few. War with England came. Abel Brown supported the Revolution with his oath and his sons with their bodies. There the Browns remained, persevered and prospered. Most certainly they multiplied; Abel Brown himself contributed vigorously to the population's growth. The old British law of primogeniture required that property be only inherited by the eldest surviving son, so unless a place could be found in the military, professions or trades, the other sons were forced to seek their fortunes elsewhere. After independence the new states began to abandon the law of primogeniture, but land was limited.. Some headed west after the Revolution, and even more followed after the War of 1812. On the new frontier they were joined by the sons and families of New England who were also finding their pickings slim and good land near the northern coast growing scarce. As conditions permitted, those fortune seekers helped occupy and populate Ohio, Indiana, Illinois, Kentucky, Missouri and territories westward. With the Revolution's new freedoms of worship, many Americans, including the Browns, relaxed their adherence to the Anglican Church. They became Baptists, Methodists, or nothing at all. They were free. They were Americans. Their stories, if we could find them, are here. Let us honor them all.

FIRST GENERATION

---

1. William BROWNE, born about 1475. William died about 1540 in Snelston, Derbyshire, England. His family was of estates near Snelston, Derbyshire, a town just southwest of Ashbourne in the Archbishopric of Derbyshire and Diocese of Lichfield. William Browne's will of 13 Apr 1540 (Diocese Registry at Lichfield) named Thomas Browne Senior and Jarvis Calvert as executors, and mentioned Thomas Browne son and Margaret daughter [-in-law]. This line was discussed by John Pym Yeatman in *The Browns of Bechworth Castle*: ..., 1903., Chs. IX, "The Brownes of Snelston," and X, "On the Early History of the Brownes of Derbyshire," and by Scull and Jacobus, to be mentioned later. Yeatman earlier wrote *The Feudal History of the County of Derby*, 1886. In both he offered his belief that the Browne family was of the oldest gentried families of the county. Although Yeatman, in his caution, did not attempt to outline an earlier pedigree than William, he repeatedly mentioned possible connections among the county's Brownes (under various Norman variations of spelling) as early as Rudulph de Burun, listed in William the Conqueror's 11th Century *Domesday Book*, continuing with Roger de Buron, a knight during the reigns of Henry II and Richard I, an Elias Brown, archer at the Battle of Agincourt in 1415, and perhaps a Lord Mayor of London — or two — as the following suggests.

The New England Browns, descendants of Connecticut's Nathaniel Browne, held a family legend that they were descended from a Sir Stephen Browne, Lord Mayor of London. In fact, it was a descendant's query to the New England Historical and Genealogical Society that led the genealogist G. D. Scull of Oxford to write and donate a treatise regarding the Browne and allied Rich families, which that society still owns in original manuscript *(Sir William Browne, Knight, 1556-1610; and Sir Nathaniel Rich, Knight, 1636*, 1882). In it, Scull proposed that Sir Stephen Browne, Sheriff of London in 1431, Lord Mayor in 1439 and 1448, was a grandson of Sir Anthony Browne, "K.B. [Knight Bachelor, a title given to knights of royal orders who are not peers] at the court of Richard II 1377," and probable son of John Browne of New Castle upon Tyne. Scull based his supposition on the resemblance of the arms granted to the Snelston Brownes and those of the Bechworth Brownes, themselves descended from Sir Stephen's brother Sir Robert Browne, and similar arms on Brown gravestones found in New England reinforced the possibility (Scull, pp. 81-2). It may then be, Scull declared, that William Browne was a near descendant of Sir Stephen, who was a resident of Derbyshire when not living in London. All very tenuous of course, but worthy of note.

Derbyshire County Court Rolls (held at Britain's Public Records Office or P.R.O , now called National Archives) include these from possible Snelston ancestors: 588/49 "2 Henry VIII [1511], Snelston, William Browne"; P.R.O 590/49 ,4 Henry VIII [1513] Snelston,- "William Browne, prosecuted for an offense against brewing"; Subs. 91/195 14 and 15 Henry VIII [1523, 1524] Snelston 1525 – "Thomas Browne £10 Land, Wm. Browne (goods) 40s."; Court Rolls P.R.O. 604/50, 23 Henry VIII [1532], Snelston 1536 - "Thomas Browne, Frankpledge, William Browne, on Jury"; Subs. 92/245 (wrongly dated at the P.R.O. as 23 Elizabeth, according to Yeatman who believed that the date is probably 35 Henry VIII, 1540) Snelston, 1554- "Thomas Browne, in lands £8, William Browne, in goods"; 91/152, 35 Henry VIII [1544] , Snelston, 1543- "Thomas Browne, sen., goods, £9. Thomas Browne, jun., goods, 40s " (Yeatman, pp. 90-91). These last were taxes, large sums at that time and evidence of wealth. William Browne's will of 13 Apr 1540 (Diocese Registry at Lichfield) named Thomas Browne Senior and Jarvis Calvert as executors, and mentioned Thomas Browne son and Margaret daughter [-in-law] (Yeatman 92). Children:

    2   i.   Thomas (about 1499 - about 1544)
    3   ii.   Margaret (daughter-in-law)

The two earlier genealogists just mentioned were approximate contemporaries but Yeatman did not know of Scull's efforts, nor vice versa, Although they produced similar pedigrees, they yielded far different biographical sketches, clearly based on different sources, as will be noted in following pages.

BROWNE OF SNELSTON

SECOND GENERATION

Family of William BROWNE (1)

2. Thomas BROWNE, son, born about 1499 in Snelston, Derbyshire, England. Thomas died about 1544 in Snelston, Derbyshire, England. The barrister and historian John Pyme Yeatman spent considerable effort in study of the Derbyshire Brownes, who were allowed to bear the arms of the well-known Brownes of Bechworth [now Beechworth] Castle in County Surrey. That permission was granted to the Derbyshire Brownes at the Herald's visitation of 1552, and Yeatman sniffed, asserting that it was "just such a pedigree as a soldier encamped in the Low Countries might scratch upon his shield with the point of his sword" (Yeatman, "The Brownes of Snelston," Ch. IX, *The Brownes of Bechworth Castle*, p. 89). Yeatman's chronology is faulty; in 1552 William would have been a child, certainly not a soldier "encamped in the Low Countries." The arms were granted to Nicolas Browne, William's father. Furthermore, Sir William did not "encamp"; his Flushing home was the city's palace (Stadhaus) where, according to letters, he entertained nobility.

Yeatman allowed that in every likelihood "the Brownes of Derby are from the family of Bechworth Castle [. . .], and from the elder branch of it, Sir George Browne, of that place, whose fourth brother it was who was progenitor of the Viscount's [Montague] family" (Yeatman, *Feudal History*, p. 6). That family descended from Henry, Earl of Derby, a Plantagenet and kin to the later Kings Henry. It might be then suggested (Yeatman continued to speculate) that the Browne line issued from Sir Anthony Browne K.B. whose son was Sir Robert Browne, father of Thomas Brown Knight. Sir Thomas was beheaded in 1460. His son was George Browne (Sheriff of Kent, d 1577). Following were Walter Brown and Mary Gvar, who in turn had sons Thomas, Richard and Walter. Sir George's brother was Sir Anthony Brown, first Viscount Montague, so dubbed by the very Catholic Queen Mary; nevertheless the following Viscounts Montague remained staunchly Catholic, even during the rein of Queen Elizabeth, and may have given Yeatman his errant thoughts about our Brownes' supposed Catholicism.

No will or administration survives of Thomas Browne. This line comes per Scull, Yeatman, and D. L. Jacobus, "The House of Rich," *The American Genealogist*, 21 (1944), pp. 234-8; 22 (1945), pp. 27-37. 157-165, 240-8; 23 (1946), pp. 101-9. Yeatman could not certify Nicholas as a son of Thomas, saying that "there is an unfortunate gap in the wills and no proof," but Jacobus, writing almost a century later and having read Scull, had no such qualm.

Thomas married Margaret CHETHAM or CHATHAM, born about 1503 in Of Snelston, Derbyshire, England. Daughter of --- Chetham, "of the family of Chetham near Manchester and related to Humphrey Chetham founder of the Cheatham Free library and Blue Coat School at Manchester" (Jacobus, Pt. III, p. 157; Waters, p. 873). They had the following children:

4	i.	Ralf (- before 1587)
5	ii.	Nicolas (1525 - about 1587)
6	iii.	Thomas

3. Margaret BROWNE, Daughter. Per Yeatman, p. 92.

SUMMARY OF PUBLISHED BROWNE PEDIGREES

Yeatman, in *The Browns of Bechworth Castle*, p. 89, produced this after the Herald's pedigree.

Thomas Browne of Snelston = Margaret, dau. of Chatham of Lancaster
    CH: Rudulphus
          Nicolas of Snelston = Eleanor dau. of Ralph Shirley of Snelston
              CH: *William = a Dutchwoman*
                      CH: *William*
                  Gertrude
        Thomas

Yeatman (p. 92) then appended an earlier pedigree of his own device:

William Browne of Snelston
    CH: *Thomas Browne the Elder*
              CH: *Thomas Browne the Younger* [Thomas Browne of Snelston, above]
        Margaret

Scull (*Sir William Browne*, p. 80), independently produced this pedigree which joined Yeatman's two, added descendants, but did not include Thomas' father William:

Thomas Browne of Snelston = Magaret daughter to ----- Chatham
    CH: *Rudulphus Browne*
          Nicholas Browne = Elianor Shirley
              CH: *Sir William Browne = Mary Savage*
                    CH: *William Browne*
                            Anne Browne
                            Barbara Browne
                            Percy Brown = Rich Dau.
                            CH: *Nathaniel Browne*
                                        Robert Browne
                                        Samuel Browne
                                        ----- *Browne*
                      Mary Browne
                Gertrude Browne
    Thomas Browne

THIRD GENERATION

Family of Thomas BROWNE (2) and Margaret CHETHAM

4. Ralf BROWNE, Grandson. Ralf died before 1587 in Snelston, Derbyshire, England. Mentioned in Nicolas Browne's will of 24 Jan 1587 as "my late brother" (Yeatman 93), and in pedigree, Yeatman 89. Jacobus (Pt. III, p. 158) adds that he was probably the Ralph buried 18 Apr 1577 in which case Robert b 1587 and Edward b 1602 were not his sons. His name was Latinized as "Radulphus" in the family pedigree. Also Rauph in Snelston Vital Records Index. Children:

    7   i.   Robert (1587-)
    8   ii.   ature;Edward (1602-)

5. Nicolas BROWNE Esquire, Grandson, born in 1525 in Snelston, Derbyshire, England. Nicolas died about 18 Jan 1587 in Snelston, Derbyshire, England (date of burial). "Easter, 4 and 5 Phillip and Mary [1557/8], Nicolas Browne fined [taxed] with George Vernon, K[nigh]t, and Matilde his wife, for land called Milneholme Meadow, and Pipehaye, for which Nicolas agreed to pay a rent of 47s. and 8d. This is the first certain notice of the name of Nicolas" (Yeatman 92). In a deed dated 8 Jan 28 Elizabeth (1586), George Allen married Barbara Vernon, daughter-in-law of Nicolas (Yeatman 93), of his wife's first marriage. The will of 24 Jan 1587 of Nicolas Browne Esq. (at Lichfield Diocese Registry) gave to his wife Ellenor lands in Snellston [sic] and Staffordshire for life, paying £6 13s 4d yearly to his son William. His inventory of estate was valued at £285, an amount then signifying great wealth (Yeatman 93). His burial was noted in the Norbury Register, near Snelston.

The coat-of-arms "Sable [black], three lions passant [walking] in bend cotised Argent [in a silver diagonal sash with double border], in chief [upper corner] a trefoil slipped Ermines [a three-leaf stemmed clover black with white spots]" was awarded to Nicolas Browne of Snelston by the herald Gilbert Dethick or Deltic, Garter, 15 Aug 5 Edward VI (1552). A gryphon is added in drawings. Notably, the coat is similar to that owned by the Brownes of Bechworth (Beechworth) Castle in Essex. Furthermore, the Herald's visitation of London 1633-5 included two other Browne pedigrees with the same coat of arms. One began with George Brown of Snelston and ended with Gervase Browne of London b. 1616; another commenced with John Browne of Gloucester and ended with Henry Browne of London (*The Visitation of London Anno Domini 1633, 1634, 1635*, Vol. I (1880), pp. 111, 113). Yet another similar Browne coat belonged to a Ralph Browne of The Woodlands, County Shropshire. Connection with our Brownes is probable but specifics are not known. Yeatman simply stated that "It is a singular fact that a considerable portion of the numerous Brownes of Derbyshire descend from the family of the Brownes of Bechworth Castle, whilst one branch (that of Snelston) were allowed by the Heralds to assume the Bechworth Arms, others bearing the arms of Sir John Browne, Lord Mayor of London" (Brownes of Derby, Ch. II, p. 7). Sir John and beforementioned Sir Steven were both Lord Mayors of London.

Nicolas married Eleanor SHIRLEY, daughter of Ralph SHIRLEY and Amee LOLLE, born about 1528 of Staunton Harold, Leicestershire, England. Eleanor died on 28 Apr 1595 in Snelston, Derbyshire, England (date of burial). "D[aughte]r and heiress to Ralph Shirley of Shirley, Derbyshire, of Staunton Harold and Braylesford co. Leichester. Her first husband was Thomas Vernon, 2d son of Humphrey Vernon of Clifton and Harleston, Derbyshire, as by the marriage settlement made 5 May 1545. The Shirleys of Shirley and of Staunton Harold were represented in 1611 by a Baronet, in 1677 by Baron Ferrars, and in 1711 by Earl Ferrars of Staunton Harold" (Waters 873). She may have been the Ellen Browne mentioned in the Snelston Court Calendar of 27 Feb 1545/6 (Yeatman 92). . They had the following children:

    9   i.   William (1556-1610)
    10   ii.   Gertrude (about 1560-)

This line ascends (per G. B. Roberts, *The Royal Descents of 500 Immigrants to the American Colonies or the United*

States, p. 334) fourteen generations back to William I the Lion, King of Scotland, who died in 1214, thus: 14. Eleanor Shirley married Nicholas Browne; 13. Ralph Shirley married Amee Lolle; 12. Robert Shirley married [--?--]; 11. John Shirley married Eleanor Willoughby; 10. Ralph Shirley married Margaret Staunton; 9. Sir Ralph Shirley married Joan Basset; 8. Beatrix de Braose married Joan de Percy; 6. William de Braose married Eleanor de Bavant; 5. Mary de Ros married William de Braose; 4. Sir Robert de Ros married Isabel d'Aubigny; 3. Sir William de Ros married Lucy FitzPiers; 2. Isabel of Scotland (illegitimate by a daughter of Richard Avenal) married Robert de Ros, Magna Charta Surety; 1. William I the Lion, King of Scotland married Ermengarde de Beaumont [but see No. 2.].

Additionally, D. L. Jacobus in "The House of Rich," *The American Genealogist*, 25, I (July 1946, pp. 107-9) gave the line from Charlemagne forward to the Brownes. It is very briefly this: 1. Charlemagne and Hildegard; 2. Louis The Pious and Judith; 3. Charles the Bald and Ermentrude; 4. Louis II and Adelaide; 5. Louis the Simple and Eadgifu; 6. Louis IV and Gerberga; 7. Duke Charles and Adelaide; 8. Adelaide of Lorraine and Count Albert I; 9. Albert II and Reginlinde; 10. Albert III and Ida; 11. Count Godfrey and Sybil; 12. Elizabeth of Namur and Count Gervaise; 13. Milicent of Rethel and Robert Marmion II; 14. Robert Marmion III and Elizabeth; 15. Robert Marmion IV and Maude de Beauchampe; 16. Robert Marmion V and Juliane; 17. Philip Marmion and Joan de Kilpeck; 18. Mazera Marmion and Ralph de Cromwell; 19. Joan de Cromwell and Alexander de Freville; 20. Baldwin de Freville and ---; 21. Sir Baldwin de Freville and Elizabeth de Montfort; 22. Baldwin de Freville and Joane Greene; 24. Margaret de Freville and Hugh Willoughby; 25. Eleanor Willoughby and John Shirley; 26. Robert Shirley and ---; 27. Ralph Shirley and Amee Lolle; 28. Eleanor Shirley and Nicolas Browne; 29. Sir William Brown and Mary Savage; 30. Percy Browne and --- Rich; 31. Nathaniel Browne

6. Thomas BROWNE, Grandson. Snelston Court Rolls No. 1543 (P.R.O. 91/152. 35 Henry VIII) show Thomas Brown Sen. and Jun. taxed goods £9 and £40 respectively. They were persons of wealth (Yeatman 90-91).

According to the Somershall-Herbert register it is possible that this Thomas Browne was buried in 1670; daughter Lucia and Thomasine his wife buried in 1671, daughter Maria buried 1680, and son Charles buried 1684 (Yeatman, p. 105). Although Jacobus (Pt. III, p. 158) stated that he died without issue, known children were:

11	i.	John (1581-)
12	ii.	William (1583-)
13	iii.	Walter (1585-)
14	iv.	Edmund (1590-)

FOURTH GENERATION

Family of Ralf BROWNE (4)

7. Robert BROWNE, born in 1587 in Snelston, Derbyshire. Date of baptism 17 Dec 1587 per Snelston Vital Records Index.

8. Edward BROWNE, born in 1602 in Snelston, Derbyshire. Date of baptism 31 Oct 1602 per Snelston Vital Records Index.

Family of Nicolas BROWNE Esquire (5) and Eleanor SHIRLEY

9. Sir William BROWNE, G Grandson, born in 1556 in Snelston, Derbyshire, England. William died in Aug 1610 in Flushing (Vlissingen), Netherlands. Convinced that the Brownes of Snelston were rigid Catholics, the Derbyshire historian John Pym Yeatman declared that William Browne, once a large landholder, suffered persecution as a "recusant," that is, Catholic, and was ruined financially by Queen Elizabeth, whereupon he fled to the Continent; that he served several years in the Low Countries as Lieutenant Governor of Flushing under the Earl of Leicester "where he could at least fight" and later "crept home," a broken man.

Better evidence attests to the contrary. G. D. Scull's very thorough work amply demonstrated that Sir William's Anglican "trew faythe" was never put to question; that he was entrusted with delicate and dangerous tasks in the Low Countries, was duly honored and knighted by the Queen herself; was knighted again to the Order of the Garter by King James; and that both he and his widow received handsome honors, grants and stipends.

Browne came on scene when England joined the Eighty Years' War on the side of the Dutch Protestant United Provinces, led in revolt by William I of Orange, and against Spain, which controlled much of the Low Countries. Pope Sixtus V then granted Papal authority to overthrow Elizabeth and place a Catholic on the throne of England. Spain intended to do just that. Queen Elizabeth sent an army of 6,000, and later many more, to the Low Countries in 1585, where the towns of Brill and Flushing (in Dutch, Vlissingen) were declared "cautionary" cities to coordinate the campaign in outlying regions, and required that those cities pay the Crown's expenses for their protection against the Catholics of France and Spain. In command was Sir Phillip Dudley, Earl of Leicester. Sir Phillip died in 1588 and Sir Robert Sydney, Lord Governor of Flushing, inherited his brother's estates, was later Viscount de L'Isle and Earl of Leicester. Captain William Browne had served under Phillip and Robert since the beginning of hostilities. In 1586 he was chosen, as the officers rolled dice on a drumhead, to head a company into Catholic territory under truce. He was taken by treachery in an incident was called "the Surprise of Graveline" (sic), surrendered in accordance with previous orders, and ransomed, but the heroism of Browne and his troops probably saved thousands of lives. (Coastal Gravelines in 1588 was near the site of the major sea battle between the English and Spanish Armada. On land Spanish land forces under the Duke of Parma were to meet with the Armada and be ferried across the channel and attack England, but the rendezvous failed. Scull's anecdote may refer to that action.) A 19 December 1595 letter from Rowand Whyte to Sir Robert (then in England, and a replacement needed for the lieutenant governor's position as the previous one, Sir Edmond Veudale, had received the Queen's permission to return to England) declared that he knew that "you had in this Town at this howre Capt. Brown, a Gentleman your Lordſhip knew to be difcrete, valiant, well affected in Religion, well languaged & one that was ſpecially well acquainted with the Humors of the Burgers and Mariners, and every Way as ſuch a one as your Lordſhip would be anſwerable for," and that the Queen had given her consent to the appointment (Collins, Vol. I, p. 381; Scull, p. 3). Browne was thus made Lieutenant Governor of Flushing, a post he held until his death in August of 1610. As for his being "languaged," there is evidence in his correspondence that he knew Latin, Dutch and French.

Sir William Browne's many letters to Sir Robert Sydney are preserved at the Centre for Kentish Studies in Maidstone, Kent, which houses the family library of the present descendant of Sir Robert, Viscount De L'Isle, including hundreds of letters dating from 23 July 1594 to 13 Mar 1610/11, shortly before Sir William's death. Some of those letters were transcribed and published, together with other Sydney family correspondence spanning 120 years, by Arthur Collins in 1746 under the title *Letters and Memorials of State*. Browne wrote almost daily, sometimes repeatedly in a day, concerning battles, skirmishes, plots and negotiations between the English garrisons and the French, the Spanish, and the Hollanders, and also his frequent visits to England on matters of state or military action. Sir William's life spanned matters of military and diplomacy, and the letters demonstrate that his affairs were sensitive, dangerous, and hectic.

To offer an example, several of Browne's communications to his commander Sir Robert Sydney detailed, in 1597, an armed offensive mounted from England to Ireland, where they had learned that the Spanish had made plans to mount a mass invasion. Brown at that time served in an attack force bound for Ireland under the Earl of Sussex. Sir Walter Raleigh was one of the other commanders of the English force, comprising many ships and 6,000 troops. The assault was turned back by rough seas, but the Spanish fleet apparently suffered likewise, and there was no confrontation (Scull, p. 8). Scull wrote that "it must have been on the return of their officers through London, that Captain Browne was knighted by Queen Elizabeth. On the 28th October 1597 she made 9 knights, viz., [...a list including Browne...], all of whom were from the garrison of Flushing (Scull, p. 13). And so it was. It was officially reported to Sir Robert Sydney by Rowland Whyte, Court Secretary, in a letter of 29 Oct. 1597 (Collins, Vol. II, p. 74). Until 1597 Browne was normally referred to as "Captain." Thereafter he was known as "Sir William" in letters.

Sir William often served as ambassador, courier, and envoy. He was at Court in 1599 to plead his commander Sir Robert's request for a leave of absence from the garrisons, which the Queen first refused and later accepted (Scull 13-15; Sir Robert was not much of a soldier-diplomat, made long stays in London and left on-site command to Browne). Then in 1601 a brief drama took place when Sir William Browne heard that he was on Queen Elizabeth's "bloody bed roll," of persons to be punished for treason. He was alarmed when an anonymous letter dated 15 Jun 1601 spoke of what happened when "great and lofty potentates fal from the top of fortune" and "Sundrye others are forced to tumble downe headlong wythe them," and invoked the fate of the Earl of Essex, a rebellious noble who had been executed just months before, in February 1601. William immediately sent a letter to the Queen's Privy Council declaring his allegiance to the Crown, and then hastened to England where Her Majesty received him personally and greeted him in the most friendly terms, declaring that "she had as good affiance in my loiolty, as any Mans that served her" (underline his), refused to let him kneel in her presence and insisted that he stand, and chatted with him at length concerning politics and warfare. This all he described on 12 Aug 1601 in a gushing letter to Sir Robert, in a tone of relief justly accorded to those who can now keep their heads. His letter to the Privy Council had been sent, for secrecy, via a French merchant and with cover in French, from "Guillaume Browne" (Scull, pp. 21-24). Browne's actual cover letter to the Privy Council was pasted into Scull's manuscript in a clear sign that Scull had free access to certain archived documents, and in this case perhaps helped himself. That letter is here reproduced. It is written in 17th Century hand, and so a transcription is also provided.

Some idea of Sir William's appearance is seen in a letter from a Capt. William to him, dated 22 Mar 1604, which said: "Your letter came in tyme, ells I would have been so bould as to have chiden you for forgetting your poor Friend; however the common oppinion is that Redbearded Men are unfaythfull yet I have never found any more honest . . . " (Scull, p. 35).

Sir William's will named numerous tracts of lands and messuages (dwellings) in Sneltson, Norbury, Cubley, Edleston (all near Snelston), comprising "fortie acres of Land, twentie acres of meadows, one hundred acres of pasture and twentie acres of wood," also in Alveston (in Warwickshire) with "one hundred acres of land, fortie acres of meadows, three hundred acres of pasture and fortie acres of wood as "estate in ffee simple as afore sayd and hould the same by Sucadge Tenures." Socage referred to lands bound to the Crown by rent but exempt from military service. The low tax assessments in Snelston listed by Yeatman may have been because of concessions granted by the Crown.

On 14 Mar 1603/4 William Browne, of Sussex, Lieutenant Governor of Flushing, was made a Knight Bachelor of the Order of the Garter by King James I at the Tower of London (Shaw, W. A., *The Knights of England*, Vol. 2, p. 129). The Order of the Garter was, and is, Britain's most prestigious order of chivalry. A Knight Bachelor was a member of the Order who was not a peer. The phrase "of Sussex" is important as well, because it establishes him as the Sir William Browne "of Chichester, kt," and "of Losely, County Surrey knt" and signatory in a "covenant to suffer a common recovery" in Sussex dated 30 Dec 1604, by Sir John Morely, (3300 acres) and 6 Jun 1608, a grant of income from a manor in Sussex to John Draper. These may have been properties, not Browne's but taken from Morely under Elizabeth and returned under James to the former owners. The signatures on these documents are similar to that of his 1601 letter, and a wax seal on one, what can be made of it, seems to be that of our Browne family.

A bill at Parliament was read on 4 June 1604 for the naturalization of his children who were born overseas (William, Ann, Barbara, with Percy and Mary apparently being too young). A codicil written 7 Jul 1604 by William indicated that William's oldest son was not yet 20, and hinted that William Jr. had died. In a letter to Sir Robert dated 2 Nov 1605 and regarding the recent Gunpowder Plot in London, of which the Earl of Northumberland (a Percy) and his kinsman Thomas Percy were accused, William wrote; "I am sory that ever I honored him and mor sory thay I have a Chyld that caryes his name." Percy's naturalization was granted in 1522 in accordance with William's will, and by an act of Parliament. Sir William Russell, Knight, was trustee of the surviving children Percy and Mary when their father died, and the will was proved by Mary Browne, relict, 23 Jan 1611.

In about 1609 William Browne was one of the initial investors in the Virginia Company, in the amount of £10.00.0; Sir Robert Sydney, then Earl of Leicester, invested £90, and Sir Robert Rich, then Earl of Warwick, £75 (Scull, 56).

An uneasy peace with Spain was achieved in 1604, but English troops remained on the Continent for a time. King James I himself granted the widow, Lady Browne, a lifelong income of 100 marks out of the Flushing garrison's proceeds, and in 1616, when the King received £13,000 from Flushing and Brill as the posts were vacated, that fund was divided among the officers and Lady Browne was paid £300 at Brill in tribute to her late husband (Scull, pp. 3-4). These were large sums at the time. Since Mary's two surviving children were not naturalized as English until 1622, it may be surmised that Mary and her family remained in the Low Countries for some years following William's death.

Sir William Browne's repute is seen in the following citations. Sir Francis Vere wrote of his three younger brothers "having, when mere boys, embraced the profession of arms, placing themselves under the care of the good soldier Sir William Browne, who had served for many years in the Low Countries." He and his brother Sir Horatio, both soldiers, always referred to Sir William as "your loving sonn." The will of one John Sparhawke, Commissary for Musters for the King, 25 Oct 1605, proved 25 Jun 1608. stated: "I have ever bynne from my cradle a true protestant in heart and soul, detesting from the very inward parts of my heart the Pope with all his shavelings and all their papistical trumperies and most ungodly and execrable courses in religion. My old good friend Sir William Browne, knight, Lieuftetennte Governor of Vlishinge whome I have heretofore with an entire affection dearly loved."

In pre-dictionary England, spelling tended to be a matter of taste and whim; thus his name was variously rendered as Brown, Broun, Browne and Broune, though his signature seemed to favor Broune.

On 11 Oct 1569 William married Mary SAVAGE, in Low Countries, born about 1550 in Ghent. Mary died after 1632 in Snelston, Derbyshire, England. Waters said Mary was born in Germany but according to Yeatman, she was Dutch. To Scull goes the last word: she was Belgian. In a 6 April 1623 letter of safe conduct, Lady Mary Browne "of Ghent" was allowed to leave England and go abroad for three years. Mary was naturalized in 1600 (Waters p. 873; Scull 3, which specified 27 January). The Herald (known as "Knight of Arms" who verified the right to bear coats of arms and crests) in his 1611 "visitation of Derby" (not to imply that he actually went there) indicated William Browne, dead by that date, to be in the Low Countries, with a son William, begotten by whom he rudely called the "Dutchwoman, as if she were a Boer or a Hottentot" (so harrumphed Yeatman, pp. 88, 95). Sir William Browne's will, written 18 Mar 34 Elizabeth (1592) but not proved until 23 Jan 1611, mentioned but did not name four sons and unnumbered daughters, plus Mary his wife; it asked that all of his children be made "free denizens," having been born "out of the Realm." That request was partially carried out by acts of Parliament with the naturalization of William, Ann and Barbara in 1604, and in 1622 for that of the two younger and the only surviving children, Percy and Mary. Sir William's wife Mary was listed in the Snelston court rolls (P.R.O. 93/358, 8 Charles I [1633]), as Dame Mary Browne, widow, with 40s. in land income (Yeatman, 90), which the historian termed a "miserable pittance." But see above. They had the following children:

    15   i.   William (-1595)
    16   ii.   William (- before 1622)
    17   iii.   Ann (- before 1609)
    18   iv.   Barbara (- before 1609)
    19   v.   Percy (1603 - before 1637)
    20   vi.   Mary
    21   vii.   ---
    22   viii.   ---

10. Gertrude Browne, G Granddaughter, born about 1560 in Snelston, Derbyshire, England.

Family of Thomas BROWNE (6)

11. John BROWNE, born in 1581 in Snelston, Derbyshire. Date of baptism was 16 Mar 1581/2 per Snelston Vital Records Index.

12. William BROWNE, born in 1583 in Snelston, Derbyshire. Date of baptism 22 Dec 1583 per Snelston Vital Records Index.

13. Walter BROWNE, born in 1585 in Snelston, Derbyshire. Date of baptism 22 Feb 1585/6 per Snelston Vital Records Index.

14. Edmund BROWNE, born in 1590 in Snelston, Derbyshire. Date of baptism 1 Nov 1590 per Snelston Vital Records Index.

Ryght Honorable

I am bold to wryte in generall to yr LLs of her Maties Most hon: privy Counsell and to send herein enclosed a libelling letter wch was yesterday delivered to my man by an ordinary dutch post, he wold thereby make mee beleeve yt I were as very a villen as hee, or at least yt I were thoght so to bee: I shold take itt as a great plague from God, if there were any such conceyt of mee, if itt bee butt a slander of a seditious roge, I shall account itt as a great honour to bee numbered among so many most honorable and vertuous p'sonages as there traiterous mallice endeveurets by scandelous libells to defame, if itt shold bee so yt such opinions were held of mee, my lyfe and goods must answere wth shame my base disloyalty: as in generall I desyre to bee knowne by all the Counsell to be a p'fect honest subject in such respects, so do I p'ticularly beeseech your honor above the rest (because I honor yew most) yt to yew I may bee known to be such a one as is worthy to be well accounted of: and even so wth my harty prayers to God for your honor I humble take leave. Flushing this 8th of July 1601.

Your honors as much At
Command as any servant yew
have
William Browne

[Following and apparently on the page's reverse:]

To the ryght honorable Syr Robert Cecill Knight-principall
Secretary to her Majesty, and master of the wards at the Court.

SIR WILLIAM BROWNE'S LETTER TO THE QUEEN'S PRIVY COUNCIL, 1601
(the original parchment found in Scull's manuscript)

FIFTH GENERATION

Family of Sir William BROWNE (9) and Mary SAVAGE

15. William BROWNE, GG Grandson, born in Low Countries. William died in May 1595. Jacobus added the burial date 5 May 1595 (Pt. III, p. 158) and postulated two sons named William as did Yeatman.

16. William BROWNE. William died before 1622. Naturalized by Parliament 1604. The Herald's 1611 visitation of Snelston mentioned him. Yeatman posited two adult Williams, Sr. and Jr., as soldiers in the Low Countries. I have found no evidence of a William Junior adult, and Scull stated that he did not survive. Ann's 1622 will mentioned Percy and Mary as the only surviving children.

17. Ann BROWNE, GG Granddaughter. Ann died before Jul 1609. Naturalized by Parliament but did not survive.

18. Barbara BROWNE, GG Granddaughter. Barbara died before Jul 1609. Naturalized by Parliament 1604 but did not survive.

19. Percy BROWNE, GG Grandson, born in Nov 1603 in Low Countries. Percy died before 1637. He was named, according to Scull, after Thomas Percy (kinsman of Henry Percy, 9th Earl of Northumberland). William Browne and Thomas Percy had served together in 1885 under Robert Dudley in the Low Countries. Accused of complicity in the 1605 "Gunpowder Plot," Thomas Percy died of wounds suffered on capture and his kinsman the Earl was imprisoned for 15 years. The charges against the Earl were probably false but Thomas was evidently involved. When the plot was known, William Browne wrote to express his chagrin at having a son so named.

Sir William Browne wrote to Sir Robert Sydney on 28 Nov 1603 concerning the birth of a son (Browne Letters, 8/367). In a 1605 letter to Sir Robert Sydney he alluded to having a son named Percy (see above). On 21 Jul 1609 Sir William wrote of his concern for his son and daughter (Browne Letters, 8/817) and so the three eldest children had apparently died before that date. As Percy and his siblings were born in the Netherlands, they were all naturalized as citizens of England by acts of Parliament as follows: William, Ann and Barbara, who did not survive, in 1604, and Percy and Mary in 1622. Percy probably did not live in Snelston; those properties were sold after William's death. In fact, Scull and Jacobus report Percy's son Nathaniel's birth to have been in London, and the following bears that out.

Percy Browne was evidently a London businessman engaged in selling arms. In an 18 Feb 1635 accounting of the Providence Island Company of London were mentioned three types of cannon, "two Mynions at £25:00:0 4 Domions at 139:2:0 and 2 Drakes at 18:0:0," that Mr. Browne (the Mr. denoting a person of stature, a gentleman) was shipping to Providence Island aboard the ship Blessing and for which he was to be paid by the company. In mid-1635 "Mr. Browne" was a creditor of the company in the amount of £800, to which was later added £32 of interest that it owed him, perhaps for the sale of arms (Kupperman, Reel I, n.p.). That was a large sum. He probably knew much about artillery because his father was a lifelong soldier, and he himself was raised in a military garrison.

In a letter dated 18 Dec 1641 Lord Mandeville in London wrote to Thomas Durham mentioning Robert as "the son of Mr. Browne" i.e., Percy, with regard to Sir Nathaniel Rich's estate (Kupperman, Reel I; see Robert Browne, below).

In about 1620 Percy married Anne RICH, daughter of Richard RICH and Jane Ann MACHELL, born about 1603 in England. Anne died after 1637. Several sources give Anne as her Christian name, but was simply the unnamed daughter of Richard Rich and Ann Machell in Jacobus, 22, 1. Her death has been estimated as before 1633, but in a letter from the Somers Island Company of London to Thomas Durham of August 1637 and regarding Southampton (in Bermuda) shares resulting from Nathaniel Rich's will, Lord Mandeville specified that "one of the shares is for Robin [i.e., Robert] Browne, and for same Browne two of Mistress Browne's." That would be Percy's widow Anne. Waters in 1907 had said that Percy's wife was daughter of Col. Nathaniel Rich of Standon, Essex, who was Richard Rich's son. That appears to be incorrect. They had the following children:

23	i.	Robert (about 1620-1660)
24	ii.	Nathaniel (about 1622-1658)
25	iii.	Samuel
26	iv.	---
27	v.	Elizabeth

20. Mary BROWNE, GG Granddaughter. Naturalized in 1622. Her later life is unknown.

21. --- BROWNE.

22. --- BROWNE.

SIXTH GENERATION

Family of Percy BROWNE (19) and Anne RICH

23. Rev. Robert BROWNE, GGG Grandson, born about 1620 in England. Robert died in 1660 in Bermuda. The Oxfordian G. D. Scull wrote on a pedigree chart of the Derbyshire Brownes that Percy's son "Robert Browne went to the Providence Islands, West Indies. Named after Robert Sydney, Earl of Leicester. Was ordained a minister and appointed to a church in Somers Islands in 1655 and died 1660" (p. 80). Robert Browne, by Nathaniel Rich's Nov. 1635 London will, received a share in the ownership of Bermuda, having already received one share from Sir Nathaniel's sister Margaret (Wroth). The will not only named Sir Nathaniel Rich's nephew Robert "residing in Somers [not Providence] Island" but also other nephews Samuel (place of residence not there noted, but see Samuel Browne) and Nathaniel Browne of New England (see Waters 872-3; J. E. Mercer, *Bermuda Settlers of the 17th Century*, pp. 17-19; Scull; and Jacobus).

The Riches, in-laws of the Brownes, were heavily invested in Providence Island. Henry Rich, Earl of Holland, Robert Rich, Earl of Warwick, and Sir Nathaniel Rich were all charter "adventurers" i.e. stockholders. Although Robert's father Percy sold goods to the Providence Island Company, there is no evidence that Robert lived there other than Scull's note on the family pedigree. He is not mentioned in any of the surviving passenger lists or accounts of the Island. A Robert Browne age 18 was a passenger on the ship Expedition, its master Peter Blackler, which left the English port of Gravesend on 20 Nov 1635 bound for "the Barbadoes," a catchall name for any place in the West Indies (M. Tepper, *Passengers to America*, 1988, p. 71). If it was he, Robert was born in 1517.

Lord Mandeville of London, on settling Sir Nathaniel Rich's estate, on 18 Dec 1641 wrote to Thomas Durham in Bermuda concerning the abovementioned two shares, and specified: "To the son [Robert] of Mr. Browne [Percy] there is assigned the two shares that lie easterly [in Southampton Tribe Bermuda], being in possession of Henry Wethersby [note that Robert was not occupying that parcel]. The particulars of these 8 shares [6 others of Rich's already listed, and their occupiers] are to be received by Robert Browne, being to that purpose assigned by me on request of the executors of Mr. Grfd. [?], that the rent of 6 of them may be sent for the use of the ward of Mr. Gr. [?], and the rent of one of the other two for the use of Sam Browne who is in London. The rent of the other share bought off Robert Browne with the other four shares [listed] are set apart for the school [...] in pursuance of your late master's [i.e., Sir N. Rich] will. [...] Postscript. The rent of the westward share you may deliver to Robert Browne to be sent hither for the [--?--] of Mr. Gr's. decease. You may save the other part and send it to me" ("Shorthand Letterbook of Providence Island Company," P.R.O. Add MS 36584 A Transcribed by K.L. Perrin," Kupperman, Reel I, p. 256). This indicates that Robert was not in Bermuda in 1641, and there is no further sign of him there until 1655. He may have sold the share, and returned to England to study.

This question must be asked: Was the Robert of Rich's 1635 will identical to the Robert who assumed the ministry in 1655? Jacobus did not question the matter. Jacobus' source seems to have been Scull, who lived in Oxford. From information contained in it, Scull's manuscript shows intimate knowledge of, and access to, family records, and so I must take it as accurate. He appears to have had access to the De Lisle private collection; I have only succeeded in examining synopses of the letters and read those later published by Collins. Convincing evidence that Scull had access to family records is the actual letter written by Sir William in 1601 to the Queen's Privy Council, which is inserted in Scull's manuscript. A written hint that Robert had been in Bermuda and then returned an ordained minister is found in a 1656 Council letter describing him as "Doctor Browne *now* a preacher" ((Lefroy, Vol. II, p. 82, italics mine).

Bermuda, Barbados and Providence Island were all on the same trade route. The Providence Islands, near the present Nicaraguan coast, were briefly a stronghold of Puritans, subscribed by those same wealthy Puritans who underwrote the Bermuda and Virginia Companies, until the islands were taken over by the Spanish. They now belong to Colombia.

As for Bermuda, Robert Browne was sent there from England by the Bermuda Company in September 1655, a family man, and known as "Reverend Doctor Robert Browne D.D.," to serve as rector. Given his Puritan family connections and despite the 2nd Earl of Warwick Robert Rich's having decreed on 4 Nov 1645 a declaration establishing freedom of worship on the island, he was surely a Puritan minister, as this was during Cromwell's Puritan dictatorship in England. His enrollment at either Cambridge, Oxford, or Leiden, has not been located in those universities' few surviving records. Cambridge's Emmanuel College was a Puritan academic Mecca.

Although most parish records are lost, early Bermudan council records, reproduced in Lefroy, J.H., *Memorials of the Discovery and Early Settlement of the Bermudas or Somers Islands 1515-1685* (2 Vol., 1877) shed a certain light on Browne's life there. In its listing of ministers, it is stated that he was officiating in St. George's in January 1656, and in Smith and Hamilton Parishes in September 1658, and that there were marriages and baptisms performed by him in Pembroke Parish registers 1658-59 and 1660 (Lefroy, Vol. I Appendix IV, p. 694).

Bermuda Council minutes of 22 January 1655/6 show "Mr. Robert Browne minister makeing demand by his petition that the Gleabe at George wth the house might be deliuered Vnto him, that thereby he might the better provide for his family if he should like to staie in the Islands. It was concluded that he should have the disposuer of the Land, soe as to agree with the Tennants as he thought fitt himselfe. And it was likewise then ordered that he should be tolerated to officiate in the ministry accordinge to his obligation wth the company" (Lefroy, Vol. II, p. 68).

At a time when Puritan or "Independent" ministers were often arrogant and troublesome, his repute was good. The beforementioned 1656 letter from the Company in London to Governor Forster further read: "What is conteyned in yr Generall Letter tuching Doctor Browne now a preacher in the Somr Islands And what is mentioned in his petition have been considered of by us And wee have thought fitt to order Doctor Browne £40 to be paid unto him or his assignes for one yeares service ending at midsummer last past. And upon that information wee have had of the generall approbation of him by the people wee further thinke fitt to continue him minister in the Somr Isl. upon triall and until further order And for other particulars in his petition wee shall consider of them in due tyme" (Lefroy, Vol. II, pp. 82-3).

And: "Vpon the 8th of December 1656 the maior part of the parrish of Georges Towne were assembled together to consult what was best to be done about the Gleab house wherein Mr Robert Browne minister thereto, hath made his dwelling during his abode in thes Islands; vpon viewe, and finding yt to be out of repaier, they thought yt requisite to take vpon them the repairacon thereof at their own charges, so that the house and the rents of the land may be at their disposing in tyme of vacancy of ministers [. . .] Att the same tyme Mr Browne abouesd did promise to leave the said gleb house in as good repaier as yt shal be deliuered to him at his entrance, both within and without at all points" (Lefroy, Vol. II, p. 97). That obligation was to fall upon his heir James, as will be seen.

On 18 May 1657 he wrote to the Company in London stating that they judge him "fitt and able" to remain in his post, or not. The Council approved of his continuance (Vol. II., p 100). The Council on 13 Sep 1658 extended his ministry to Smith and Hamilton Tribes, and also to "haue and enioy the gleabe lands there, with all profits and comodities thereto belonging" (Vol. II, p. 122). This was likely because of a lack of ministers, which the London Company complained on 3 Sep 1660 in a letter to Governor Sayle, adding that it had also authorized a £20 gratuity to Rev. Browne (Lefroy, Vol. II. p. 135), although he had likely died by that date.

On 30 Aug 1661 the Company sent Sayle news that Thomas Abercrombie would be sent out to occupy a ministry, and also the "Parsonage house and Land late Mr Robert Browne, belonging to Smiths and Hamilton Tribes, and the rents and profits of the two shares of Gleabe land there" (Vol. II, p. 153). Widows were usually entitled to glebe privileges when ministers died, so it may be taken that Mrs. Browne was deceased before her husband.

Robert is said to have married Sarah ---. Sarah died before 1660. Given name Sarah per *Descendants of John Darrell*, but no source provided. She may have married Robert in England and came as a minister's wife with children. Nothing more is known of her. They had the following children:

    28   i.   James (-1677)
    29   ii.   Katherine
    30   iii.   Abell (about 1640-1701)
    31   iv.   ---

24. Nathaniel BROWNE, GGG Grandson, born about 1622 in London, Middlesex, England. Nathaniel died in Aug 1658 in Middletown, Middlesex Co. CT. Under the charge of the Rev. Thomas Hooker (a fiery Puritan of both England and

New England), Nathaniel Browne went to Connecticut in New England about 1633, married Eleanor Watts, moved from Hartford to Middletown Connecticut and died there in 1658, according to Waters pp. 873-4. His date of burial was 26 Aug 1658. Nathaniel and Eleanor Browne's lineage, as follows, is primarily taken from Jacobus' article series "The House of Rich," except those of Deana Carlson and Alice Marie Beard who provided good sources. I have hesitated to add other data regarding the extensive Connecticut line found elsewhere.

In 1647 Nathaniel married Ellinor WATTS, daughter of Richard WATTS and Elizabeth OSBORNE, in Hartford, Hartford Co. CT, born in 1625. Ellinor died on 28 Sep 1703 in Hartford, Hartford Co. CT. They had the following children:

32	i.	Nathaniel (1648-)
33	ii.	Hannah (1651-)
34	iii.	Nathaniel (1654-1712)
35	iv.	Thomas (1655-1717)
36	v.	John (1657-1719)
37	vi.	Benoni (1658-1688)

25. Samuel BROWNE, GGG Grandson. Mention of Samuel appeared in a letter from Lord Mandeville in London to Thomas Durham in Bermuda on 18 Dec 1641 regarding the disposition of two island shares from Sir Nathaniel Rich's will that went "to the son of Mr. [Percy] Browne," i.e., Robert. Robert had already sold one share and rents from the other were to go to "Sam Browne who is in London" (Kupperman, p. 255). Jacobus observed that he may heve been the Samuel Browne of Essex who was admitted Fellow-Commoner at Emmanuel, Cambridge, 24 Apr 1649 (Jacobus, "The House of Rich" Pt. III, 158). Emmanuel College of Cambridge was a center of Puritan activity, led by the Rev. Thomas Hooker before that churchman fled to New England.

26. --- BROWNE, GGG Grandson. Not named but "educated by the Countess of Leicester, widow of Robert Sydney, first Earl of Leicester of the Sydney family; his name was supposed to be William, as a William Browne was out in the Providence Islands" (Waters, p. 873). In point of information, a Will Brown was condemned to death there in 1639 and the outcome was not recorded.

27. Elizabeth BROWNE.

Bermuda, about 1615
from Capt. John Smith"s "Generall Historie"

SEVENTH GENERATION

Family of Rev. Robert BROWNE (23) and Sarah ---

28. James BROWNE, GGGG Grandson. James died in 1677 in Bermuda. "At a council meeting October 4, 1660 The Governor propounded to the Council that what tobacco was standing upon the Glebe Land or ground belonging to Smith's and Hamilton Tribe at the day of the death of Mr. Robert Browne late Rector should be sequestered for the repairing of said Glebe House or Parsonage. Several of the creditors of Mr. Robt. Browne lately deceased (1660) having importuned the Governor that Mr. James Browne, sonne to aforsaid Robert be put to his Oath whether he hath now of his father's estate in his hands sufficient wherewith to satisfy his late father's creditors." On 22 Feb 1668, James Brown appointed his "loving wife, Mistress Hannah Brown," his attorney. He made a will on 4 Sep 1669 "being about to make a voyage to Jamaica, [and] made wife Hannah and John Bristow attorneys, named stepdaughters or daughters in law Judith and Hannah Hollowaie [perhaps from his wife's first marriage], and his children Robert and Katherine. On 11 Jun 1672 James Browne appeared in court to guarantee any debts of Andrew Norwood, who was in New York (Mercer, p. 143). On 28 Jan 1675 (*Book 1 E*, p. 234) he made another will then naming daughter Katherine, sons Robert, John, James, Samuel. Named friend Anthony Jenour Senr and brother John Bristow executors, James and Thomas Wright. His will was proved 23 Apr 1677, giving real estate to son Robert, and Robert was to pay his brother John, James and Samuel the valuations made by the executors. *Deeds Book 4*, p. 99 18 Jul 1698 ordered that since "the Testator is now dead and the Executors are also dead and the lands enjoyed by Robert who is now dead leaving one [unnamed] son [...] no money was ever paid to the other brothers of whom John is now dead [...] Captain John Tucker is one of the executors and he is requested by the legatees to settle the estate to Tucker [and] requests the Guardian of young [unnamed] Brown, Robert's son, to pay to James and Samuel the sum of 56 pounds between them within one month." (Mercer, pp. 17-19).

Strangely, Norwood's survey of the Bermudas made in 1663 does not mention any of the Browne siblings, nor lands held by James. As a merchant, he may have lived in the town and so was not enumerated, as the survey was of agricultural lands and holders. A Roger Browne lived in St. George, and a John Browne lived in Tucker Town. Both were small tenants. John Browne, who may have been James' son, was a local troublemaker, to judge from Council records.

Before 1660 James married Hannah TUCKER, daughter of John TUCKER, in Bermuda. Hannah died before 1675. This per *Descendants of John Darrell*, n.p., citing her father's will. Hannah (Tucker) Hallowie brought her daughters Hannah and Judith Hollowaie to the second marriage, whom James Browne named as daughters-in-law or stepdaughters in his 1669 will. James Brown's 1669 will mentioned "brother" John Bristow but Darrell says she was a Tucker. Katherine Browne married John Bristow so "brother" likely meant brother-in-law. See also Robert of James' guardianship 19 Sep 1683. Hannah was not named in James' 1675 will, but her inventory was recorded 19 Sep 1683. They had the following children:

38	i.	Robert (about 1669 - before 1698)
39	ii.	Katherine (before 1669 - after 1674)
40	iii.	John (after 1669 - before 1698)
41	iv.	James (after 1669 - after 1721)
42	v.	Samuel (after 1669 - before 1710)

29. Katherine BROWNE, GGGG Granddaughter. Per *Descendants of John Bristow*, n.p. Bermuda Council records show that on two occasions, she (as Dame Bristow and as Katherine Bristow) was empanelled to examine women accused of witchcraft, looking for any "marke or spotts" on the body which may indicate guilt. She and other women examined Elizabeth Page in 1654, and "Goodwife" Moore in 1658. Neither produced signs of suspicion, but on other evidence Elizabeth Page was hanged in January 1654/5 (Lefroy, Vol. II, pp. 626, 629).

Before 1658 Katherine married John BRISTOW, in Bermuda. John died after May 1677 in Bermuda. Per *Descendants of John Bristow*, n.p., also Mercer p. 16, which states that he was made Provost Marshall in 1658, came to Bermuda with wife Katherine (doubtful), son John and perhaps other children; in his will he had second wife Sarah and additional children Sarah (Tucker?) and Katherine. Hannah Browne witnessed his 1680 will. They had the following children:

    43   i.   John (- after 1679)
    44   ii.   Judith (- after 1727)

30. Abell BROWNE, GGGG Grandson, born about 1640 in England (?). Abell died in Feb 1701 in Anne Arundel Co. MD. It has been long claimed that Abell Browne came from Dumfries, Scotland to the Maryland province in about 1660 together with two nephews Robert and James, sons of a brother James who lived in Barbados. There is no supporting evidence of that. Rather, the family was from England and Abell's brother, father and nephews lived and died in Bermuda. Abell may have left Bermuda for Maryland approximately when his father Rev. Robert Browne died, in 1660.

Abell Browne was a gentried Maryland landholder in 1675, He was Associate Justice in 1678 and later became a Maryland Council Member (much like a member of the legislature) in 1680 and High Sheriff (the highest civil post, much more powerful than sheriffs now) during the exciting years of upheaval in England. It was the High Sheriff's duty to collect taxes, but the changing political situation made it necessary for Abell Browne to supplement uncollected funds from his own pocket. His term of office expired in 1692 and he asked the Commissioners to extend it in order that he might recover his losses. They didn't. He also appeared in documents as a State Commissioner in 1692. Meanwhile . England saw the Great Revolution, when Catholic sympathizer James II gained and lost the throne, William of Orange, with his wife Mary, paraded grandly from Holland to the throne, and the Anglican Church was saved.

Abell Browne witnessed land sales in 1665 (4 Nov.), 1682, 1683 (2), 1688, and 1689. The 1665 date is the first in Anne Arundel known of him, and that signature as witness to a land sale reflects his status as an established Anne Arundel resident by that date. He was also an adult, and so his year of birth is thus estimated.

He purchased 200 acres (later found to hold 169 acres) called Cumberton on 20 Jan 1692 from John Cumber. The property, located in Anne Arundel County on "Swamp Herring Creek," was resurveyed in 1692 and 1693 at his request (*Proceedings of the Council of Maryland*, Vol. VIII, p. 433, and Vol. XX, p. 221; *Book W.H. 4*, pp. 211-214, 261). Browne then sold on 4 Aug 1697 to John Giles for £100 (Land Records of Anne Arundel County, p. 211).

Abell Browne purchased "Harwood" from Anthony Demondidier for 7,000 lbs. of tobacco on 4 Oct 1675 (Anne Arundel *Land Records Book IT 5 1676-1752*, pp. 1-6). In 1684 he patented "Abell's Lot" of 300 acres, located on the head of Bush River, in that portion of Baltimore County which later became Harford County (*Liber N.S. #B*, Folio 93). He witnessed wills in 1682 and 1688. When Abell Browne took out the patent on Abell's Lot, in Baltimore County (*Liber 25, Patent Certificates, 1682-2*, 110:32/93), and when he wrote his 1698 will, he identified himself as a "gentleman." This indicates that he was of high social status, a man who, in Chesapeake society would have paraded down the muddy streets followed by a servant or slave, wearing delicate silks and lace, gloves, boots and spurs, feathers in a large hat. (Although Browne, the son of a Puritan minister, may not have indulged in such finery, his household inventory indicated no lack of quality items.) Abell's negro Roger Bishop was baptized 12 Mar 1698/9 at All Hallows' Church. His will of 1698 (no date; Anne Arundel County *Wills Book 11*, p. 214, proved 7 Sep 1702) mentioned his "only son" Robert but Samuel Browne later made claim in court to proceeds from "Harwood," speaking of "his father" Abell. Robert contested the claim and prevailed (Anne Arundel *Land Records Book IT 5 1676-1752*, pp. 1-6). Samuel may have been illegitimate because Abell's 1698 will laid much emphasis on the legitimacy of his son Robert's future heir or heirs, i.e., quality of the blood line (very important in Chesapeake society). Robert sold both of his father's plantations in 1715. Abell's will also stipulated that in the event of death of his "only son" while under age or without issue, the estate was to pass to Samuel and James, sons of brother James who "dwelt" in Bermuda.

Although Abell's father was a Puritan minister who gave Abell his typically Puritan, Biblical, name, all evidence suggests that Abell himself, who left Bermuda in about 1660 at his father's death and the collapse of the Puritan government in England, established himself in Annapolis as a thoroughgoing and devout "Book of Common Prayer" Anglican. He named his son Robert after grandfather Robert, a naming practice typical of those in Cavalier society, not the Puritans. Early Anne Arundel church records are scarce and for a reason: there were none. The July 1694 report by the state council regarding churches (and at that time there was only one recognized church, that of England), stated that "Ann-Arrundell County has ffour Parishes laid out but noe Churches built nor noe Minister" (*Proceedings*, Vol. XX, p. 107). Incidentally, Mr. Abell Browne was among the commissioners who issued the report.

Surviving records indicate that numerous persons owed him large sums of money at one time or another. His estate's inventory (personal goods only; land and buildings were never inventoried) listed 39 farm animals (including 6 horses), 7 slaves and goods amounting to £381.15.11, a large sum at the time. His estate also posted a crop of tobacco worth £3,150, plus some £10,427 owed him by some 22 individuals. His estate's inventory was reported on 14 Sep 1702 (*Testamentary Proceedings of the Prerogative Court*, Vol. 23, pp. 137-139). During his last year of life James Couch paid off a debt to him in August 1701, Henry Chapell in March 1702, and Henry Sewell in November 1702 (Ibid, p. 157). The latter were clearly posthumous and probably paid to his estate, but they do not appear in his inventoried accounts receivable. All this suggests that he was engaged in commerce of some sort, perhaps moneylending. One sum of £505 was owed to him "for his Prodawsse" which may be produce.

Abell Browne's burial was 25 February 1701/2 at All Hallows' Church, Anne Arundel. That church was located in the South River area of present-day Davidsonville near Annapolis.

Additional published sources for family and nearer descendants are Albert S. Brown, "An Imperfect Chronological Record of the House of Brown," a manuscript held at the University of Maryland College Park; H. D. Richardson, *Sidelights on Maryland History*, 1913, pp. 302-9; J. D. Warfield, *Founders of Anne Arundel and Howard Counties, Maryland*, 1980, pp. 168-170; E. McCallahan, "A Brown family of Maryland," *Maryland Genealogical Society Bulletin*, 19, 1 (Winter 1978), pp. 1-16; G. N. Mackenzie, *Colonial Families of the United States of America*, Vol. I, pp. 46-49; James W. Brown, "Anne Arundel's Abell Browne and Descendants: Review, Critique, Addenda," *Maryland Genealogical Society Bulletin*, 45, 3 (Spring 2004), pp. 241-258; and "Anne Arundel's Abell Browne - Part Two," *Maryland Genealogical Society Bulletin*, 46, 1 (Winter 2005), pp. 3-13.

In about 1680 Abell married Elizabeth PHILLIPS, daughter of Commander Samuel PHILLIPS, in Anne Arundel Co. MD. Elizabeth died before Aug 1697. Identified as "daughter of Samuel Phillips, of Calvert County, a sister of Mary, wife of Michael Taney, who with Abell Browne, was an executor of their brother-in-law, Ambrose Landerson [or Sanderson], of Calvert" in his will of 21 Sep 1682 - 1 Feb 1682/3 (Warfield, p. 168). Samuel Phillips, master of the ship "Crown Malago," entered the Province in 1678, so his daughter Elizabeth would have probably married after that date. When Abell Browne sold Cumberton on 4 Aug 1697 to John Giles, no waver of dower was mentioned; thus Elizabeth was dead by that date. They had the following children:

45	i.	Samuel (Illegitimate) (-1713)
46	ii.	Robert (about 1684-1769)

Shelton (p. 118) conjured another wife for Abell, (---) Landerson, on basis of that same will, guessing that Abell's unnamed sister was Landerson's wife. That is a leap of faith. Landerson died without wife or heirs and his will specified only Abell Browne as an in-law (Warfield's "their" above was inaccurate and should have said "his"). Abell could have been Landerson's brother-in-law by sharing sibling sisters in any of three ways: Browne sisters, Taney sisters, or Landerson sisters. Ambrose Landerson was probably Ambrose Sanderson, a minister.

31. --- BROWNE, GGGG Granddaughter. Unnamed, but there was an Elizabeth Browne who received ten pounds and certain linen from Lady Elizabeth (Rich) Morgan, in her will of 1632. If this is she, Lady Elizabeth would have been Elizabeth Browne's aunt.

Family of Nathaniel BROWNE (24) and Ellinor WATTS

32. Nathaniel BROWNE, born in Jan 1648/9 in Springfield, Westfield Co. CT. Died young.

33. Hannah BROWNE, born on 15 Apr 1651.

On 5 Nov 1669 when Hannah was 18, she married Isaac LANE, in Middletown, Middlesex Co. CT. Isaac died on 18 Jul 1711 in Middletown, Middlesex Co. CT. They had the following children:

47	i.	Hannah (1670-1734)
48	ii.	Elizabeth (1672-1708)
49	iii.	Eleanor (1674-)
50	iv.	Isaac (1675-1675)
51	v.	John (1675-1675)
52	vi.	John (1676-1677)

53	vii.	Sarah (1676-1677)
54	viii.	Sarah (1678-1737)
55	ix.	Samuel (1679-1679)
56	x.	John (1680-1716)
57	xi.	Isaac (1683-1745)
58	xii.	Benoni (1684-1688)
59	xiii.	Mary (1687-1687)
60	xiv.	Mary (1688-)
61	xv.	Abigail (1690-1690)
62	xvi.	Nathaniel (1694-1702)

34. Nathaniel BROWNE, born on 15 Jul 1654 in Middletown, Middlesex Co. CT. Nathaniel died in Middletown, Middlesex Co. CT, on 9 May 1712; he was 57.

On 2 Jul 1677 when Nathaniel was 22, he married Martha HUGHES, born in Guilford CT. Martha died on 30 May 1729 in Middletown, Middlesex Co. CT. They had the following children:

63	i.	Mary (1677-1751)
64	ii.	Martha (1679-1698)
65	iii.	Eleanor (1681-1712)
66	iv.	Nathaniel (1683-1735)

35. Thomas BROWNE, born on 31 Oct 1655 in Middletown, Middlesex Co. CT. Thomas died in Colchester, Hartford Co. CT, on 15 Apr 1717; he was 61.

On 8 Mar 1687 when Thomas was 31, he married Hannah LEE, daughter of Walter LEE and Mary ---, in Springfield, Hampden Co. MA, born on 9 Jan 1667 in Westfield, Hampden Co. MA. They had one child:

67	i.	Samuel (1692-)

36. John BROWNE, born on 15 Apr 1657 in Middletown, Middlesex Co. CT. John died in 1719 in Middletown, Middlesex Co. CT.

On 1 Apr 1685 when John was 27, he married Anna PORTER. They had the following children:

68	i.	Thomas (1685-)
69	ii.	Hannah (1688-1716)
70	iii.	John (1690-1744)
71	iv.	Mary (1693-1716)
72	v.	Nathaniel (1695-)
73	vi.	Thomas (1698-)
74	vii.	Martha (1700-)
75	viii.	Abigail (1701 - before 1765)

37. Benoni BROWNE, born on 15 Mar 1658/9. Benoni died in Hartford, Hartford Co. CT, on 8 May 1688; he was 30.

EIGHTH GENERATION

Family of James BROWNE (28) and Hannah TUCKER

38. Robert BROWNE, 5G Grandson, born about 1669 in Bermuda. Robert died before 1698 in Bermuda. On 19 Sep 1683 Robert Brown son of James Brown deceased, aged 14 years, chose his brother-in-law (i.e., step-brother) Anthony Jenour and his great uncle Henry Tucker Junior of St. Georges to be his guardians (Mercer, p. 19). Child:
    76   i.   ---

39. Katherine BROWNE, 5G Granddaughter, born before 4 Sep 1669 in Bermuda. Katherine died after 1674 in Bermuda. Perhaps married Anthony Jenour, according to Robert of James' 1683 guardianship. Robert, age 14, named brother-in-law Anthony Jenour and great uncle Henry Tucker Jr. as his guardians. Estimated year of death *per Darrell Family Record*, n.p.

Katherine married Anthony JENOUR.

40. John BROWNE, 5G Grandson, born after 4 Sep 1669 in Bermuda. John died before 1698 in Bermuda. Declared dead in court order of *Deeds 4*, p. 99 of 18 Jul 1698. He could have been the troublemaking John Browne alluded to elsewhere.

John married Sarah ---. They had the following children:
    77   i.   Sarah
    78   ii.   Solomon

41. James BROWNE, 5G Grandson, born after 4 Sep 1669 in Bermuda. James died after 8 Oct 1721 in Bermuda. Wives per *Descendants of John Darrell*, n.p. Thomas Gilbert's will of 1699 mentioned land currently rented to James Browne. It also mentioned Gilbert's daughter-in-law Sarah Browne. James is one of the two nephews mentioned in Abell Browne's 1698 will as sons of his brother James, who "dwelt" in Bermuda.

James first married Sarah GILBERT.

James second married Mary TUCKER, daughter of Henry TUCKER. They had one child:
    79   i.   Robert (after 1700 - after 1752)

42. Samuel BROWNE, 5G Grandson, born after 4 Sep 1669 in Bermuda. Samuel died before 19 Jul 1710 in Bermuda. Marriage and children per A.C.T. Hallett, *Early Bermuda Records 1619-1826*. Died intestate, his inventory dated Southampton 19 Jul 1710, recorded in 1 Aug 1710's *Book 4*, p. 81 (Probate Registry). Samuel is one of the two nephews mentioned in Abell Browne's 1698 will as sons of his brother James, who "dwelt" in Bermuda.

On 26 Dec 1697 Samuel married Elizabeth ---, in Bermuda. They had the following children:
    80   i.   Sarah (about 1698-)
    81   ii.   Bristow (about 1699-)
    82   iii.   John (about 1703-)

Family of Katherine BROWNE (29) and John BRISTOW

43. John BRISTOW Jr., 5G Grandson. John died after 4 Mar 1679/80 in Warwick, Bermuda. Will dated 4 Mar 1679/80, Warwick Bermuda. Served on His Majesty's Council as listed 23 Aug 1673.

John married Sarah TUCKER. Sarah died after 4 Mar 1679/80. Alive at the writing of John Bristow Jr's will. They had the following children:
```
83      i.    Sarah
84      ii.   Katherine
```

44. Judith BRISTOW, 5G Granddaughter. Judith died after 1727.

Family of Abell BROWNE (30) and Elizabeth PHILLIPS

45. Samuel BROWNE, 5G Grandson. Samuel died in 1713 in Baltimore Co. MD. Probably illegitimate. Following the 1704 fire which destroyed county documents, in 1705 Samuel Brown attempted to lay claim to his father's tract of land, "Harwood." Robert Brown contested Samuel's claim and testified that four years before he had mortgaged the land to a Wornell Hunt and Patrick Simpson had paid off the mortgage, but that Hunt had since departed and had kept the original deed. He added that the original seller to Abell Browne had been Anthony Demondidier, who in court then testified that he sold to Abell Brown on 4 October 1675 for 7,000 lb. of tobacco, whereupon the court (perhaps on examination of Abell's will) honored Robert Brown's claim and not Samuel's. According to Warfield's opinion, since Samuel had in 1692 obtained a naval commission from his grandfather Phillips, Abel may have seen fit not to name him as heir. I have not found reference to Samuel's naval commission. On the other hand, Abell's will put such emphasis on the legality of any heirs, plus his pointedly naming Robert as his "only son," suggests that Samuel was illegitimate. County records that might have brought clarity to the matter were lost in the 1704 fire. A Samuel Browne was Justice of Anne Arundel County in 1680, commanded a troop of horse 1697-8, and became Naval Officer of Anne Arundel County, Patuxent District in 1692. His career and some lineage listed here are per McKenzie, but are ascribed to Samuel Brown nephew of Abell (the Samuel of Bermuda, clearly in error). McKenzie was probably unaware that Abell had two sons, Samuel and Robert.

About illegitimacy in the Chesapeake area: unlike the Puritans, "Cavalier" gentlemen, forerunners of Southern plantation society, were encouraged to exercise their manhood in a broad range. Nevertheless, blood lines were strictly defended, so those offspring of male adventures (with widows, lowborn women, servants, slaves) went unrecognized by the courts in matters of inheritance.

Samuel married Mary ---. They had the following children:
```
85      i.    Thomas (about 1660-)
86      ii.   James
87      iii.  Abel
88      iv.   Elizabeth
89      v.    Mary
```

46. Robert BROWNE, 5G Grandson, born about 1684. Robert died in 1769 in Anne Arundel Co. MD. Robert Browne was a resident of Anne Arundel County, that part of which became Howard County. He was about fifteen years of age and unmarried at the 1698 writing of his father's will, which was to give him, on Abell's death, Harwood in Anne Arundel and Abell's Lot in Baltimore County. Probably older stepbrother Samuel made claim to Harwood in 1705, but Robert prevailed (being then barely at age 21 or 22). He sold from both in 1715 (*Liber IBZ*, pp. 211-213) but retained part of Harwood. His will (*Liber WD2*, p. 66 30 Jun 1765 proved 2 Mar 1769) named his surviving children. That will gave Rocky Ridge to a minor grandson Frederick, his son James' son. In a deposition of Baltimore County dated 15 Apr 1747 Robert Brown of Anne Arundel County "age about 63" (placing his birth in about 1683) stated that he had examined his land borders in Baltimore County 28-29 years earlier (*Abstracts of Baltimore County Land Commissions*, p. 29; *Liber HWS #4*, folio 51) and in other depositions was 66 in 1749, 74 in 1758, 82 in 1764 (Chancery Court of Maryland). In Maryland Prerogative Court (administration of estate) dated 4 Sep 1769 Anne Arundel County *Liber 100*, Folio 121, his estate was worth 573 pounds, 3 shillings, 4 pence, named kin were John (perhaps an otherwise unidentified son) and

James Brown, executor James Brown. His and children's All Hallows' and Queen Caroline's Parish dates here are per Wright *(Anne Arundel County Church Records 17th and 18th C.*, 1989, 1994, pp. 14 -24) because Wright had access to the original texts and the later typed copies were sometimes found to be in error.

Writer McCallahan confused two Roberts, one the son of Abell and the other "of Wrighton," which Richardson had clarified years earlier. Further, Robert Browne's mother is widely reputed to have been Nancy Cockey by Abell's first marriage, but no evidence has been identified. I think this to be a misreading of Scharf's history, which names Nancy Cockey as Abel Brown Jr.'s wife, but who was actually Ann Cockey, Elias' wife *(History of Western Maryland,* p. 870). Additionally, no record of another marriage has surfaced other than Richardson's and Warfield's unsupported assertions.

On 18 Jun 1702 Robert first married Katherine (CHENEY) PARNELL, daughter of Richard CHENEY and Elliner ---, in All Hallows' Parish, Anne Arundel County MD, born on 12 Mar 1679 in All Hallows' Parish, Anne Arundel County MD. Katherine died in Mar 1713 in All Hallows' Parish, Anne Arundel County MD. Buried on 13 Mar 1713 in All Hallows' Parish, Anne Arundel County MD. The Cheney line, including this family, is noted in Doliante, S.S., *Maryland and Virginia Colonials: Genealogies of Some Colonial Families* (1991), pp. 117-119. Katherine was daughter of Richard Cheney and Ellinor and widow of James Parnell who died in 1701. She had two daughters previously with Parnell (per Richardson). Since it is unlikely that she was still having children at 58, especially as she was recorded as being buried 13 Mar 1713, another wife named Katherine is probable but no record is found in church archives or elsewhere. They had the following children:

90	i.	Abel (about 1704 - about 1796)
91	ii.	Robert (1707 - before 1716)
92	iii.	Priscilla (1709 - after 1765)
93	iv.	Comfort (1710-1769)
94	v.	Hester (1712-)

In about 1715 Robert second married Catherine ---. Catherine died before 1765.

Catherine, wife of Robert Browne of Anne Arundel County, waived dower in a property sale, 1715, of "Abell's Lott" in Baltimore County (Baltimore County Land Records *TR#A*, Folio 365). She also waived dower in a 1749 land sale *(Anne Arundel Deeds, RB* 3, Folio 20406). She was not mentioned in Robert's will, so her death occurred between 1749 and 1765. They had the following children:

95	i.	Robert (1716-1764)
96	ii.	Benjamin (1722-1768)
97	iii.	Sarah (1723 - before 1765)
98	iv.	William (1727 - before 1769)
99	v.	Rebecca (1729-)
100	vi.	James (1731-)
101	vii.	Samuel (1737-)

Family of Hannah BROWNE (33) and Isaac LANE

47. Hannah LANE, born on 27 Mar 1670/1 in Middletown, Middlesex Co. CT. Hannah died in Glastonbury CT, on 27 May 1734; she was 64.

On 27 Jul 1704 when Hannah was 34, she married Benjamin SMITH, in Hartford, Hartford Co. CT, born about 1652. Benjamin died on 20 Jul 1730/1 in Glastonbury CT. They had the following children:

102	i.	Richard (1705-1774)
103	ii.	Jeduthan (1709-1781)
104	iii.	Manoah (1711-1752)

48. Elizabeth LANE, born on 24 Jan 1672/3 in Middletown, Middlesex Co. CT. Elizabeth died in 1708 in New Haven CT.

In May 1693 Elizabeth married Joseph CLARK, in New Haven CT, born on 27 Oct 1668 in New Haven CT. Joseph died in 1703 in New Haven CT. They had the following children:

105	i.	Hannah (1693 - about 1764)

106	ii.	Joseph (1695-1765)	
107	iii.	Sarah (1698-)	
108	iv.	Mehitabel (1701-1723)	
109	v.	Silence (1703-1794)	

49. Eleanor LANE, born on 9 Apr 1674.

On 11 Feb 1695/6 when Eleanor was 20, she first married Ebenezer BROWN, in New Haven CT, born on 12 Nov 1670 in New Haven CT. Ebenezer died in 1707 in New Haven CT. Per Jacobus, but New Haven did not then exist; the towns of Milford and Orange were the previous political units in that area. They had the following children:

110	i.	Hannah (1696-1787)
111	ii.	Eleanor (1698-)
112	iii.	Ebenezer (1700-1722)
113	iv.	Rebecca (1703-)
114	v.	Mary (1706-1789)

On 2 Jan 1709/10 when Eleanor was 34, she second married Samuel BLAKESLEE, in New Haven CT, born on 28 Jan 1685 in New Haven CT. Samuel died in Roxbury CT, on 24 Dec 1753; he was 68. They had the following children:

115	i.	Miriam (about 1711-)
116	ii.	Sarah (about 1713-1796)
117	iii.	Thankful (1714-1752)
118	iv.	Samuel (1718-1775)

50. Isaac LANE (twin), born on 22 Dec 1675 in Middletown, Middlesex Co. CT. Isaac died in Middletown, Middlesex Co. CT, on 25 Dec 1675; he was less than 1.

51. John LANE (twin), born on 22 Dec 1675 in Middletown, Middlesex Co. CT. John died in Middletown, Middlesex Co. CT, on 26 Dec 1675; he was less than 1.

52. John LANE (twin), born on 28 Jan 1676/7 in Middletown, Middlesex Co. CT. John died in Middletown, Middlesex Co. CT, on 10 Apr 1677; he was 1.

53. Sarah LANE (twin), born on 28 Jan 1676/7 in Middletown, Middlesex Co. CT. Sarah died in Middletown, Middlesex Co. CT, on 6 May 1677; she was 1.

54. Sarah LANE, born on 29 Sep 1678 in Middletown, Middlesex Co. CT. Sarah died in Middletown, Middlesex Co. CT, on 30 Sep 1737; she was 59.

On 19 Nov 1702 when Sarah was 24, she married Zaccheus CANDEE, in New Haven CT, born on 5 Jan 1675/6 in New Haven CT. Zaccheus died in New Haven CT, on 29 Dec 1743; he was 68. They had the following children:

119	i.	Zaccheus (1703-1777)
120	ii.	Isaac (1704-)
121	iii.	Theophilus (1706-1782)
122	iv.	Sarah (1708-)
123	v.	Hannah (1711-)
124	vi.	Abigail (1714-1743)
125	vii.	Mary (1716-)

55. Samuel LANE, born on 24 Nov 1679 in Middletown, Middlesex Co. CT. Samuel died in Middletown, Middlesex Co. CT, on 11 Dec 1679; he was less than 1.

56. John LANE, born on 10 Jan 1680/1 in Middletown, Middlesex Co. CT. John died in Middletown, Middlesex Co. CT, on 3 May 1716; he was 36. In addition to Jacobus, source for the following Lane-Peterson line is Alice Marie Beard.

In Oct 1712 John married Anna ALLEN, born on 12 Sep 1677 in Middletown, Middlesex Co. CT. They had the following children:

126	i.	John (1713-)
127	ii.	John (1715-1761)

57. Isaac LANE, born on 5 Nov 1683 in Middletown, Middlesex Co. CT. Isaac died in Feb 1745 in Middletown, Middlesex Co. CT.

Isaac first married Mindwell MERRY, born in Hartford, Hartford Co. CT. Mindwell died on 3 Nov 1732. They had the following children:
128	i.	Mary (1709-)
129	ii.	Isaac (1711-)
130	iii.	Mindwell (1714-1778)
131	iv.	Nathaniel (1717-1754)
132	v.	Samuel (1719-)
133	vi.	Cornelius (1722-)
134	vii.	Zaccheus (1724 - about 1755)
135	viii.	Hannah (1726-)
136	ix.	Ashbel (1729-1807)

Isaac second married Isabel WHITMORE.

Isaac third married Elizabeth CORNWELL.

58. Benoni LANE, born on 13 Feb 1684/5 in Middletown, Middlesex Co. CT. Benoni died in Middletown, Middlesex Co. CT, on 10 Dec 1688; he was 4.

59. Mary LANE, born on 25 Apr 1687 in Middletown, Middlesex Co. CT. Mary died in Middletown, Middlesex Co. CT, on 4 Aug 1687; she was less than 1.

60. Mary LANE, born on 30 Aug 1688 in Middletown, Middlesex Co. CT.

61. Abigail LANE, born on 8 Apr 1690 in Middletown, Middlesex Co. CT. Abigail died in Middletown, Middlesex Co. CT, stillborn, on 8 Apr 1690; she was less than 1.

62. Nathaniel LANE, born on 28 Mar 1694 in Middletown, Middlesex Co. CT. Nathaniel died in Nov 1702 in Middletown, Middlesex Co. CT.

Family of Nathaniel BROWNE (34) and Martha HUGHES

63. Mary BROWNE, born on 2 Mar 1677/8 in Middletown, Middlesex Co. CT. Mary died in Guilford CT, on 30 Mar 1751; she was 74.

On 21 Apr 1713 when Mary was 36, she married James EVARTS, born on 15 Feb 1699/70 in Guilford CT. James died in Guilford CT, on 3 Jan 1738/9; he was 38. They had the following children:
137	i.	Eleanor (1714-)
138	ii.	Rueben (1719-1776)
139	iii.	Elizabeth (1719-1750)

64. Martha BROWNE, born on 3 Feb 1679/80 in Middletown, Middlesex Co. CT. Martha died in Middletown, Middlesex Co. CT, on 30 Apr 1698; she was 19.

65. Eleanor BROWNE, born on 30 Jun 1681 in Middletown, Middlesex Co. CT. Eleanor died in Middletown, Middlesex Co. CT, on 11 Jan 1712/13; she was 30. Did not marry.

66. Nathaniel BROWNE, born on 18 Sep 1683 in Middletown, Middlesex Co. CT. Nathaniel died in Middletown, Middlesex Co. CT, on 7 May 1735; he was 51.

Nathaniel married Sarah BACON, born on 14 Sep 169? Sarah died after 1742 in probably Lyme CT. They had one child:
140	i.	Sarah (1709-1796)

Family of Thomas BROWNE (35) and Hannah LEE

67. Samuel BROWNE, born on 8 Jun 1692 in Westfield, Hampden Co. MA.

On 12 Mar 1713 when Samuel was 20, he first married Elizabeth COLLINS. Elizabeth died on 2 Jul 1714 in Colchester, New London Co. CT.

On 11 Apr 1715 when Samuel was 22, he second married Priscilla KENT, in Suffield, Hartford Co. CT, born on 24 Feb 1694/5 in Suffield, Hartford Co. CT. They had one child:
    141   i.   Samuell (1723-)

Family of John BROWNE (36) and Anna PORTER

68. Thomas BROWNE, born on 3 Mar 1685/6 in Middletown, Middlesex Co. CT. Died young.

69. Hannah BROWNE, born on 28 Oct 1688 in Middletown, Middlesex Co. CT. Hannah died in Middletown, Middlesex Co. CT, on 7 Jan 1716/17; she was 27.

70. John BROWNE, born on 2 Dec 1690 in Middletown, Middlesex Co. CT. John died in 1744 in Middletown, Middlesex Co. CT. "On 11 May 1714, Richard Smith, late of Hartford, now of Windsor, petitioned for divorce from Elizabeh Cole, late of Hartford, now of Middletown, 'and a married wife to John Brown of Middletown.' alleging that she was married to Brown in the fall of 1712 (by Nathaniel Chauncy of Durham), and that she has a child by Brown. The divorce was granted" (Jacobus, op. cit., Vol 23, I, p. 106., after *Connecticut Archives, Crimes and Misdemeanors, Vol. 3.*).

On 24 Oct 1711 when John was 20, he married Elizabeth SMITH, born in Hartford CT? They had the following children:
    142   i.   Elizabeth (1712-)
    143   ii.   Dorothy (1715-)
    144   iii.   Hannah (1717-)
    145   iv.   Nathaniel (1718 - about 1746)
    146   v.   Lydia (1720-)
    147   vi.   John (1722-)
    148   vii.   Mary (1725-1763)

71. Mary BROWNE, born on 8 Nov 1693 in Middletown, Middlesex Co. CT. Mary died in Middletown, Middlesex Co. CT, on 31 Jan 1716/17; she was 22.

72. Nathaniel BROWNE, born on 1 Sep 1695 in Middletown, Middlesex Co. CT. D. young.

73. Thomas BROWNE, born in 1698 in Middletown, Middlesex Co. CT. D. young.

74. Martha BROWNE, born in 1700 in Middletown, Middlesex Co. CT.

75. Abigail BROWNE, born on 5 Feb 1701/2 in Middletown, Middlesex Co. CT. Abigail died before 1765 in Middletown, Middlesex Co. CT.

On 4 Oct 1720 when Abigail was 19, she married Thomas STEVENS, in Middletown, Middlesex Co. CT. Thomas died in Oct 1757 in Middletown, Middlesex Co. CT. They had the following children:
    149   i.   Aaron (about 1721-)
    150   ii.   Hannah (1722-)
    151   iii.   Thomas (1725-)
    152   iv.   Aaron (1728-)
    153   v.   John (1731-)

154	vi.	Robert (1732-)
155	vii.	Hannah (1735-)
156	viii.	Abigail (1738-)
157	ix.	Sarah (1741-)
158	x.	Mary (1743-)

NINTH GENERATION

Family of Robert BROWNE (38)

76. --- **BROWNE**, 6G Grandson. Had a guardian, unnamed, in 1698, Bermuda.

Family of John BROWNE (40) and Sarah ---

77. Sarah BROWNE, 6G Granddaughter. "Sarah of Tuckers Town daughter of John and Sarah Brown puts herself apprentice" to David Ming of Cooper's Island 20 Sep 1672 (*Book V A*, p. 424); on 19 Sep 1675 assigns of David Ming [deceased] returned to her parents, and on 19 Sep 1675 her brother Solomon Brown became apprentice of Joseph Ming.

78. Solomon BROWNE, 6G Grandson.

Family of James BROWNE (41) and Mary TUCKER

79. Robert Browne, 6G Grandson, born after 1700 in Warwick, Bermuda. Robert died after 18 Jun 1752 in St. George's, Bermuda. Per *Descendants of John Darrell*. Will dated 18 Jun 1752.

Robert married Elizabeth ---.

Family of Samuel BROWNE (42) and Elizabeth ---

80. Sarah BROWNE, 6G Granddaughter, born about 1698 in Bermuda. Baptized 5 Aug 1698, Southampton Parish, Bermuda (Hallett).

81. Bristow BROWNE, 6G Grandson, born about 1699 in Bermuda. Baptized 5 Sep 1699, Southampton Parish, Bermuda (Hallett). Bristow Brown son of Bristow of Warwick Parish baptized 20 Jan 1744 Warwick Parish Bermuda; Robert Brown son of Bristow Brown and Lois baptized 26 Nov 1749 (Hallett). I would guess these to be grandchildren of Bristow Sr.

82. John BROWNE, 6G Grandson, born about 1703 in Bermuda. Baptized 1 May 1703, Southampton Parish, Bermuda (Hallett).

Family of John BRISTOW Jr. (43) and Sarah TUCKER

83. Sarah BRISTOW, 6G Granddaughter.

84. Katherine BRISTOW, 6G Granddaughter.

Family of Samuel BROWNE (45) and Mary ---

85. Thomas BROWNE, 6G Grandson, born about 1660. Listed by Mackenzie. He "was evidently the eldest child, as his father conveyed to him large estates before his death" (Vol. I, p. 46). Probably by a previous marriage, and thus not mentioned in his father's will. The descendants of Thomas Browne are per Mackenzie (Vol. I, pp. 47-49), adding that Thomas married a widow, had also several daughters names unknown. Possible wife Katherine. Children:

159	i.	Samuel
160	ii.	John
161	iii.	Vachel
162	iv.	Joshua

86. James BROWNE, 6G Grandson. Listed by Mackenzie. May or may not be the James by second marriage.

87. Abel BROWNE, 6G Grandson. Listed by Mackenzie. Probable owner of the tract named Discovery and other properties amounting to 2,590 acres in Baltimore County purchased 1725 and listed in Coldham, P.W., *Settlers of Maryland 1679-1783*, p. 84. Discovery patent was of 200 acres, listed in *P.L. #6*, Folio 191.

88. Elizabeth BROWNE, 6G Granddaughter. Listed by Mackenzie.

89. Mary BROWNE, 6G Granddaughter. Listed by Mackenzie.

Family of Robert BROWNE (46) and Katherine (CHENEY) PARNELL

90. Abel BROWN Sr., 6G Grandson, born about 1704 in All Hallows' Parish, Anne Arundel County MD. Abel died about Jul 1796 in Baltimore (later Carroll) Co. MD. Abel Brown's baptism dated 25 Jun 1704 was noted in he All Hallows' Parish Registry. He received one shilling in his father Robert's will, probably because of previous gifts of land (see below). He witnessed John Dorsey's gifts of land to children in Anne Arundel County Maryland, 2 Aug 1735. In March 1745/6 he was one of several co-signers of a petition to increase allowances to court jurors (*Calendar of Maryland State Papers, The Black Books*, #511). He served as Vestryman at Christ Church Anne Arundel County 1738. On 5 Oct 1748 Abel Brown and Elizabeth sold 137.5 acres known as Brown's Topyard in Anne Arundel County to James MacGill. That land had been patented 20 May 1725 by Robert Browne and had been granted to Abel 27 Apr 1742 (*Liber RB 7*, Folio 139; *Liber RB 7*, Folios 52-4). Likewise, Abel and Elizabeth Brown sold 100 acres in Anne Arundel County on the same day, 5 Oct 1748, to James MacGill, land that was patented 10 Jun 1734 by Robert Brown and then granted to Abel (*Liber RB 7* Folios 52-4). Listed as "planter" in Anne Arundel County 1747, a "gentleman" of Anne Arundel County in 1749. He purchased Owens (Owings) Outland Plains, 400 acres, on 5 Nov 1747, from John Paca (witnessed by Robert Browne), and John's Chance, 400 acres, from John Hammond on 22 Jul 1749, signing as "Abell of Anne Arundel County, planter."

He abandoned his Anne Arundel church pew (shared with Robert) about 1749, "having removd out of this parrish." On 13 Nov 1749 he and Elizabeth sold 400 acres in Prince George County (later Frederick) to Edward Crow, purchased in 1741 (*Liber RB 3*, Folios 202-3), calling himself a planter of Anne Arundel. Rocky Ridge, 70 acres purchased 28 Jun 1741in Anne Arundel, was sold 7 Jul 1759 by Abel Brown "of Baltimore County" and Elizabeth to Robert Brown, perhaps his father, of Anne Arundel County (*Liber BB 2*, Folio 303). In the 1754 tax list he owned Owings Outland Plains, Hunter's Chance, and Fine Soil Forest. He was called a "planter" of Baltimore County in the 1758 tax list. He purchased Bynam's Run in Baltimore County, a tract originally patented by Abell his grandfather and sold by Robert to Benjamin Bond. When he remarried and as a protection for the sons of his first marriage, he gave in 1763 large tracts to each son who had come of age. He is found in 1763 on tax list. In Baltimore County's St. Thomas Parish Register, he signed an oath of affirmation to the King on 7 May 1754 and "The Test of Nontransubstantiation in the Holy Sacrament" 1753; was Church Warden in the years 1754-55. Four sons' names (Abel, Jacob, David, Samuel) were given in his indenture of 16 Apr 1763 which gave lands to each, but his much later will, plus other documents, indicate a larger family that other searchers have overlooked.

As congregations grew another meeting-place was needed and in 1771 Abel Brown contributed to the establishment of St. Barnabas' Church or the Chapel of Ease on the forks of the Patapsco River in Delaware Hundred. He served as overseer of a road until 1782, until replaced by Peter Tevis, who was later replaced by Francis Snowden, all connected by marriages. In the 1783 tax list he owned John's Chance of 320 acres and Owings Outland Plains of 420 acres. In 1784 the aged Abel Brown Sr. petitioned the county to confirm his land boundaries. In days of "metes and bounds" surveys this was probably a wise move to avoid controversy regarding the division of his estate.

In 1786 he sold his remaining interest to the old family property in Anne Arundel County, Harwood, to Vachel Dorsey, of Vachel (Warfield, p. 169). His 3 Aug 1788 - 9 Jul 1796 will Baltimore County *Will Book 5*, p. 382 named children alive at that time (Elias, Moses, Jacob, Abel, John, Nancy, Ruth, and Rebecca), wife Susannah, and specified his ownership of John's Chance and Deavers' Forest. The 1790 Census of Baltimore County's Delaware Hundred on p. 53 enumerated Abel Brown Sr.: 2022-18 (2 white males over 16, 2 white females, 2 "other", and 18 slaves). His property was next to Abel Jr., and Absolom and Adam Shipley. George Horvath's *1798 Particular Assessment List for Baltimore County* (p. 102) listed him with one slave, occupants Joshua Brown (perhaps his great-grandson) and Joseph Gray, ownership of 330 acres part of Hunter's Chance, an old log dwelling house, log cabin, smokehouse.

The administration of his estate begun in 1796 and settled in 1801 named Elias and Moses Brown as administrators, Stephen Cockey and Thomas Phillips posted security. In his will, Abel expressed the wish that he be buried in his own orchard. That was the "Brown Cemetery" cited by McCallahan and further described in *Carroll County Cemeteries Vol. 1 Southeast* (Westminster MD: Carroll County Genealogical Society, 1989), p. 85 as the "Brown/Owings Cemetery," and quite sentimentally described in Albert Brown's family manuscript. That cemetery, read in 1897 and in poor condition, is now grown over and its stones lost. Why did he not choose to be buried in the St. Thomas Parish churchyard? One guess is that after the Revolution, the Virginian Church of England lost its power to tax and tithe, to fine those who did not attend, and to summarily select residents for vestryman or warden service. The Browns, and others, then drifted away from church life or changed denomination although Moses and Elias remained in the church and its activities. Finding fewer descendant Browns in post-Revolutionary church records reflects this drift. In fact, the rector of St. Thomas Parish, a Tory, "fled to England" in 1775 after the populace had turned against him, and as a result there was no minister there for some years, save for the occasional itinerant Methodist preacher (*Centennial of Wesley Chapel*, p. 9).

For other accounts of Abel's lineage, see also Nancy Etta Brown Southard's DAR membership 22446 (DAR *Lineage Book* Vol. 23, p. 179, although some details regarding are, in my opinion, erroneous), and SAR #102209, 110830. Valuable information on this line was found in the aforementioned 1897 manuscript of Albert S. Brown held at the University of Maryland College Park. That author emphasized Abel Brown's title, given "when the term Gentleman was not so elastic as now, when it is made to fit all classes of individuals who wear pantaloons." McCallahan's data on the following family came evidently from the manuscript of Albert S. Brown via an intermediary, Charles Butler Rogers, who wrote in the 1920s and whose papers on the Cockey family are found at the Maryland Historical Society; Brown was also, perhaps, the purveyor if not author of Abell Browne's widespread legend of Scottish origin.

Abel first married Elizabeth ---. Elizabeth died about 1758 in Baltimore (later Carroll) Co. MD. Elizabeth Brown signed off on her husband's land sales, as above, in 1748, 1749, and 1759. She was not mentioned when Abel gave land to his sons in anticipation of a second marriage. They had the following children:

163	i.	Abel (about 1735-1817)
164	ii.	David (about 1740 - before 1775)
165	iii.	Jacob (- about 1798)
166	iv.	John (about 1742-1801)
167	v.	James (about 1743 - about 1782)
168	vi.	Samuel (about 1745-1777)
169	vii.	Nancy

In about 1760 Abel second married Susannah SHIPLEY, daughter of Adam SHIPLEY and Catherine HAMILTON, in Baltimore (later Carroll) Co. MD, born in 1742. Susannah died after 1796 in Baltimore (later Carroll) Co. MD. Buried in Brown Family Cemetery. The Shipleys, Abraham and Adam, lived near the Browns; see 1790 Baltimore 2 Delaware Hundreds Census, p 53. For more on the Shipleys see D. S. Granger, *The Shipleys of Maryland*. They had the following children:

170	i.	Adam (1764-)
171	ii.	Elias (1765-1800)
172	iii.	Moses (1768-1817)
173	iv.	Ruth Ann (1770-1816)

| 174 | v. | Susannah (1773-) |
| 175 | vi. | Rebecca (1774-1852) |

91. Robert BROWNE, 6G Grandson, born on 4 May 1707, baptized 25 Jul 1707 (or 2 Jun 1709) in All Hallows' Parish, Anne Arundel County MD. Robert died before 1716. This Robert apparently died, because another son Robert followed.

92. Priscilla BROWNE, 6G Granddaughter, born in 1709 in All Hallows' Parish, Anne Arundel County MD. Priscilla died after 1765. Baptized 2 Jun 1709. She received one shilling in her father's will as Priscilla Crafts. Sharf's *History* mentioned that one of Abel's sisters was murdered in about 1775 by Indians near Harper's Ferry while on her way westward.

Priscilla married --- CRAFTS.

93. Comfort BROWNE, 6G Granddaughter, born on 3 Jul 1710 in All Hallows' Parish, Anne Arundel County MD. Comfort died in 1769-1778 in Tryon Co. NC. Baptized 21 Oct 1713. She received one shilling in her father's will as Comfort Lanham. The Lanham-Osborne family and descendants are per Pj Sisseck, Kristin Dougherty, Colleen Mhyre, and Richard Bates. Mhyre and Sisseck list her name as Barbely Comfort.

In about 1748 Comfort married John LANHAM, son of William LANHAM and Alice TALBOTT, in York Co. SC, born on 12 Dec 1723 in Prince George's Co. MD. John died in 1765 in Mecklinburg Co., NC. John Lanham was once held captive by either hostile Indians, or as a political prisoner during the Revolutionary War. A co-prisoner was Caleb Osborne, uncle of Comfort Lanham Osborne's husband. Ref.: "Early Osbornes and Alleys" (per Cisseck). The surname is also rendered as Langham. They had the following children:

176	i.	Comfort Lana Renne (1749 - about 1824)
177	ii.	Sarah
178	iii.	Esther
179	iv.	Jean
180	v.	William (about 1755-)
181	vi.	August Abel (1762-1837)

94. Hester BROWNE, 6G Granddaughter, born in 1712 in All Hallows' Parish, Anne Arundel County MD. Baptized 21 Apr 1712. Assumedly died or married and left the area before 30 Jun 1765 because she was unmentioned in Robert's will of that date.

Family of Robert BROWNE (46) and Catherine ---

95. Robert BROWN, 6G Grandson, born in 1716 in All Hallows' Parish, Anne Arundel County MD. Robert died on 9 Aug 1764 in Conocoteague, MD.

96. Benjamin BROWN, 6G Grandson, born on 12 Feb 1722 in Anne Arundel Co. MD. Benjamin died in Jun 1768 in Anne Arundel Co. MD. Received one shilling in his father's will. Benjamin Brown's will dated 9 Jun 1768 was proved 12 Jun 1768 (*Liber 36*, Folio 746). Anne Arundel *Will Book 36*, p. 476 named wife Susannah, son Samuel. Others were Rachel Todd, Ruth Todd, Joshua, Vachel, Susannah, Richard, Charles, Ephraim, Rebecca and Benjamin Brown Jr. The Maryland Prerogative Court of Anne Arundel County dated 18 Apr 1770 (*Liber 103*, Folio 92) valued his estate at 241 pounds, 14 shillings 6 pence, kin Joshua Brown, Aquila Randall, executors Susannah Brown, Samuel Brown. His plantation was Good Fellowship. Sources: Warfield p. 491, son Samuel's family from *Ohio Chapter of Florida DAR*, Vol. II, p. 73; Shelton pp. 118-21; and "A Brown Family," a well-crafted but anonymous manuscript in Maryland Historical Society Archives, Filing Case A.

Benjamin married Susannah RANDALL, daughter of Christopher RANDALL and Ann CHEW, born about 1728 in Anne Arundel Co. MD. Susannah died on 28 Apr 1819 in Anne Arundel Co. MD. Benjamin's cousin. They had the following children:

182	i.	Samuel (1747-1833)
183	ii.	Rachel (about 1742-1809)
184	iii.	Ruth
185	iv.	Joshua

186	v.	Vachel
187	vi.	Susannah
188	vii.	Richard
189	viii.	Charles
190	ix.	Ephraim
191	x.	Rebecca
192	xi.	Benjamin

97. Sarah BROWN, 6G Granddaughter, born on 9 Apr 1723 in Queen Caroline now Howard Co. Sarah died before 1765. Assumedly died or married and left the area before 30 Jun 1765 because she was unmentioned in Robert's will of that date.

98. William BROWN, 6G Grandson, born on 5 Jul 1727 in Queen Caroline now Howard Co. William died before 1769. Received one shilling in his father's 1765 will. Shipley family information has had it that William married Elizabeth Shipley, but that has not been confirmed. A William Brown married an Elizabeth Shipley in Anne Arundel County much later, in 1800, hence a possible confusion.

William married --- ---. They had one child:
| 193 | i. | Elijah (before 1765-) |

99. Rebecca BROWN, 6G Granddaughter, born on 3 Sep 1729 in Queen Caroline now Howard Co. She received one shilling in her father's will as Rebecca Harrison.

Rebecca married --- Harrison.

100. James BROWN, 6G Grandson, born on 2 Mar 1731 in Queen Caroline now Howard Co. James Brown received his father's personal goods (excluding lands) and was appointed executor of his father's estate in Robert Brown's will of 30 June 1765. James Browne was listed in 1762-1765 Index to Aquila Hall's *Assessment Ledger of Baltimore County*. Child:
| 194 | i. | Frederick (before 1764-) |

101. Samuel BROWN, 6G Grandson, born on 1 Jul 1737 in Queen Caroline now Howard Co. Samuel assumedly died before 30 Jun 1765 because he was unmentioned in Robert's will of that date.

Family of Hannah LANE (47) and Benjamin SMITH

102. Richard SMITH, born on 8 Aug 1705 in Wethersfield CT. Richard died in Glastonbury CT, on 16 May 1774; he was 68.

On 25 Nov 1730 when Richard was 25, he first married Abigail CLARK, in Glastonbury CT. Abigail died on 27 Jul 1752 in Glastonbury CT. They had the following children:
195	i.	Benjamin (1731-1803)
196	ii.	Abraham (1733-1733)
197	iii.	Abraham (1734-)
198	iv.	Isaac (1735-1796)
199	v.	Israel (1737-1783)
200	vi.	Elihu (1740-1758)
201	vii.	Irene (1742-)
202	viii.	Tirzah (1743-1790)
203	ix.	Asaph (1745 - before 1781)
204	x.	Samuel (1749-1749)
205	xi.	Achsah (1751-1759)

On 2 May 1754 when Richard was 48, he second married Hannah BIDWELL, in Glastonbury CT, born on 6 May 1716.

103. Jeduthan SMITH, born on 23 Oct 1709 in Wethersfield CT. Jeduthan died in Glastonbury CT, on 20 Nov 1781; he was 72.

Jeduthan first married Mary KIMBERLY, born on 8 Jun 1712 in Glastonbury CT. Mary died in Glastonbury CT, on 6 Oct 1751; she was 39. They had the following children:

206	i.	Mary (about 1733 - after 1816)
207	ii.	Hannah (about 1735-)
208	iii.	Anne (about 1737-)
209	iv.	Bathsheba (about 1739 - after 1811)
210	v.	Thomas (about 1741-1773)
211	vi.	Jeduthan (1744-1749)
212	vii.	Elizabeth (about 1746-1825)
213	viii.	Ruth (1748-1750)

Jeduthan second married Hannah ---, born about 1726. Hannah died on 17 Dec 1798 in Glastonbury CT. They had the following children:

214	i.	Prudence (1756-1811)
215	ii.	Mercy (- after 1811)
216	iii.	Thankful
217	iv.	Jedidiah (1764-1826)

104. Manoah SMITH, born on 19 Feb 1711 in Wethersfield CT. Manoah died in Glastonbury CT, on 29 Aug 1752; he was 41.

Manoah married Lucy ---. They had the following children:

218	i.	Lucy (about 1745-1822)
219	ii.	Jemima (-1824)
220	iii.	Dorothy (about 1750-1831)
221	iv.	Sarah (1751-1830)

Family of Elizabeth LANE (48) and Joseph CLARK

105. Hannah CLARK, born on 21 Feb 1693/4 in New Haven CT. Hannah died about 1764.

In 1717 Hannah first married John BINGLEY. John died about 1736. They had the following children:

222	i.	William (1718-)
223	ii.	Hannah (1722-1802)

Hannah second married Joseph COLLINS. They had one child:

224	i.	Ann (1737-1822)

106. Joseph CLARK, born on 15 Feb 1695/6 in New Haven CT. Joseph died in Middletown, Middlesex Co. CT, on 8 Jun 1765; he was 70.

Joseph married Miriam CORNWELL, born on 27 Sep 1702 in Middletown, Middlesex Co. CT. Miriam died in Middletown, Middlesex Co. CT, on 27 May 1772; she was 69. They had the following children:

225	i.	Miriam (1726-1754)
226	ii.	Sybil (1728-)
227	iii.	Joseph (1731-1731)
228	iv.	Joseph (1733-1797)
229	v.	Benjamin (1736-)
230	vi.	Elizabeth (1739-)
231	vii.	Timothy (1742-1807)

107. Sarah CLARK, born on 7 Aug 1698 in New Haven CT.

108. Mehitabel CLARK, born on 17 Jul 1701 in New Haven CT. Mehitabel died in New Haven CT, on 25 Oct 1723; she was 22.

Mehitabel married Thomas DOWNS, born on 7 Jun 1699 in New Haven CT. Thomas died in West Haven CT, on 1 Oct 1785; he was 86. Per Jacobus, but New Haven was not incorporated at that time. Thus this family lived in either the towns of Milford or Orange. They had one child:

    232   i.   Mehitabel (1723-1795)

109. Silence CLARK, born on 31 Oct 1703 in New Haven CT. Silence died in Derby CT, on 10 Nov 1794; she was 91.

Silence married John LUM.

Family of Eleanor LANE (49) and Ebenezer BROWN

110. Hannah BROWN, born on 31 Jan 1696/7 in New Haven CT. Hannah died in 1787 in West Haven CT.

On 9 Feb 1725/6 when Hannah was 29, she married Ebenezer TROWBRIDGE, in New Haven CT, born on 25 Jul 1702 in West Haven CT. Ebenezer died in West Haven CT, on 24 Nov 1777; he was 75. They had the following children:

    233   i.   Hannah (1726-)
    234   ii.   Ebenezer (1728-1767)
    235   iii.   Sarah (1731-)
    236   iv.   Mary (about 1733-)

111. Eleanor BROWN, born on 1 Mar 1698/9 in New Haven CT.

Eleanor married Daniel HODGE, born on 28 Jan 1693/4 in New Haven CT. Daniel died in New Haven CT, on 10 Jun 1777; he was 84. They had the following children:

    237   i.   Sarah (1726-1802)
    238   ii.   Jesse (1727-)
    239   iii.   Daniel (1720-1787)
    240   iv.   Benjamin (1731-1776)
    241   v.   Eleanor (1734-1745)
    242   vi.   Mary (1736-1805)
    243   vii.   Martha (1740-)
    244   viii.   Rebecca (1743-)

112. Ebenezer BROWN, born on 25 Feb 1700/1 in New Haven CT. Ebenezer died in New Haven CT, on 17 Apr 1722; he was 22.

113. Rebecca BROWN, born in Oct 1703. Rebecca died young.

114. Mary BROWN, born on 17 Mar 1706 in New Haven CT. Mary died in Roxbury CT, on 26 Feb 1789; she was 82. Per Jacobus, but as in the case of New Haven, Roxbury did not yet exist. Roxbury was formed in 1796 from Woodbury.

On 7 Feb 1728/9 when Mary was 21, she married Tilley BLAKESLEE, in Roxbury CT, born on 18 Mar 1705 in New Haven CT. Tilley died in Roxbury CT, on 8 Mar 1769; he was 63. They had the following children:

    245   i.   Mary (1729-1748)
    246   ii.   Tilley (1731-)
    247   iii.   Jonathan (1732-)
    248   iv.   Justus (1736-)
    249   v.   Sarah (1736-1759)
    250   vi.   Dan (about 1741-1811)
    251   vii.   Eleanor (about 1743-1828)
    252   viii.   Ebenezer (1745-1770)
    253   ix.   David (1749-1821)

Family of Eleanor LANE (49) and Samuel BLAKESLEE

115. Miriam BLAKESLEE, born about 1711 in Woodbury CT.

On 9 Feb 1731/2 Miriam married David FOOTE, in Woodbury CT, born on 7 Jul 1707. David died in 1797 in Washington CT. They had the following children:

254	i.	Miriam (1735-1738)
255	ii.	David (1737-)
256	iii.	Miriam (1738-)
257	iv.	Isaac (1741-1826)
258	v.	Esther
259	vi.	Dorothy
260	vii.	Mary (about 1749-1820)
261	viii.	Eleanor (1751-)
262	ix.	Aaron

116. Sarah BLAKESLEE, born about 1713 in Woodbury CT. Sarah died on 4 Nov 1796 in Washington CT. Per Jacobus, but Washington was incorporated in 1779 from Woodbury, Litchfield and New Milford.

In Jan 1733 Sarah married Ephraim BAKER, in Woodbury CT, born in 1706/7 in Washington CT. Ephraim died in 1784 in Washington CT. They had the following children:

263	i.	Samuel (about 1734-)
264	ii.	Nathan (1735-)
265	iii.	Daniel (about 1737-)
266	iv.	Sarah (about 1739-1821)
267	v.	Mary
268	vi.	Ephraim
269	vii.	Mehitabel

117. Thankful BLAKESLEE, born on 20 Oct 1714 in Woodbury CT. Thankful died in Woodbury CT, on 8 Oct 1752; she was 37.

Thankful married Elijah BAKER, born on 16 May 1718 in Woodbury CT. Elijah died in Roxbury CT, on 25 Oct 1804; he was 86. They had the following children:

270	i.	Thankful (about 1740-)
271	ii.	Elijah (about 1742-)
272	iii.	Comfort (1744-1817)
273	iv.	Anna (about 1746-)
274	v.	Elijah (about 1748-)
275	vi.	--- (1752-1752)

118. Samuel BLAKESLEE, born on 22 Nov 1718 in Woodbury CT. Samuel died in Roxbury CT, on 8 Apr 1775; he was 56.

Samuel married Ruth HURD. They had the following children:

276	i.	Samuel
277	ii.	Ruth (about 1743-)
278	iii.	Rebecca (1745-)
279	iv.	--- (1746-1746)
280	v.	Miriam (about 1747-)
281	vi.	Abraham
282	vii.	Anna (about 1752-1753)
283	viii.	Isaac (about 1754-)
284	ix.	Anna (about 1756-)
285	x.	Joseph (about 1758-)
286	xi.	James (about 1760-)
287	xii.	Eleanor (about 1765-)
288	xiii.	Sabra (1767-)

Family of Sarah LANE (54) and Zaccheus CANDEE

119. Zaccheus CANDEE, born on 6 Jun 1703 in Middletown, Middlesex Co. CT. Zaccheus died in 1777 in Middletown, Middlesex Co. CT.

On 10 Nov 1726 when Zaccheus was 23, he married Desire ROBERTS, in Middletown, Middlesex Co. CT. Desire died after 1772. They had the following children:

289	i.	Dinah (1727 - before 1772)
290	ii.	Desire (1728-)
291	iii.	Theophilus (1736-)
292	iv.	Sarah (about 1738-)
293	v.	Zaccheus (about 1740-)
294	vi.	Mary (about 1744-)
295	vii.	Rebecca (about 1746-)
296	viii.	Rhoda (about 1749-)

120. Isaac CANDEE, born on 13 Dec 1704 in Middletown, Middlesex Co. CT.

121. Capt. Theophilus CANDEE, born on 20 Dec 1706 in Middletown, Middlesex Co. CT. Theophilus died in Middletown CT, on 2 May 1782; he was 75.

Theophilus first married Hannah BACON, born on 19 Apr 1712. Hannah died on 29 Oct 1762; she was 50. They had the following children:

297	i.	Hannah (1739-1739)
298	ii.	Samuel (1740-)
299	iii.	Hannah (1743-)
300	iv.	Isaac (1745-1765)
301	v.	John (1750-1821)
302	vi.	Abigail (1752-)

Theophilus second married Ann (CAMP) CORNELL. Ann died on 19 May 1790. widow of Capt. Daniel Cornwell.

122. Sarah CANDEE, born on 3 May 1708 in Middletown, Middlesex Co. CT.

On 9 Mar 1731/2 when Sarah was 22, she married John HIGBY, in Middletown CT, born on 16 Jul 1707 in Middletown CT. John died in 1791 in Middletown CT. They had the following children:

303	i.	John (1732-)
304	ii.	Zaccheus (1734-)
305	iii.	Sarah (1739-)
306	iv.	Abigail (1742-1761)
307	v.	Lois (1744-)
308	vi.	Ephraim (1747-)
309	vii.	Jeduthan (1749-)
310	viii.	Amos (1753-)

123. Hannah CANDEE, born on 20 May 1711 in Middletown, Middlesex Co. CT.

On 10 Feb 1731/2 when Hannah was 19, she married Timothy BAKER, in Middletown CT. Timothy died in 1761 in Middletown CT. They had the following children:

311	i.	Timothy (1732-1732)
312	ii.	Thankful (1733-)
313	iii.	Bayzie (1736-1758)
314	iv.	Susanna (1738-1763)
315	v.	Timothy (1741-)
316	vi.	Hannah (1741-)

317	vii.	Eleanor (1747-1752)
318	viii.	Jeremiah (1749-)
319	ix.	William (1752-)

124. Abigail CANDEE, born on 9 May 1714 in Middletown, Middlesex Co. CT. Abigail died in Middletown CT, on 26 May 1743; she was 29.

On 29 Dec 1737 when Abigail was 23, she married Joseph CORNWELL, in Middletown CT, born on 7 Apr 1711 in Middletown CT. They had the following children:

320	i.	Joseph (1738-1763)
321	ii.	Abigail (1739-1745)
322	iii.	Elizabeth (1741-1742)
323	iv.	--- (1743-1743)

125. Mary CANDEE, born on 20 Aug 1716 in Middletown, Middlesex Co. CT.

On 8 Aug 1750 when Mary was 33, she married Joel ADKINS, in Middletown CT, born on 24 Apr 1725 in Middletown CT. They had the following children:

324	i.	Elisha (1750-1839)
325	ii.	Elizabeth (1752-)
326	iii.	Mary (1752-1762)
327	iv.	Joel (1754-1776)
328	v.	Olive (1756-)

Family of John LANE (56) and Anna ALLEN

126. John LANE, born on 13 Aug 1713 in Middletown, Middlesex Co. CT. Died young.

127. John LANE, born on 1 Nov 1715 in Middletown, Middlesex Co. CT. John died in Middletown CT, on 12 May 1761; he was 45.

On 15 Oct 1747 when John was 31, he first married Anna BACON, in Middletown CT. Anna died on 21 Feb 1752/3. They had the following children:

329	i.	Anna (1751 - before 1780)
330	ii.	John (1752 - before 1777)

On 5 Jun 1754 when John was 38, he second married Letitia HOWELL, in Middletown CT, born about 1732. Letitia died after 1790. They had the following children:

331	i.	Isaac (1755-)
332	ii.	Letitia (1757-)
333	iii.	Allen (1758-)
334	iv.	Sarah (1760 - before 1790)

Family of Isaac LANE (57) and Mindwell MERRY

128. Mary LANE, born on 30 Dec 1709 in Middletown, Middlesex Co. CT.

Mary married Ebenezer EGGLESTON Jr., born on 4 Apr 1712 in Middletown CT. Ebenezer died in Middletown CT, on 28 Apr 1761; he was 49. They had the following children:

335	i.	Mary (1734-)
336	ii.	Elizabeth (1736-)
337	iii.	Ebenezer (1740-1782)
338	iv.	Elihu (1742-)

339	v.	Mindwell (1744-)
340	vi.	Thomas (1747-)
341	vii.	Sybil (1752-)

129. Isaac LANE, born on 18 Feb 1711/12 in Middletown, Middlesex Co. CT. Isaac died young.

130. Mindwell LANE, born on 24 Sep 1714 in Middletown, Middlesex Co. CT. Mindwell died in Middletown CT, on 15 Mar 1778; she was 63.

On 20 Feb 1745/6 when Mindwell was 30, she married Joseph CORNWELL, in Middletown CT, born on 7 Apr 1711 in Middletown CT. They had the following children:
342	i.	Isaac (1747-)
343	ii.	Abigail (1751-)
344	iii.	Mindwell (1755-)

131. Capt. Nathaniel LANE, born on 4 Dec 1717 in Middletown, Middlesex Co. CT. Nathaniel died in Middletown CT, on 6 Jan 1754/5; he was 36.

Nathaniel married Elizabeth GILBERT. Elizabeth died on 16 Dec 1757. They had the following children:
345	i.	Nathaniel (1749-1770)
346	ii.	Elizabeth (1753-1753)
347	iii.	Elizabeth (1754-)

132. Samuel LANE, born on 9 May 1719 in Middletown, Middlesex Co. CT. Died young.

133. Cornelius LANE, born on 25 Sep 1722 in Middletown, Middlesex Co. CT. Served in the 7th Co., 1st Regt., French and Indian War.

Cornelius married --- ---.

134. Zaccheus LANE, born on 10 Feb 1724/5 in Middletown, Middlesex Co. CT. Zaccheus died about 4 Oct 1755 in the French and Indian War.

135. Hannah LANE, born on 12 Jan 1726/7 in Middletown, Middlesex Co. CT.

On 15 Aug 1754 when Hannah was 28, she married Charles DUPEE, in Middletown CT. They had the following children:
348	i.	Charles (1755-)
349	ii.	Hannah (1758-)
350	iii.	Samuel (1761-)
351	iv.	James (1767-)
352	v.	Nancy (1767-)
353	vi.	SARAH (about 1770-)

136. Ashbel LANE, born on 13 Sep 1729 in Middletown, Middlesex Co. CT. Ashbel died in 1807 in Canaan CT.

On 1 Jan 1751/2 when Ashbel was 21, he married Prudence WILLIAMS, in Middletown CT. They had the following children:
354	i.	Hannah (1752-)
355	ii.	Isaac (1754-)
356	iii.	Mindwell (1757-)
357	iv.	Lydia (1769-)
358	v.	Martha "Mattie" (1763-)
359	vi.	Ashbel (1765-)
360	vii.	Cornelius
361	viii.	Nathaniel
362	ix.	Elizabeth

Family of Mary BROWNE (63) and James EVARTS

137. Eleanor EVARTS, born on 9 Dec 1714 in Guilford CT.

Eleanor married Jeremiah GUILD, born on 3 Jul 1711 in Dedham MA. They had the following children:
- 363   i.   Mary
- 364   ii.   Samuel (1743-1815)
- 365   iii.   Jeremiah (1746-1822)

138. Rueben EVARTS (twin), born on 25 Mar 1719 in Guilford CT. Rueben died in Guilford CT, on 31 Jul 1776; he was 57.

On 5 Jun 1751 when Rueben was 32, he married Onner EVARTS, in Guilford CT. They had the following children:
- 366   i.   James (1753-)
- 367   ii.   Elizabeth (1755-)
- 368   iii.   Jeremiah (1761-1778)
- 369   iv.   Reuben (1763-)
- 370   v.   John (1765-)

139. Elizabeth EVARTS (twin), born on 25 Mar 1719 in Guilford CT. Elizabeth died in Guilford CT, on 8 Oct 1750; she was 31.

On 5 May 1742 when Elizabeth was 23, she married Abraham TURNER, in Guilford CT, born on 17 Sep 1718 in Guilford CT. They had the following children:
- 371   i.   Ezra (1743-)
- 372   ii.   Martha (1745-1787)
- 373   iii.   Elizabeth (1749-1752)

Family of Nathaniel BROWNE (66) and Sarah BACON

140. Sarah BROWNE, born on 14 Mar 1709/10 in Middletown, Middlesex Co. CT. Sarah died in Lyme CT, on 3 Jun 1796; she was 87.

In about 1729 Sarah married Rev. George BECKWITH, born on 28 Apr 1703 in Lyme CT. George died in Dec 1793 in Lyme CT. Buried on 22 Dec 1793. A.B. Yale 1728, A.M. and minister at North Church, Lyme; chaplain in the French and Indian War; fellow of the Yale Corporation. They had the following children:
- 374   i.   Rebecca (1732-1732)
- 375   ii.   Sarah (1734-1738)
- 376   iii.   Barzillai (about 1738-1818)
- 377   iv.   Nathaniel Brown (about 1742 - about 1777)
- 378   v.   Penelope (about 1744-1770)
- 379   vi.   George (about 1747-1824)
- 380   vii.   Baruch (about 1751-1778)

Family of Samuel BROWNE (67) and Priscilla KENT

141. Samuell BROWNE, born on 10 Mar 1723 in Colchester, Hartford Co. CT.

Family of John BROWNE (70) and Elizabeth SMITH

142. Elizabeth BROWNE, born on 17 Nov 1712 in Middletown, Middlesex Co. CT. Died young.

143. Dorothy BROWNE, born on 12 Jan 1715 in Middletown, Middlesex Co. CT.

Dorothy married Ebenezer HURLBUT, born on 8 Aug 1711 in Middletown CT. They had the following children:
381	i.	Martha (about 1735-)
382	ii.	Elizabeth (1738-)
383	iii.	Ebenezer (1740-)
384	iv.	John (1742-)
385	v.	Mary (1745-)

144. Hannah BROWNE, born before 7 Apr 1717 in Middletown, Middlesex Co. CT (baptism). D. young.

145. Nathaniel BROWNE, born on 25 Dec 1718 in Middletown, Middlesex Co. CT. Nathaniel died without issue about 1746 in Middletown, Middlesex Co. CT.

146. Lydia BROWNE, born on 4 Dec 1720 in Middletown, Middlesex Co. CT.

In about 1746/7 Lydia married Samuel SHIPMAN. They had the following children:
386	i.	Lois (about 1749-)
387	ii.	Benjamin (about 1749-)
388	iii.	Asahel or Azel (about 1751-)
389	iv.	Elizabeth
390	v.	Phebe (1759-)
391	vi.	Stephen (1762-)

147. John BROWNE, born before 9 Sep 1722 in Middletown, Middlesex Co. CT (baptism). Died young.

148. Mary BROWNE, born on 9 Jul 1725 in Middletown, Middlesex Co. CT. Mary died in 1763 in East Hartford CT. Per Jacobus, but East Hartford was incorporated in 1783 from Hartford.

In 1745 Mary married Jonathan COLE. Jonathan died in 1759 in East Hartford CT. They had the following children:
392	i.	Elisha (about 1750-)
393	ii.	Elizabeth (about 1753-)
394	iii.	Jonathan (about 1754-)
395	iv.	Daniel (about 1757-)

Family of Abigail BROWNE (75) and Thomas STEVENS

149. Aaron STEVENS, born about 1721 in Middletown, Middlesex Co. CT. Died young.

150. Hannah STEVENS, born on 18 Mar 1722/3 in Middletown, Middlesex Co. CT. Died young.

151. Thomas STEVENS, born on 16 Jul 1725 in Middletown, Middlesex Co. CT.

Thomas married Mary ---. They had the following children:
396	i.	Elnathan
397	ii.	Diana
398	iii.	Huldah
399	iv.	Daniel
400	v.	Abigail
401	vi.	Phebe
402	vii.	Aaron (1773-)

152. Aaron STEVENS, born on 25 Apr 1728 in Middletown, Middlesex Co. CT.

153. John STEVENS, born on 3 Sep 1731 in Middletown, Middlesex Co. CT. John died young.

154. Robert STEVENS, born on 25 Feb 1732/3 in Middletown, Middlesex Co. CT. Served in the French and Indian War 1759, 1761, 1762.

155. Hannah STEVENS, born before 1 Jun 1735 in Middletown, Middlesex Co. CT (baptism).

156. Abigail STEVENS, born before 28 May 1738 in Middletown, Middlesex Co. CT (date of baptism). Unmarried in 1765.

157. Sarah STEVENS, born on 26 Apr 1741 in Middletown, Middlesex Co. CT.

Before 1765 Sarah married William MILES, in Middletown, Middlesex Co. CT.

158. Mary STEVENS, born on 14 Aug 1743 in Middletown, Middlesex Co. CT. Unmarried in 1765.

Stephen Osborne Home
Courtesy PJ Sisseck

TENTH GENERATION

Family of Thomas BROWNE (85)

159. Samuel BROWNE, 7G Grandson.

160. John BROWNE, 7G Grandson.

161. Vachel BROWNE, 7G Grandson.

162. Joshua BROWNE, 7G Grandson.

Family of Abel BROWN Sr. (90) and Elizabeth ---

163. Abel BROWN Jr., 7G Grandson, born about 1735 in Anne Arundel Co. MD. Abel died in 1817 in Baltimore (later Carroll) Co. MD. Abel Brown Jr. served as vestryman at Christ Church in Anne Arundel County 1758-60 where he was also taxed as a bachelor in 1761. (Those unmarried males over 25 and worth more than £100 were taxed as a measure to finance the defense against threatened Indian attacks.) Assumedly keeping two residences for a time, his own and his father's in Baltimore County, he was also taxed as a bachelor in Baltimore County 1760, 1761, 1762 but not 1763 when he probably was married. In Baltimore County Abel Sr. gave him land 1763. He was known as Abel Jr. during his father's lifetime. He was named on 1763 tax list as a landowner. In the 1773 tax list William Purer, James, Oitter (servants?) were also listed as residents on his property. In 1777 Abel Brown Jr. furnished a substitute to serve for him in the 4th Maryland Regiment (*Calendar of Maryland State Papers No. 5*, p. 95), which at his age was forgivable. He did, however, sign the loyalty oath to the Revolution. In the 1783 tax list he owned a part of Hunters Chance, 300 acres, the gift from his father twenty years before. In a 1785 deposition Abel Jr. gave his age as "about 50 yrs." In the 1790 Census, p. 53 of Baltimore County Delaware Hundreds, Abel Brown Jun. was listed as 3340-0 (6 white males, 4 white females, no "other," no slaves). John, Jacob were nearby. Near also were John Elder, Elias Brown. The 1798 Tax List showed Abel Brown "Sr.," because there was a younger nephew Abel Brown, his brother John's son, in the neighborhood (this was a common practice among namesakes that did not restrict "junior" and "senior" to son and father) and listed one slave, 300 acres part of Hunter's Chance, occupants Joshua Brown and Joseph Gray, and property listed as owning an old log dwelling house, 20x16, 1 story; log cabin 16x15; smoke house 14x10 (Horvath, G., *The Particular Assessment Lists for Baltimore and Carroll Counties Maryland, 1798*, p. 201). Abel Brown Senr in the 1810 Census of Baltimore County's Delaware Lower Hundred, p. 707 listed as: 10101-10031-3-1. The 1813 Baltimore County *Assessment Records* District 6, p. 6 enumerated Abel Brown Sr., showing 300 acres part Hunter's Chance, 2 slaves. In the 1820 Census Baltimore County Election District 6 p. 61 he was again enumerated, still 45 and up (he would have been about 85): 000001-00000-00000-0-1. DAR # 22446 gives what is in my opinion a confused version of this family.

As Abel Brown Jr. died intestate, according to a court-ruled division his property was to go equally to his eight children and two grandchildren. The heirs disagreed as to the partition and as a result Josiah Brown purchased the whole for $17.00 an acre. Ref.: 1 Aug 2005 letter from descendant Howard Smith, who also provided much family data.

Abel married Sarah GOSNELL, daughter of Peter Gosnell. See Peter Gosnell's will of 9 Jul 1785 - 17 Apr 1787 Baltimore County. The 1823 Baltimore County Assessment District 6 p. 4 listed Sarah Brown, widow and owner part Hunters Chance 50 acres, $50 improvements, 1 slave, plus Able, Brice, Ann Boring Widow, Rachel, Zachariah, and

Josiah Brown owning parts of Hunters Chance, all amounting to about 300 acres as Abel had, thus certifying them as Abel's widow, remarried, and family. Abel and Ann had the following children:

403	i.	Abel
404	ii.	David
405	iii.	Brice
406	iv.	Rachel (about 1778-1857)
407	v.	Zachariah (- about 1835)
408	vi.	Josiah (1781-1864)
409	vii.	Nancy Ann

164. David BROWN, 7G Grandson, born about 1740 in Anne Arundel Co. MD. David died before 20 Feb 1775 in Baltimore (later Carroll) Co. MD. Abel Sr. gave him 300 acres of land in 1763 at Fine Soil Forest. Listed in the 1763 Tax List, also in the 1773 Tax List with John Hammersbale, Jesse Grant, John Roule, Fib[---torn] in his household. He signed an oath of affirmation to the King in 1766 and the "Test of Nontransubstantiation in the Holy Sacrament" (St. Thomas Registry entry undated but about 1753-7). Served as Church Warden at St. Thomas Parish, Baltimore County 1769-1770. He apparently died intestate as his estate was filed in the Maryland Prerogative Court, Baltimore County, *Liber 121*, Folio 358, 11 May 1775, for 209 pounds, 8 shillings, 10 pence. Appraisers were Richard Shipley (son of Adam) and Nicholas Dorsey. Kin named were Abel Brown, Jacob Brown, administrator Abel Brown Jr. John Elder and John Townson posted security for his administration, which was settled in 1778. David may have been the brother of Abel mentioned in Scharf's *History of Western Maryland* Vol. II (881-2) who was killed fighting with Braddock, i.e., 10 Oct 1774, at the Battle of Point Pleasant during the French and Indian War.

In about 1762 David married Naomi TEVIS, daughter of Robert TEVIS and Margaret TREADWAY, in MD, probably Baltimore Co. (See note in *Maryland Genealogical Society Bulletin*, Vol. 35, No. 1, Winter 1994, p. 42 .) Naomi's parents per Donna Suggs. Also per will of her sister Rachel Crown, Baltimore County *Will Book 8*, p. 284. She must have been the "Monomy" Brown who sold land (acreage not mentioned) to Moses in 1785. They had one child:

410	i.	David (1763-)

165. Jacob BROWN, 7G Grandson, born in Anne Arundel Co. MD. Jacob died about 1798. Abel Sr. gave him 300 acres in 1763, part of Fine Soil Forest in Baltimore County Delaware Lower Hundred, where he was entered in the tax list as: 1161-2-5. He sold 60 acres in 1777 and 180 acres in 1782. In the 1783 tax list he owned 150 acres. Jacob and John Brown signed oaths of allegiance to the Revolution before Peter Shepherd in 1776, 1778. He was serving as Pvt. in the Baltimore Artillery Co. on 16 Oct 1775, with John Brown. He witnessed the will of Andrew Grangett on 5 Feb 1785. The 1790 Census Baltimore Delaware Hundred p. 58 listed Jacob Brown 3330-0. His will was entered in 1798 (*Will Book 5*, p. 382), and in particular assessments of 1798.

In about 1775 Jacob married Catherine STOCKSDALE, daughter of Edward STOCKSDALE and Catherine ---, in Baltimore (later Carroll) Co. MD, born in Baltimore (later Carroll) Co. MD. Family per Bill Reynolds, Kathleen Field (per Nancy Lesure). Refs.: Reynolds: Richards and Jay, *Roots and Fruits, Family Records of Tobias Stocksdale*; Edward Stoxdale will 16 Aug 1779, Baltimore Co. *Will Book 3*, Baltimore Co. Chancery Court Edward Brown v Thomas Cockey et al, 9 Aug 1798; In a Chancery Court Case in Baltimore County, Maryland (9 Aug 1798), Edward Brown petitioned the court to recover a Slave that was left to his mother Catherine through the Will of her father Edward Stocksdale. Edward Stocksdale's will indicated that the slave was to go to grandson Edward Brown upon the death of Catherine. Apparently, Jacob Brown was in financial straits and was even jailed for a while. He had sold the slave to a Mr. Philips, although based on the will of Edward Stocksdale, he did not have the right do sell. Subsequently, Mr. Philips sold the slave and 5 children to Elias Brown, Thomas Cockey, Moses Brown and John Brown (Reynolds). There is indication whether any of these people were related to Edward Brown. He may be the Edward Brown who is mentioned in the will of Richard Brown 3 Jul 1825 in Baltimore County, Maryland. If so, then he had a brother named Richard. I have no information on that Edward Brown or Richard., except an Edward Brown married Jane Boyle, license issued 3 Sep 1807 Baltimore Co. Jacob and Catherine Brown had the following children:

411	i.	Abel
412	ii.	Edward (about 1775-)
413	iii.	Elizabeth

166. John BROWN, 7G Grandson, born about 1742 in Anne Arundel Co. MD. John died in 1801 in Baltimore Co. MD. On remarrying, his father Abel Brown Sr. gave him and brothers land in 1763, presumably to protect his and brothers' inheritance. He was listed in the 1762-*1765 Index to Aquila Hall's Assessment Ledger of Baltimore County*. In 1763 tax list, also listed. In 1768 John Brown signed the Joppa Petition as "John, son of Abell." Also signing were both Abel Sen.,

Junr., David, Dixson, Henry, Jacob, James, Robert, Saml., Thomas, and William Brown, not all identified. John and Jacob Brown were listed as privates in Capt. Henry Sheaff's Baltimore Artillery Company on October 16, 1775 (*Maryland State Papers: Red Books*, No. 4, Pt. 2, p. 8), and John was later listed in Sheaff's company as sergeant on June 16, 1777 (Maryland Archives Original Manuscript Acc. 4582-162). He may have again joined with a brother at a later time: Henry Peden's *Maryland and Delaware Patriots, 1775-1783*, p. 31 listed James and John Brown as 1780 recruits from Baltimore County. The 1780 tax list listed him as owner of 250 acres of Fine Soil Forest near land belonging to Jacob, Abel Sr. and Jr., Benjamin Brown, John Elder (probable future son-in-law). The 1783 tax list showed John Brown as owner of part of Hunters Chance 200 acres. In his 1785 deposition regarding his father's property boundary lines, he gave his age as 43 years, and son of Abel Sr. The 1790 Census Delaware Hundred of Baltimore County, p 57 enumerated John Brown thus: 233-3 (5 males, 2 under 16, and 3 females, 3 slaves). Horvath's *1798 Particular Assessment Lists for Baltimore and Carroll*, p. 102, listed John Brown, Sr. with seven slaves, part of the tract Hunter's Chance comprising 198 acres, a frame dwelling house 24x24 1 story; a log cabin 16x12; a stone dairy 10x10; a smoke house 12x12 and others, valued at $792.00. In Baltimore County *Will Book No 6*, pp. 377-8, 10 Mar 1799 – 11 Apr 1801, John Brown "Planter" named the children listed below, executor son John, witnesses Elias, Abel, David Brown, his land Hunters Chance. Mentioned no wife. His estate listed 1801 and settled in 1804 named John Brown adm., Moses Brown and Frances Snowden security. And this household drama: Sarah ---, an unidentified servant to John Brown, was charged with bastardy in November Court, 1772 and fined £1.10.0 (Peden, *Bastardy Cases in Baltimore County, Maryland 1673-1783*, p. 172). John Brown of Baltimore County freed his slaves Rachel on 25 Aug 1783, and Samuel on 3 Feb 1789.

John married Mary Catherine ---. John Brown's birth in 1759 named John and Katherine as his parents (St. Thomas Parish Register, p. 47). Mary Catherine Brown may be presumed deceased by her husband's will date of writing as she was not named. They had the following children:

414	i.	John (1759-)
415	ii.	Abel (-1834)
416	iii.	Robert (about 1779 - after 1860)
417	iv.	Elizabeth
418	v.	Rosanna or Susannah
419	vi.	Sarah
420	vii.	Isaiah (about 1785-)
421	viii.	Rachel
422	ix.	Archibald (1790-1838)
423	x.	Jesse (- about 1844)

167. James BROWN, 7G Grandson, born about 1743 in Anne Arundel Co. MD. James died about May 1782 in Baltimore (later Carroll) Co. MD. James Brown didn't receive land from his father in 1763 as others did because he was then a minor. He signed as "James of Abel" an oath of allegiance to the Revolution in 1777, entered the military as a recruit in Baltimore County 1780, was a private in the Extra Regiment at Fort Whetstone Point in Baltimore 1781 (*Revolutionary Patriots of Maryland and Delaware*, p. 31). He received as a gift from his father Abel on 2 Dec 1780 a 175 acre tract called Addition to Treadway's Quarter (Baltimore County Land Records, *Liber WG#F*, Folio 101), at which time his father Abel's wife, then Susannah, waived her dower rights at sale. His will dated 26 Apr 1782 and proved 29 May 1782 gave his personal property and his land or proceeds from the sale of his land to his (then) six children by Elizabeth Twist. The will was witnessed by Peter Tevis and Elijah Elder, neighbors. The will also named brothers Abel, John, Jacob, Elias and Moses. James Brown's estate was filed in 1783, with Elizabeth Twist granted letters of administration and Peter Tevis and Charles Knight posting security. No settlement date was found. In the 1785 Baltimore County Maryland *Will Book 3*, pp. 484-5 James Brown named his brothers Abel, John, Jacob, Elias, Moses, witness Elijah Elder. He mentioned no wife, but acknowledged as his children Elizabeth, William, Marry (sic), Charlote (sic), Ann and Rebecca, all children of Elizabeth Twist. Another, Rachel, was yet to be born. Horvath's *1798 Particular Assessment Lists for Baltimore and Carroll Counties*, p. 102) listed in the name of "James Brown heirs," 175 acres in Treadway's Quarter, a log house 20x18 and a large tobacco house 68x24 (p. 201).

He did not marry Elizabeth TWIST. Thanks to Nancy Lesure for finding this episode in the Brown history. Baltimore County *Orphans Court Proceedings, Book 2*, Folio 50 of Saturday, 22 Jan 1787 stated: "Elizabeth, William, Mary Ann, Charlotte, Anna, Rebecca and Rachel Brown (alias) Twist Orphan children of James Brown deceased under 14 years Comes into Court and the Court appoints Benjamin Watkins their Guardian who is Present here in Court accepts the Guardianship and offers Leonard Swingle and George Swingles his Security who are approved of by the Court and Bonds are Ordered Accordingly." Thus all children were born 1773 or after. Further: "Ordered that Ephraim Lansbeth and Elizabeth his wife Administratrix of James Brown deceased Deliver into the hands of Benj- Watkins app'd Guardian of the Children of the Said J. B. the Amount of their Respective Shares of the deceased Fathers Estate." A Benjamin

Watkins was found in the 1790 Census of Anne Arundel County as 3-0-5-0-21 (3 males 21 or up, 5 females, 21 slaves), which does not coincide with the orphan children with whom he was entrusted. At least a portion of James' land, Addition to Treadway's Quarter, remained in the family, belonging later to half brother Elias and later Elias' widow Ann (1823 Tax Assessment, p. 6). James Brown and Elizabeth Twist had the following children:

424	i.	Elizabeth (after 1773-)
425	ii.	William (about 1777 - after 1850)
426	iii.	Mary Ann (after 1773 - after 1840)
427	iv.	Charlotte (after 1773-)
428	v.	Ann (after 1773-)
429	vi.	Rebecca (after 1773-)
430	vii.	Rachel (about 1783-)

168. Samuel BROWN, 7G Grandson, born about 1745 in MD. Samuel died on 17 Aug 1777. He enlisted as a Revolutionary Minute Man under Governor Thomas Johnson and was killed in combat, Battle of Brandywine. Died unmarried. Didn't receive land given previously brothers in 1763 because he was still a minor.

169. Nancy BROWN, 7G Granddaughter, born in MD. Mentioned in Abel's will but not included among the "four youngest" who were children of Susannah

Nancy married John BAKER. Resident of southwest Virginia (Albert S. Brown).

Family of Abel BROWN Sr. (90) and Susannah SHIPLEY

170. Adam BROWN, 7G Grandson, born on 3 Feb 1764 in Carroll Co. MD. Died young (per McCallahan and Albert S. Brown).

171. Elias BROWN, 7G Grandson, born on 29 Mar 1765 in Baltimore (later Carroll) Co. MD. Elias died in Baltimore (later Carroll) Co. MD, on 17 Sep 1800; he was 35. Buried on 6 Nov 1800 in Brown Family Cemetery, Carroll Co. MD. McCallahan's stated year of marriage of 1792 is questionable as two children were born before that date. Elias' year of death given by McCallahan as 1837 was that of Ann Cockey Brown, his wife. Elias' headstone year of death was illegible at the time of its reading, but see below. Elias served as vestryman at St. Thomas' Parish in 1792-3. Elias and Moses were witnesses of Robert Tevis Sr.'s will 25 Oct 1796. Elias witnessed the will of Hillen Ogg 2 Apr 1798. Served in the state legislature 1796 - 1798 as was his brother Moses a few years later. Elias was named in Abel Sr's will as one of four youngest children. He erected on his property a stone saw and flour mill. All four sons were said to have fought in the War of 1812 (Scharf, p. 874). 1798's Particular Assessment Lists for Baltimore and Carroll Counties, p. 102, listed him as owner of 18 slaves, 1198 acres and many buildings and structures, marking him as one of the wealthiest gentry in the county. He was listed on St. James Parish (north of Baltimore City) Register 1787-1815, but this is likely a shared reporting from St. Thomas'. Baltimore County Maryland *Will Book 6*, p. 303 contains his will dated 3 Aug 1800 – 25 Oct 1800 naming son Thomas Cockey Brown, minor sons Stephen, Elias, William, daughters Prudence, Ann, brother Moses, and wife Ann. The will specified ownership of Brown's Inheritance which he had patented on 12 Dec 1798 including a gristmill, sawmill, etc., plus land in Anne Arundel County. Witnesses were Francis Snowden, Thomas Beasman, Benjamin Tevis. His administration (posted in 1800 and settled in 1806) named Moses and Ann Brown co-administrators, Francis Snowden and Geo. F. Warfield security. Value of personal property at inventory: $4,498, including 15 slaves. His date of death is from the Baltimore Federal Gazette of 24 Sep 1800. At his death in the mid-30s, family lore had it that he died from eating cherries and their seed (Albert S. Brown manuscript). Additional source: St. Thomas' Parish Registers 1732-1850.

About 17 May 1788 when Elias was 23, he married Ann COCKEY, daughter of Thomas COCKEY and Prudence GILL, in Baltimore County MD (date of license). She was born on 29 Apr 1760. Ann died in Carroll Co. MD, on 5 Jun 1837; she was 77. Buried in Brown Family Cemetery, Carroll Co. MD. Mentioned in Stephen Cockey's will as sister Ann Brown, which also named her son Stephen Cockey Brown as Stephen's "nephew Stephen Brown who received also one-half of the [Stephen] Cockey realty in Anne Arundel Co." (Newman, p. 19). Left at an early age as a widow with a large estate, she managed the property well, built in 1808 the well-known "Brown Mansion." The 1813 Baltimore County Assessment Records, District 6, p. 5, reported Ann Brown as owning part of Owings Outland Plains, part of Hammond's Fine Soil Forest, part of Brown's Free and Ins. Project [?], part of Hunter's Chance, part of Treadaway Quarter (James' former property) for 1075 acres total, plus $200 of improvements and 9 slaves. 1823 Baltimore County Assessment District 6, p. 4 reported Ann Brown owner of Addition to Treadway's Quarter, 33 acres, 3 slaves, a considerable decline in property ownership. Her will of 4 Aug 1836 - 12 Aug 1837 (Carroll County *Will Book 1837-1852* No. 12, Folio 22) named son Elias, daughter [-in-law] Susannah E. Brown, son William and William's sons unnamed. Scharf's *History of Western Maryland*, Vol 2, p. 870 claimed that Thomas C. Brown's father (meaning Elias) married Nancy Cockey. No other source agrees with this. It was Ann Cockey. He further reported, erroneously, that that same father Elias was an immigrant from England. The Albert Brown manuscript of 1897 recorded that her headstone in the Brown family burial plot said "Ann: wife of E. Brown, died June 5th 1837, aged 77 yrs 1 mo and 5 dys" (Albert S. Brown). They had the following children:

431	i.	Thomas Cockey (1789-1822)
432	ii.	Stephen Cockey (1791-1814)
433	iii.	Elias (1793-1857)
434	iv.	William (1796-1838)
435	v.	Prudence Ann (1799-1808)

172. Major Moses BROWN, 7G Grandson, born on 8 Jul 1768 in Baltimore (later Carroll) Co. MD. Moses died in Baltimore (later Carroll) Co. MD, on 3 Sep 1817; he was 49. In 1786 he purchased from his half-brother David's widow 60 acres for £86. David had died in 1775, and had received that land from his father Abel Sr. in 1863. On 25 Apr 1797 his marriage license was issued in Baltimore County, and he was married on 30 April at St. Thomas' Church by Rev. Mr. William West and also at St. Peter's Roman Catholic Church by Father Francis Beeston, as Mary Snowden, his bride, was from a Catholic family. He was named in Abel Sr.'s will as one of the four youngest children, i.e., children of Abel's second wife. In Baltimore County *Will Book 3*, p. 484 the will of James Brown in 1785 named brothers Abel, John, Jacob, Elias, Moses, witness Elijah Elder. Moses and Elias Brown witnessed Robert Tevis Sr.'s will 25 Oct 1796 (half brother David Brown had married Naomi Tevis). Like his father and brothers he was a tobacco planter. Horvath's *1798 Particular Assessment Lists for Baltimore and Carroll Counties*, p. 102 listed him with 6 slaves, 516 acres in John's Chance and Fine Soil Forest By 1798 he owned nearly 1,000 acres valued at $4,409 with improvements, including a mill. The 1804 Tax Assessment of Delaware Hundred (No. 8260) listed his land holdings as Part of John's Chance 320 acres, part of Fine Soil Forest 50 acres, part of Forest Level 191 acres, part of Owings Outland Plains 15 acres, for a total of 576 acres, plus 11 slaves, 8 horses, 28 cattle, 18 hogs and 22 sheep.

He was the only Brown to remain active in St. Thomas' Church after the Revolution; he served as Vestryman from 1808 to 1810. He served as Republican state legislator in 1803-1804, again in 1806-11. The 1810 Census Baltimore County's Delaware Lower Hundred p. 706 listed his family as 11010-3101. The 1813 Baltimore County Assessment Records, District 6, p. 5 (No. 12502), listed him as owning 931 acres in these properties: part of John's Chance, part of Forest Level, part of Fine Soil Forest, and one tract unnamed but was no doubt part of Treadway's Quarter, plus 14 slaves, 7 horses, 38 cattle, 26 hogs, 30 sheep. He was buried in the Brown Cemetery. The old gravestone (now lost) had been read in late 1800s and gave his year of death as 1826 (McCallahan p. 11), before birth of his known children, but his age on stone was reputed to have said 58; nevertheless an obituary gave the date of his death of 3 Sep 1817 (*Federal Gazette and Baltimore American*. 8 Sep 1817), and his will was written 19 Jul 1817 and probated 15 Sep 1817. That will (*Will Book 10*, p. 350) named his wife Mary, children Francis Snowden Brown, Elias Joseph Brown, Mary Ann Brown, Eleanor Elizabeth Brown, Rebecca Brown, Theresia Brown, Ann Brown, and nephew Elias as executor. His mansion called Stony Ridge was located on Liberty Road still stands and is listed on the National Register of Historic Places. His obituary appearing in the *Federal Gazette and Baltimore American* called him "Major" and simply stated that he left a family of small children. The rank of major stemmed from his service in the Maryland Militia from 1794, but during the War of 1812 he held the rank of sergeant in Captain John Coat's Company, 36th Baltimore County Regiment. His reduced rank may have been because of his age, said his biographer Marks (see below). The Tax Assessment of 1818 listed 937 acres under "Moses Brown Heirs" and 75 acres under Mary Brown, his widow, and in 1823 800 acres belonging to Francis S. Brown, Moses' son and heir. By 1831 the last of his estate was sold off by executors, and most of his surviving family left in caravan for the West.

McCallahan erroneously added to his family another daughter, Mary, who married James A. (sic) Broadhead, and was among those Browns and others who left for Missouri by wagon train. That was James Overton Broadhead, who became a US Senator and prominent Missouri leader during and after the Civil War, but he was married to Mary Dorsey, not Brown. McCallahan misread Warfield.

A major source for the Moses Brown family is Lillian Bayly Marks' "Moses Brown 1768 -1817," a well-crafted 1982 typescript held at the Carroll County Historical Society Library.

On 30 Apr 1797 when Moses was 28, he married Mary "Polly" SNOWDEN, daughter of Col. Francis SNOWDEN and Eleanor MILES, in Baltimore Co. MD. Mary "Polly" died after 1841 in Pike Co. MO. Her 25 Apr 1797 marriage license was issued in Baltimore County, followed by two ceremonies, one Protestant and one Catholic. Mary Snowden Brown received legacies from her grandfather Snowden, who died in 1810, and from her parents who died in 1812. The 1820 Census of Baltimore County Election District 6 p. 206 showed Mary Brown: 010100-312100-700 (one male 10-15, one male 16-25, three females under 10, one 10-15, two 16-25, one 26-44, seven persons engaged in agriculture) plus 24 slaves. Together with Snowdens and others, Mary and her surviving children (except for daughters Susanna and Mary Ann) joined the wagon train for the West in about 1831. She and her family settled in Pike County Missouri, where she was still living in 1841 (Marks, p. 2). They had the following children:

436	i.	Francis Snowden (1798 - after 1834)
437	ii.	Susannah Eleanor (1799-1883)
438	iii.	Moses
439	iv.	Mary Ann (1802 - before 1850)
440	v.	Eleanor Elizabeth "Ellen" (1804-1892)
441	vi.	Ruth Ann (about 1805-1826)
442	vii.	Rebecca (about 1808-)
443	viii.	Elias Joseph (1810-1829)
444	ix.	Theresia Josephine (1812-1889)
445	x.	Ann Alexis (1813-1889)

173. Ruth Ann BROWN, 7G Granddaughter, born on 30 Jan 1770 in Baltimore (later Carroll) Co. MD. Ruth Ann died in Carroll Co. MD, on 2 May 1816; she was 46. Buried in Cockey Family Cemetery. Named in Abel Sr.'s will as one of four youngest children. Both she and her husband were buried in the Cockey family cemetery on their plantation Arlington, but that cemetery's stones were moved to All Saints' Episcopal Church in Reiserstown when the farm left Cockey ownership (McCallahan, p. 12).

On 11 Mar 1788 when Ruth Ann was 18, she married Thomas COCKEY, son of Thomas COCKEY and Prudence GILL, in Baltimore Co. MD, by Rev. Richards, born on 15 Apr 1754 in Baltimore (later Carroll) Co. MD. Thomas died about Nov 1813 in Baltimore Co. MD. Marriage license issued 10 Mar 1788. Will 26 Jun 1812 - 20 Nov 1813 (Baltimore County *Will Book 9*, p. 369). They had the following children:

446	i.	William Henry
447	ii.	Andrew Rodney
448	iii.	Thomas John
449	iv.	Elias Brown (- about 1838)
450	v.	Susanna Brown (-1822)
451	vi.	Georgius Rex
452	vii.	John Robert (1807-1867)
453	viii.	Mordecai Gist (1802-1872)
454	ix.	Ruth Brown (-1852)
455	x.	Dolly Brown (1804-1848)
456	xi.	Charles C.

174. Susannah BROWN, 7G Granddaughter, born on 5 Feb 1773 in Baltimore (later Carroll) Co. MD. Mentioned in Abel Sr.'s will as one of his four youngest. Died in infancy according to McCallahan but obviously survived to 10 in order to be mentioned in her father's will of that year. She may have been the Anne Brown who married Morris Baker 1800 in Brooke County Virginia as claimed in Frederick County Historical Society's "Brown Papers."

175. Rebecca BROWN, 7G Granddaughter, born on 24 Dec 1774 in Baltimore (now Carroll) Co. MD. Rebecca died on 4 Mar 1852; she was 77. Mentioned in Abel Sr.'s will as one of his four youngest, meaning that she was a child of Abel's second wife. Dates per Scharf's *History of Western Maryland*, Vol. II, p. 881.

On 1 Nov 1795 when Rebecca was 20, she married George Frazier WARFIELD, son of Azel WARFIELD and Susannah MAGRUDER, in Baltimore Co. MD, born on 20 Mar 1769. George Frazier died on 11 Dec 1849; he was 80. Marriage license was issued 30 Oct 1795, Baltimore County. His family plantation was Dorsey's Dilemma, 315 acres. Warfield's brother gave the tract Groveland to the Episcopal Church to found Warfield College (per Warfield). He had four children listed in McCallahan, but Scharf listed seven, given here (*History of Western Maryland*, Vol. II, p. 881). The 1820 Census Baltimore County District 6, p. 206: enumerated "Mr." G. W. Warfield: 002000-0021110-700 plus 8 slaves. He was said to be brother of Dr. Charles Alexander Warfield, who "in October 1773 proceeded to Annapolis and not only destroyed the tea but burned the ship Peggy Stewart in which it was brought here" (Albert S. Brown manuscript). They had the following children:

457	i.	Lewis
458	ii.	George F.
459	iii.	Warner W. (1788-1867)
460	iv.	William H.
461	v.	Susannah (-1894)
462	vi.	Rebecca
463	vii.	Elizabeth Ann

Family of Comfort BROWNE (93) and John LANHAM

176. Comfort Lana Renne LANHAM, 7G Granddaughter, born in 1749. Comfort Lana Renne died about 1 Dec 1824 in Pound Gap, Scott Co. TN. Also named Comfort Longhorn Lanham per Cisseck.

Comfort Lana Renne married Stephen OSBORNE, son of Gen. Ephraim OSBORNE Sr. and Elizabeth Wells HOWARD, born in 1750 in Scott Co. VA. Stephen died in 1820 in Scott Co. VA. Operated a trading post at Osborne's Ford (now Dungannon), Scott County North Carolina. See sketch provided by Timothy J. Barron to Pj Sisseck. The site is now in the Registry of Historic Places. They had the following children:

464	i.	Solomon (before 1765-1828)
465	ii.	Mary "Polly" (about 1766-1856)
466	iii.	Robert (about 1770-1851)
467	iv.	Jonathan (1772-1861)
468	v.	Virginia Jane "Jenny" (1774-1851)
469	vi.	James (1775-)
470	vii.	William (1777-1865)
471	viii.	Sarah "Sally" (about 1781-)
472	ix.	John (1783-1853)
473	x.	Jemima (1783-1853)
474	xi.	Elizabeth "Betsey" (1786 - about 1824)
475	xii.	Esther Louise (1790-1865)

177. Sarah LANHAM, 7G Granddaughter, born in Mecklenburg Co. NC.

Sarah married --- HAGARTY.

178. Esther LANHAM, 7G Granddaughter.

Esther married --- DEAN.

179. Jean LANHAM, 7G Granddaughter.

Jean married --- MCCOY, born about 1755.

180. William LANHAM, 7G Grandson, born about 1755.

181. August Abel LANHAM, 7G Grandson, born on 1 Jan 1762 in Mecklenburg Co. NC. August Abel died in Claiborne Co. TN, on 25 Aug 1837; he was 75. Buried in Lanham Cemetery, Tazewell TN. Full name, dates per Myhre and Sisseck. Mhyre says born 1760. Family and line per Bates.

On 3 Dec 1777 when August Abel was 15, he first married Jean KUYKENDAL, in Tryon Co. NC, born in 1762. Jean died on 29 Aug 1810 in Claiborne Co. TN. They had the following children:

476	i.	Elizabeth (1780-)
477	ii.	Robert (1786-)
478	iii.	Solomon (1788-1867)

479	iv.	Abel (1790-)
480	v.	William (1792-)
481	vi.	Joseph (1794-)
482	vii.	Ann (1796-)
483	viii.	Samuel (1799-)
484	ix.	John (1801-)
485	x.	Randal (1804-)
486	xi.	Melissa Morgan (1808-)

August Abel second married Sarah NUNN, born in 1787. Sarah died after 1853 in KY. They had the following children:

487	i.	Malinda (1819-)
488	ii.	Samivarnes (1820-)
489	iii.	Abel (1822-)
490	iv.	Sarah (1823-)
491	v.	Matilda (1824-)
492	vi.	Lee (1832-)
493	vii.	Luther (1832-)

Family of Benjamin BROWN (96) and Susannah RANDALL

182. General Samuel BROWN, born on 9 Jan 1747 in MD. Samuel died in OH on 6 Oct 1833; he was 86. Date of birth per Samuel Brown Bible. Served in the Revolutionary War. Commissioned 2nd. Lieutenant 2 Mar 1778 in Col. Charles Hammond's Elk Ridge Militia Battalion, Capt. John Dorsey's Co. Promoted to general at the close of the war. Howard County plantation was named Walnut Hill. It passed to Samuel Brown Jr. See Peden, *Revolutionary Patriots*, p. 20; Newman p. 276. In 1812 he took an active part in war affairs but was too old for service. He signed the military commissions for his three sons Samuel, Vachel and John Riggs Brown (MacKenzie, Vol. I, p. 47). His family Bible list dated 2 Dec 1817 is found copied at the Maryland Historical Society Archive, Filing Case A.

On 30 Nov 1773 when Samuel was 26, he married Achsah RIGGS, daughter of John RIGGS and Mary DAVIS, born on 27 Jan 1745 in MD. Achsah died in OH on 9 Sep 1817; she was 72. This family primarily per a Bible record owned by Vachel Jeremiah Bown, copy filed in Maryland Historical Society Filing Case A. The record was dated 1780 14th Day of August on the back of the frontispiece, and inscribed by Samuel Brown Sen. 2 Dec 1817; also per Virkus, Vol. III, p. 58. They had the following children:

494	i.	Elisha (1774-1832)
495	ii.	John Riggs (1775-1814)
496	iii.	Mary (1777-)
497	iv.	Susannah (1781-1804)
498	v.	Samuel (1783-1847)
499	vi.	Vachel (1784-1834)
500	vii.	Joseph (1786-)
501	viii.	Achsah Riggs (1787-1837)

183. Rachel BROWN, born about 1742 in MD. Rachel died in 1809 in Frederick Co. MD.

Rachel married Alexander TODD, born on 7 Sep 1736 in Anne Arundel Co. MD. Alexander died in 1808 in Frederick Co. MD. They had the following children:

502	i.	Benjamin (about 1759-1841)
503	ii.	Basil (about 1762 - after 1810)
504	iii.	Elizabeth (about 1765-)
505	iv.	Alexander (about 1766-1810)
506	v.	Joshua (about 1768-)
507	vi.	Samuel (about 1770-)
508	vii.	Rachel (1773-1842)
509	viii.	Warfield (about 1775-1837)
510	ix.	Susannah (about 1781-)

184. Ruth BROWN.

Ruth married --- TODD.

185. Joshua BROWN. Joshua and Vachel Brown owned, at the 1823 Tax Assessment of Baltimore County District 6, 224 acres parts of Favour and Ease, with $75 of improvements and one slave.

Joshua married Patience ---. They had one child:
    511   i.   John

186. Vachel BROWN. Joshua and Vachel Brown together owned, at the 1823 Tax Assessment of Baltimore County District 6, 224 acres parts of the tract Favour and Ease, with $75 of improvements and one slave.

187. Susannah BROWN.

188. Richard BROWN.

189. Charles BROWN.

190. Ephraim BROWN.

191. Rebecca BROWN.

192. Benjamin BROWN.

Family of William BROWN (98) and --- ---

193. Elijah BROWN, 7G Grandson, born before 30 Jun 1765 in Anne Arundel Co. MD. Per his grandfather Robert's will, Anne Arundel Co., according to which he was to receive the family lands if Frederick died or there were no other lawful heirs of James.

Family of James BROWN (100)

194. Frederick BROWN, 7G Grandson, born before 1764 in Montgomery Co. MD.

Son of James per Grandfather Robert's will, Anne Arundel County, in which he (a minor) received Robert's "Plantation whereon I now live on one tract of Land called Rockey Ridge containing Seventy Acres according to the Meets and Bounds thereof likewise part of a Tract of Land called Browns Enlargement Containing Sixty Acres." Also received livestock and furniture "to be delivered to him the aforesaid Frederick Brown when he arrives at the Age of Twenty one Years." Resided in Howard District Anne Arundel County, that portion which later became Howard County (1810 Census), then in Frederick County (1820 Census), New Market, Frederick County (1840 Census).

This family and line comes from Gregory S. Priebe and an undated manuscript authored by his uncle Marshall Brown, which Mr. Priebe has kindly shared.

Frederick first married --- ---.

In 1788 Frederick second married Sarah WILLSON, in Montgomery Co. MD. They had one child:
    512   i.   Robert (1793-)

Family of Richard SMITH (102) and Abigail CLARK

195. Benjamin SMITH, born on 6 Sep 1731 in Glastonbury CT. Benjamin died in Glastonbury CT, on 28 Nov 1803; he was 72.

196. Abraham SMITH, born on 13 May 1733 in Glastonbury CT. Abraham died in Glastonbury CT, on 14 Jun 1733; he was less than 1.

197. Abraham SMITH, born on 4 Jun 1734.

Abraham married Damaris HOLLISTER.

198. Isaac SMITH, born on 16 Dec 1735 in Glastonbury CT. Isaac died in Glastonbury CT, on 31 Aug 1796; he was 60.

On 14 Nov 1758 when Isaac was 22, he married Ruth HOLLISTER, in Glastonbury CT.

199. Israel SMITH, born on 17 Dec 1737 in Glastonbury CT. Israel died in Glastonbury CT, on 17 Jul 1783; he was 45.

On 6 Nov 1760 when Israel was 22, he married Mary TREAT, in Glastonbury CT, born on 16 May 1736 in Glastonbury CT.

200. Elihu SMITH, born on 15 Apr 1740 in Glastonbury CT. Elihu died in Glastonbury CT, on 13 Dec 1758; he was 18.

201. Irene SMITH, born on 18 Mar 1742 in Glastonbury CT.

202. Tirzah SMITH, born on 26 Sep 1743 in Glastonbury CT. Tirzah died in Enfield CT, on 23 Aug 1790; she was 46.

Tirzah married Noadiah PEASE, born in Jul 1737 in Enfield CT.

203. Asaph SMITH, born on 7 May 1745 in Glastonbury CT. Asaph died before 1781 in Glastonbury CT.

On 25 Feb 1768 when Asaph was 22, he married Dorothy PEASE.

204. Samuel SMITH, born on 14 Jun 1749 in Glastonbury CT. Samuel died in Glastonbury CT, on 14 Jun 1749; he was less than 1.

205. Achsah SMITH, born on 20 May 1751 in Glastonbury CT. Achsah died in Glastonbury CT, on 21 Jan 1759; she was 7.

Family of Jeduthan SMITH (103) and Mary KIMBERLY

206. Mary SMITH, born about 1733. Mary died after 1816.

Mary married John TREAT, born on 22 Jul 1728 in Glastonbury CT. John died in New York, a prisoner of war, on 13 May 1778; he was 49.

207. Hannah SMITH, born about 1735 in Glastonbury CT.

Hannah married Capt. Wait GOODRICH, born on 8 Feb 1736 in Wethersfield CT. Wait died in Wethersfield CT, on 21 Sep 1809; he was 73.

208. Anne SMITH, born about 1737 in Glastonbury CT.

On 22 Nov 1764 Anne married Samuel WRIGHT, born about 1737. Samuel died on 25 Feb 1815 in Glastonbury CT.

209. Bathsheba SMITH, born about 1739 in Glastonbury CT. Bathsheba died after 1811.

210. Thomas SMITH, born about 1741 in Glastonbury CT. Thomas died on 18 Aug 1773 in Glastonbury CT.

On 15 Jun 1768 Thomas married Margaret OLCOTT, born on 1 Apr 1745 in Hartford CT.

211. Jeduthan SMITH, born on 30 Sep 1744 in Glastonbury CT. Jeduthan died in Glastonbury CT, on 21 Jul 1749; he was 4.

212. Elizabeth SMITH, born about 1746 in Glastonbury CT. Elizabeth died on 11 Nov 1825 in Glastonbury CT.

On 2 Apr 1767 Elizabeth married Philip SELLEW, born about 1743 in Martha's Vineyard. Philip died on 12 Jun 1828 in Glastonbury CT.

213. Ruth SMITH, born on 3 Feb 1748 in Glastonbury CT. Ruth died in Glastonbury CT, on 21 Nov 1750; she was 2.

Family of Jeduthan SMITH (103) and Hannah ---

214. Prudence SMITH, born on 31 Dec 1756 in Glastonbury CT. Prudence died in Stamford, Delaware Co. NY, on 3 May 1811; she was 54.

On 14 Jul 1790 when Prudence was 33, she married Joshua WEBSTER, born on 16 Apr 1750 in Glastonbury CT.

215. Mercy SMITH, born in Glastonbury CT. Mercy died after 1811.

216. Thankful SMITH, born in Glastonbury CT.

Thankful married Alvin BIGELOW.

217. Jedidiah SMITH, born before 9 Sep 1764 in Glastonbury CT (baptism). Jedidiah died in Glastonbury CT, on 4 Apr 1826; he was 61.

Jedidiah married Mary TREAT, born before 22 Feb 1767 in Glastonbury CT (baptism). Mary died on 17 Mar 1832; she was 65.

Family of Manoah SMITH (104) and Lucy ---

218. Lucy SMITH, born about 1745 in Glastonbury CT. Lucy died on 4 Oct 1822 in Derby CT.

On 17 Feb 1768 Lucy married Jonathan MILES, in Glastonbury CT, born about 1745 in Derby CT. Jonathan died on 25 Feb 1830 in Seymour (Derby) CT.

219. Jemima SMITH, born in Glastonbury CT. Jemima died in 1824 in East Harford CT.

On 2 Oct 1771 Jemima married William WADSWORTH, in Glastonbury CT.

220. Dorothy SMITH, born about 1750 in Glastonbury CT. Dorothy died on 8 Oct 1831 in Glastonbury CT.

On 23 Nov 1769 Dorothy married Josiah BENTON, in Glastonbury CT, born on 3 Oct 1745. Josiah died on 15 Nov 1820; he was 75.

221. Sarah SMITH, born on 2 May 1751 in Glastonbury CT. Sarah died in Glastonbury CT, on 12 Oct 1830; she was 79.

On 19 Oct 1769 when Sarah was 18, she married Deacon John SELLEW, in Glastonbury CT, born about 1745 in Martha's Vineyard. John died on 5 Aug 1824 in Glastonbury CT.

Family of Hannah CLARK (105) and John BINGLEY

222. William BINGLEY, born on 27 Jun 1718 in New Haven CT. William died in New Haven CT, young.

223. Hannah BINGLEY, born on 17 Jul 1722 in New Haven CT. Hannah died in New Haven CT, on 5 Mar 1802; she was 79.

Family of Hannah CLARK (105) and Joseph COLLINS

224. Ann COLLINS, born on 26 Aug 1737 in Oxford CT. Ann died in 1822 in Oxford CT.

Ann married Isaac BUNNELL, born on 12 Jun 1734 in Milford CT. Isaac died in 1808 in Oxford CT.

Family of Joseph CLARK (106) and Miriam CORNWELL

225. Miriam CLARK, born on 15 Mar 1726/7 in Middletown, Middlesex Co. CT. Miriam died in Middletown, Middlesex Co. CT, on 12 Jul 1754; she was 28.

On 12 Jun 1746 when Miriam was 20, she married Stephen TREAT, in Middletown, Middlesex Co. CT, born on 10 Oct 1715 in Milford CT. Stephen died in Middletown, Middlesex Co. CT, on 13 Nov 1794; he was 79.

226. Sybil CLARK, born on 7 Jan 1728/9 in Middletown, Middlesex Co. CT.

On 21 Feb 1750/1 when Sybil was 22, she married Josiah BACON, in Middletown, Middlesex Co. CT, born on 24 Sep 1727 in Middletown, Middlesex Co. CT. Josiah died in Middletown, Middlesex Co. CT, on 24 Feb 1779; he was 51.

227. Joseph CLARK, born on 11 Jul 1731 in Middletown, Middlesex Co. CT. Joseph died in Middletown, Middlesex Co. CT, on 30 Jul 1731; he was less than 1.

228. Joseph CLARK, born on 26 Feb 1733/4 in Middletown, Middlesex Co. CT. Joseph died in Middletown, Middlesex Co. CT, on 27 Jun 1797; he was 64.

Joseph first married Mary BALCAM. Mary died on 17 Jun 1762.

Joseph second married Phebe STOW.

229. Benjamin CLARK, born on 26 May 1736 in Middletown, Middlesex Co. CT.

On 15 Sep 1763 when Benjamin was 27, he married Abiah HALL.

230. Elizabeth CLARK, born on 28 Jul 1739 in Middletown, Middlesex Co. CT.

On 25 Sep 1764 when Elizabeth was 25, she married Joseph RUSSELL, born on 3 Feb 1729/30 in Derby CT. Joseph died in 1802 in Derby CT.

231. Timothy CLARK, born on 2 May 1742 in Middletown, Middlesex Co. CT. Timothy died in 1807 in Middletown, Middlesex Co. CT.

On 7 Jan 1768 when Timothy was 25, he married Ruth WARNER, born on 29 Mar 1746.

Family of Mehitabel CLARK (108) and Thomas DOWNS

232. Mehitabel DOWNS, born on 4 Oct 1723 in New Haven CT. Mehitabel died in New Haven CT, on 29 Sep 1795; she was 71.

Family of Hannah BROWN (110) and Ebenezer TROWBRIDGE

233. Hannah TROWBRIDGE, born on 13 Mar 1726/7 in New Haven CT.

Hannah married Nathan SMITH, born on 1 Mar 1713. Nathan died on 12 Apr 1787; he was 74.

234. Ebenezer TROWBRIDGE, born on 26 Feb 1728/9 in New Haven CT. Ebenezer died in 1767.

Ebenezer first married Esther CATLIN, born on 24 Mar 1733.

Ebenezer second married Obedience BEECHER, born on 27 Jan 1723/4. Obedience died in Jan 1807.

235. Sarah TROWBRIDGE, born on 22 Apr 1731 in New Haven CT.

Sarah married Levi CLINTON, born about 1732 in New Haven CT. Levi died on 23 Jan 1782. Baptized 27 Dec 1732.

236. Mary TROWBRIDGE, born about 1733.

Mary married John BENHAM, born on 27 Sep 1736 in New Haven CT. John died in Aug 1821 in Amenia NY.

Family of Eleanor BROWN (111) and Daniel HODGE

237. Sarah HODGE, born on 19 May 1726 in West Haven CT. Sarah died on 20 Mar 1802; she was 75.

Sarah married Jonathan BROWN.

238. Jesse HODGE, born on 11 Mar 1727/8 in West Haven CT.

239. Daniel HODGE, born on 12 Dec 1720 in West Haven CT. Daniel died in West Haven CT, on 29 Aug 1787; he was 66.

Daniel married Sarah PLATT, born on 14 Feb 1741/2. Sarah died on 7 Apr 1825; she was 84.

240. Benjamin HODGE, born on 22 Feb 1731/2 in West Haven CT. Benjamin died on 20 Sep 1776; he was 45.

241. Eleanor HODGE, born on 25 May 1734 in West Haven CT. Eleanor died on 20 Sep 1745; she was 11.

242. Mary HODGE, born on 24 Jun 1736 in West Haven CT. Mary died on 8 Oct 1805; she was 69.

Mary married Nathaniel DOWNS, born on 28 Oct 1731. Nathaniel died in Nov 1801.

243. Martha HODGE, born on 24 Apr 1740 in West Haven CT.

244. Rebecca HODGE, born on 26 May 1743 in West Haven CT.

Family of Mary BROWN (114) and Tilley BLAKESLEE

245. Mary BLAKESLEE, born on 25 Jul 1729 in New Haven CT. Mary died in Roxbury CT, on 25 Jul 1748; she was 19.

246. Tilley BLAKESLEE, born on 14 Jun 1731 in New Haven CT. Served in the French and Indian War.

On 16 Mar 1758 when Tilley was 26, he married Mercy BAKER, born before 13 Aug 1738 in New Haven CT (baptism). Mercy died on 28 Apr 1792; she was 53.

247. Jonathan BLAKESLEE, born on 3 Feb 1732/3 in New Haven CT. Served in the French and Indian War.

248. Justus BLAKESLEE, born on 9 Mar 1736 in Roxbury CT. Served in the French and Indian War.

249. Sarah BLAKESLEE, born on 5 Aug 1736 in Roxbury CT. Sarah died on 10 Jan 1759; she was 22.

250. Dan BLAKESLEE, born before 14 Jun 1741 (baptism) in Roxbury CT. Dan died on 8 Nov 1811 in Roxbury CT.

251. Eleanor BLAKESLEE, born before 18 Sep 1743 in Roxbury CT (baptism). Eleanor died on 17 Feb 1828 in Roxbury CT.

On 15 Feb 1764 Eleanor married Zaccheus WELLER.

252. Ebenezer BLAKESLEE, born on 22 Oct 1745 in Roxbury CT. Ebenezer died in 1770.

253. David BLAKESLEE, born on 25 Jul 1749 in Roxbury CT. David died on 10 Jul 1821; he was 71.

On 28 Feb 1776 when David was 26, he married Phebe HALL.

Family of Miriam BLAKESLEE (115) and David FOOTE

254. Miriam FOOTE, born on 3 Aug 1735 in Washington CT. Miriam died in Jun 1738.

255. David FOOTE, born on 13 Feb 1737/8 in Washington CT. Served in the French and Indian War.

256. Miriam FOOTE, born on 12 Jan 1738/9 in Washington CT.

257. Isaac FOOTE, born in Jun 1741 in Washington CT. Isaac died in 1826 in Charlotte VT. Served in the French and Indian War.

Isaac married Anna HURLBUT, born on 3 May 1745. Anna died on 9 Nov 1815; she was 70.

258. Esther FOOTE, born in Washington CT.

259. Dorothy FOOTE, born in Washington CT.

260. Mary FOOTE, born about 1749 in Washington CT. Mary died in Jan 1820 in Washington CT. Baptized 3 Sep 1749.

261. Eleanor FOOTE, born on 28 May 1751 in Washington CT.

Eleanor married Joseph ROOD.

262. Aaron FOOTE.

On 28 Dec 1780 Aaron married Content --- HURD.

Family of Sarah BLAKESLEE (116) and Ephraim BAKER

263. Samuel BAKER, born about 1734 in Woodbury CT. Baptized 3 Nov 1734. Served in the French and Indian War.

264. Nathan BAKER, born on 6 Apr 1735 in Woodbury CT.

265. Daniel BAKER, born about 1737 in Woodbury CT. Baptized 15 May 1737.

On 6 Jan 1763 Daniel married Jerusha HURD, in Washington CT, born of Roxbury.

266. Sarah BAKER, born about 1739 in Woodbury CT. Sarah died on 2 Nov 1821 in Washington CT. Baptized 22 Jul 1739.

On 3 Feb 1756 Sarah married John WOODRUFF, in Washington CT, born about 1732. John died in 1806 in Washington CT.

267. Mary BAKER.

Mary married --- CLARK.

268. Ephraim BAKER.

Ephraim first married Elizabeth EASTON. Elizabeth died in 1777.

Ephraim second married Mary (JOHNSON) SPERRY, born on 9 Aug 1747 in New Haven CT. Mary died on 30 Sep 1822; she was 75.

269. Mehitabel BAKER.

In 1766 Mehitabel married Joseph EASTON.

Family of Thankful BLAKESLEE (117) and Elijah BAKER

270. Thankful BAKER, born about 1740 in Woodbury CT. Baptized 6 Jan 1740.

On 23 Feb 1758 Thankful married William CASTLE.

271. Elijah BAKER, born about 1742 in Woodbury CT. Baptized 24 Feb 1742.

272. Comfort BAKER, born on 17 Mar 1744 in Roxbury CT. Comfort died in May 1817 in Roxbury CT.

On 8 Aug 1765 when Comfort was 21, she married Ebenezer HURLBUT, born on 21 Jan 1736 in Woodbury CT. Ebenezer died in Woodbury CT, on 10 Nov 1788; he was 52.

273. Anna BAKER, born about 1746 in Roxbury CT. Baptized 11 Mar 1746.

Anna married Benjamin CHITTENDEN, born of Spencertown NY.

274. Elijah BAKER, born about 1748 in Roxbury CT. Baptized 17 Apr 1748.

275. --- BAKER, born on 22 Mar 1752 in Roxbury CT. --- died in Roxbury CT, on 23 Mar 1752; he was less than 1.

Family of Samuel BLAKESLEE (118) and Ruth HURD

276. Samuel BLAKESLEE, born in Roxbury CT.

277. Ruth BLAKESLEE, born before 11 Jan 1743/4 (baptism) in Roxbury CT.

On 15 Jun 1763 Ruth married Edward COLLINS, in Roxbury CT.

278. Rebecca BLAKESLEE, born on 22 Aug 1745 in Roxbury CT.

On 20 Feb 1766 when Rebecca was 20, she married Asahel HURD, in Washington CT.

279. --- BLAKESLEE, born on 27 Dec 1746 in Roxbury CT. --- died in Roxbury CT, on 27 Dec 1746; he was less than 1.

280. Miriam BLAKESLEE, born before 17 Jan 1747/8 in Roxbury CT (baptism).

281. Abraham BLAKESLEE, born in Roxbury CT.

282. Anna BLAKESLEE, born before 9 Feb 1752 in Roxbury CT (baptism). Anna died on 2 Jun 1753 in Roxbury CT.

283. Isaac BLAKESLEE, born before 14 Jul 1754 in Roxbury CT (baptism).

284. Anna BLAKESLEE, born before 15 Aug 1756 in Roxbury CT (baptism).

285. Joseph BLAKESLEE, born before 12 Oct 1758 in Roxbury CT (baptism).

286. James BLAKESLEE, born before 26 Oct 1760 in Roxbury CT (baptism).

On 26 Nov 1786 James married Ruth ROOT, in Roxbury CT.

287. Eleanor BLAKESLEE, born before 10 Mar 1765 in Roxbury CT (baptism).

288. Sabra BLAKESLEE, born before 16 Aug 1767 in Roxbury CT (baptism).

Sabra married Ransom HUNT.

Family of Zaccheus CANDEE (119) and Desire ROBERTS

289. Dinah CANDEE, born on 31 Dec 1727 in Middletown, Middlesex Co. CT. Dinah died before 1772.

Dinah married --- DURHAM.

290. Desire CANDEE, born on 21 Mar 1728/9 in Middletown, Middlesex Co. CT.

On 28 Nov 1751 when Desire was 23, she married Samuel STOW, in Middletown, Middlesex Co. CT.

291. Theophilus CANDEE, born on 2 Aug 1736 in Middletown, Middlesex Co. CT.

On 28 May 1761 when Theophilus was 24, he first married Rebecca CHURCHILL, in Middletown CT.

Theophilus second married Mary COUSENS, born of Brookline MA.

292. Sarah CANDEE, born before 17 Dec 1738 in Middletown CT (baptism).

Sarah married --- DUNHAM.

293. Zaccheus CANDEE, born before 11 Jan 1740/1 in Middletown CT (baptism).

294. Mary CANDEE, born before 22 Jul 1744 in Middletown CT (baptism).

Mary married Isaac HOW, born of Canaan CT.

295. Rebecca CANDEE, born before 10 Aug 1746 in Middletown CT (baptism).

296. Rhoda CANDEE, born before 7 May 1749 in Middletown CT (baptism).

Rhoda married --- CHURCHILL.

Family of Capt. Theophilus CANDEE (121) and Hannah BACON

297. Hannah CANDEE, born on 18 Oct 1739 in Middletown CT. Hannah died in Middletown CT, on 27 Oct 1739; she was less than 1.

298. Samuel CANDEE, born on 2 Feb 1740/1 in Middletown CT.

299. Hannah CANDEE, born on 31 Mar 1743 in Middletown CT.

On 10 Dec 1763 when Hannah was 20, she married Jeremiah BACON, in Middletown CT.

300. Isaac CANDEE, born on 28 Jun 1745 in Middletown CT. Isaac died in May 1765 in Middletown CT.

301. John CANDEE, born on 16 Apr 1750 in Middletown CT. John died in Trenton, Oneida Co. NY, on 13 Apr 1821; he was 70.

On 14 Sep 1775 when John was 25, he first married Hannah GILBERT, in Middletown CT, born about 1754. Hannah died on 16 Apr 1781.

John second married Mary ELLIS.

302. Abigail CANDEE, born on 10 Jun 1752 in Middletown CT.

Abigail first married Capt. Ebenezer EGGLESTON (337), son of Ebenezer EGGLESTON Jr. and Mary LANE (128), born on 8 Jun 1740 in Middletown CT. Ebenezer died in 1782 in Middletown CT.

Abigail second married Elisha ADKINS (324), son of Joel ADKINS and Mary CANDEE (125), born on 17 Oct 1750 in Middletown CT. Elisha died in Jun 1839 in Killingly CT. Yale College 1773, pastor at Killingly 1784-1839.

Family of Sarah CANDEE (122) and John HIGBY

303. John HIGBY, born on 17 Dec 1732.

304. Zaccheus HIGBY, born on 20 Nov 1734 in Middletown CT.

On 16 Oct 1760 when Zaccheus was 25, he married Rebecca WILCOX, in Middletown CT.

305. Sarah HIGBY, born on 24 Mar 1739 in Middletown CT.

Sarah married --- RATHBURN.

306. Abigail HIGBY, born on 27 Dec 1742 in Middletown CT. Abigail died on 21 Aug 1761; she was 18.

307. Lois HIGBY, born on 9 Aug 1744 in Middletown CT.

On 15 Feb 1770 when Lois was 25, she married Joseph GRAVES Jr.

308. Ephraim HIGBY, born on 19 Dec 1747 in Middletown CT.

On 16 Jan 1772 when Ephraim was 24, he married Hannah CORNWELL, in Middletown CT.

309. Jeduthan HIGBY, born on 16 Sep 1749 in Middletown CT.

310. Amos HIGBY, born on 15 May 1753 in Middletown CT.

Family of Hannah CANDEE (123) and Timothy BAKER

311. Timothy BAKER, born on 24 Jun 1732 in Middletown CT. Timothy died on 30 Jul 1732; he was less than 1.

312. Thankful BAKER, born on 25 Oct 1733 in Middletown CT.

Thankful married William MARSH.

313. Bayzie BAKER, born on 1 Sep 1736 in Middletown CT. Bayzie died in Lake George, on 22 Sep 1758, in the French and Indian War. He was 22.

314. Susanna BAKER, born on 11 Mar 1738/9 in Middletown CT. Susanna died in Canaan CT, on 5 Apr 1763; she was 25.

On 2 Jun 1762 when Susanna was 24, she married David FELLOWS, in Canaan CT.

315. Timothy BAKER, born on 20 Oct 1741 in Middletown CT.

316. Hannah BAKER, born on 28 May 1741 in Middletown CT.

317. Eleanor BAKER, born on 15 Feb 1747 in Middletown CT. Eleanor died on 10 Apr 1752; she was 5.

318. Jeremiah BAKER, born on 9 May 1749 in Middletown CT.

On 4 Mar 1773 when Jeremiah was 23, he married Ann STEVENS, in Canaan CT.

319. William BAKER, born on 16 Nov 1752 in Middletown CT.

Family of Abigail CANDEE (124) and Joseph CORNWELL

320. Joseph CORNWELL, born on 7 Oct 1738 in Middletown CT. Joseph died in 1763 at sea.

Joseph married Phebe STOW.

321. Abigail CORNWELL, born on 10 Dec 1739 in Middletown CT. Abigail died on 30 Mar 1745; she was 5.

322. Elizabeth CORNWELL, born on 27 Nov 1741 in Middletown CT. Elizabeth died in Apr 1742.

323. --- CORNWELL, born on 17 May 1743 in Middletown CT. --- died on 22 May 1743; he was less than 1.

Family of Mary CANDEE (125) and Joel ADKINS

324. Elisha ADKINS, born on 17 Oct 1750 in Middletown CT. Elisha died in Jun 1839 in Killingly CT. Yale College 1773, pastor at Killingly 1784-1839.

Elisha first married Abigail CANDEE (302), daughter of Capt. Theophilus CANDEE (121) and Hannah BACON, born on 10 Jun 1752 in Middletown CT.

On 13 Jul 1825 when Elisha was 74, he second married Lydia DYKE, in Thompson CT.

325. Elizabeth ADKINS (twin), born on 30 Jan 1752 in Middletown CT.

326. Mary ADKINS (twin), born on 30 Jan 1752 in Middletown CT. Mary died on 10 Oct 1762; she was 10.

327. Joel ADKINS, born on 17 Sep 1754 in Middletown CT. Joel died in 1776. Died in the Revolutionary War serving in Capt. Joseph Churchill's Co., 3rd Battalion, Wadsworth's Brigade.

328. Olive ADKINS, born on 23 Jun 1756 in Middletown CT.

Family of John LANE (127) and Anna BACON

329. Anna LANE, born on 21 Jul 1751 in Middletown CT. Anna died before 1780.

Anna married Benjamin BIDWELL, born of Chatham CT.

330. John LANE, born on 21 Feb 1752/3 in Middletown CT. John died before 7 Apr 1777.

Family of John LANE (127) and Letitia HOWELL

331. Isaac LANE, born on 6 Jan 1755 in Middletown CT. Revolutionary soldier, resident (1811) at Salina, Onondoga Co. NY.

On 9 Feb 1779 when Isaac was 24, he married Mabel HOLLISTER.

332. Letitia LANE, born on 15 Aug 1757 in Middletown CT.

On 29 Jun 1777 when Letitia was 19, she married John PRIOR.

333. Allen LANE, born on 2 Sep 1758 in Middletown CT. Revolutionary soldier, Captain Shepherd's Company, resident in 1812 of Smithfield, Lycoming Co. PA. Alice Marie Beard wrote that the minister "miswrote Lane initially as 'Lain,' then wrote over. As result, 100 years later, a copyist misread name as 'Lewis.' Genealogist Donald Lines Jacobus saw only hand copy and perpetuated error in print." Beard has rectified the error.

Allen first married Esther GRANNIS, born about 1760 in Cheshire, New Haven Co. CT. Esther died after 2 Aug 1792.

Allen second married Susanna ---. They had one child:
    513   i.   Allen (1787 - before 1838)

334. Sarah LANE, born on 18 Sep 1760 in Middletown CT. Sarah died before 1790.

On 7 Jan 1781 when Sarah was 20, she married Eldad GRANNIS, born on 28 Jan 1758 in Wallingford CT.

Family of Mary LANE (128) and Ebenezer EGGLESTON Jr.

335. Mary EGGLESTON, born on 29 Aug 1734 in Middletown CT.

On 12 Nov 1761 when Mary was 27, she married James MASTERS.

336. Elizabeth EGGLESTON, born on 13 Oct 1736 in Middletown CT.

Elizabeth married Stephen SCOVILLE, born on 1 Mar 1728/9. Stephen died about 1820 in NY.

337. Capt. Ebenezer EGGLESTON, born on 8 Jun 1740 in Middletown CT. Ebenezer died in 1782 in Middletown CT.

Ebenezer married Abigail CANDEE (302), daughter of Capt. Theophilus CANDEE (121) and Hannah BACON, born on 10 Jun 1752 in Middletown CT.

338. Elihu EGGLESTON, born on 1 Aug 1742 in Middletown CT.

339. Mindwell EGGLESTON, born on 27 Sep 1744.

On 12 Sep 1763 when Mindwell was 18, she married Elisha ROBERTS, in Middletown CT.

340. Thomas EGGLESTON, born on 29 Jan 1747/8 in Middletown CT.

341. Sybil EGGLESTON, born on 12 Jan 1752 in Middletown CT.

On 17 Nov 1774 when Sybil was 22, she married Abisha DOOLITTLE, born on 5 Feb 1752 in Middletown CT.

Family of Mindwell LANE (130) and Joseph CORNWELL

342. Isaac CORNWELL, born on 30 Jun 1747 in Middletown CT. Revolutionary soldier.

On 15 May 1775 when Isaac was 27, he married Hannah ROBERTS, born about 1754. Hannah died on 1 Feb 1805.

343. Abigail CORNWELL, born on 31 Jul 1751 in Middletown CT.

On 5 Jan 1777 when Abigail was 25, she married Joseph HARRIS.

344. Mindwell CORNWELL, born on 15 May 1755 in Middletown CT.

Mindwell married Aaron NORTON.

Family of Capt. Nathaniel LANE (131) and Elizabeth GILBERT

345. Nathaniel LANE, born on 9 Oct 1749 in Middletown CT. Nathaniel died on 31 May 1770; he was 20.

346. Elizabeth LANE, born on 2 Jan 1753 in Middletown CT. Elizabeth died on 2 Feb 1753; she was less than 1.

347. Elizabeth LANE, born on 30 Jul 1754 in Middletown CT.

Elizabeth married Ebenezer BARNARD, born of Hartford.

Family of Hannah LANE (135) and Charles DUPEE

348. Charles DUPEE, born on 29 Dec 1755 in Middletown CT.

349. Hannah DUPEE, born on 23 Oct 1758 in Canaan CT.

350. Samuel DUPEE, born on 25 Nov 1761 in Canaan CT.

351. James DUPEE (twin), born on 27 Jun 1767 in Canaan CT.

352. Nancy DUPEE (twin), born on 27 Jun 1767 in Canaan CT.

353. SARAH DUPEE, born about 1770 in Canaan CT. Baptized 8 Jul 1770.

Family of Ashbel LANE (136) and Prudence WILLIAMS

354. Hannah LANE, born on 28 Nov 1752 in Middletown CT.

On 18 Jul 1771 when Hannah was 18, she married Ira ROWLINSON, in North Canaan CT.

355. Isaac LANE, born on 28 Dec 1754 in Canaan CT.

Isaac married Sabra ---.

356. Mindwell LANE, born on 16 Aug 1757 in Canaan CT.

357. Lydia LANE, born in 1769 in Canaan CT.

Lydia married --- BACON.

358. Martha "Mattie" LANE, born on 10 Mar 1763.

Martha "Mattie" married --- MORTON.

359. Ashbel LANE, born on 24 Jul 1765 in Canaan CT.

360. Cornelius LANE, born in Canaan CT.

361. Nathaniel LANE.

362. Elizabeth LANE.

Elizabeth married --- CHITTENDEN.

Family of Eleanor EVARTS (137) and Jeremiah GUILD

363. Mary GUILD.

Mary married --- MARSHALL.

364. Samuel GUILD, born on 3 Jan 1743 in Middletown CT. Samuel died in Middletown CT, on 5 Aug 1815; he was 72. Served in the French and Indian War, 1761.

Samuel married Abigail DOOLITTLE, born on 17 Mar 1743 in Middletown CT. Abigail died in Middletown CT, on 3 Jan 1813; she was 69.

365. Jeremiah GUILD, born on 3 Jan 1746 in Middletown CT. Jeremiah died in Warren CT, on 31 Jan 1822; he was 76.

On 15 Jan 1775 when Jeremiah was 29, he first married Hannah HALE, born on 27 Jun 1756 in Middletown CT. Hannah died on 9 May 1800; she was 43.

Jeremiah second married Lucinda FENTON, born on 13 Nov 1768. Lucinda died on 22 Feb 1849; she was 80.

Family of Rueben EVARTS (twin) (138) and Onner EVARTS

366. James EVARTS, born on 13 May 1753 in Guilford CT. moved in 1787 to Georgia VT.

367. Elizabeth EVARTS, born on 15 Dec 1755 in Guilford CT.

368. Jeremiah EVARTS, born on 25 Feb 1761 in Guilford CT. Jeremiah died on 21 Jan 1778; he was 16. Served in he Revolution, 7th Regt., CT Line.

369. Capt. Reuben EVARTS, born on 7 Jan 1763 in Guilford CT. moved in 1787 to Georgia VT.; first town clerk of Georgia; representative 1796.

Reuben married Sarah ALLEN, born in 1771 in Georgia VT.

370. John EVARTS, born on 15 Dec 1765 in Georgia VT.

Family of Elizabeth EVARTS (twin) (139) and Abraham TURNER

371. Ezra TURNER, born on 6 Feb 1743 in Guilford CT. Served in the French and Indian War, Middletown Co., 1761.

372. Martha TURNER, born on 13 Nov 1745 in Guilford CT. Martha died in 1787 in East Guilford CT.

373. Elizabeth TURNER, born on 15 Jul 1749 in Guilford CT. Elizabeth died on 16 Jan 1752; she was 2.

Family of Sarah BROWNE (140) and Rev. George BECKWITH

374. Rebecca BECKWITH, born on 27 Mar 1732 in Lyme CT. Rebecca died on 29 Mar 1732; she was less than 1.

375. **Sarah BECKWITH, born** on 30 Jan 1734 in Lyme CT. Sarah died in Oct 1738.

376. **Barzillai BECKWITH, born** about Apr 1738 in Lyme CT. Barzillai died on 22 Feb 1818.

Barzillai married Lucinda ---, born about 1751. Lucinda died on 18 Jan 1813.

377. **Nathaniel Brown BECKWITH, born** about 1742 in Lyme CT. Nathaniel Brown died about 1777. A.B. Yale 1766., A.M.

378. **Penelope BECKWITH, born** about 1744 in Lyme CT. Penelope died on 30 Aug 1770.

Penelope married Ozias BIDWELL.

379. **George BECKWITH, born** about 1747 in Lyme CT. George died in Oct 1824 in Lisle, Broome Co. NY. A.B. Yale 1766, A.M., minister at Wilkes-Barre PA 1770 and at Litchfield South Farms (now Morris) CT. 1772-81.

In about 1773 George married Rachel MARSH, born about 1743.

380. **Baruch BECKWITH, born** about 1751 in Lyme CT. Baruch died on 15 Sep 1778. A.B. Yale 1773, A. M.

Family of Dorothy BROWNE (143) and Ebenezer HURLBUT

381. **Martha HURLBUT, born** about 1735/6 in Middletown CT. Baptized 18 Jan 1735/6.

382. **Elizabeth HURLBUT, born** before 9 Apr 1738 in Middletown CT (baptism).

383. **Ebenezer HURLBUT, born** before 24 Aug 1740 in Middletown CT (baptism).

384. **John HURLBUT, born** on 16 Jan 1742/3 in Middletown CT.

385. **Mary HURLBUT, born** before 14 Aug 1745 in Rockway NY (baptism).

Family of Lydia BROWNE (146) and Samuel SHIPMAN

386. **Lois SHIPMAN, born** before 30 Apr 1749 in Morristown [Sic: Probably Litchfield South Farms] CT (baptism).

387. **Benjamin SHIPMAN, born** before 30 Apr 1749 in Morristown CT (baptism).

388. **Asahel or Azel SHIPMAN, born** about 1751 in Morristown CT.

Asahel or Azel married Electa RIGGS.

389. **Elizabeth SHIPMAN, born** in Morristown CT.

Elizabeth married John GARRIGAN, born on 30 Jun 1760.

390. **Phebe SHIPMAN, born** on 7 Oct 1759 in Morristown CT.

391. **Stephen SHIPMAN, born** on 25 Jul 1762 in Morristown CT.

Family of Mary BROWNE (148) and Jonathan COLE

392. Elisha COLE, born before 1750 in East Hartford CT (baptism).

393. Elizabeth COLE, born before 18 Feb 1753 in East Hartford CT (baptism).

394. Jonathan COLE, born before 1754 in East Hartford CT (baptism).

395. Daniel COLE, born before 1757 in East Hartford CT (baptism).

Family of Thomas STEVENS (151) and Mary ---

396. Elnathan STEVENS, born in Durham CT.

397. Diana STEVENS, born in Durham CT.

On 19 Aug 1779 Diana married Charles SEARS, in Durham CT.

398. Huldah STEVENS, born in Durham CT.

399. Daniel STEVENS, born in Durham CT.

400. Abigail STEVENS, born in Durham CT.

401. Phebe STEVENS, born in Durham CT.

402. Aaron STEVENS, born on 11 Jul 1773 in Durham CT. French and Indian War service as Cpl., 1756, Sgt., 1758-62, Middletown County.

Aaron married Lucrecia SIZAR?.

ELEVENTH GENERATION

Family of Abel BROWN Jr. (163) and Sarah Gosnell

403. Abel BROWN. In the 1820 Census Baltimore County District 6, p. 206, Abel Brown was living alone: 0000010000001 (one male 45+, one person engaged in agriculture).

Abel married Magdalen ---. Her given name per Howard Smith.

404. David BROWN, 8G Grandson. "David of Abel" listed in 1810 Census, Baltimore Delaware Hundred, p. 710: 20010-2101000.

405. Brice BROWN.

406. Rachel BROWN, born about 1778. Rachel died at age 79 on 13 Dec 1857 in Marriottsville MD at the home of her nephew Thomas A. Cooper (Obituary, *Westminster Democrat Advocate*, 31 Dec 1857). Her farm on Piney Falls, two miles from Marriottsville, was sold for her heirs in May 1858 (*Democrat Advocate*, 6 May 1858).

407. Zachariah BROWN. Zachariah died about 1835 in Anne Arundel Co. MD.

1813 Baltimore County Assessment Records, District 6, p. 5 listed Zachariah Brown but no property shown. His estate administration was in Anne Arundel County *Liber TH No.1*, p. 233.

Zachariah married Sarah H. ---.

Named as Zachariah Brown's widow in 22 Apr 1835 administration proceeding. They had the following children:
514	i.	Joshua D.
515	ii.	Lloyd
516	iii.	Zachariah

408. Josiah BROWN, born in 1781. Josiah died in 1864 in Marriottsville MD. Baltimore County's 1823 Tax Assessment District 6 showed Josiah Brown in ownership of 93 1/2 acres, $70 improvements and no slaves. Tract name was not given. The 1837 Tax Assessment showed Josiah Brown as owner of Hunter's Chance, which his grandfather Abel had purchased in 1749. Much information in the line of Josiah Brown comes by courtesy of descendant Howard Smith.

Josiah married Nancy Scrivnor. They had the following children:
517	i.	John Wesley (1811-1877)
518	ii.	Caroline (1814-1878)
519	iii.	Eleanor (1818-1887)
520	iv.	Julia Ann (1825-1874)
521	v.	Elizabeth Ann (1830-)

409. Nancy Ann BROWN.

"Morris Baker and Anne Baker of Brooke Co. Va appoint John Baker of same their attorney to get from Elias and Moses Brown, executors of Abel Brown dec'd of Baltimore County Md., money due as legatees." 27 Sep 1800. "Received £50 currency of Maryland from surviving executor Moses of legacy owed to daughter Anne--- now Anne Baker." 20 Oct 1800 (Maryland Archives Correspondence File, n.p.).

Nancy Ann married Morris BAKER.

Family of David BROWN (164) and Naomi TEVIS

410. David BROWN Jr., 8G Grandson, born on 3 Dec 1763 in Baltimore (later Carroll) Co. MD. Birth noted in Baltimore County St. Thomas Parish Registry, p. 31. Also per *Orphans Court Proceedings,* Vol. 1, p. 45. The *1798 Particular Assessment Lists for Baltimore and Carroll Counties*, p. 102 listed him with one slave, 178 acres at Turkey Thicket, an old tobacco house, log dairy house, log dwelling house 2 stories, cabin, smoke house. The 1813 Baltimore County Assessment Records, District 6, p. 6 showed David Brown part owner of the tract Dorsey Industry, Mary's Victory, part of Lawrence Pleasant Valley, 383 acres in total and $135 in improvements, no slaves.

About 5 Nov 1791 (license date) when David was 27, he married Jemima ELDER, daughter of John ELDER Jr. and Sarah ---, in Baltimore Co. MD, by Rev. Richards. He was born on 1 Mar 1774 in Baltimore Co. MD. They had one child:
    522   i.   Harriot (1791-)

Family of Jacob BROWN (165) and Catherine STOCKSDALE

411. Abel BROWN, 8G Grandson. The 1798 Tax list p. 102 listed "Abel of Jacob" owner of 75 acres at Deavour's Forest in Baltimore County Delaware Lower Hundred. The 1823 Baltimore County Assessment District 6, p. 4 included Able Brown owner of Dever's Forest 60 acres, $10 in improvements, no slaves.

412. Edward BROWN, 8G Grandson, born about 1775. Baltimore Co. 1798; Edward Brown vs. Thomas Cockey. "Edward Brown of Baltimore County says Edward Stocksdale of Baltimore County being owner of a certain slave, Dinah on the 8 February 1775 in consideration for love and affection which he bore his daughter Catherine, the wife of Jacob Brown of same county by his deed . . . give and grant unto his daughter Catherine Brown ... the negro . . . 13 years old ... immediately after her decease do grant to my grandson, Edward Brown (son of Catherine and Jacob Brown) the said negro and all her increase . . . give and grant unto my granddaughter, Elizabeth Brown . . . Jacob sold Dinah and her child to Thomas Phillips on 6 November 1783. Catherine Brown now greatly advanced in age and infirmities. Some of the slaves now in possession of Elias Brown. One in possession of Thomas Cockey, son of Thomas. Another in possession of Moses Brown, another in possession of John Brown." 1813 Baltimore County Assessment Dist. 6, p. 4: "Edw. Brown of Jac." part Fine Soil Forest, 60 acres, $10 in improvements, no slaves. 1820 Census Baltimore County District 6, p. 206: one male 26-45, one male 45+, one person engaged in agriculture, no slaves. 1823 Baltimore County Assessment Dist. 6 p. 4: Fine Soil Forest, Deven's Forest," 120 acres, $20 in improvements, no slaves.

413. Elizabeth BROWN, 8G Granddaughter.

Family of John BROWN (166) and Mary Catherine ---

414. John BROWN, 8G Grandson, born in May 1759 in MD. Baltimore County St. Thomas' Parish Registry noted John Brown son of John Brown and Katherine, born May 1759 (p. 31). John Brown was listed in the 1810 Census of Baltimore County Delaware Lower Hundred, p. 707: 00020-20110. The 1820 Census Baltimore County Election District 7 enumerated John Brown thus: 002211-010012-0002.

415. Abel BROWN, 8G Grandson. Abel died in 1834 in Baltimore (Later Carroll) Co. MD. The 1810 Census of Baltimore County Maryland, Delaware Lower Hundred p. 706, listed Abel Brown age 26-44 thus: 00110-0000-0-0; in 1813 Baltimore County Assessment Records, District 6, p. 6: Abel Brown "Jr." owned part of Dorsey Forest 50 acres, $15 improvement, no slaves. The 1820 Census of Baltimore County Election District 6, p. 60, he was still in the broad age category 26-44: 000010-00000-10000000000. His will was written 9 Feb 1831 and proved 9 Apr 1834 (*Will Book 14*, p. 500), and named mother Mary Catherine Brown, sisters Betsy and Rachel, brother and executor Jesse, witnesses Archibald, Zachariah and Josiah Brown.

416. Robert BROWN, 8G Grandson, born about 1779 in Baltimore County later Carroll Co. MD. Robert died after 1860 in OH. Robert married Sarah Elder, their marriage license dated 11 Aug. 1803 (*Baltimore County Marriage Licenses 1798-1803*, p. 8), and marriage 14 Aug 1803 (*Baltimore Telegraph* 16 Aug 1803). It can be noted that Sarah, born about 1781 in Maryland, could be his second wife since Lloyd's year of birth was always recorded as about 1800-1. After leaving Maryland, the Browns were found near Steubenville in East Bethlehem Township Ohio in the 1820 Census p 244; thence in the 1830 Census of Perry County, Jackson Township (453), and thereafter Monroe Township of Perry County (1840 Census 141, 1850 Census p. 262). Robert purchased no land on record. In 1860 Robert and Sarah Brown were living in Zanesville with their son Elijah, the only known son who remained in the area.

As for their son Lloyd, Robert Brown put Lloyd into indentured apprenticeship in Frederick County, 1815 (*Frederick County Maryland Inventories Liber R.B. 2, 1808-1815*, pp 484-5), then left for the "West" - Pennsylvania, then Ohio. Two years later Lloyd ran away from his "master" and sought out his parents, while a reward was posted in Ohio for his return (*Western Herald and Steubenville Gazette*, 2 May 1817).

On 14 Aug 1803 Robert married Sarah Ann ELDER, possible daughter of John ELDER Jr. and Sarah ---, in Baltimore Co. MD, born about 1781 in MD. Sarah Ann died after 1860 in OH. Sarah is not listed in parish records. Her three half-siblings Michael (born 1763), Helen (born 1765), and Providence (born 1767), all children of Honor Elder who died 19 June 1771 are shown in birth records; also her siblings John (born 1772), Jemima (born 1774), Onour (or Honor, born 1776), and Owen (born 1778). During and following the Revolution years, St. Thomas and its offshoot Holy Trinity Parish languished until the church was later repatriated under the Episcopal banner in about 1792. Thus parish records of the period are not complete. John and Sarah had at least two other unregistered children: Elizabeth (born about 1781, and Mary (see Robert Barnes, *The Green Spring Valley*, Vol. II); and another, Sarah, is possible.
They had the following children:

523	i.	Lloyd (about 1801 - about 1884)
524	ii.	Elijah (1812-)
525	iii.	William (1815-)
526	iv.	Elias (1819-1875)
527	v.	Henry (1821-1862)

417. Elizabeth BROWN, 8G Granddaughter.

About 23 Apr 1789 (date of license) Elizabeth married Mordecai MOBLEY, son of John MOBLEY and Chloe CROUCH, in Baltimore Co. MD, First Baptist Church. He was born on 5 Feb 1763 in PA. Mordecai died in Clark Co. IN, on 12 Oct 1838; he was 75. The following Mobley line and notes come courtesy Dianne Mueller and Vern Beckman. Warren stated that Mordecai Mobley was descended from M. Moberly of England, who supposedly came to America with William Penn in 1692 and married the governess of Penn's children Phoebe Lovejoy. They had the following children:

528	i.	John Lewis (1790-1842)
529	ii.	Edward (after 1790-)
530	iii.	Elias (before 1790-)
531	iv.	Elizabeth
532	v.	Mordecai

418. Rosanna BROWN, 8G Granddaughter. Or Susannah (per Field).

419. Sarah BROWN, 8G Granddaughter.

420. Isaiah BROWN, 8G Grandson, born about 1785. 1820 Census Cecil County Election District 4, p. 172 enumerated Isaiah Brown. Later of Baltimore City, according to Vincent Brown's estate sale.

421. Rachel BROWN, 8G Granddaughter, born. The 1850 Maryland Census of Carroll County, 5th District enumerated Rachel Brown age 57 as having no family but 800 acres, next to nephew John W. Brown and family.

422. Archibald BROWN, 8G Grandson, born on 30 Dec 1790 in MD. Archibald died in Baltimore Co. MD, on 3 May

1838; he was 47. This family and descendants per Bosler and Young, with exceptions noted. Archibald Brown served in the War of 1812. The 1813 Baltimore County Assessment Records of District 6, p. 6: list Archibald Brown, owner of part Pedicord Hope 113 acres, no improvement (i.e., structures). The 1820 Census of Baltimore County Maryland, Election District 6, p. 60 enumerated Archabald [sic] Brown thus: 200113-00100-3000001. He bought property in 1822. The 1823 Baltimore County Assessment District 6, p. 4 showed him owner of Petticoat's Hope, "Elder's Plague" for a total of 100 acres, $25 improved. The 1830 Census of Baltimore County's 6th District, p. 207 enumerated Archibald Brown thus: 2211011000000-1012001000000 (he being then age 40-50). His property was in Baltimore, later Carroll, County constituting parts of Elder's Plague and Petticoat's [Pedicord's] Hope. McPherson claimed his date of birth was 30 Dec 1780 and that he died 3 Mar 1836 per "another source."

On 30 Mar 1812 when Archibald was 21, he married Harriet ELDER, daughter of John Owen ELDER and Ann DORSEY, in MD, born on 18 Nov 1791 in Baltimore Co. MD. Harriet died in Carroll Co. MD, on 28 Mar 1877; she was 85. Marriage license issued 29 Mar 1801 Baltimore County. Death date recorded in Vincent Brown's estate sale. McPherson says she was born in 1792 per "another source." They had the following children:

533	i.	Eliza
534	ii.	Joshua
535	iii.	Sarah Rebecca
536	iv.	John W. (1811-1877)
537	v.	Cordelia (about 1818-)
538	vi.	Lloyd (about 1820-1874)
539	vii.	Isaiah (1822-1880)
540	viii.	Vincent (1824-1875)
541	ix.	Archibald (1832-1836)
542	x.	Harriet Elizabeth or Eliza (1833-1897)

423. Jesse BROWN, 8G Grandson. Jesse died about 1844 in Carroll Co. MD. His will of 28 Jun 1839 and probated 2 Apr 1844 (*Carroll County Wills 1837-1852*, No. 172, Folio 305) named brother Edward and sister Rachel. Edward is not identified in the family, but Edward Brown's will of 28 Apr 1843 and proved 16 Jan 1846 (*Carroll County Wills 1837-1852*, No. 227, Folio 417) mentioned brother Jesse and sister Rachel.

Family of James BROWN (167) and Elizabeth TWIST

424. Elizabeth TWIST alias BROWN, 8G Granddaughter, born after 1773.

425. William TWIST alias BROWN, 8G Grandson, born about 1777. William died after 1850. William Twist age 73 appeared in the 1850 Census, District 1 of Baltimore County, p. 301, living in the home of Margaret Lovet age 33 and family. Margaret Lovett was found in the previous 1840 Census Baltimore County Ward 8, p 52: 0200110000-00100100000000. Whether she was Twist's daughter-in-law, grand-daughter-in-law or other is not determined, but she had listed in 1850 these children, who may well be Browns by blood: Margaret S. Lovet b about 1830; William Lovet b about 1832; Samuel Lovet b about 1835. Children:

543	i.	Hillary (about 1810-)
544	ii.	Margaret (about 1813-)

426. Mary Ann TWIST alias BROWN, 8G Granddaughter, born after 1773. Mary Ann died after 1840. Mary Twist was enumerated in the 1820 Census, Baltimore County District 1, p. 201: 000000 - 00101 - 00 (one female age 16-25, one female 45 and upward; near neighbors Moses, Samuel and Henry Brown. Mary Twist also found in the 1840 Census, Baltimore County District 1, p. 367: 0000000000000 - 0000010010000 (one female 30-40, one female 60-70. Nearby was Saml. Brown.

427. Charlotte TWIST alias BROWN, 8G Granddaughter, born after 1773.

428. Ann TWIST alias BROWN, 8G Granddaughter, born after 1773.

429. Rebecca TWIST alias BROWN, 8G Granddaughter, born after 1773. Rebecka Twist is found in the 1820 Census, Baltimore County District 1: 010000 - 00010 - 01 (one male 10-15, one female 26-44, one person engaged in agriculture). Near neighbors are Mary Twist, Moses, Samuel and Henry Brown. She was absent in the 1840 Census but Hilary was found in District 1 (p. 370) with his family; it may have been he living with her, his aunt, in previous years.

430. Rachel TWIST alias BROWN, 8G Granddaughter, born about 1783. Not mentioned in James Brown's will; probably yet unborn at that date.

Family of Elias BROWN (171) and Ann COCKEY

431. Thomas Cockey BROWN, 8G Grandson, born on 23 Mar 1789. Thomas Cockey died in Baltimore (later Carroll) Co. MD, on 24 Jan 1822; he was 32. Date of Birth per McCallahan. The 1810 Census Delaware Hundred enumerated Thomas C. Brown (p. 708) as follows: 00100-00000, a single man. He married the next year and was soon to be a participant in the War of 1812. He marched to the defense of Baltimore when it was attacked (Albert S. Brown manuscript). His recorded marriage is after the birth of son Stephen, which was also reported by McCallahan. 1813 Baltimore County Assessment Records, District 6, p. 5 listed him as owner of part of Brown's Inheritance, part Everett's Progress 327 acres, improvements consisting of a gristmill valued at $200, sawmill $60, 7 slaves. He purchased Brown's Inheritance, which lay north of Piney Road, in about 1820. His estate was known as Walton. His biography and portrait (together with a quite muddled genealogy) are found in Scharf's *History of Western Maryland*, pp. 870 ff. His burial place is also in the Brown family plot (Albert S. Brown manuscript 1897). Stones are lost.

In about 23 Apr 1811 Thomas Cockey married Susannah SNOWDEN, daughter of Col. Francis SNOWDEN and Eleanor MILES, in Baltimore Co. MD. Date of license, born on 1 Feb 1791 in Baltimore (later Carroll) Co. MD. Susannah died in Carroll Co. MD, on 19 Sep 1861; she was 70. Younger sister of her husband's uncle Moses Brown's wife. The 1823 Baltimore County Assessment of District 6, p. 4 listed Susanah (sic) Brown owner of Brown's inheritance, Everett's Progress for 497 acres total, plus a grist mill valued at $300 and a saw mill at $20, 13 slaves. She was living with the Steven T. Brown family in the 1850 Carroll County, Census p. 221, at age 59. They had the following children:

545	i.	Louis H. (1816-)
546	ii.	Prudence Ann (1817-1883)
547	iii.	Stephen Thomas Cockey (1820-1876)

432. Stephen Cockey BROWN, 8G Grandson, born on 4 Apr 1791. Stephen Cockey died in Nov 1814. His birth 4 Apr 1791 and baptism 28 May 1792 were noted in Baltimore County's St. Thomas Parish Registry p. 35. A legatee of Stephen Cockey, received land in Anne Arundel County from the latter's will written 21 Feb 1797 and probated 3 Jun 1797. He served in the War of 1812 as a lieutenant on the Canadian frontier and, it is said, died from consumption and exposure (Warfield, p. 169). His will written 1814 (no date) and probated 7 Dec 1814 (*Will Book 9*, p. 508) named brothers Thomas C. Brown, Elias Brown, William Brown, mother Ann Brown, Francis C. Brown son of Moses, Francis' unnamed sisters, Elias Joseph Brown son of Moses, cousin Prudence Gill, and witness was his brother Elias. His estate was valued at some $60,000. That will stipulated that his brother Elias was to "encompass half an acre of ground with a good stone or brick wall, five feet with an iron gate around the burying ground of our family on the old plantation," and if not done, the executor was to forfeit his share of the estate. It was not done (Albert S. Brown manuscript 1897). The reference was to the Brown Cemetery near Sykesville, now lost. He also held tracts of land in Anne Arundel County on his death.

433. Honorable Elias BROWN Jr., 8G Grandson, born on 5 May 1793 in Baltimore (later Carroll) Co. MD. Elias died in Carroll Co. MD, on 3 Jul 1857; he was 64. Buried in Brown Family Cemetery, Carroll Co. MD. Elias Brown's baptism of 15 Jun 1793 was noted in St. Thomas Parish of Baltimore County Maryland Register, p. 35. Participant of the War of 1812 and in the defense of Baltimore, Sept. 1814. His marriage to Susannah E. Brown was noted in St. Thomas' Parish Registry p. 40. Susannah was a cousin, daughter of Moses Brown and so they are both listed twice here. Elias was vestryman at St. Thomas' Parish in 1821-23. He witnessed his brother's will of 1814 and was executor of his uncle Moses' will of 1817. The 1823 Baltimore County Assessment District 6, p. 4 showed him as owner of Owings Outland Plains and "Fine Soile Forrest," Prospect Hills, totaling 757 acres, plus $300 in improvements and 8 slaves. Captain of militia in 1824.

Elias Brown Jr. was a notable personage: he was a U.S. congressman, elected as a Jacksonian Democrat-Republican (Whig) to the House of Representatives of the U.S. Congress from 1829 to 1833, Maryland's House of Representatives 1834-35, the Maryland Senate 1836-38, served at the Maryland State Constitutional Convention in 1836 and was a presidential elector in the1820 ballot for Monroe, and in 1828, for Jackson. Baltimore County opponents of Van Buren and Johnson invited Elias Browne to a public meeting to discuss the upcoming election (*The Carrolltonian*, 5 Sep 1835).

While in the state senate, he was the body's sole opponent of the motion to form Carroll County out of Baltimore County on 19 January 1837. At 57 he appeared in the 1850 Census of Carroll County Maryland, 5th District p. 233 (nearby to John W. Brown and Rachel Brown) on property valued at $13,000, with Susannah 50, Ann 26, Elias 24, and Bazzell 31, the latter a "laborer" and probably Basil Perry Brown son of William. He and his family lived on Ridge Road in Carroll County and were buried in the Brown Cemetery near Sykesville, now lamentably lost, but his headstone reportedly stated: "In memory of Hon Elias Brown died July 3rd 1857 aged 64 yrs 1 mo 28 dys." (Albert S. Brown).

Concerning Elias Brown's death, Arthur S. Brown related in his 1897 manuscript that Elias Brown "was one of the victims of the most atrocious case of wholesale poisoning ever made in this or any other country, known as the 'National Hotel Case.' It was an attempt to murder President James Buchanan and his Cabinet by placing poison in the food and drink served at a banquet given them by his friends, after his inauguration in March 1857. It caused the death of more than 100 persons and the serious illness of more than 600 more. The authors of this dastardly outrage and wholesale murder was never discovered, but there is well founded reason for believing it to have been instigated by the Abolitionists who placed no limit to their vindictiveness as the history of this country records." Conspiracy theorists, assuming it to have been a case of arsenic poisoning, have blamed Abolitionists, Catholic Jesuits and others for the numerous illnesses and deaths among distinguished guests at the National Hotel in Washington of February 1857 (which was before, not after, the inauguration). Later epidemiological theory has it that a sewage backup had contaminated the hotel's plumbing and caused a particularly virulent dysentery. Mr. Brown's numbers of casualties have not been verified.

On 7 Sep 1819 when Elias was 26, he married Susannah Eleanor BROWN (437), 8G Granddaughter, daughter of Major Moses BROWN (172) and Mary "Polly" SNOWDEN, in St. Thomas Parish, Baltimore Co. MD, born on 2 Dec 1799 in Baltimore (later Carroll) Co. MD. Susannah Eleanor died in Carroll Co. MD, on 9 Nov 1883; she was 83. A minor at the time of her father's death, she received $2,000 in legacy. Her husband's cousin. Buried in the Brown family plot, dates provided by Albert S. Brown who fondly remembered her as a "dear old lady." They had the following children:

548	i.	Ann Cockey (1823-1857)
549	ii.	Elias (1826-1900)
550	iii.	Ruth Ann (1828-1828)

434. William BROWN, 8G Grandson, born on 8 Jul 1796 in Baltimore (later Carroll) Co. MD. William died in Carroll Co. MD, on 1 Mar 1838; he was 41. McCallahan gave his date of birth as 8 Jul 1799; the above date per Albert S. Brown. William Brown served in the War of 1812 at the age of 18 as Adjutant in Col. Beall Randall's Battalion, and participated in the Battle of North Point. Family history related that his mother objected to his going off to war, and in anger he fired a pistol ball into a Lombardy poplar tree some 50 yards behind the house; that years later the tree was cut down and imbedded ball was recovered (Albert S. Brown). He was Presidential Elector for General Andrew Jackson in the campaign of 1824 (note the names of two of his children). He inherited much land. The 1820 Census of Baltimore County, District 6, p. 206 included S. [Steven's estate?] and William Brown: 100110-0220200-1100 (3 females and 6 males) plus 21 slaves. The 1823 Baltimore County Assessment District 6, p. 4 reported him as owning Browns Prospect and other tracts, plus Prospect Hills totaling 880 acres, with $60 in improvements, 7 slaves. He died about March 1838, intestate (Shaffer says 1 March, source unreported), and his estate was partitioned in 1842 (*Chancery Book 2*, pp. 60-72, Equity #90, reproduced in Chancery Books of Carroll County Vols. 1-20, 1984, p. 8, in which children and year of death, properties, are listed). McCallahan listed his year of death as 1836, which is incorrect. His year of birth per Scharf is in doubt as well, as he would have been an officer in the War of 1812 at age 13. Buried in the Brown family cemetery with a stone, now lost, that simply said "W. B. Mar 1 1838" (Albert S. Brown). He was a very robust person but killed when he was thrown from a sleigh, broke ribs and died from the resultant inflammation.

A letter to his brother Elias dated March 14, 1837, gave some depth to his political career and his allegiance to Andrew Jackson: "I and my four sons had this day the honor of wagging the bone (shaking the hand) of Old Hickory whilst he was at Sykesville" (Albert S. Brown).

On 1 Dec 1818 when William was 22, he married Ann Waters PERRY, daughter of Basil Magruder PERRY and Delilah Elizabeth WATERS, in Baltimore (later Carroll) Co. MD, born on 9 Nov 1801. Ann Waters died in Carroll Co. MD, on 18 Jul 1860; she was 58. Her husband William and her brother Elias Perry were buried in the Brown Cemetery, but she was buried in the Mount Olivet Cemetery, Frederick Co. MD with her daughter Lucinda and son-in-law William Reich. The children of this family were all educated at he Oakland Academy. They had the following children:

551	i.	Basil Perry (1819-1883)
552	ii.	Elizabeth Ann (1821-1824)
553	iii.	Thomas Cockey (1822-1883)

554	iv.	William Andrew Jackson (1823-1842)
555	v.	Benjamin Franklin (1825-1898)
556	vi.	Jemima Elizabeth (1827-1876)
557	vii.	Lucinda Rachel Jackson (Twin) (1828-1910)
558	viii.	Rebecca Ann Worthington (Twin) (1828-)
559	ix.	Mary Ann (1830-)
560	x.	Susannah Delila (1831-1897)
561	xi.	Ann Virginia (1833-)

435. Prudence Ann BROWN, 8G Granddaughter, born on 21 Apr 1799. Prudence Ann died in 1808. Her birth and baptism (the latter 25 May 1800) were noted in St. Thomas' Parish Register p. 28. Albert S. Brown gave her date of birth variously as 1 Apr and 30 Apr 1799 and she died, he said, in 1808. Buried in Springfield Cemetery.

Family of Major Moses BROWN (172) and Mary "Polly" SNOWDEN

436. Francis Snowden BROWN, 8G Grandson, born in 1798 in Baltimore (later Carroll) Co. MD. Francis Snowden died after 1834 in MO. Also known as Frank. Francis Brown, son of Moses and brother of Elias Joseph Brown, son of Moses was mentioned in Stephen C. Brown's will. The 1823 Baltimore County Assessment District 6, p. 4 claimed his ownership of part of Forest Level and John's Chance totaling 800 acres, plus $250 of improvements and 16 slaves. Despite his inherited holdings, he and his family went west by wagon caravan in 1831, together with Edward Dorsey, Col. Steele, Dr. Edmonston, and others mentioned here. Many settled in Kentucky, Illinois, Missouri, and elsewhere (Warfield, McCallahan, Marks).

Before 1831 Francis Snowden married Lucinda Rebecca EDMONDSON, daughter of Col. Robert EDMONDSON, born in 1812 in Montgomery Co. MD. Lucinda Rebecca died on 26 Apr 1834 in Louisville, KY. Marks (p. 3) stated that the couple had two children, but only one is known by name. They had one child:
| 562 | i. | Moses |

437. Susannah Eleanor BROWN, 8G Granddaughter, born on 2 Dec 1799 in Baltimore (later Carroll) Co. MD. Susannah Eleanor died in Carroll Co. MD, on 9 Nov 1883; she was 83. A minor at the time of her father's death, she received $2,000 in legacy. Buried in the Brown family plot, dates provided by Albert S. Brown who fondly remembered her as a "dear old lady." Since she was her husband's cousin, their entries are found twice in this listing.

On 7 Sep 1819 when Susannah Eleanor was 19, she married Elias BROWN Jr. (see 433). They had the following children:
548	i.	Ann Cockey (1823-1857)
549	ii.	Elias (1826-1900)
550	iii.	Ruth Ann (1828-1828)

438. Moses BROWN. Not mentioned in his father's will. Apparently died young.

439. Mary Ann BROWN, 8G Granddaughter, born on 18 Jan 1802 in Baltimore (later Carroll) Co. MD. Mary Ann died before 1850. Baptized in the Catholic Church at St. Peter's, on 26 Feb 1802. Mentioned in her father's will receiving $2,000 as Mary Ann Brown, thus was unmarried in 1817. Not listed with Wesley Bennett in the 1850 Census p. 218 and presumably dead by that time. See also Warfield p. 169.

On 9 Oct 1820 when Mary Ann was 18, she married Wesley BENNETT, son of Elisha BENNETT and Mary E. WARFIELD, in Baltimore (later Carroll) Co. MD, born on 1 Sep 1797 in Oakland MD. Wesley died in Oakland MD, on 31 Dec 1875; he was 78. Buried at Sykesville. Much of this family information comes also thanks to Kathleen Field's research provided by Nancy Lesure. See also 1850 Census Carroll Co. MD Dist. 5, p. 218. They had the following children:
563	i.	Mary Ellen (1821-1888)
564	ii.	Susan Ann (1823-1908)
565	iii.	Caroline (1825-1909)
566	iv.	Miranda (1827-1917)

440. Eleanor Elizabeth "Ellen" BROWN, 8G Granddaughter, born on 26 Feb 1804 in Baltimore (later Carroll) Co. MD. Eleanor Elizabeth "Ellen" died in 1892 in San Joaquin Co. CA. Baptized in the Catholic Church at St. Peter's on 26 Feb 1804 (Parish Register, p. 145). A minor at the time of her father's death, she received $2,000 in her father's will. Called Ellen in McCallahan's article and by Shelton, her full name was Eleanor Elizabeth Brown as mentioned in her father Moses' will and in the register of marriage, noted in the St. Thomas' Parish Register Baltimore Co. MD, p. 70, elsewhere reported as 26 Oct 1824. E.E. Dorsey age 76 MD was living in the James O. Broadhead home St. Louis MO 1880 (see James O. Broadhead and Mary Brown).

On 9 Apr 1822 when Eleanor Elizabeth "Ellen" was 18, she married Edward Worthington DORSEY, son of John Worthington DORSEY and Comfort WORTHINGTON, in St. Thomas' Parish, Baltimore Co. MD, born on 3 Oct 1793 in Anne Arundel Co. MD. Edward Worthington died in Pike Co. MO, on 10 Jul 1858; he was 64. Sergeant in the War of 1812, Capt. Burgess' Co., 32nd Rgt., Anne Arundel County Militia (widow's pension, NARA). This family moved west in the caravan often mentioned here, and except for the two eldest daughters, are found in the 1850 Census, Cuivre Township, Pike County Missouri, p. 171. His will was dated 19 Jul 1859 Pike Co. MO. They had the following children:

567	i.	Comfort W. (about 1823-)
568	ii.	Mary Snowden (1825 - after 1888)
569	iii.	John Worthington (1827-)
570	iv.	Edward W. (about 1829-)
571	v.	Thomas Beale (1832-)
572	vi.	Eleanor Elizabeth (about 1833-)
573	vii.	Caleb (about 1834-)
574	viii.	Ann (about 1840-)
575	ix.	Susan (1844-)
576	x.	Edward A. (1846-)

441. Ruth Ann BROWN, 8G Granddaughter, born about 1805 in Baltimore (later Carroll) Co. MD. Ruth Ann died on 19 May 1826 in Baltimore (later Carroll) Co. MD. Died young. She received $2,000 in her father's will. Her will (*Will Book 12*, p. 276 dated 25 Nov 1824 - 31 Jul 1826) identified her as daughter of Moses and named brothers Francis F. (sic) Brown, Elias J. Brown, sister Therecia, witnesses J. B. Snowden, Elias and (cousin?) William Brown. Shelton reported that she married Col. Samuel B. Steele of Oldham Co. KY on 5 Sep 1832, which was Ann Alexis, not Ruth Ann, Brown. Buried in the Brown Family Cemetery near Sykesville. Her early death was reportedly due to tight lacing (Albert S. Brown).

442. Rebecca BROWN, 8G Granddaughter, born about 1808 in Baltimore (later Carroll) Co. MD. Baptized in the Catholic Church on 16 Dec 1811 at her grandfather Snowden's home (St. Peter's Register, p. 485). A minor at the time of her father's death, she received $2,000 from his estate.

On 24 Apr 1832 Rebecca married Dr. Benjamin EDMONDSTON. Brother of Gov. Frank Brown's wife. These Edmonstons also joined the family's westward caravan of the early 1830s.

443. Elias Joseph BROWN, 8G Grandson, born on 20 Nov 1810 in Baltimore (later Carroll) Co. MD. Elias Joseph died in Baltimore (later Carroll) Co. MD, on 17 Sep 1829; he was 18. Buried in the Brown Family Cemetery. Died young and unmarried. Mentioned in Stephen Cockey Brown's 1814 will and in Moses', his father's, will. His estate's inventory, entered on 2 Nov 1829, amounted to $338.79 1/2 plus a legacy from Stephen Brown's estate due him for $500 (*Liber 38*, pp. 153-4, 155). It was said that he died tragically on the William Brown Plantation while cutting bush along the Piney Falls stream, he was impaled on a sharp branch and died from infection (Albert S. Brown).

444. Theresia Josephine BROWN, 8G Granddaughter, born on 31 Oct 1812 in Baltimore (later Carroll) Co. MD. Theresia Josephine died in Lincoln Co. MO, on 2 Apr 1889; she was 76. Named as Theresa by McCallahan, Shelton and Shirk but as Theresia Brown in her father Moses' will, also in sister Ruth Ann's will. Theresia is identified in Shirk, p. 92, as daughter of Moses and Mary (Snowden) Brown, which further states that Moses was son of Abel, son of Robert, son of Abel, and which corroborates a major thesis of this work.

On 14 Jan 1840 when Theresia Josephine was 27, she married Larkin LAWRENCE, son of Levin LAWRENCE and Rebecca DORSEY, in Pike Co. MO, born in 1792 in Howard Co. MD. Larkin died on 15 Mar 1857 in Pike Co. IL. Served in the War of 1812 as a Pvt. in Capt. James Hammond's Co., 32nd Anne Arundel Regt., Militia. He and his family went to Missouri in 1834 by wagon train with Col. Edward Dorsey and others (McCallahan, Richardson, Shirk, Marks). For this family see especially Shirk, p. 92, also Shelton, pp. 38-40. They had the following children:

577	i.	Mary Elizabeth (1840-)
578	ii.	Sarah Ann (1842-1882)
579	iii.	Rebecca Ann (1844-1882)
580	iv.	Jennie Dorsey (1848-1917)
581	v.	Larkin Dorsey (1850-1855)
582	vi.	Levin (1851-)
583	vii.	Francis

445. Ann Alexis BROWN, 8G Granddaughter, born in 1813 in Baltimore (later Carroll) Co. MD. Ann Alexis died on 11 Apr 1889 in KY. She received $2,000 as a minor child in her father's will. Not mentioned by Shelton. Her marriage with Col. Steele took place at the home of Edward Dorsey in Baltimore County, officiated by Rev. A.J. Elder (Catholic). It may be noted here that the Elder family had both Catholic and Protestant branches.

On 5 Sep 1832 Ann Alexis married Col. Samuel Bledsoe STEELE, son of Andrew STEELE and Margaret MCFERRAN, born on 24 Sep 1801 in Oldham Co. KY. Samuel Bledsoe died on 14 Dec 1878; he was 77. Left for the West with other kin. He and family were enumerated in the 1850 Census Division 1, Oldham County Kentucky, p. 152. They had the following children:

584	i.	Margaret (1836-)
585	ii.	Teresa (1838-)
586	iii.	Florence Elizabeth (1840-)
587	iv.	Samuel B. (1842-)
588	v.	Susannah (1845-)
589	vi.	Thomas (1843-)

Family of Ruth Ann BROWN (173) and Thomas COCKEY

446. William Henry COCKEY, 8G Grandson, born in Baltimore Co. MD.

William Henry married Providence ---.

447. Andrew Rodney COCKEY, 8G Grandson.

448. Thomas John COCKEY, 8G Grandson.

449. Elias Brown COCKEY, 8G Grandson. Elias Brown died about Mar 1838 in Baltimore Co. MD. His will dated 21 Apr 1835 (Baltimore County *Will Book 16*, p. 463) proved 12 Mar 1838, named nephew William H. Cockey son of Charles C. Cockey and Elizabeth his wife, also John R. Cockey, Rebecca Stocksdale daughter of Thomas E. Stocksdale and Ruth; Mordecai G. and Lewis H. Stocksdale brothers of Rebecca, nephew Charles C. Cockey Stocksdale and his brothers John T. Stocksdale, Solomon Tevis Stocksdale and William H. Stocksdale sons of Solomon Stocksdale and Dolly Stocksdale. The will did not name his wife or children.

Elias Brown married Eliza BARNETT. They had the following children:

590	i.	William
591	ii.	Samuel
592	iii.	Edward
593	iv.	Susannah

450. Susanna Brown COCKEY, 8G Granddaughter. Susanna Brown died in 1822 in Baltimore Co. MD. Found in the 1818 tax list living with Dolly Cockey near the Abel Brown Jr. estate, owning two slaves (p. 25). Dolly was later to marry Solomon Stocksdale, in 1822.

451. Georgius Rex COCKEY, 8G Grandson.

452. John Robert COCKEY, 8G Grandson, born on 13 Mar 1807 in Baltimore Co. MD. John Robert died in Baltimore Co. MD, on 10 Nov 1867; he was 60.

On 23 Dec 1837 when John Robert was 30, he married Deborah Stansbury POWELL, daughter of Capt. John POWELL and Ann STANSBURY. They had the following children:

594	i.	Thomas Robert (1838-1940)
595	ii.	John Powell (1840-)
596	iii.	Annie Stansbury (1842-1935)
597	iv.	Mordecai Gist (1849-1939)
598	v.	Mary Elizabeth (1854-)

453. Mordecai Gist COCKEY, 8G Grandson, born on 22 Feb 1802 in Baltimore Co. MD. Mordecai Gist died in Carroll Co. MD, on 19 Jul 1872; he was 70. Buried at the Finksburg Cemetery.

Mordecai Gist married Urath BRAMWELL. Given as Bramble by McCallahan. They had the following children:

599	i.	Elizabeth
600	ii.	Virginia
601	iii.	Ann Rebecca (1831-1885)
602	iv.	Urath

454. Ruth Brown COCKEY, 8G Granddaughter, born in Baltimore Co. MD. Ruth Brown died on 16 Feb 1852.

On 10 Oct 1816 Ruth Brown married Thomas Edward STOCKSDALE, son of Edmund Howard STOCKSDALE and Naomi EVANS, in Baltimore Co. MD, born on 26 Aug 1790. Thomas Edward died in Carroll Co. MD, on 10 Aug 1876; he was 85. Sources are 1850 Census Carroll County Maryland, Lutheran Church tombstones of Reiserstown MD, Maryland Marriages. They had the following children:

603	i.	Rebecca (1820-1864)
604	ii.	Mordecai Cockey (1824-1890)
605	iii.	Lewis Henry (1826-1909)
606	iv.	Thomas Franklin (1827-1828)
607	v.	Stephen Thomas (1829-1848)

455. Dolly Brown COCKEY, 8G Granddaughter, born on 21 Feb 1804. Dolly Brown died in Carroll Co. MD, on 5 May 1848; she was 44. Shaffer gave her name as Dolly Buchanan Cockey.

On 31 Dec 1822 when Dolly Brown was 18, she married Solomon STOCKSDALE, son of Edmund Howard STOCKSDALE and Naomi EVANS, in Baltimore Co. MD, born on 17 Feb 1795. Solomon died on 17 Nov 1864; he was 69. Buried at Lutheran Cemetery, Reiserstown, Carroll County Maryland. See Elias Brown Cockey. They had the following children:

608	i.	John Thomas Cockey (1824-1898)
609	ii.	Elias Cockey (1825-1882)
610	iii.	William Jackson (1828-1863)
611	iv.	Solomon Tevis (1832-)
612	v.	Stephen Brown (1835-1910)
613	vi.	Ruth Ann Elizabeth (1838-1906)
614	vii.	Edmund Howard (1841-)

456. Charles C. COCKEY, 8G Grandson. Middle name confused. Could be Charles Cornwallis Cockey per *Anne Arundel Gentry* Vol. III, or Charles Brown Cockey by McCallahan.

Charles C. married Elizabeth GRIFFITH. They had one child:

615	i.	William Henry

Family of Rebecca BROWN (175) and George Frazier WARFIELD

457. Lewis WARFIELD, 8G Grandson.

458. Dr. George F. WARFIELD, 8G Grandson.

459. Warner W. WARFIELD, 8G Grandson, born on 20 Mar 1788. Warner W. died on 28 Jul 1867; he was 79.

460. William H. WARFIELD, 8G Grandson.

461. Susannah WARFIELD, 8G Granddaughter. Susannah died in 1894. Never married, but on her parents' death she mistress of the large estate at Groveland. An article on the Browns in the *Sykesville Herald* of 14 May 1936 stated that "Miss Susanna Warfield was particularly active in founding a chapel for the accommodation of the English operatives of the cotton mills owned by Mr. James Sykes, for whom Sykesville is named. The St. Barnabas Church (Episcopal) is a standing memorial to her in this behalf. The work of Miss Susannah Warfield and George E. Holmes, her nephew, was to establish a rectory for the church. She willed to the diocese 50 acres with buildings for the Warfield Academy for Boys, a school to be under the rectory of the St. Barnabas Church."

Susannah married Richard HOLMES.

462. Rebecca WARFIELD, 8G Granddaughter.

463. Elizabeth Ann WARFIELD, 8G Granddaughter.

Elizabeth Ann married M.C. WADE. Lawyer, Boston.

Family of Comfort Lana Renne LANHAM (176) and Stephen OSBORNE

464. Solomon OSBORN, 8G Grandson, born before 1765 in Lee Co. VA. Solomon died in 1828 in Vermillion Co. IL.

In 1788 Solomon married Mary "Polly" STEWART, daughter of John STEWART and Hannah BOONE, in Yadkin, Rowan Co. NC, born on 9 May 1766 in Rowan Co. NC. Mary "Polly" died in 1832 in Danville, Vermillion Co. IL. They had the following children:
616	i.	Joseph (1789-1870)
617	ii.	James (1790-1844)
618	iii.	John (1791-)
619	iv.	Sarah (1795-)
620	v.	Noah (1797-1846)
621	vi.	Richard (1798-1876)
622	vii.	Samuel M. (1802 - about 1850)
623	viii.	Mahala (1803-)
624	ix.	William (1804 - before 1850)
625	x.	Tabitha (1806-1862)

465. Mary "Polly" OSBORNE, 8G Granddaughter, born about 1766 in NC. Mary "Polly" died on 18 Oct 1856 in Clifty, Decatur Co. IN. Family and descendants per Lori Griffith.

In 1786 Mary "Polly" married Samuel Jay ALLEY, born on 25 Jun 1761 in Henrico Co. VA. First County Clerk of Scott County Virginia when it was formed in 1814. They had one child:
| 626 | i. | Doddridge (1788-) |

466. Robert OSBORNE, 8G Grandson, born about 1770. Robert died in 1851 in Bates Co. MO.

Robert married Mary Caroline PRICE, born about 1778. Mary Caroline died after Oct 1851. They had the following children:
627	i.	Ruth (1798-1871)
628	ii.	Joseph (1799 - before 1850)
629	iii.	Naomi (about 1800-)
630	iv.	Zachariah (1801-)
631	v.	James (1804-1888)
632	vi.	Joanna (1809-)
633	vii.	Enoch (1814-1869)

634	viii.	Martha (about 1817-)
635	ix.	Mary Catherine (about 1819-)
636	x.	Thomas (about 1820-)

467. Jonathan OSBORNE, 8G Grandson, born in 1772 in NC. Jonathan died in 1861 in Scott Co. VA.

Jonathan married Martha "Mattie" GRAY.

468. Virginia Jane "Jenny" OSBORNE, 8G Granddaughter, born in 1774 in New River VA. Virginia Jane "Jenny" died on 10 Feb 1851 in Scott Co. VA.

In 1791 Virginia Jane "Jenny" married William KILGORE.

469. James OSBORNE, 8G Grandson, born in 1775. Year of Birth per Myhre.

James first married Matilda "Fanny" RICHMOND. Given name Matilda per Myhre.

James second married Matilda RICHMOND.

470. William OSBORNE, 8G Grandson, born on 4 Jul 1777 in Washington Co. VA. William died in Aug 1865 in Franklin Co. MO. Month of death given per Myhre. Sisseck gave 15 Sep 1865.

On 29 Sep 1803 when William was 26, he married Rebecca RICHMOND, daughter of John RICHMOND Jr., in Osborne's Ford, born in 1784. Rebecca died in 1860. They had the following children:

637	i.	Jane (1803-)
638	ii.	Elizabeth (about 1810-)
639	iii.	Hiram (about 1810-)
640	iv.	Stephen (1812-)
641	v.	Comfort (1814-)
642	vi.	Sarah "Sally" (1816-1876)
643	vii.	Mary Ann "Polly" (about 1820-)
644	viii.	Malinda (about 1821-)
645	ix.	Jemima (about 1823-)
646	x.	Lucinda (1827-)
647	xi.	John (about 1829-)

471. Sarah "Sally" OSBORNE, 8G Granddaughter, born about 1781 in Washington Co. VA.

Sarah "Sally" married Jeremiah "Jerry" HARROLD. Given name per Myhre, Sisseck.

472. John OSBORNE, 8G Grandson, born in 1783 in Scott Co. VA. John died on 18 Jan 1853 in Floyd Co. VA. These dates per Myhre. Sisseck says born 4 Jul 1777.

John first married Celia "Sealy" COCKRELL. Given name per Myhre. Surname Cotrell per Sisseck.

John second married Betty FLANNERY.

473. Jemima OSBORNE, 8G Granddaughter, born in 1783. Jemima died on 18 Jan 1853. These dates per Myhre.

Jemima married John DOLLARHIDE. They had one child:
| 648 | i. | Annis |

474. Elizabeth "Betsey" OSBORNE, 8G Granddaughter, born in 1786 in Washington Co. VA. Elizabeth "Betsey" died about 1824. Dates per Myhre, Sisseck.

Elizabeth "Betsey" married Jonathan OSBORN, son of James OSBORN and Mary WHITTAKER, born in 1779 in Russell Co. VA. Jonathan died on 6 Apr 1874 in Marion Co. IN. Cousin. They had the following children:
| 649 | i. | Stephen (-1876) |

650	ii.	Elizabeth (- before 1875)
651	iii.	Comfort (about 1801 - after 1875)
652	iv.	Hester (about 1803-)
653	v.	Mary A. (about 1812-1876)

475. Esther Louise OSBORNE, 8G Granddaughter, born in 1790. Esther Louise died in 1865. Middle name per Myhr.

Esther Louise married Isaac RICHMOND, born in 1783 in VA. Isaac died in 1871 in Lee Co. VA. They had the following children:

654	i.	Sarah (1804-)
655	ii.	Jonathan (1805-)
656	iii.	William (1808-)
657	iv.	Elizabeth "Betsy" (about 1810 - about 1824)
658	v.	Fanny (about 1812 - about 1813)
659	vi.	Esther (about 1814-)
660	vii.	Isaac (about 1817 - about 1827)
661	viii.	Caroline Ann (1819-1865)
662	ix.	Comfort (1821-)
663	x.	Rebecca Sherrill (1822-1907)
664	xi.	Polly Ann Sublett (1826-1902)
665	xii.	Jane (1829-)
666	xiii.	Louisa (about 1831-)
667	xiv.	Baby

Family of August Abel LANHAM (181) and Jean KUYKENDAL

476. Elizabeth LANHAM, 8G Granddaughter, born on 4 Mar 1780.

477. Robert LANHAM, 8G Grandson, born on 15 Dec 1786.

478. Solomon LANHAM, 8G Grandson, born on 1 Jan 1788 in Claiborne Co. TN. Solomon died in Hunt Co. TX, on 21 Apr 1867; he was 79. Buried in Oddfellows Cemetery, Hunt Co. TX.

Solomon married Mary Margaret BURLESON, born on 26 Aug 1789. Mary Margaret died in Smith Co. TX, on 25 Aug 1863; she was 73. Buried in Ebenezer Cemetery, Smith Co. TX. They had the following children:

668	i.	Franklin (1810 - after 1880)
669	ii.	Jane (1812-)
670	iii.	Lucinda (1814-1866)
671	iv.	Mary (1816-)
672	v.	Randolph (1818-1900)
673	vi.	Minerva Ann (1826-1905)
674	vii.	Bedford (1830-1881)
675	viii.	Margaret (1832-)
676	ix.	Samuel (1832-1855)
677	x.	Cynthia (1833-1912)
678	xi.	William (1839-)

479. Abel LANHAM Jr., 8G Grandson, born on 1 Jan 1790.

480. William LANHAM, 8G Grandson, born on 4 Jan 1792.

William married Vina MCCRARY.

481. Joseph LANHAM, 8G Grandson, born on 12 Mar 1794.

Joseph married Ann BERRY.

482. Ann LANHAM, 8G Granddaughter, born on 22 Jan 1796.

483. Samuel LANHAM, 8G Grandson, born on 12 Nov 1799.

484. John LANHAM, 8G Grandson, born in Oct 1801.

485. Randal LANHAM, 8G Grandson, born on 11 Nov 1804.

486. Melissa Morgan LANHAM, 8G Granddaughter, born on 22 Nov 1808.

Family of August Abel LANHAM (181) and Sarah NUNN

487. Malinda LANHAM, 8G Granddaughter, born on 2 Jun 1819.

488. Samivarnes LANHAM, 8G Grandson, born on 6 Dec 1820.

489. Abel LANHAM Jr., 8G Grandson, born on 21 Jul 1822.

490. Sarah LANHAM, 8G Granddaughter, born in 1823.

491. Matilda LANHAM, 8G Granddaughter, born in 1824.

492. Lee LANHAM, 8G Grandson, born in 1832.

493. Luther LANHAM, 8G Grandson, born in 1832.

Family of General Samuel BROWN (182) and Achsah RIGGS

494. Elisha BROWN, born on 16 Oct 1774. Elisha died on 19 Jan 1832; he was 57. Served in War of 1812. Received the family plantation Brown's Purchase from his unmarried brother Samuel on the latter's death.

On 5 Jan 1805 when Elisha was 30, he married Anne RAY. Their marriage license was issued 20 Dec 1804, Baltimore County. They had the following children:

679	i.	Lucracia
680	ii.	Samuel (-1826)
681	iii.	James R. (about1812-1838)
682	iv.	Elizabeth Ann (about 1815-1838)

495. Major John Riggs BROWN, born on 27 Oct 1775. John Riggs died on 3 Oct 1814; he was 38. Commissioned lieutenant in Captain Samuel Hammond's Co. Militia 1812. He was wounded in the battle of North Point., promoted to major and died in 1814, it is said, from his wounds suffered in the war.

On 14 Dec 1797 when John Riggs was 22, he married Sarah Griffith GASSAWAY, daughter of Brice John GASSAWAY and Dinah WARFIELD, born in 1776. Sarah Griffith died in 1858. They had the following children:

683	i.	Louisa Worthington (1799-1868)
684	ii.	Mary Ann (1800-)
685	iii.	Henry Gassaway (1803-)
686	iv.	Eliza (1805-)
687	v.	Achsah (1807-)
688	vi.	Elizabeth A. (1808-)
689	vii.	Samuel (1810-1880)
690	viii.	Katherine Ann Warfield "Kitty" (1812- about1896)
691	ix.	John Riggs (1815-1890)

496. Mary Brown, born on 6 Apr 1777. Mentioned only by Newman p. 276 as sister of Samuel and Vachel Brown and in "Brown Family" Manuscript at the Maryland Historical Society, Filing Case A.

Mary first married Henry HOWARD.

On 9 Sep 1815 when Mary was 38, she second married Isaac PAUL, in Baltimore Co. MD.

497. Susannah Brown, born on 17 Jul 1781. Susannah died on 6 Feb 1804; she was 22.

498. Samuel Brown, born on 12 Apr 1783. Samuel died on 4 Jan 1847; he was 63. Died unmarried. Officer in the War of 1812. Recipient of Walnut Hill from his father, and then willed it, as he was a bachelor, to his brother Vachel. Also received Brown's Purchase and deeded it to his brother Elisha. Longtime Register of Wills for Anne Arundel County (Warfield 491).

499. Vachel Brown, born on 26 Oct 1784. Vachel died on 9 Jan 1834; he was 49. Served in the War of 1812. Received Walnut Hill from his brother Samuel and later sold it to Capt. Pendleton of VA (Warfield, p. 491).

On 25 Oct 1821 when Vachel was 36, he married Elizabeth Ann BERRY, daughter of Jeremiah BERRY and Mary ---. They had the following children:

692	i.	Jonathan "John" (1823-)
693	ii.	Richard (1824-)
694	iii.	William (1826-)
695	iv.	Vachel (1828-)
696	v.	Ann Elizabeth (1829-)
697	vi.	Samuel L. (1831-)
698	vii.	Thomas Alexander (1835-)

500. Joseph Brown, born on 25 Feb 1786.

501. Achsah Riggs Brown, born on 13 Oct 1787. Achsah Riggs died on 31 Dec 1837; she was 50. Their marriage license was issued 25 Oct 1806, Baltimore Co. Newman and others listed her death as 9 Sep 1817, but the above, in the "51st year of her age," is from the family Bible.

On 28 Oct 1806 when Achsah Riggs was 19, she married Thomas Beale Dorsey Jr., born in 1761. Thomas Beale died on 4 Sep 1828. Will 16 Mar 1827 - 20 Oct 1828. This family per Newman, p. 139. They had the following children:

699	i.	Thomas Beale (1808-)
700	ii.	Achsah Riggs (1810-)
701	iii.	Ann Worthington (1811-)
702	iv.	Sarah "Sally" (1813-1848)

Family of Rachel BROWN (183) and Alexander TODD

502. Benjamin TODD, born about 1759 in Columbiana Co. OH. Benjamin died on 2 Dec 1841 in Columbiana Co. OH.

Benjamin married Charlotte CLARY, born about 1788. Charlotte died on 19 Apr 1876 in Columbiana Co. OH. They had the following children:

703	i.	Mary Ann (about 1813-)
704	ii.	Janet (about 1813-)
705	iii.	John H. (about 1815-1821)
706	iv.	Sarah A. (about 1817-1833)
707	v.	Elizabeth (1821-)
708	vi.	Nancy (about 1824-1910)

503. Basil TODD, born about 1762 in MD. Basil died after 1810.

On 29 Aug 1782 Basil married Sarah GRIMES, in Frederick Co. MD. They had the following children:
- 709 i. Alexander (1786-1876)
- 710 ii. Samuel (about 1794-)

504. Elizabeth TODD, born about 1765 in MD.

On 9 Jan 1783 Elizabeth married Henry BARRINGTON.

505. Alexander TODD, born about 1766 in MD. Alexander died in 1810 in Fayette Co. PA.

On 8 Oct 1787 Alexander married Verlinda CONDON, in MD, born about 1767. Verlinda died after 1810.

506. Joshua TODD, born about 1768 in MD.

On 29 Oct 1792 Joshua married Sophia HYATT, in Frederick Co. MD, born about 1772 in MD. They had the following children:
- 711 i.   Edna (about 1794-)
- 712 ii.   Anna (about 1797-)
- 713 iii. Vachel (about 1798-)
- 714 iv.   Rachel (about 1801-)
- 715 v.   Lucy (about 1803-)
- 716 vi.   Susan (about 1804-)
- 717 vii. George W. (about 1806-1849)
- 718 viii. William (about 1810-)
- 719 ix.   Joshua (about 1812-)
- 720 x.   Howard (about 1812-1849)

507. Samuel TODD, born about 1770 in MD.

508. Rachel TODD, born on 25 Dec 1773 in MD. Rachel died in Wayne Co. OH, on 7 Aug 1842; she was 68.

On 24 Jun 1791 when Rachel was 17, she married Jacob BIDDLE, in Bedford Co. PA, born about 1770 in Frederick Co. MD. Jacob died on 26 Jun 1851 in Morrow Co. OH.

509. Warfield TODD, born about 1775 in MD. Warfield died on 11 Feb 1837.

On 22 Nov 1796 Warfield married Eleanor BALL, in the German Reformed Church, Frederick, Frederick Co. MD, born about 1774 in MD. Eleanor died after 1830. They had the following children:
- 721 i.   Samuel (about 1804 - after 1880)
- 722 ii. Alexander (about 1807 - about 1857)
- 723 iii. Charles Warfield (1810-1890)
- 724 iv. Vachel B. (about 1813-1880)

510. Susannah TODD, born about 1781 in MD.

On 17 Dec 1799 Susannah married Zachariah CONDON, in MD, born before 1776.

Family of Joshua BROWN (185) and Patience ---

511. John BROWN.

Family of Frederick BROWN (194) and Sarah WILLSON

512. Robert BROWN, 8G Grandson, born on 26 Feb 1793 in Montgomery Co. MD. Baptized 3 Apr 1793 Prince George

Parish, Montgomery Co. 1820 Census Montgomery Co. 1850 Census, Triadelphia. Per Marshall Brown manuscript provided by Gregory S. Priebe.

Robert first married --- ---.

On 13 Apr 1817 when Robert was 24, he second married Jane BOND, in Montgomery Co. MD, born about 1785. Jane died after 1879. They had the following children:
725	i.	James (1822-)
726	ii.	George (1824-)
727	iii.	Robert B. (1831-1905)

Family of Allen LANE (333) and Susanna ---

513. Allen LANE II, born on 1 Nov 1787 in Wells Twp., Rutland Co. VT. Allen died before 17 Oct 1838 in Athens Co. OH.

Allen married Hannah COOK. Of Tioga Co. PA. They had one child:
728	i.	Cilinda (1810-1849)

TWELFTH GENERATION

Family of Zachariah BROWN (407) and Sarah H. ---

514. Joshua D. BROWN. Possible son and legatee named in Zachariah Brown's 1835 administration.

515. Lloyd BROWN. Possible son, legatee in Zachariah Brown's 1835 administration.

516. Zachariah BROWN. Possible son, legatee in Zachariah Brown's 1835 administration.

Family of Josiah BROWN (408) and Nancy Scrivnor

517. John Wesley BROWN, born on 9 Oct 1811 in Marriottsville MD. John Wesley died in Marriottsville MD, on 7 Mar 1877; he was 65. Served as private in Co. K, Ist. Virginia Cavalry, CSA. Buried at the Wesley Freedom Cemetery.

John Wesley married Elizabeth ---, born on 27 Oct 1811. Elizabeth died in Marriottsville MD, on 12 Jul 1890; she was 78. Buried at the Wesley Freedom Cemetery. They had the following children:

729	i.	John Henry (1834-1902)
730	ii.	Benjamin Franklin (1839-1892)
731	iii.	Josiah (1847-1942)
732	iv.	Annie (1850-1921)
733	v.	Mary Jane (1845-1894)

518. Caroline BROWN, born on 14 Apr 1814 in Marriottsville MD. Caroline died in Marriottsville MD, on 17 Jul 1878; she was 64. Unmarried.

519. Eleanor BROWN, born in 1818 in Marriottsville MD. Eleanor died on 10 May 1887 in Marriottsville MD.

On 16 Jan 1862 Eleanor married Francis ALLEN.

520. Julia Ann BROWN, born in 1825 in Marriottsville MD. Julia Ann died on 6 Aug 1874 in Eldersburg MD.

On 5 Jun 1856 Julia Ann married William G. LINDSAY.

521. Elizabeth Ann BROWN, born in 1830.

Family of David BROWN Jr. (410) and Jemima ELDER

522. Harriot BROWN, 9G Granddaughter, born on 1 Nov 1791 in Baltimore (later Carroll) Co. MD. Birth noted in

Baltimore County St. Thomas Parish Registry, p. 35, with baptism 1 May 1782. It is noted that the birth preceded parents' recorded marriage.

Family of Robert BROWN (416) and Sarah Or Honor ELDER

523. Lloyd BROWN, 9G Grandson, born about 1801 in Baltimore or Frederick Co. MD. Lloyd died about 1884 in Anderson IN. Year of birth variously reported from 1798-1812, year of marriage not reported but estimated at 1825, year of death also estimated at 1884 and reported so by Ruby Rynearson, niece. Lloyd was apprenticed to a mill owner in Frederick Co. MD 1815 (*Frederick County Indentures RP1*, pp. 484-5), but ran away (reward notice *Western Herald and Steubenville Gazette*, 2 May 1817). Married in or near Perry Co. OH (James Pargin 1829 will mentioned Sally Brown), moved later to Knightstown (1840 Census), then Anderson IN as did brothers William and Elias. He settled first in Lafayette Twp., Madison Co. (Hardin's *Pioneer*, p. 36, *Deed Book 10*, pp. 280-81), then bought with Frank Davis a half interest in a mill 1845, which he operated on and off till 1856. Miller, farmer, land speculator (Refs.: 1830, 40, 50, 60, 70, 80 Censuses, and 1850 Census of Manufacturers). Burial probably in Moss Island Cemetery where most headstones and markers, if they ever existed, are lost.

In about 1825 Lloyd married Sarah Ann PARGIN, daughter of James PARGIN and Margaret ---, in Perry or Muskingum Co. OH, born about 1810 in OH. Sarah Ann died about 1858 in Anderson IN. Maiden surname given in son Elijah's 1913 death certificate as Pardgen; mentioned in father James Pargin's 1829 Perry County will as Sally Brown. Signed off ("X") dower right on various property sales with Lloyd in Madison County. They had the following children:

734	i.	Eli (1827 - after 1870)
735	ii.	Anderson (1829 - after 1900)
736	iii.	Obadiah (about 1832 - before 1880)/
737	iv.	Elijah (1835-1913)
738	v.	Rebecca A. (about 1842-)
739	vi.	Sarah I. (1843-1923)
740	vii.	Catherine (1846-1913)

524. Elijah BROWN, 9G Grandson, born in 1812 in MD or PA, born about 1812 in Maryland (1850 Census Muskingum County, District 112, Falls Township, p. 120. 1860 Census p. 45 said age 40 or born 1820, which is unlikely as he would have married at 12), married Rebecca Ann Spillman on 9 Aug 1832 by A. Wilkins JP (*Muskingum County Marriages 1818-1835* Vol., 2 p. 18); in 1850 was a millworker in W. Zanesville in 1850 (where Lloyd had been in 1830). In 1860 he was no longer a miller; he was a "billiard table keeper" and his parents Robert and Sarah had left Perry County to live there with him and his family (1860 Census, Muskingum Co., Falls Twp., W. Zanesville, p 45). The children in 1860 were Margaret age 18, Amos 15, Clara 9, Charles 4, Lucy 1, with wife Rebecca 44 born Ohio, plus in the home his parents Robert age 83 and Sarah 78, both born in Maryland.

On 9 Aug 1832 Elijah married Rebecca Ann SPILLMAN, in Muskingum Co. OH, born in 1816 in Ohio. They had the following children:

741	i.	Margaret (1842-)
742	ii.	Amos (1845-)
743	iii.	Clara (1851-)
744	iv.	Charles (1856-)
745	v.	Lucy (1859-)

525. William BROWN, 9G Grandson, born in 1815 in MD. Suspected brother of Lloyd Brown, born about 1815 Pennsylvania or Maryland, was mentioned by the historian Harden as having arrived with Lloyd as one of the two Browns who settled early in Jackson Township. But with two or three early Browns there (one William son of unrelated Martin Brown of VA), it is difficult to separate him out from others. He did not appear in the 1850 Census but did in 1860 when he, 45, wife Harriett 43, had six children including an "Eligah" age 14. Harriett must have died 1860-1870 and other events occurred, for in 1870 he was a farmhand living with brother Elias Brown, and his family was scattered among nearby homes, with Wm. Guelson, Isaac and L. Hoppis. In 1880 he was living in the family of Francis Hoppis, father-in-law of the wife Mary A., age 25. His and Harriett's children were Caroline born 1843, Eligah born 1846, Martha born 1849, Sarah born 1851, Mary born 1855, and William born 1857. His son may have been the Elijah Brown who served in the Civil War from Madison County and was mustered out a corporal.

William married Harriett ---. Harriett died before 1860. They had the following children:
- **746** i. Caroline (1843-)
- **747** ii. Elijah (1846-)
- **748** iii. Martha (1849-)
- **749** iv. Sarah (1851-)
- **750** v. Mary Ann or Lydia (1855-1905)
- **751** vi. William (1857-)

526. Elias BROWN, 9G Grandson, born in 1819-21 in PA. Elias died on 25 Apr 1875 in Anderson IN, measles. Buried in Moss Cemetery, Anderson, born about 1821 in PA, was living in Perry Co. OH next to Robert and Sarah in 1850 with wife Mary Ann and daughter Mary 3; but in 1860 was in Anderson Township, IN, married to Catherine (Moss, daughter of John Moss) with daughter Mary 13 b OH, plus Robert 8 b IN. By 1870 Elias and Catherine had lost Robert and had Rosa 3. The 1870 Census shows E. Brown age 50 farming on $4000 worth of land and $700 property. His wife Catherine was then 42, born in Ohio, and daughter Rosa was 3, born in Indiana. There was also at the household a farmhand William Brown aged 55 born in Pennsylvania, probably Lloyd's younger brother. Elias died 25 Apr 1875 of Measles according to an *Anderson Democrat* obituary, and was buried at the Moss Island Cemetery (headstone). Catherine died 21 Jun 1879 of cancer (*Anderson Democrat* obituary), and her headstone is also found at the Moss Island Cemetery, together with that of another child, Francis M Brown, d 5 Sep 1863 at the age of one year, six months and two days.

Elias first married Mary Ann ---, in OH, prob. Perry Co. Mary Ann died about 1855. They had the following children:
- **752** i. Mary (1847-)
- **753** ii. Robert (1852-)

Elias second married Catherine MOSS, in Madison Co. IN, born on 8 May 1828 in OH. Catherine died in Anderson IN, cancer, on 21 Jun 1879; she was 51. Buried in Moss Cemetery, Anderson. They had the following children:
- **754** i. Rosa (1857-)
- **755** ii. Francis M. (1862-1863)

527. Henry BROWN, 9G Grandson, born in 1821 in PA. Henry died on 22 Nov 1862 in Nashville TN. Lung disease, Civil War. The 1860 Census of Perry County, Monroe Township p. 236 listed Henry Browne age 39 born Pennsylvania, wife Caroline 37, children Isaiah 10, George 7. Graham's 1883 "History of Fairfield and Perry Counties Ohio" stated that Henry, "son of Robert Brown, of Monroe Township, this county [Perry]" (p. 476), served in the Civil War. He enlisted at Chapel Hill Ridge, Perry County, on 7 Aug 1861 as a private in Co. A, 31st Regiment Ohio Volunteers, and died of hepatitis and chronic diarrhea in Military Hospital 13 in Nashville Tennessee 22 Nov 1862 (Widow's Pension 7719, National Archives).

On 23 Dec 1847 Henry married Caroline M. MAINS, daughter of George MAINS and Hannah SELBY, in Perry Co. OH, by Joseph Casper M.G, born in Mar 1823 in OH. Caroline M. died on 10 Mar 1902 in OH (Widow's Pension File No. 7719, National Archives). Caroline was daughter of Hannah Selby and grand-daughter of Ruth (Shipley) Selby (*The Shipley Family of Maryland*, 1st ed., 1938, p. 111). The Shipleys figure heavily in the Brown family line, as can be noted in this study. Other refs.: 1870 Census Perry County, Ohio, p. 212, 1900 Census Perry County, Pike Township, p. 196. They had the following children:
- **756** i. Isaiah M. (1850-)
- **757** ii. George W. (1852-)

Family of Elizabeth BROWN (417) and Mordecai MOBLEY

528. John Lewis MOBLEY, 9G Grandson, born on 5 Feb 1790. John Lewis died in IN on 15 Sep 1842; he was 52. This family moved to Clark County Indiana about 1820, then to Bartholomew County Indiana (Vern Beckman). See 1830 Census Clark County Indiana, p. 18; 1840 Census Clifty Township, Bartholomew County Indiana, p. 102; 1850 Census Clifty Township, Bartholomew County Indiana. Warren also listed wife and children. John Mobley died Typhoid fever. John farmed and raised livestock.

In about 1812 John Lewis married Ruth ELDER, in MD, born on 10 Mar 1796 in Baltimore MD. Ruth died in Bartholomew Co. IN, on 6 Apr 1883; she was 87. Major Mobley source cited by informant Vern Beckman is *The Mobley Family*. It stated that "she lived the last years of her life in a small log house. She would sit in a chair in front of the fire and smoke her corn cob pipe, peel apples for children and tell them stories. She usually wore a long sleeved black dress." In the 1850 Census Clifty Township, County Indiana, p. 400 she was a widow. In the 1860 Census, Clifty Township, Bartholomew County Indiana, p. 101 living with John. Also 1870 Census Clifty, Bartholomew County, p. 19. They had the following children:

758	i.	Elizabeth A. (1815-1897)
759	ii.	Jesse Ralph (1818-1895)
760	iii.	Alameda (1820-1893)
761	iv.	Lucretia (1821-)
762	v.	John Henry (1823-1897)
763	vi.	Mahala (1826-1912)
764	vii.	Sarah (1828-1909)
765	viii.	Lewis (1830-1902)
766	ix.	Reason D. (1831-1903)
767	x.	Catherine Minerva (1833-1906)
768	xi.	William (1835-1865)
769	xii.	Warren Wesley (1838-1907)

529. Edward MOBLEY, 9G Grandson, born after 1790.

530. Elias MOBLEY, 9G Grandson, born before 1790.

531. Elizabeth MOBLEY, 9G Granddaughter.

532. Mordecai MOBLEY, 9G Grandson.

Family of Archibald BROWN (422) and Harriet ELDER

533. Eliza BROWN, 9G Granddaughter.

Eliza married Joshua ORAM.

534. Joshua BROWN, 9G Grandson. Named, with siblings, in the partition of Lloyd Brown's estate, *Chancery Book 25*, pp. 222-248, Equity #1519, 1875. There were several Joshua Browns in the area, difficult to distinguish. The 1810 Census Baltimore County, Delaware Lower Hundred, shows Joshua Brown p. 707 enumerated thus: 21110-11000. He may have had these children: Elizabeth Bond Brown, Mary Ann Brown, John Thomas Brown (per cousin Martha Brown's will 13 Feb 1784), but relationships are not substantiated. There was a Joshua son of Joshua and Mary Brown born 15 Jun 1799 (St. Thomas Parish Records p. 39). These latter were Joshua Brown and Mary (Lee) Brown, married by license on 17 Nov 1792, Baltimore County Maryland, by Rev. Bend.

535. Sarah Rebecca BROWN, 9G Granddaughter.

536. John W. BROWN, 9G Grandson, born on 9 Oct 1811 in MD. John W. died on 7 Mar 1877; he was 65. Buried in Wesley Freedom Methodist Church, Carroll Co. MD. Farmer in 1850 Census Carroll County District 5, p. 915.

John W. married Elizabeth ---, born on 27 Oct 1811 in MD. Elizabeth died in MD on 12 Jul 1890; she was 78. They had the following children:

770	i.	John W. (1835-)
771	ii.	Benjamin F. (1839-1892)
772	iii.	Margaret E. (1843-)
773	iv.	Mary Jane (1845-1894)
774	v.	Josiah (1847-1942)

537. Cordelia BROWN, 9G Granddaughter, born about 1818.

On 19 May 1834 Cordelia married Levi ELDER, born about 1812. They had the following children:

775	i.	Margaret E.

776	ii.	Sarah E.
777	iii.	Levi Marshall
778	iv.	Emma E.
779	v.	James M.
780	vi.	William E.
781	vii.	Alessa

538. Lloyd BROWN, 9G Grandson, born about 1820 in MD. Lloyd died in Oct 1874 in Carroll Co. MD. Partition of his estate is found in *Chancery Book 25*, pp. 222-248, 1875, Equity #1519, naming various family members. Property included tracts part of Elder's Plague and Petticoat's (Petticord's) Hope. Lloyd was a stonemason in Carroll County Dist. 5, 1850 Census, p. 664.

Lloyd married Mary E. WILLCOCK or WILCOX, born in 1821. Mary E. died after 1875. They had the following children:

782	i.	Archibald (1843-1917)
783	ii.	John T. (1846-)
784	iii.	Charles E. (1847 - about 1923)
785	iv.	Lewis E. (1850-)
786	v.	Georgianna
787	vi.	Lloyd A. (1853-1921)
788	vii.	Amelia W.
789	viii.	Saib D. (1857-1926)
790	ix.	Isaiah (1860-1931)
791	x.	Jefferson J. (about 1863-)

539. Isaiah BROWN, 9G Grandson, born on 3 Apr 1822 in MD. Isaiah died in MD on 5 Jul 1880; he was 58. Resident of Baltimore City.

540. Vincent BROWN, 9G Grandson, born on 20 Mar 1824. Vincent died in Mechanicsburg, Carroll Co. MD, on 27 Jul 1875; he was 51. Resident of the Sykesville area. Partition of his estate in *Chancery Book 29*, pp. 355-373 1877, Equity #1758. His death was noted in the *Democratic Advocate*, Westminster MD, 7 Aug 1875, where his age was given as 51 years. He was buried in the Mt. Pleasant Methodist Church Cemetery, Gamber, Carroll Co.

On 13 Dec 1848 when Vincent was 24, he first married Adahzilah CARTER, in Carroll Co. MD, born about 1832 in MD. Adahzilah died on 3 Nov 1867 in Westminster, Carroll Co. MD. Death noted in the *Democratic Advocate*, Westminster MD, 7 Nov 1867, giving her age as 35 years. They had the following children:

792	i.	Alice (about 1858-)
793	ii.	Granville (about 1855-)
794	iii.	Clara Josephine (1857-1916)
795	iv.	Vincent (about 1860-)

On 1 Jul 1865 when Vincent was 41, he second married Matilda Ann ZENZ, born on 10 Jul 1835 in Carroll Co. MD. Matilda Ann died in Carroll Co. MD, on 2 Apr 1904; she was 68. They had one child:

796	i.	Jerome N. (about 1869-)

541. Archibald BROWN, 9G Grandson, born on 7 Feb 1832 in MD. Archibald died in MD on 7 Jul 1836; he was 4.

542. Harriet Elizabeth or Eliza BROWN, 9G Granddaughter, born on 18 Oct 1833 in Marollsville, Howard Co. MD. Harriet Elizabeth or Eliza died on 23 Mar 1897; she was 63.

Harriet Elizabeth or Eliza married Joshua ORAM.

Family of William TWIST alias BROWN (425)

543. Hillary TWIST, born about 1810. Refs.: First M.E. Church and St. Paul's Parish Records, Baltimore; 1830 Census Baltimore County District 1, p. 34; 1840 Census Baltimore County District 1, p. 17; 1850 Census Baltimore County

District 1, p. 370.

On 26 Feb 1829 Hillary married Martha Ann BURKS, in First M. E. Church, Baltimore. They had the following children:
797	i.	Rebecca (about 1830-)
798	ii.	William H. (about 1831-)
799	iii.	John (about 1832-)
800	iv.	James (about 1837-)
801	v.	Eliza E. (about 1841-)
802	vi.	Norbury G. (about 1844-)
803	vii.	Samuel (about 1846-)
804	viii.	Sarah (about 1847-)

544. Margaret TWIST, born about 1813. 1840 Census Baltimore Ward 8, p. 52, Margaret Lovet and family. Wm. Twist age 73 b MD was living with Margaret Lovet and family at the time of the 1850 Census (Baltimore County Dist. 1, p. 301).

Margaret married Ephraim (?) LOVETT. Ephraim (?) died before 1840. Baltimore County 1830 Census, District 6, p. 193, enumerated Ephraim Lpt [sic] living near Moses, Samuel and David Brown. They had the following children:
805	i.	Margaret S. (about 1830-)
806	ii.	William (about 1832-)
807	iii.	Samuel (about 1835-)

Family of Thomas Cockey BROWN (431) and Susannah SNOWDEN

545. Louis H. BROWN, 9G Grandson, born in 1816. Married and lived in Missouri (Albert S. Brown manuscript).

Louis H. married Susan HUDSON. They had the following children:
808	i.	Emma (1846-1903)
809	ii.	Louisiana
810	iii.	Ruth (-1894)
811	iv.	George
812	v.	Louis
813	vi.	Horatio

546. Prudence Ann BROWN, 9G Granddaughter, born on 21 Jun 1817 in Baltimore (later Carroll) Co. MD. Prudence Ann died in Howard Co. MD, on 10 Jan 1883; she was 65. Marriage reported in the 17 Jun 1742 *Carroltonian*. Buried at the Springfield Presbyterian Church of Sykesville.

On 31 May 1842 when Prudence Ann was 24, she married George PATTERSON, son of William "Billy" PATTERSON and Dorcas SPEAR, in Carroll Co. MD, born on 26 Aug 1796. George died on 19 Nov 1869; he was 73. Resident of Carroll County, Maryland on a tract of about 3,000 acres originally belonging to the Brown family and known as Brown's Inheritance, which Patterson bought and renamed as Springfield. Raised prize imported Devon stock on his farm Springfield. He owned many slaves, and it was said that the John Brown of song and legend visited Springfield and attempted to induce the slaves to rise up and join him, but they would not (Albert S. Brown citing his father B.F. Brown). Buried at the Springfield Presbyterian Church of Sykesville. George was brother of Elizabeth or Betsy Patterson, who gained international fame and notoriety when she married Jerome Bonaparte, brother of Napoleon Bonaparte. When their daughter Florence inherited the plantation, her cousin Gov. Frank Brown purchased it and sold to the state to be used as an asylum for the mentally ill, known as Springfield Hospital Center. They had the following children:
814	i.	George (1844-1849)
815	ii.	Florence (1847-1878)

547. Stephen Thomas Cockey BROWN, 9G Grandson, born on 12 Nov 1820 in Baltimore (later Carroll) Co. MD. Stephen Thomas Cockey died in Carroll Co. MD, on 6 Dec 1876; he was 56. He inherited his father's Carroll County tract, Brown's Inheritance, when he reached 21, his mother and brother having held it in trust until he reached that age, in 1841. State legislator and county commissioner. He was co-founder of the Springfield Presbyterian Church (Warfield p. 169; *Sykesville Herald*, 15 May 1936; 1850 Census Carroll County District 5, p. 221). Buried at Springfield Presbyterian

Cemetery, Sykesville MD. This Brown family line was staunchly Democrat in its politics, according to Albert S. Brown, and, to judge by the latter's remarks, sympathetic to the Confederate cause.

In 1842 Stephen Thomas Cockey married Susan Ann BENNETT (564), 9G Granddaughter, daughter of Wesley BENNETT and Mary Ann BROWN (439), in Baltimore Co. MD, born in 1823 in Baltimore (later Carroll) Co. MD. Susan Ann died in 1908. Her husband's cousin. She lived in Baltimore after her husband's death; was among the financial supporters for the foundation of the Maryland Agricultural College. Buried at Springfield Presbyterian Cemetery, Sykesville MD. They had the following children:

816	i.	Mary Ridgely (about 1844-)
817	ii.	Francis (Frank) (1846-1920)

Family of Honorable Elias BROWN Jr. (433) and Susannah Eleanor BROWN (437)

548. Ann Cockey BROWN, 9G Granddaughter, born on 12 Apr 1823. Ann Cockey died in Carroll Co. MD, on 6 Jul 1857; she was 34. Buried in Brown Family Cemetery. "A little child of V W and A C Brown was buried alongside its grandfather Elias the 2nd, his little daughter Ruth Ann who died in 1830 lies in the NE corner near her aunt Ruth Ann who died in 1826 and whose grave is marked R.A.B. with the date" (Albert S. Brown manuscript 1897). Those stones are now lost.

On 22 Oct 1853 when Ann Cockey was 30, she married Vachel W. BEASMAN, son of John BEASMAN and Rebecca GRIFFEE, in Baltimore Co. MD, born in 1819 in Baltimore Co. MD. Vachel W. died in 1881 in Baltimore Co. MD. They had the following children:

818	i.	Elias Brown (-1857)
819	ii.	Aletha V. (Adopted)

549. Elias BROWN, 9G Grandson, born on 2 Sep 1826 in Baltimore (later Carroll) Co. MD. Elias died in 1900 in Ellicott City MD. Lived on the tract Owings Outland Plains which his great-grandfather Abel had purchased in 1747. Children except Samuel T., are from the 1880 Census, Election District 53, Carroll County Maryland, p. 379B.

On 9 Dec 1852 when Elias was 26, he married Catherine E[liza?]. J. BARNETT, born on 4 Dec 1831 in MD. Catherine E. J. died in Carroll Co. MD, on 28 Nov 1896; she was 64. Named Eliza in the 1880 Census. Middle initials also given as E.I. but Albert S. Brown knew her personally used E.J. They had the following children:

820	i.	Elias (1853-1855)
821	ii.	William M. (1855-)
822	iii.	Edward D. (1859-1919)
823	iv.	Catherine E. (1861-1861)
824	v.	Samuel Thomas (1866-1934)
825	vi.	Susannah Amelia (1868-)

550. Ruth Ann BROWN, born on 19 May 1828. Ruth Ann died on 19 May 1828; she was less than 1.

Family of William BROWN (434) and Ann Waters PERRY

551. Basil Perry BROWN, 9G Grandson, born on 12 Nov 1819 in Baltimore (later Carroll) Co. MD. Basil Perry died in Aug 1883 in Carroll Co. MD. Unmarried (per McCallahan). Listed a Laborer age 31 at the home of Elias Brown in 1850 Census of Carroll County, 5th District, p. 233. Buried in the Brown family plot. A soldier in the Mexican War, Col. Watson's Regiment, he was discharged in Texas for matters of health, traveled to California where he remained for some time (Albert S. Brown). Albert S. Brown reported his death as Aug 1883; others have said 1891.

552. Elizabeth Ann BROWN, 9G Granddaughter, born in 1821 in Baltimore (later Carroll) Co. MD. Elizabeth Ann died in 1824 in Baltimore (later Carroll) Co. MD.

553. Thomas Cockey BROWN, 9G Grandson, born on 5 Apr 1822 in Baltimore (later Carroll) Co. MD. Thomas Cockey died in Carroll Co. MD, on 15 Feb 1883; he was 60. Scharf (*History of Western Maryland,* Vol. II, p. 870) reported that

Thomas C. Brown's mother was Nancy Cockey (actually a reference to Ann Cockey his grandmother), and was the third child in the family. Scharf (and nephew Albert S. Brown) continued to relate that in 1848 he went to Louisiana to manage a sugar plantation with 360 slaves owned by James A. Sedden, Confederate Secretary of War, and was there during the Union Army's siege of New Orleans. On his return to Maryland he was arrested and tried for treason by a U.S. military commission but subsequently acquitted and released. In 1866 he bought the plantation Wilton, 186 acres, near Finksburg. He served as Democratic state congressman in 1873-4. At 6'6" and 325 pounds he was presented with a special chair at the state body's meetings, and prized it thereafter. Died of a self-inflicted wound and was buried at Freedom Cemetery, Carroll County (Albert S. Brown).

554. William Andrew Jackson BROWN, 9G Grandson, born on 5 Dec 1823 in Baltimore (later Carroll) Co. MD. William Andrew Jackson died in Baltimore (later Carroll) Co. MD, on 4 Mar 1842; he was 18. Worked as a clerk in a bookstore in Baltimore but died as a young man of 19 years (Albert S. Brown).

555. Benjamin Franklin BROWN, 9G Grandson, born on 7 Mar 1825 in Baltimore (later Carroll) Co. MD. Benjamin Franklin died in MD on 11 Sep 1898; he was 73. Buried in Mt. Olivet Cemetery, Frederick Co. MD. Dealer in coal, grain, real estate. This family lived in Fredericksburg MD, also home of the Reichs. Like his family, he was a lifelong Democrat and apparently at odds with the Union cause. During the Civil War he was imprisoned for 56 days in 1862 at Washington D.C., then released without charge; imprisoned again in 1864 for 60 days in Baltimore with his brother Thomas, charged with treason. A military tribunal released them (per Albert S. Brown, his son). Additional ref.: 1880 Census Frederick, Frederick Co. MD p. 77D.

On 2 Nov 1852 when Benjamin Franklin was 27, he married Dorcas H. REICH, daughter of Phillip REICH and Rebecca ---, born in Oct 1836. Dorcas H. died after 1900. 1900 Census Frederick, Frederick Co. MD, p. 93, Dorcas H. Brown widow, age 63, living with son Albert S. Brown, son, Lawyer age 36. The census enumeration further stated that she had had seven children, three were then living. They had the following children:

826	i.	Florence (1853-)
827	ii.	Fannie (1857-)
828	iii.	Albert S. (1863 - after 1930)
829	iv.	Mildred Lee (1865-1890)
830	v.	Miriam E.

556. Jemima Elizabeth BROWN, 9G Granddaughter, born on 14 Sep 1827 in Baltimore (later Carroll) Co. MD. Jemima Elizabeth died in Carroll Co. MD, on 12 Jan 1876; she was 48. Buried at Wesley Freedom Cemetery.

In 1852 Jemima Elizabeth married John Gorsuch PEARCE, born on 2 Mar 1818 in Baltimore (later Carroll) Co. MD. John Gorsuch died in Carroll Co. MD, on 20 Aug 1890; he was 72. Buried in Wesley Freedom Chapel Cemetery, Carroll Co. MD. Farmer of Carroll County MD. They had the following children:

831	i.	William Brown (1852-)
832	ii.	John Thomas (1854-1916)
833	iii.	Elias Joseph (1856-1876)
834	iv.	George Marshall (1857-)
835	v.	Mary Virginia (1859-)
836	vi.	Charles Cockey (1861-1916)

557. Lucinda Rachel Jackson BROWN, 9G Granddaughter, born on 12 Nov 1828 in Baltimore Co. MD. Lucinda Rachel Jackson died in 1910. Twin sister. Buried at Mt. Olivet Cemetery, Frederick County Maryland.

In Feb 1853 Lucinda Rachel Jackson married William REICH, son of John REICH and Phebe ---, born on 5 Oct 1815 in Frederick Co. MD. William died in 1901 in Frederick Co. MD. Buried Mt. at Olivet Cemetery, Frederick County Maryland. They had the following children:

837	i.	William John (1854-)
838	ii.	Lucy Brown (1855-)
839	iii.	Phillip Valentine (1857-1912)
840	iv.	Elenore (1859-)
841	v.	Benjamin Franklin (1861-)

558. Rebecca Ann Worthington BROWN, 9G Granddaughter, born on 12 Nov 1828 in Baltimore Co. MD. Twin sister. Albert S. Brown reported her name as Rebecca Martha Washington Brown.

In about 1850 Rebecca Ann Worthington married Christian SHRYOCK, in Baltimore Co. MD. Christian died before 1897. Farmer of Frederick County MD. He was a widower with a child when married. They had the following children:

842	i.	William Brown (1853-)
843	ii.	Henrietta (about 1855 - before 1897)
844	iii.	Leonora P. "Lena" (1857-)

559. Mary Ann BROWN, 9G Granddaughter, born on 5 May 1830 in Baltimore Co. MD.

In 1852 Mary Ann married Alfred A. TILYARD, in Baltimore Co. MD. Alfred A. died in 1893. Resident of Baltimore. Clerk, Register of Wills, Baltimore County. They had the following children:

845	i.	John S. (1855-)
846	ii.	Charles H. (1859-)
847	iii.	Mattie

560. Susannah Delila BROWN, 9G Granddaughter, born on 12 May 1831 in Baltimore (later Carroll) Co. MD. Susannah Delila died in Pikesville MD, on 30 Jul 1897; she was 66. She was her husband's 2nd cousin. Additional source: "Cockey Bibles," *The Maryland Genealogical Society Bulletin*, 26, 2 (Spring 1985), pp. 186-188.

On 17 Mar 1852 when Susannah Delila was 20, she married Charles Thomas COCKEY, son of Edward Augustus COCKEY and Urath Cromwell OWINGS, in Carroll Co. MD, born on 6 Dec 1829 in Baltimore (later Carroll) Co. MD. A gentleman farmer, described by Alfred S. Brown in 1897 as "by large odds the wealthy man of the family." Vestryman at St. Thomas' Parish 1885-98. The estate of this family was Garrison Forest, near Pikesville. Lands totaling 1079 acres held at the time of his will were Melinda's Prospect, 458 acres; Garrison. 450 acres; Liele Park, 124 acres; plus 40 acres near Catonsville and 7 acres near Reiserstown, tracts unnamed. They had the following children:

848	i.	Edward Augustus (1853-1922)
849	ii.	Ann A. (1855-)
850	iii.	Thomas Beale (1857-)
851	iv.	Urath Cromwell (1859-)
852	v.	William Brown (1861-)
853	vi.	Charles Thomas (1863-)

561. Ann Virginia BROWN, 9G Granddaughter, born on 12 Apr 1833 in Baltimore Co. MD. Albert S. Brown reported her date of birth as 12 Oct 1832.

Ann Virginia married Phillip H. TILYARD, in Baltimore Co. MD. Brother of Alfred Tilyard; resident of Reiserstown MD and Baltimore. Attorney's clerk. They had the following children:

854	i.	Tyson (1863-)
855	ii.	Mattie Virginia (1866-)
856	iii.	Walter (1867-)
857	iv.	Irene (1869-)
858	v.	Florence Patterson (1871-)

Family of Francis Snowden BROWN (436) and Lucinda Rebecca EDMONDSON

562. Moses BROWN, 9G Grandson. Resided in Missouri.

Family of Mary Ann BROWN (439) and Wesley BENNETT

563. Mary Ellen BENNETT, 9G Granddaughter, born on 16 Aug 1821 in Oakland MD. Mary Ellen died in Oakland MD, on 23 Feb 1888; she was 66. Age 27 in the 1850 Census Carroll Co. Dist. 5 p. 218, living with father Wesley and two sisters.

Mary Ellen married Elisha H. BENNETT, cousin and son of Col. Jesse BENNETT and Sarah ---, in Baltimore Co. MD,

born on 7 Mar 1828 in Oakland MD. Elisha H. died in Reisterstown MD, on 23 Mar 1900; he was 72. They had one child:
    859   i.   Laura Ella (1856-1946)

564. Susan Ann BENNETT, 9G Granddaughter, born in 1823 in Baltimore (later Carroll) Co. MD. Susan Ann died in 1908. Her husband's cousin. She lived in Baltimore after her husband's death, was among the financial supporters for the foundation of the Maryland Agricultural College. Buried at Springfield Presbyterian Cemetery, Sykesville MD.

In 1842 Susan Ann married Stephen Thomas Cockey BROWN (547) , 9G Grandson, son of Thomas Cockey BROWN (431) and Susannah SNOWDEN, in Baltimore Co. MD, born on 12 Nov 1820 in Baltimore (later Carroll) Co. MD. Stephen Thomas Cockey died in Carroll Co. MD, on 6 Dec 1876; he was 56. He inherited his father's Carroll County tract, Brown's Inheritance, when he reached 21, his mother and brother having held it in trust until he reached that age, in 1841. State legislator and county commissioner. He was cofounder of the Springfield Presbyterian Church (Warfield p. 169; *Sykesville Herald*, 15 May 1936; 1850 Census Carroll County District 5, p. 221). Buried at Springfield Presbyterian Cemetery, Sykesville MD. This Brown family line was staunchly Democrat in its politics, according to Albert S. Brown, and, to judge by the latter's remarks, sympathetic to the Confederate cause. They had the following children:
    816   i.   Mary Ridgely (about 1844-)
    817   ii.   Francis (Frank) (1846-1920)

565. Caroline BENNETT, 9G Granddaughter, born in 1825 in Baltimore (later Carroll) Co. MD. Caroline died on 11 Feb 1909 in Carroll Co. MD. Age 23 in the 1850 Census Carroll Co. Dist. 5 p. 218, living with father Wesley and two sisters. See will 10/345.

566. Miranda BENNETT, 9G Granddaughter, born on 26 Oct 1827 in Baltimore (later Carroll) Co. MD. Miranda died in Carroll Co. MD, on 26 Sep 1917; she was 89. Marandy age 27 in the 1850 Census Carroll Co. Dist. 5 p. 218, living with father Wesley and two sisters. Buried All Saints' Cemetery, Reisterstown.

On 27 Oct 1851 when Miranda was 24, she married Mordecai Cockey STOCKSDALE (604) , 9G Grandson, son of Thomas Edward STOCKSDALE and Ruth Brown COCKEY (454), in Carroll Co. MD, born on 25 Apr 1824 in Baltimore Co. MD. Mordecai Cockey died in Carroll Co. MD, on 4 Feb 1890; he was 65. Buried All Saints' Cemetery, Reisterstown. They had the following children:
    860   i.   Florence
    861   ii.   Annie

Family of Eleanor Elizabeth "Ellen" BROWN (440) and Edward Worthington DORSEY

567. Comfort W. DORSEY, 9G Granddaughter, born about 1823 in Baltimore (later Carroll) Co. MD. She and her husband accompanied other family members on their westward trek, much mentioned here.

On 25 Feb 1840 Comfort W. married Gilchrist PORTER, in Pike Co. MO, born about 1820 in MD. Congressman from the Hannibal District of Missouri before the Civil War (Albert S. Brown manuscript). They had the following children:
    862   i.   Mary Eleanor (about 1841-)
    863   ii.   Julia (about 1848-)
    864   iii.   Margaret D. (1849-)

568. Mary Snowden DORSEY, 9G Granddaughter, born in 1825 in Baltimore (later Carroll) Co. MD. Mary Snowden died after 1888 in MO?

On 13 May 1847 Mary Snowden married James Overton BROADHEAD, in Pike Co. MO, born about 1819. Lawyer. Also called Broadshear, Brodhead. Minister to Switzerland during the Cleveland presidency, and a member of the Missouri Legislature. They had one child:
    865   i.   Edward (about 1849-)

569. John Worthington DORSEY, 9G Grandson, born in 1827 in MD. living in California 1858.

570. Edward W. DORSEY, born about 1829. Died young.

571. Thomas Beale DORSEY, 9G Grandson, born in 1832 in MD. Living in California 1858.

572. Eleanor Elizabeth DORSEY, 9G Granddaughter, born about 1833. Died in infancy.

573. Caleb DORSEY, 9G Grandson, born about 1834 in MD.

574. Ann DORSEY, 9G Granddaughter, born about 1840 in MO.

575. Susan DORSEY, 9G Granddaughter, born in 1844 in MO.

576. Edward A. DORSEY, 9G Grandson, born in 1846 in MO. Called "Edna" in father's will.

Family of Theresia Josephine BROWN (444) and Larkin LAWRENCE

577. Mary Elizabeth LAWRENCE, 9G Granddaughter, born on 30 Oct 1840 in Lincoln Co. MO. Called Marry Ellen "Tip," by Shelton.

On 16 Oct 1860 when Mary Elizabeth was 19, she married James William WILLIAMS.

578. Sarah Ann LAWRENCE, 9G Granddaughter, born on 26 Dec 1842 in Lincoln Co. MO. Sarah Ann died in 1882.

Sarah Ann married Washington Green MCCARDIE.

579. Rebecca Ann LAWRENCE, 9G Granddaughter, born on 5 Apr 1844 in Lincoln Co. MO. Rebecca Ann died on 10 Sep 1882; she was 38. Called Ann Rebecca by Shelton.

On 14 Nov 1866 when Rebecca Ann was 22, she married her first cousin George Benton LAWRENCE, son of Hammond Dorsey LAWRENCE and Louise SHIPLEY, in MO, born on 18 Jul 1841 in MD. They had the following children:
866	i.	Hammond (1868-1900)
867	ii.	Ida Lee (1872-)
868	iii.	France Edward (1875-)
869	iv.	Claude (1878-)

580. Jennie Dorsey LAWRENCE, 9G Granddaughter, born on 25 Aug 1848 in Louisville, Lincoln Co. MO. Jennie Dorsey died in Ralls Co. MO, on 7 Sep 1917; she was 69. Called Jane Dorsey Lawrence by Shelton.

On 26 Dec 1872 when Jennie Dorsey was 24, she married John Henry MCCLINTOCK, son of Robert Miller MCCLINTOCK and Lorain RIBBLE, in Lincoln Co. MO, born on 3 Feb 1844 in Pike Co. IL. They had the following children:
870	i.	Clemmie Irene (1874-)
871	ii.	James Henry (1876-)
872	iii.	George Edward (1879-)
873	iv.	Robert Levin (1882-)
874	v.	Nettie Myrtle (1884-)
875	vi.	Orie Lawrence (1888-)

581. Larkin Dorsey LAWRENCE, 9G Grandson, born on 20 Sep 1850 in Louisville, Lincoln Co. MO. Larkin Dorsey died in 1855 in Lincoln Co. MO.

582. Levin LAWRENCE, 9G Grandson, born on 12 Jul 1851 in Lincoln Co. MO.

On 7 Jan 1876 when Levin was 24, he married Florence MURPHEY, born on 27 Jun 1855 in Bloomington IN. They had the following children:
| 876 | i. | Musa (1877-1877) |
| 877 | ii. | Charles Larkin (1879-1923) |

878	iii.	Verdie (1883-1905)
879	iv.	Leone (1890-)
880	v.	Everett Curtis (1892-)
881	vi.	Raymond Vance (1895-)

583. Francis LAWRENCE. Per Albert S. Brown but not elsewhere mentioned.

Family of Ann Alexis BROWN (445) and Col. Samuel Bledsoe STEELE

584. Margaret STEELE, 9G Granddaughter, born in 1836 in KY.

585. Teresa STEELE, 9G Granddaughter, born in 1838 in KY.

586. Florence Elizabeth STEELE, 9G Granddaughter, born on 24 Sep 1840 in KY.

Florence Elizabeth first married --- MARTIN. They had one child:
| 882 | i. | Harry |

In 1880 Florence Elizabeth second married Zebulon Baird VANCE, son of David VANCE and Mira BAIRD, born on 13 May 1830 in Buncombe Co. NC. Zebulon Baird died on 14 Apr 1894; he was 63. He was known as North Carolina's "Civil War Senator." His political career started as a Whig candidate when he won his first election for a seat in the State House of Commons at the young age of twenty-four. One of the dominant personalities of the South for nearly half a century, Zeb Vance served in public office for thirty years. In 1858, at the age of 28 he won his first congressional seat and was the youngest member of Congress but resigned when North Carolina voted for secession. In May of 1861, he was captain of the "Rough and Ready Guards" of Raleigh, which later became a part of the Fourteenth Regiment. In August of that year Vance was elected colonel of the Twenty-sixth North Carolina Regiment. In January of 1865 Vance was arrested and taken into custody by federal troops. He spent time as a prisoner in Washington D.C until the end of 1865 when he was paroled and sent home. He became governor as the "soldier's candidate" in 1862, 1864 and his third and final term in 1876. He won his first seat in the U.S. Senate in 1870 but was not allowed to serve because he was still on parole. In 1878 Zebulon B. Vance again won the Senate seat and held that office until his death on April 14, 1894. This couple had no children.

587. Samuel B. STEELE, 9G Grandson, born in 1842 in KY.

588. Susannah STEELE, 9G Granddaughter, born in 1845 in KY.

589. Thomas STEELE, 9G Grandson, born in 1843 in KY.

Family of Elias Brown COCKEY (449) and Eliza BARNETT

590. William COCKEY.

591. Samuel COCKEY.

592. Edward COCKEY.

593. Susannah COCKEY.

Family of John Robert COCKEY (452) and Deborah Stansbury POWELL

594. Thomas Robert COCKEY, 9G Grandson, born on 7 Nov 1838 in Baltimore Co. MD. Thomas Robert died in Hutchins KS, on 11 Nov 1940; he was 102.

On 29 Aug 1864 when Thomas Robert was 25, he married Clara BROOKS, in Baltimore Co. MD.

595. John Powell COCKEY, 9G Grandson, born on 12 Jan 1840 in Baltimore Co. MD. He died in the Civil War battle of Bunker Hill in Virginia and was buried there, but his remains were then returned to the family plantation Arlington by his father; they were later re-interred at All Saints' Episcopal Church, Reiserstown (McCallahan, p. 13). Regarding Bunker Hill: there were five recorded skirmishes, none called battles, in the period 1861-4 at Bunker Hill near Berkeley, now in West Virginia.

596. Annie Stansbury COCKEY, 9G Granddaughter, born on 16 Apr 1842 in Baltimore Co. MD. Annie Stansbury died in Baltimore Co. MD, on 15 Sep 1935; she was 93. Buried at Woodlawn Cemetery, Baltimore.

Annie Stansbury married Edward Dawes MCCONKY, in Baltimore Co. MD. They had the following children:
883	i.	Mary Grafton (1867 - about 1879)
884	ii.	Edward Dawes (1877-1963)

597. Mordecai Gist COCKEY, 9G Grandson, born on 10 May 1849 in Baltimore Co. MD. Mordecai Gist died in Baltimore Co. MD, on 17 Nov 1939; he was 90. Inherited the estate Arlington, dedicated to managing it, but when his sons decided not to pursue farming, he sold the property.

On 24 Apr 1873 when Mordecai Gist was 23, he married Olivia "Ollie" SLADE, in Baltimore Co. MD. They had the following children:
885	i.	Mary Etta (1874-1965)
886	ii.	John Robert (1875-)
887	iii.	Edward Randolph (1877-1913)
888	iv.	Anna Griselda (1879-1974)
889	v.	William Warfield (1880-1923)
890	vi.	Mordecai Gist (1884-)
891	vii.	Sally Montgomery (1892-1969)
892	viii.	James Powell (1892-)

598. Mary Elizabeth COCKEY, 9G Granddaughter, born on 14 Oct 1854 in Baltimore Co. MD.

On 23 Dec 1875 when Mary Elizabeth was 21, she married William Henry BOSLEY, son of John BOSLEY and Rachel Harryman COLE, in Baltimore Co. MD. Banker and civic leader of Baltimore. They had the following children:
893	i.	William Henry
894	ii.	John Robert
895	iii.	Marie Elise
896	iv.	Chauncey Brooks
897	v.	Harrryman Gist (1894-)
898	vi.	Mollie

Family of Mordecai Gist COCKEY (453) and Urath BRAMWELL

599. Elizabeth COCKEY, 9G Granddaughter.

600. Virginia COCKEY, 9G Granddaughter.

601. Ann Rebecca COCKEY, 9G Granddaughter, born on 1 Jul 1831. Ann Rebecca died in Finksburg MD, on 8 Feb 1885; she was 53.

On 25 Oct 1865 when Ann Rebecca was 34, she married Stephen Brown STOCKSDALE (612), 9G Grandson, son of Solomon STOCKSDALE and Dolly Brown COCKEY (455), in Carroll Co. MD, born on 10 Aug 1835 in Baltimore Co. MD. Stephen Brown died in Finksburg, Carroll Co. MD, on 25 Jun 1910; he was 74. This per the Beasman Family Bible held by Ruth Snider Cummings (cited by Field). They had the following children:
899	i.	Harry Cockey (1867-1898)

900	ii.	Georgia Virginia (1871-1872)
901	iii.	Mordecai Bramwell (1875-1926)

602. Urath COCKEY, 9G Granddaughter.

Family of Ruth Brown COCKEY (454) and Thomas Edward STOCKSDALE

603. Rebecca STOCKSDALE, 9G Granddaughter, born on 8 Apr 1820. Rebecca died on 20 May 1864; she was 44.

604. Mordecai Cockey STOCKSDALE, 9G Grandson, born on 25 Apr 1824 in Baltimore Co. MD. Mordecai Cockey died in Carroll Co. MD, on 4 Feb 1890; he was 65. Buried All Saints' Cemetery, Reisterstown.

On 27 Oct 1851 when Mordecai Cockey was 27, he married Miranda BENNETT (566) , 9G Granddaughter, daughter of Wesley BENNETT and Mary Ann BROWN (439), in Carroll Co. MD, born on 26 Oct 1827 in Baltimore (later Carroll) Co. MD. Miranda died in Carroll Co. MD, on 26 Sep 1917; she was 89. Marandy was age 27 in the 1850 Census Carroll Co. Dist. 5 p. 218, living with father Wesley and two sisters. Buried All Saints' Cemetery, Reisterstown. They had the following children:

860	i.	Florence
861	ii.	Annie

605. Lewis Henry STOCKSDALE, 9G Grandson, born on 31 Mar 1826. Lewis Henry died on 1 Jul 1909; he was 83.

On 14 Mar 1853 when Lewis Henry was 26, he married Catherine E. GARDNER, in Carroll Co. MD, born on 14 Apr 1834. Catherine E. died on 31 Aug 1911; she was 77. In 1860 Census Carroll Co., his children listed as Ida (Annie Ida below) age 2 and Louisianna age 1. Louisianna must have died in infancy. They had the following children:

902	i.	Emma R. (1854-1854)
903	ii.	Annie Ida (1857-1922)
904	iii.	Louisianna (about 1859-)
905	iv.	William G. (1865-1902)
906	v.	Harry Cockey (1868-1869)

606. Thomas Franklin STOCKSDALE, 9G Grandson, born on 25 Oct 1827. Thomas Franklin died on 28 Jun 1828; he was less than 1.

607. Stephen Thomas STOCKSDALE, 9G Grandson, born on 26 May 1829. Stephen Thomas died on 10 Sep 1848; he was 19.

Family of Dolly Brown COCKEY (455) and Solomon STOCKSDALE

608. John Thomas Cockey STOCKSDALE, 9G Grandson, born on 1 Feb 1824 in Baltimore Co. MD. John Thomas Cockey died on 26 Mar 1898; he was 74.

On 21 Jun 1853 when John Thomas Cockey was 29, he married Eliza COOK, born on 4 Jan 1830. Eliza died on 26 Jul 1905; she was 75. They had the following children:

907	i.	George Tevis (1854-1938)
908	ii.	Dolly Maud (1855-1943)
909	iii.	Clara May (1858-1941)
910	iv.	Annie Howard (1859-1930)
911	v.	John Thomas Cockey (1862-1913)
912	vi.	Lillie Eliza (1864-)
913	vii.	Gertrude (1866-1950)
914	viii.	Arthur Lee (1870-1922)
915	ix.	Howard Hewett (1875-)

609. Elias Cockey STOCKSDALE, 9G Grandson, born on 8 Dec 1825 in Baltimore Co. MD. Elias Cockey died on 2 Mar 1882; he was 56.

On 6 Dec 1848 when Elias Cockey was 22, he first married Martha WHALEN, daughter of William WHALEN and Susannah REISTER, in Carroll Co. MD, born in 1826. Martha died on 18 Jun 1863 in Reisterstown, Carroll Co. MD. Or died 17 Jun 1863 (Field). They had the following children:
916	i.	William Vinton (1850-1855)
917	ii.	Rebecca Jane (1852-1938)
918	iii.	Susannah (1857-1868)
919	iv.	Elias Cockey (1857-1912)

Elias Cockey second married Elizabeth A. BOWEN, born in 1827. Elizabeth A. died on 14 Mar 1879.

610. William Jackson STOCKSDALE, 9G Grandson, born on 24 Jan 1828 in Baltimore Co. MD. William Jackson died on 26 Apr 1863; he was 35.

611. Solomon Tevis STOCKSDALE, 9G Grandson, born on 15 Jun 1832 in Baltimore Co. MD.

612. Stephen Brown STOCKSDALE, 9G Grandson, born on 10 Aug 1835 in Baltimore Co. MD. Stephen Brown died in Finksburg, Carroll Co. MD, on 25 Jun 1910; he was 74. Beasman Family Bible held by Ruth Snider Cummings (per Field).

On 25 Oct 1865 when Stephen Brown was 30, he first married Ann Rebecca COCKEY (601), 9G Granddaughter, daughter of Mordecai Gist COCKEY (453) and Urath BRAMWELL, in Carroll Co. MD, born on 1 Jul 1831. Ann Rebecca died in Finksburg MD, on 8 Feb 1885; she was 53. They had the following children:
899	i.	Harry Cockey (1867-1898)
900	ii.	Georgia Virginia (1871-1872)
901	iii.	Mordecai Bramwell (1875-1926)

On 28 Apr 1891 when Stephen Brown was 55, he second married Mary Jane "Jennie" PATTERSON, born on 14 Mar 1862. Mary Jane "Jennie" died on 1 Jul 1939; she was 77. They had one child:
920	i.	Rebecca Jane (1899-)

613. Ruth Ann Elizabeth STOCKSDALE, 9G Granddaughter, born on 16 Oct 1838 in Carroll Co. MD. Ruth Ann Elizabeth died on 21 Apr 1906; she was 67. Source: Baseman family Bible per Field.

On 22 Oct 1857 when Ruth Ann Elizabeth was 19, she married Theodore Wesley BASEMAN (or Beasman throughout), son of Sylvester Wesley BASEMAN and Ellen Ann BEDFORD, in Carroll Co. MD, born about 1834 in Baltimore Co. MD. Theodore Wesley died on 20 Dec 1890 in Carroll Co. MD. They had the following children:
921	i.	Emma Dolly (1858-1924)
922	ii.	Fannie Howard (1860-1941)
923	iii.	Julie Ann (1862-1925)
924	iv.	Ellen Bedford (1864-)
925	v.	Dora Florence (1866-)
926	vi.	Grant T. (1868-)
927	vii.	Littlewood Alfred (1872-1878)
928	viii.	Rosa Estella (1874-1878)
929	ix.	Grace Ruth Ann (1876-)
930	x.	Ray F. (1879-1882)
931	xi.	May Pauline (1879-1882)

614. Edmund Howard STOCKSDALE, 9G Grandson, born on 26 Apr 1841.

Family of Charles C. COCKEY (456) and Elizabeth GRIFFITH

615. William Henry COCKEY, 9G Grandson. Named in uncle Elias B. Cockey's will.

Family of Solomon OSBORN (464) and Mary "Polly" STEWART

616. Joseph OSBORN, 9G Grandson, born in 1789 in NC. Joseph died on 12 Nov 1870 in McDonough Co. IL.

Before 1804 Joseph married Nancy PENNINGTON, daughter of Moses PENNINGTON and Anna OSBORN, in Barren Co. KY, born in 1790 in KY. They had the following children:

932	i.	Solomon (1804-1878)
933	ii.	Lydia (1809-1859)
934	iii.	John (1810-)
935	iv.	Stephen Jones (1812-)
936	v.	Sabrina (1818-)
937	vi.	Andrew Jackson (1825 - after 1880)

617. James OSBORN, 9G Grandson, born on 30 Jan 1790 in NC. James died in Champaign, Champaign Co. IL, on 23 Dec 1844; he was 54.

In 1815 James married Ruth OSBORN (627), 9G Granddaughter, daughter of Robert OSBORNE (466) and Mary Caroline PRICE, in IN, born on 18 Jun 1798 in Rowan Co. NC. Ruth died in Champaign, Champaign Co. IL, on 16 Mar 1871; she was 72. They had the following children:

938	i.	Solomon (about 1816-)
939	ii.	Amalthea (1821-)
940	iii.	Robert Patient (about 1825-)
941	iv.	Elizabeth (1827-)
942	v.	Clarissa (about 1830-)
943	vi.	Noah (about 1832-)
944	vii.	Julia Ann (about 1834-)
945	viii.	Jonathan B. (about 1837-)
946	ix.	Martha C. (about 1839-)
947	x.	Elmira (about 1841-)

618. John OSBORN, 9G Grandson, born in 1791.

619. Sarah OSBORN, 9G Granddaughter, born in 1795.

Sarah married --- PETTIT.

620. Noah OSBORN, 9G Grandson, born in 1797. Noah died on 31 May 1846 in Champaign Co. IL.

621. Richard OSBORN, 9G Grandson, born on 23 Jan 1798 in NC. Richard died in 1876 in Fulton Co. IL.

On 10 Dec 1820 when Richard was 22, he married Mary SHAW, in Crawford Co. IN, born about 1800.

622. Samuel M. OSBORN, 9G Grandson, born in 1802 in Barren Co. KY. Samuel M. died about 1850 in Louisville, Jefferson Co. KY.

On 15 May 1828 Samuel M. married Cynthia STEWART, in Floyd Co. IN.

623. Mahala OSBORN, 9G Granddaughter, born on 12 Dec 1803 in IN.

Mahala married William MCCALL.

624. William OSBORN, 9G Grandson, born in 1804 in Barren Co. KY. William died before 1850.

On 4 Jul 1830 William married Elizabeth HUMPHREYS, in Vermillion Co. IL, born about 1805. Elizabeth died on 2 Feb 1851 in Champaign Co. IL.

625. Tabitha OSBORN, 9G Granddaughter, born in 1806 in Barren Co. KY. Tabitha died on 13 May 1862 in Mahomet, Champaign Co. IL.

On 15 Jul 1823 Tabitha married John ROBERTSON, in Crawford Co. IN.

Family of Mary "Polly" OSBORNE (465) and Samuel Jay ALLEY

626. Doddridge ALLEY, 9G Grandson, born on 1 Nov 1788 in Washington Co. VA.

Doddridge married Jane PHILLIPS, born on 19 Oct 1789 in VA or GA. They had one child:
948	i.	William W. (1810-)

Family of Robert OSBORNE (466) and Mary Caroline PRICE

627. Ruth OSBORN, 9G Granddaughter, born on 18 Jun 1798 in Rowan Co. NC. Ruth died in Champaign, Champaign Co. IL, on 16 Mar 1871; she was 72.

In 1815 Ruth married James OSBORN (617), 9G Grandson, son of Solomon OSBORN (464) and Mary "Polly" STEWART, in IN, born on 30 Jan 1790 in NC. James died in Champaign, Champaign Co. IL, on 23 Dec 1844; he was 54. They had the following children:
938	i.	Solomon (about 1816-)
939	ii.	Amalthea (1821-)
940	iii.	Robert Patient (about 1825-)
941	iv.	Elizabeth (1827-)
942	v.	Clarissa (about 1830-)
943	vi.	Noah (about 1832-)
944	vii.	Julia Ann (about 1834-)
945	viii.	Jonathan B. (about 1837-)
946	ix.	Martha C. (about 1839-)
947	x.	Elmira (about 1841-)

628. Joseph OSBORN, 9G Grandson, born in 1799. Joseph died before 1850.

On 18 May 1820 Joseph married Lydia COPELAND, daughter of Charles COPELAND and Hannah OSBORNE, in Crawford Co. IN, born in 1801. They had the following children:
949	i.	Cynthia (about 1822-)
950	ii.	Serena (about 1825-)
951	iii.	Angeline (about 1828-)
952	iv.	Green (about 1828-)
953	v.	Mary (about 1831-)
954	vi.	Malinda (about 1832-)
955	vii.	Lurilla (about 1834-)
956	viii.	Joseph (about 1842-)

629. Naomi OSBORN, 9G Granddaughter, born about 1800 in VA.

Naomi married Isaac EMBREE, born about 1845 in VA.

630. Zachariah OSBORN, 9G Grandson, born in 1801.

On 16 Mar 1830 Zachariah married Christina WRIGHT, in Vermillion Co. IL, born about 1811 in VA.

631. James OSBORN, 9G Grandson, born on 8 Feb 1804 in NC. James died in Mound Coty, Linn Co. KS, on 21 Sep 1888; he was 84.

On 21 Dec 1829 when James was 25, he first married Christianna "Ann" SOUDER, in Edgar Co. IL. Christianna "Ann" died before 17 Oct 1846 in Bates Co. MO. They had the following children:
957	i.	Mary A. (about 1833-)
958	ii.	Adelaide (about 1835-)
959	iii.	Phillip (about 1839-)

In 1846 James second married Mary WRIGHT, born on 23 Mar 1825 in Licking Co. OH. Mary died in Linn Co. KS, on 18 Mar 1909; she was 83. They had the following children:
960	i.	George (about 1847 - before 1883)
961	ii.	Lewis (about 1848-)
962	iii.	Martha (about 1849-)
963	iv.	Byron W. (about 1850-)

632. Joanna OSBORN, 9G Granddaughter, born in 1809 in KY.

On 24 Sep 1826 Joanna married George Washington WAKEFIELD, in Vermillion Co. IL, born about 1795 in SC. George Washington died in 1856 in Cass, MO. They had the following children:
964	i.	William (1827-)
965	ii.	John Allen (1831-)
966	iii.	Susan (1833-)
967	iv.	Almeda (1834-1878)
968	v.	Martha Adeline (1838-1911)
969	vi.	Dianna (1843-)
970	vii.	Ruth Emma (1846-)
971	viii.	George Washington (1849-1931)

633. Enoch OSBORNE, 9G Grandson, born on 25 Nov 1814 in Crawford Co. IN. Enoch died in NE on 7 Sep 1869; he was 54.

On 17 May 1838 when Enoch was 23, he married Anna STARR, daughter of John or James STARR and Hannah OSBORN, in Warren Co. IN, born on 25 Nov 1819 in Jackson Co. IN. Anna died on 12 Oct 1899; she was 79.

634. Martha OSBORN, 9G Granddaughter, born about 1817.

Martha married Michael H. JOSE.

635. Mary Catherine OSBORN, 9G Granddaughter, born about 1819 in IN.

Mary Catherine married Hiram OSBORN, born about 1812 in IN.

636. Thomas OSBORN, 9G Grandson, born about 1820 in IN.

Thomas married Mary ---, born about 1822.

Family of William OSBORNE (470) and Rebecca RICHMOND

637. Jane OSBORNE, 9G Granddaughter, born in 1803. These children per Sisseck.

638. Elizabeth OSBORNE, 9G Granddaughter, born about 1810 in VA.
639. Hiram OSBORNE, 9G Grandson, born about 1810 in VA.

640. Stephen OSBORNE, 9G Grandson, born in 1812 in Franklin Co. MO.

641. Comfort OSBORNE, 9G Granddaughter, born in 1814 in Franklin Co. MO. Six children, only Mary Elizabeth known (per Sisseck).

Comfort married Solomon DRACE, son of Thomas DRACE and Elizabeth ALKIRE. They had one child:
 972 i. Mary Elizabeth

642. Sarah "Sally" OSBORNE, 9G Granddaughter, born on 18 Dec 1816 in Franklin Co. MO. Sarah "Sally" died in Franklin Co. MO, on 4 Feb 1876; she was 59.

On 21 Jan 1836 when Sarah "Sally" was 19, she married Silas DRACE, son of Thomas DRACE and Elizabeth ALKIRE, in Franklin Co. MO, born on 4 Dec 1813 in Hampshire Co. VA. Silas died in Boles Twp., Franklin Co. MO, on 26 Jun 1879; he was 65. They had the following children:
 973 i. William Thomas "W.T." (1839 - after 1900)
 974 ii. Annie Rebecca
 975 iii. Minerva
 976 iv. Scott
 977 v. Mary Francis "Polly" (1843-1922)
 978 vi. James A.
 979 vii. S.S. "Donnie"
 980 viii. Emma Laura
 981 ix. Charles P.

643. Mary Ann "Polly" OSBORNE, 9G Granddaughter, born about 1820 in Franklin Co. MO.

On 24 Dec 1840 Mary Ann "Polly" married William O. MING.

644. Malinda OSBORNE, 9G Granddaughter, born about 1821 in Franklin Co. MO.

645. Jemima OSBORNE, 9G Granddaughter, born about 1823 in Franklin Co. MO.

On 28 Oct 1846 Jemima married James M. MING.

646. Lucinda OSBORNE, 9G Granddaughter, born in 1827 in Franklin Co. MO.

647. John OSBORNE, 9G Grandson, born about 1829 in Franklin Co. MO.

On 17 Feb 1853 John married Tabitha WILKERSON.

Family of Jemima OSBORNE (473) and John DOLLARHIDE

648. Annis DOLLARHIDE, 9G Granddaughter.

This line per Joyce Lang.

Annis married Jonathan COMPTON. They had one child:
 982 i. Margaret Susan

Family of Elizabeth "Betsey" OSBORNE (474) and Jonathan OSBORN

649. Stephen OSBORN, 9G Grandson. Stephen died in 1876.

650. Elizabeth OSBORN, 9G Granddaughter. Elizabeth died before 1875.

On 11 Oct 1831 Elizabeth married Thomas H. STEWART, in Franklin Co. IN.

651. Comfort OSBORN, 9G Granddaughter, born about 1801. Comfort died after 1875.

Comfort married William WILSON.

652. Hester OSBORN, 9G Granddaughter, born about 1803.

On 2 Aug 1821 Hester married Hiram LEWIS, in Bartholomew Co. IN, born about 1801.

653. Mary A. OSBORN, 9G Granddaughter, born about 1812. Mary A. died in 1876.

On 20 May 1827 Mary A. married Henry HARPER, in Marion Co. IN.

Family of Esther Louise OSBORNE (475) and Isaac RICHMOND

654. Sarah RICHMOND, 9G Granddaughter, born in 1804.

Sarah married William RICHMOND.

655. Jonathan RICHMOND, 9G Grandson, born in 1805.

Jonathan married Mary DICKENSON.

656. William RICHMOND, 9G Grandson, born in 1808.

William married Mary HORTON.

657. Elizabeth "Betsy" RICHMOND, 9G Granddaughter, born about 1810. Elizabeth "Betsy" died about 1824.

658. Fanny RICHMOND, 9G Granddaughter, born about 1812. Fanny died about 1813.

659. Esther RICHMOND, 9G Granddaughter, born about 1814.

Esther married Jerry EIKINS.

660. Isaac RICHMOND, 9G Grandson, born about 1817. Isaac died about 1827.

661. Caroline Ann RICHMOND, 9G Granddaughter, born in 1819. Caroline Ann died on 29 Aug 1865.

Caroline Ann married Francis Harvey STURGILL.

662. Comfort RICHMOND, 9G Granddaughter, born in 1821.

Comfort married Anderson WILLIAMS.

663. Rebecca Sherrill RICHMOND, 9G Granddaughter, born on 28 Oct 1822. Rebecca Sherrill died on 31 Jan 1907; she was 84.

Rebecca Sherrill married Preston Hamilton COLLIER, born on 6 Feb 1818. Preston Hamilton died on 29 May 1864; he was 46.

664. Polly Ann Sublett RICHMOND, 9G Granddaughter, born on 4 Apr 1826. Polly Ann Sublett died in 1902.

Polly Ann Sublett first married James BOWLIN.

Polly Ann Sublett second married William WINN.

665. Jane RICHMOND, 9G Granddaughter, born in 1829.

Jane married William HORTON.

666. Louisa RICHMOND, 9G Granddaughter, born about 1831.

Louisa married Thomas CASSIDY.

667. Baby RICHMOND, 9G Grandson.

Family of Solomon LANHAM (478) and Mary Margaret BURLESON

668. Franklin LANHAM, 9G Grandson, born in 1810 in TN. Franklin died after 1880.

In 1839 Franklin first married Mrs. Margaret JORDAN, in Bienville Parish, LA, born in 1814 in SC. Margaret died after 1856. They had the following children:
983	i.	Unity (1840-)
984	ii.	Abel (1843-)
985	iii.	Elizabeth (1846-1929)
986	iv.	Sophenia (1849-)

On 4 Nov 1860 Franklin second married Elizabeth SANDERS, in LA, born in 1830 in AL. They had the following children:
987	i.	Solomon J. (1864-)
988	ii.	Nancy J. (1865-)

669. Jane LANHAM, 9G Granddaughter, born in 1812 in AL.

Jane married Ira J. MITCHELL. They had one child:
989	i.	Frank L.

670. Lucinda LANHAM, 9G Granddaughter, born in 1814 in Bienville Parish, LA. Lucinda died in 1866 in Bienville Parish, LA.

In about 1832 Lucinda first married Angus DAWKINS. They had the following children:
990	i.	Mary
991	ii.	Jackson
992	iii.	Abigail
993	iv.	Ophelia

Aft 1840 Lucinda second married Daniel N. DAVIS, in Bienville Parish, LA. They had the following children:
994	i.	William L.
995	ii.	Christian
996	iii.	Cynthia
997	iv.	James

671. Mary LANHAM, 9G Granddaughter, born in 1816.

Mary married James WARREN.

672. Randolph LANHAM, 9G Grandson, born on 25 Feb 1818 in TN. Randolph died in Kaufman Co. TX, on 25 Sep

1900; he was 82. Buried in Conner Cemetery, Navarro Co. TX.

In about 1835 Randolph married Jalie Wood ROBERTS, daughter of Nathan ROBERTS and Abigail BISHOP, in MS, born on 15 Feb 1816 in Madison Co. AL. Jalie Wood died before 1900 in Weatherford, Porter Co. TX. They had the following children:

998	i.	Solomon Thomas (1835-)
999	ii.	Mary A. (1837-1838)
1000	iii.	Cynthia Elizabeth (1839-1905)
1001	iv.	Abel (1841-1841)
1002	v.	Joseph B. (1842-)
1003	vi.	John Castleton (1844-)
1004	vii.	Sarah Jane (1847-1926)
1005	viii.	Jailie Ann (1849-1931)
1006	ix.	Rachel Lucinda (1851-)
1007	x.	Margaret Narcissa (1853-)
1008	xi.	Samuel (1854-1854)
1009	xii.	Hannah Theodicia (1856-)

673. Minerva Ann LANHAM, 9G Granddaughter, born on 18 Sep 1826 in AL. Minerva Ann died in Victoria, Victoria Co. TX, on 28 Nov 1905; she was 79. This family information per Doris Sanders.

On 12 Sep 1849 when Minerva Ann was 22, she married Charles GILLEY, son of John GILLEY and Sarah ---, in Smith Co. TX. Family information from his and her Mexican War Pension affidavits. They had the following children:

1010	i.	Mary A.
1011	ii.	Thomas Newton
1012	iii.	John Solomon
1013	iv.	William Robert
1014	v.	Susan Margaret
1015	vi.	Eula

674. Bedford LANHAM, 9G Grandson, born on 29 Mar 1830 in AL or MS. Bedford died in Indian Territory, OK, on 20 Sep 1881; he was 51. Buried in Maysville Cemetery, Garvin Co. OK.

On 18 Sep 1850 when Bedford was 20, he married Georgia Louisiana FRIEND, daughter of Samuel Edgar FRIEND and Maria Jane CURTIS, in Monroe, Quachita Parish LA, born on 26 Dec 1832 in Monroe, Quachita Parish LA. Georgia Louisiana died in San Angelo, Tom Green Co. TX, on 26 Nov 1907; she was 74. Buried in Fairmont Cemetery, San Angelo TX. They had the following children:

1016	i.	Maria Jane Curtis (1851-1923)
1017	ii.	Samuel (1853-1854)
1018	iii.	Mary Margaret (1855-1938)
1019	iv.	James Millard (1858-)
1020	v.	Georgia Alice (1861-1889)
1021	vi.	Robert Edward Lee (1864-1884)
1022	vii.	Franklin (1865-1865)
1023	viii.	Monroe (1868-)
1024	ix.	Annie Maud (1872-1962)
1025	x.	Edwin Friend (1874-1933)

675. Margaret LANHAM, 9G Granddaughter, born in 1832 in AL.

676. Samuel LANHAM, 9G Grandson, born on 17 Jun 1832 in AL. Samuel died in Dec 1855 in Smith Co. TX. Buried in Ebenezer Cemetery, Smith Co. TX.

Before 1850 Samuel married Elizabeth ---, in Smith Co. TX, born on 25 Mar 1832 in GA. Elizabeth died in Smith Co. TX, on 25 Aug 1914; she was 82. Buried in Ebenezer Cemetery, Smith Co. TX. They had the following children:

1026	i.	William S. (1851-)
1027	ii.	Franklin C. (1854-1936)

677. Cynthia LANHAM, 9G Granddaughter, born in 1833 in MS. Cynthia died on 6 Jul 1912 in Hill Co. TX. Buried in Ebenezer Cemetery, Smith Co. TX.

On 18 Mar 1847 Cynthia first married Aaron W. WEEKS, in LA. They had one child:
    1028   i.   Samuel (1849-)

On 22 Dec 1853 Cynthia second married Ezequiel BARRON, in Smith Co. TX, born on 4 Nov 1830 in AL. Ezequiel died in 1864 at the Battle of Pleasant Hill, LA. They had the following children:
    1029   i.   Ophelia (1856-1928)
    1030   ii.   Caleb Ezekiel (1858-1946)
    1031   iii.   Solomon (1861-1934)

On 18 Dec 1867 Cynthia third married E. JARVIS, in Smith Co. TX, born on 9 Oct 1843 in Kemper Co. MS and died in Smith Co. TX, on 18 Sep 1919; he was 75. Buried in Ebenezer Cemetery, Smith Co. TX. They had the following children:
    1032   i.   Ada (1868-1947)
    1033   ii.   Rob (1872-)

678. William LANHAM, 9G Grandson, born in 1839 in AL.

Family of Elisha BROWN (494) and Anne RAY

679. Lucracia BROWN.

Lucracia married Hammond DORSEY.

680. Samuel BROWN. Samuel died in 1826.

681. James R. BROWN, born about 1812. James R. died on 4 Jul 1838.

682. Elizabeth Ann BROWN, born about 1815. Elizabeth Ann died on 4 Jul 1838.

Family of Major John Riggs BROWN (495) and Sarah Griffith GASSAWAY

683. Louisa Worthington BROWN, born on 10 Mar 1799. Louisa Worthington died on 23 Jul 1868; she was 69.

On 9 Mar 1819 when Louisa Worthington was 19, she married Caleb Dorsey DAVIS, son of Robert DAVIS and Ruth GAITHER, born on 7 Mar 1792. Caleb Dorsey died in Sep 1850. A resident of Woodstock. They had the following children:
    1034   i.   John Brown (1819-1889)
    1035   ii.   Elizabeth (1821-1827)
    1036   iii.   Henry Gassaway (1823-)
    1037   iv.   Eliza Ann (1825-)
    1038   v.   Thomas Beale (1828-)
    1039   vi.   William R. (1832-1879)

684. Mary Ann BROWN, born on 16 Oct 1800.

Mary Ann married Anthony SMITH.

685. Henry Gassaway BROWN, born on 31 Mar 1803.

Henry Gassaway married Ann FROST.

686. Eliza BROWN, born on 4 Apr 1805.

Eliza married William FROST.

687. Achsah BROWN, born on 8 Jul 1807.

Achsah married Samuel RIDGELY.

688. Elizabeth A. BROWN, born on 29 Oct 1808.

Elizabeth A. married Peter GORMAN, born in 1839 in Woodstock, MD. Resident of Woodstock. They had one child:
    1040   i.   Arthur Pue

689. Samuel BROWN, born on 18 Oct 1810. Samuel died in 1880. Member of Maryland House of Delegates for Howard County and Howard County Commissioner.

Samuel first married Elizabeth JENKINS, daughter of Henry JENKINS and Ann HARRISON, born in 1812 in Baltimore City MD. Elizabeth died in 1892 in Howard Co. MD. They had the following children:
    1041   i.   Henry
    1042   ii.   Samuel Thomas (1847-)
    1043   iii.   Charles
    1044   iv.   Frank D. (1853-)
    1045   v.   Josephine

Samuel second married Mary BARLIN.

690. Katherine Ann Warfield "Kitty" BROWN, born on 30 Jun 1812. Katherine Ann Warfield "Kitty" died about 1896.

Katherine Ann Warfield "Kitty" first married --- FAITHFUL.

Katherine Ann Warfield "Kitty" second married Henry HOOD, son of General Thomas HOOD.

691. John Riggs BROWN Jr, born on 20 May 1815. John Riggs died in 1890. Editor *Ellicott City Times*.

John Riggs married Mary FROST.

Family of Vachel Brown (499) and Elizabeth Ann BERRY

692. Jonathan "John" Brown, born on 13 Jun 1823.

693. Richard Brown, born on 1 Sep 1824.

694. William Brown, born on 19 May 1826.

695. Vachel Brown, born on 18 Jan 1828.

696. Ann Elizabeth Brown, born on 28 Sep 1829.

697. Samuel L. Brown, born on 26 Jul 1831.

698. Thomas Alexander Brown, born on 9 Jan 1835. A "posthumous son" according to the family Bible, as he was born after his father's death.

Family of Achsah Riggs Brown (501) and Thomas Beale Dorsey Jr.

699. Judge Thomas Beale Dorsey, born on 29 Jun 1808.

700. Achsah Riggs Dorsey, born on 26 Apr 1810.

Achsah Riggs married Reuben Meriwether Dorsey. His second marriage (Warfield, p. 491).

701. Ann Worthington Dorsey, born on 3 Jun 1811.

702. Sarah "Sally" Dorsey, born on 23 Jul 1813. Sarah "Sally" died on 7 May 1848; she was 34.

Sarah "Sally" married Dr. Arthur Pue Jr.. Sources: Warfield, p. 491, Newman, p. 139, Samuel Brown Family Bible.

Family of Benjamin TODD (502) and Charlotte CLARY

703. Mary Ann TODD, born about 1813 in Frederick Co. MD.

704. Janet TODD, born about 1813 in Frederick Co. MD.

In about 1844 Janet married Jacob JOHNSON, in OH. They had one child:
   1046   i.   Benjamin H.

705. John H. TODD, born about 1815 in Columbiana Co. OH. John H. died on 23 Oct 1821 in Columbiana Co. OH.

706. Sarah A. TODD, born about 1817 in Columbiana Co. OH. Sarah A. died on 23 Apr 1833 in Columbiana Co. OH.

707. Elizabeth TODD, born in 1821 in OH.

On 19 Aug 1847 Elizabeth married William JOHNSON, in Columbiana Co. OH, born about 1821 in OH. They had the following children:
   1047   i.   Tom M. (about 1848-)
   1048   ii.   Emma E. (about 1849-)

708. Nancy TODD, born about 1824 in Columbiana Co. OH. Nancy died in 1910 in Columbiana Co. OH.

Nancy married Edward PUMPHREY, born on 14 Nov 1844 in Columbiana Co. OH.

Family of Basil TODD (503) and Sarah GRIMES

709. Alexander TODD, born on 29 Jan 1786 in Frederick Co. MD. Alexander died in Columbiana Co. OH, on 31 Mar 1876; he was 90.

In 1804 Alexander married Elizabeth WITHROW, in Beaver Co. PA, born about 1791. Elizabeth died on 6 May 1855 in Columbiana Co. OH. They had one child:
   1049   i.   David Withrow (1839-1893)

710. Samuel TODD, born about 1794 in MD.

Family of Joshua TODD (506) and Sophia HYATT

711. Edna TODD, born about 1794 in MD.

Edna married Peter STALEY, born about 1790. They had one child:
    1050   i.   Warfield D. (1815-1898)

712. Anna TODD, born about 1797.

On 8 Oct 1817 Anna married Henry BUSSARD, in Montgomery Co. MD.

713. Vachel TODD, born about 1798 in MD.

714. Rachel TODD, born about 1801 in MD. She died before 1830.

On 5 Jan 1821 Rachel married Samuel SHIPLEY, in Frederick Co. MD. Samuel Shipley is found in the Baltimore Co. Dist. 6 Census of 1830, p. 193 with one adult male, three young females and one young male. Neighbors were Moses Shipley, Grove Shipley (Sr.), David Brown, Ephraim Lpt (Lovett?).

715. Lucy TODD, born about 1803 in MD.

On 11 Feb 1823 Lucy married Edward MILLER, in Baltimore Co. MD.

716. Susan TODD, born about 1804 in MD.

On 12 Mar 1823 Susan married David BUSSARD, in Frederick Co. MD, born about 1800.

717. George W. TODD, born about 1806 in MD. George W. died in 1849.

718. William TODD, born about 1810 in MD.

On 22 Aug 1831 William married Mary Ann FLUHART, in Frederick Co. MD.

719. Joshua TODD, born about 1812 in MD.

On 12 Dec 1834 Joshua married Letitia HOOD, in Frederick Co. MD.

720. Howard TODD, born about 1812 in MD. Howard died in 1849.

Family of Warfield TODD (509) and Eleanor BALL

721. Samuel TODD, born about 1804 in MD. Samuel died after 1880.

On 9 Sep 1844 Samuel married Ara ENGEL, in Frederick Co. MD, born about 1794 in MD. Ara died before 1880.

722. Alexander TODD, born about 1807 in MD. Alexander died about 1857 in Stark Co. IL.

On 31 Oct 1831 Alexander married Eliza RAMSOWER, in Frederick Co. MD, born about 1809 in MD. Eliza died after 1880. They had the following children:
    1051   i.   Mary Ellen (1833-1916)
    1052   ii.   Ira A. (about 1833 - before 1920)
    1053   iii.   Rachel Ruth (1835-1881)
    1054   iv.   Janet (about 1837 - before 1920)
    1055   v.   --- (about 1839 - before 1850)

1056	vi.	Margaret A. (about 1840 - after 1920)
1057	vii.	Susanah Cevelah (1843-1920)
1058	viii.	Benjamin Warfield (1846-1928)
1059	ix.	Martha Alice (1847-1923)
1060	x.	Cachel (1850 - before 1920)

723. Charles Warfield TODD, born on 3 Oct 1810 in MD. Charles Warfield died in Colfax, Jasper Co. IA, on 6 Aug 1890; he was 79.

On 18 Jan 1830 when Charles Warfield was 19, he first married Marcelliar W. BONHAM, in Frederick Co. MD, born about 1810. Marcelliar W. died about 1841 in IL. They had the following children:

1061	i.	Benjamin (1830-1905)
1062	ii.	Sydney Jane (about 1832-)
1063	iii.	Mary Elizabeth (about 1835 - before 1850)
1064	iv.	Ellen Warfield (about 1839-)
1065	v.	James Forrest (about 1840-)

On 4 Apr 1847 when Charles Warfield was 36, he second married Abian Ann JACKSON, in Stark Co. IL, born on 12 Mar 1809 in Goshen, Orange Co. NY. Abian Ann died in La Fayette, Stark Co. IL, on 16 Mar 1885; she was 76. They had one child:

1066	i.	Henrietta Jackson (1848-)

724. Vachel B. TODD, born about 1813 in MD. Vachel B. died in Jun 1880 in CA.

On 30 Jan 1834 Vachel B. first married Susan Brown, in Frederick Co. MD, born about 1811 in Frederick Co. MD. Susan died on 26 Sep 1871 in Galva, Henry Co. IL. They had the following children:

1067	i.	Warfield Benjamin (1837-1907)
1068	ii.	Vachel H. (1839-1904)
1069	iii.	Henrietta (about 1841-)
1070	iv.	Sarah (about 1852-)

On 6 Apr 1873 Vachel B. second married Emily S. TILDEN, in Henry Co. IL.

Family of Robert BROWN (512) and Jane BOND

725. James BROWN, 9G Grandson, born in 1822 in Montgomery Co. MD. Living with Robert B. Brown family in 1870, age 47 (Census, p. 224B).

726. George BROWN, 9G Grandson, born in 1824 in Montgomery Co. MD.

727. Robert B. BROWN, 9G Grandson, born on 18 Mar 1831 in Sunshine, Montgomery Co. MD. Robert B. died in Sunshine, Montgomery Co. MD, on 15 Mar 1905; he was 73. Sources: 1860, 1870, 1880 Census.; Christening 1879; Enlisted 21 Mar 1864, Co. I, Potomac Home Brigade Cavalry and 7 Mar 1865 Co. D., Potomac Home Brigade. Resident of Triadelphia (1870 Census, p. 224B), then near Brookville (1880 Census, p. 200C), farmer and carpenter. Per Marshall Brown.

Robert B. married Hannah R. SULLIVAN, daughter of Richard SULLIVAN, born on 9 May 1828 in MD. Family name and parents per Marshall Brown. They had the following children:

1071	i.	Thomas J. (1859-1924)
1072	ii.	Edward B. (1861-1905)
1073	iii.	Benjamin R. (1864-)
1074	iv.	Annie E. (1867-)

Family of Allen LANE II (513) and Hannah COOK

728. Cilinda LANE, born on 16 Apr 1810 in Tioga Co. PA. Cilinda died in Vermilion Co. IL, on 26 Feb 1849; she was 38. Buried Fairfield Cemetery, Vermilion Co. IL. Sources: Marriage record, Athens Co., Ohio; birth and death from gravestone. Gravestone says 38 years, 10 months, 10 days.

On 30 Mar 1826 when Cilinda was 15, she married Cornelius PETERSON, son of Abraham PETERSON Sr. and Susannah ---, in Athens Co. OH, born on 5 Oct 1806 in Maine. Cornelius died in Vermilion Co. IL, on 11 Oct 1877; he was 71. Gravestone says 70 years, 10 months, and 6 days. They had the following children:

1075	i.	Lydia (1827-)
1076	ii.	John L. (1828-1894)
1077	iii.	Elmira (1832-1907)
1078	iv.	Sarah (1834-)
1079	v.	Benjamin (1836-1916)
1080	vi.	Lucy (1837-1883)
1081	vii.	Eli (1840-1887)
1082	viii.	Mary Jane (1842-)
1083	ix.	Charlotte (1844-1873)
1084	x.	Selinda (1847-1882)

**Frank Brown and Thomas Cockey Brown,
from Scharf's *History of Western Maryland***

THIRTEENTH GENERATION

Family of John Wesley BROWN (517) and Elizabeth ---

729. John Henry BROWN, 10G Grandson, born on 22 Jun 1834. John Henry died on 24 Dec 1902; he was 68.

John Henry married Hannah LINDSAY.

730. Benjamin Franklin BROWN, 10G Grandson, born on 18 Aug 1839 in Marriottsville MD. Benjamin Franklin died in Sykesville MD, on 2 Nov 1892; he was 53. He purchased tracts named Concord, John's Mistake, and Sally's Chance, for $6,306.30 on 29 Dec 1883, from Charles W. Hood heirs. They included the large two-story house presently occupied by descendant Howard Smith. Benjamin F. Brown was buried at Springfield Cemetery, Sykesville MD.

Benjamin Franklin first married Lavina ROBB, daughter of George ROBB and Mary ---, born on 23 Oct 1839 in Tiffin OH. Lavina died in Sykesville MD, on 8 May 1891; she was 51. Buried at Springfield Cemetery, Sykesville MD. It was reported in the Sykesville *Democratic Advocate* of 8 May 1891 that when Lavinia Brown's remains lay at the Presbyterian Church after two days of lying in state at the home, her husband insisted that the coffin be reopened and he refused to allow her burial in the belief that she was merely suffering from "suspended animation" in spite of a re-examination there by a physician. The burial was postponed for a day, the remains were then taken to the Springfield Institute and again re-examined, after which burial took place (article citation courtesy Howard Smith). They had the following children:

1085	i.	George Alan (1869-1920)
1086	ii.	Francis W. (1870-1921)
1087	iii.	Walter C. (1874-1910)
1088	iv.	Benjamin Franklin (1872-1942)
1089	v.	Mary E.

On 25 Jan 1892 when Benjamin Franklin was 52, he second married Rachel SELLMAN, born on 27 Jun 1859. Rachel died on 23 Jan 1894; she was 34. Buried at Springfield Cemetery, Sykesville MD.

731. Josiah BROWN, 10G Grandson, born on 8 Sep 1847. Josiah died on 3 Feb 1942; he was 94.

Josiah married Caroline R. ARRINGTON.

732. Annie BROWN, 10G Granddaughter, born on 25 Dec 1850. Annie died on 24 Feb 1921; she was 70.

Annie married Thomas THOMPSON.

733. Mary Jane BROWN, 10G Granddaughter, born on 5 Oct 1845. Mary Jane died on 13 Jan 1894; she was 48.

Family of Lloyd BROWN (523) and Sarah Ann PARGIN

734. Eli BROWN, 10G Grandson, born in 1827-8 in OH. Eli died after 1870 (1850, 60, 70 Census). For a time he was engaged in milling (processing wool, flax, grain, and lumber) with his father Lloyd (1850 Census Anderson Indiana, 1850 Indiana Manufacturing Census), but he later sold out and was a farmer. The 1860 Census enumerated him as age 32, wife

Lavina, sons [name illeg.] and Peter 1. He was listed "able bodied" in the Madison County Volunteers on 124 August 1862 at age 33, farmer (R. Davis, "Militia Enrollments Anderson Township," p. 20, typescript, Anderson Public Library). Later he lived in Elkhart Indiana according to the 1870 Census (Goshen Ward 1, Elkhart Indiana, p. 276) then age 41, wife Jane 29 (born in Indiana), children Peter 10 and "Eddie" a girl, age 7, plus his father Loyd at age 71.

In 1851-3 Eli first married Lavina ---, in Madison Co. IN, born in 1833 in OH. They had the following children:
1090	i.	--- (1854-)
1091	ii.	Peter (1859-)

Eli second married Jane ---. Three children (above) are not identified as to mother Lavina or Jane.

735. Anderson BROWN, 10G Grandson, born in 1829 in OH. Anderson died after 1900 in Madison Co. IN. Resident of Richland Township, Madison Co. IN. In the 1850 Census he was attending school near Anderson and listed his occupation as farmer and his age as 21. In 1900 Census he was living in Richland Township (north of Anderson) with his brother Elijah Brown. No known wife or children.

736. Obadiah BROWN, 10G Grandson, born about 1832 in OH. Obadiah died before 1880 in Anderson IN. Merchant, laborer. Also known as "Obid, Obed, O.D.," b about 1832 OH, m 7 Apr 1853 to Sarah (Sarah b about 1833 in OH), d 1870-80. Obid was a farmer at age 18 and was attending school also, according to the 1850 Census, and in 1860 a merchant at 28. He was listed as a day laborer in the 1870 Census at age 39, after the Brown family had lost its fortune, and the family then included the two surviving children Alvina (12) and J.D. (9), and a domestic. By 1880 Obid had passed away and his widow was living with son James, 19, who worked in a heading factory (1880 Census Madison Co. IN, p. 7).

On 7 Apr 1853 Obadiah married Sarah WYSONG, in Anderson IN, born about 1833 in OH. Sarah died after 1880. They had the following children:
1092	i.	Alvina (about 1858-)
1093	ii.	James D. (about 1861 - after 1880)
1094	iii.	Francis (1865-1865)

737. Elijah BROWN, 10G Grandson, born on 31 Aug 1835 in Perry Co. OH. Elijah died in Perkinsville IN, on 20 Jun 1913; he was 77. Year of birth given as both 1831 and 1835. His birthplace is uncertain but it was likely Perry County OH. After marriage with Lydia, he moved from Anderson to McLean County Illinois with Lydia's ex-guardians the William Wyatts. From there he served two enlistments in the Civil War, in the 4th Illinois Cavalry and the 10th Illinois Cavalry Volunteers. Later the Brown family returned to Indiana, first to Connersville, then Hancock Co., then Perkinsville in Madison County, near his father's old mill area. Buried at Neese Cemetery, Perkinsville IN. Refs.: death certificate Madison County, obituary in an unidentified 1913 Madison Co. newspaper courtesy Eloise Brenneman, National Archives pension papers and Illinois Civil War record, Censuses of 1850, 60, 70, 80, 1900, 1910, Ruby Tate Rynearson copy of family Bible page.

In 1853 Elijah first married Mary Jane COLLIS, in Anderson IN, born about 1839. Mary Jane died in 1855 in Anderson IN, in childbirth. They had one child:
1095	i.	(Infant) (1855-1855)

In 1856 Elijah second married Lydia C. EVANS, daughter of Ambrose EVANS and Louisa MCGHEE, in Madison County IN, born about 1837 in Henry Co. IN. Lydia C. died on 10 Apr 1872 in Madison Co. IN. She died in childbirth. Earlier, she was taken into the Rev. William Wyatt family which moved from Henry County to Madison Co. IN in 1850. Enumerated in both Ambrose Evans family and Wm. Wyatt families in the 1850 Census. Elijah, Lydia, and two children moved to McLean County Illinois with the Wyatts (1860 Census), then back to IN. Date of death given by Elijah's third wife Malissa in her widow's pension application, but 10 May 1871 is given on one page and 10 Apr 1872 on the other. Lydia died at James Anderson Brown's birth, so the latter is the correct one, coinciding with son James Anderson Brown's birth certificate, as she died in giving him birth. They had the following children:
1096	i.	Ralph Clark (1857-1941)
1097	ii.	William Lloyd (1859-1950)
1098	iii.	Nettie (1861 - about 1872)
1099	iv.	Ida (1864-1937)
1100	v.	Alonzo Grant (1866-1953)
1101	vi.	Clara (1869 - before 1872)

1102	vii.	James Anderson (1872-1928)

On 3 Mar 1873 when Elijah was 37, he third married Malissa Ellen WHITE, in Anderson IN, born on 29 Oct 1856 in Davis Co. IA. Malissa Ellen died in Fayette Co. IN, on 27 Jul 1939; she was 82. Buried at Neese Cemetery, Madison County Indiana. They had the following children:

1103	i.	Elmer E. (1874-1939)
1104	ii.	Rosa B. (1877-1900)
1105	iii.	John Scherer (1880-1963)
1106	iv.	Mary C. (1883-1939)
1107	v.	Bessie M. (1890-1942)
1108	vi.	Elijah (1893-1948)
1109	vii.	Sherman (1896-1898)

738. Rebecca A. BROWN, 10G Granddaughter, born about 1842 in IN. Living at home in 1860, at 18 years of age (1860 Census). Later she went to live in the home of her brother Obadiah and his family (1870 Census). Died after 1870.

739. Sarah I. BROWN, 10G Granddaughter, born in 1843 in IN. Sarah I. died in 1923 in Anderson IN. Buried in Perkinsville Cemetery. Probably named after her mother. Census reports show her as 6 in 1850 and 16 in 1860. Her headstone in the Perkinsville Cemetery states that she was "W of L. Brown and G. Leever," which is unexplained, as she was actually Lloyd Brown's daughter.

Sarah I. married G. LEEVER, who died in 1923.

740. Catherine BROWN, 10G Granddaughter, born on 20 Feb 1846 in IN. Catherine died in Kokomo IN, on 8 Jul 1913; she was 67. Buried in Crown Point Cemetery, Kokomo. In 1800 husband Abraham was a farmer who lived near Anderson. Known children's' names per 1880 Census and Eugene Elliott, descendant.

In about 1863 Catherine married Abraham ELLIOTT, born on 18 Oct 1842. Abraham died in Kokomo IN, on 29 Jan 1934; he was 91. Buried in Crown Point Cemetery, Kokomo. The family lived in Goshen IN, then Anderson IN, and moved to Kokomo IN in 1900. This family's refs.: Eugene Elliott citing Kokomo vital records; obituaries; cemetery records; 1880 Census Anderson IN. They had the following children:

1110	i.	Montreville (about 1864-)
1111	ii.	Jennette (about 1865-1948)
1112	iii.	William Lankford (1870-1929)
1113	iv.	Frank (about 1874-)
1114	v.	Daisy M. (about 1878-)
1115	vi.	Leroy "Roy" (1885-1962)

Family of Elijah BROWN (524) and Rebecca Ann SPILLMAN

741. Margaret BROWN, 10G Granddaughter, born in 1842 in Muskingum Co. OH.

742. Amos BROWN, 10G Grandson, born in 1845 in Muskingum Co. OH.

743. Clara BROWN, 10G Granddaughter, born in 1851 in Muskingum Co. OH.

744. Charles BROWN, 10G Grandson, born in 1856 in Muskingum Co. OH.

745. Lucy BROWN, 10G Granddaughter, born in 1859 in Muskingum Co. OH.

Family of William BROWN (525) and Harriett ---

746. Caroline BROWN, 10G Granddaughter, born in 1843 in IN.

747. Elijah BROWN, 10G Grandson, born in 1846 in IN. May have been the Elijah L. Brown who served in the Civil War from Madison County.

748. Martha BROWN, 10G Granddaughter, born in 1849 in IN.

749. Sarah BROWN, 10G Granddaughter, born in 1851 in IN.

750. Mary Ann or Lydia BROWN, 10G Granddaughter, born in 1855 in Madison Co. IN. Mary Ann or Lydia died on 20 Sep 1905 in Madison Co. IN.

In Apr 1873 Mary Ann or Lydia married Francis M. HOPPES, in Madison Co. IN, born on 18 Dec 1850 in Madison Co. IN. Francis M. died in 1922 in Madison Co. IN. They had the following children:

1116	i.	Emma Frances
1117	ii.	Cary A.
1118	iii.	Minnie J.
1119	iv.	Ollie G.
1120	v.	Charles C.
1121	vi.	Thomas G.
1122	vii.	Myrtle M.
1123	viii.	Asa R.
1124	ix.	Elizabeth
1125	x.	Edward
1126	xi.	Flossie
1127	xii.	Hazel

751. William BROWN, 10G Grandson, born in 1857 in IN.

Family of Elias BROWN (526) and Mary Ann ---

752. Mary BROWN, 10G Granddaughter, born in 1847 in OH, prob. Perry Co.

753. Robert BROWN, 10G Grandson, born in 1852 in OH, prob. Perry Co.

Family of Elias BROWN (526) and Catherine MOSS

754. Rosa BROWN, 10G Granddaughter, born in 1857 in IN.

755. Francis M. BROWN, 10G Grandson, born on 3 Apr 1862 in Anderson Twp., Madison Co. IN. Francis M. died in Anderson Twp., Madison Co. IN, on 5 Sep 1863; he was 1.

Family of Henry BROWN (527) and Caroline M. MAINS

756. Isaiah M. BROWN, 10G Grandson, born on 19 Jan 1850 in Perry Co. OH. The 1870 Perry County OH Monroe Township, p. 109 gave Isaiah Brown age 20 attending school, boarding with schoolmaster. The 1880 Census of Newark, Licking Co. OH, p. 399A enumerated him as being of age 30, "R Engineer." In the home was wife Annie W., 22 and mother Caroline M. age 58. He may have remarried: LDS Pedigree Resource File CD 65 PIN 971107 contains Isaiah M. Brown, father Henry Brown, mother Caroline Mains, who married Mary Catherine Truex 14 Apr 1904, she born 12 Mar 1873 Perry County Ohio, died 18 Aug 1945, father Jasper Samson Truex, mother Mary Ellen Rogers. I have been unable to substantiate that from the LDS file's contributor.

Isaiah M. married Annie ---.

757. George W. BROWN, 10G Grandson, born on 14 Sep 1852 in Perry Co. OH.

Family of John Lewis MOBLEY (528) and Ruth ELDER

758. Elizabeth A. MOBLEY, 10G Granddaughter, born on 22 Nov 1815 in Whitely, Clark Co. IN. Elizabeth A. died in IA on 14 Mar 1897; she was 81. Source: Warren.

On 16 Feb 1836 when Elizabeth A. was 20, she married Retus DUNN, in Whitely, Clark Co. IN. They had the following children:
1128	i.	Mary
1129	ii.	Nannie

759. Jesse Ralph MOBLEY, 10G Grandson, born on 18 Mar 1818 in Williamsport, Fountain Co. IN. Jesse Ralph died in Hartsville, Bartholomew Co. IN, on 24 Nov 1895; he was 77 (Bartholomew County *Death Certificates*, p. 36). Other sources:1850, 1860, 1870, 1880 Census, Bartholomew, IN, plus a letter from Nellie Mobley Collins which stated that he served in the Civil War on the side of the Union. A letter from Don Mobley to Y. Berkanstock stated Jesse Mobley was a stonemason and brick mason, that he built homes, school houses, and the County Courthouse. The 1870 Census Clifty, Bartholomew, IN, p. 18 stated that he was born in PA, which is unexplained.

Jesse Ralph married Nellie or Ellen LAWS or MCFALLS, born about 1825 in TN. Nellie or Ellen died on 11 Feb 1898 in Hartsville, Bartholomew Co. IN. Sources: 1850, 1860, 1870, 1880 Census, Bartholomew, Indiana, Bartholomew Co. IN death certificate. Letter from Don Mobley to Berkanstock stated that Jesse wife's name was Nellie Laws. "She died on the old home place. Our family moved there and took care of her until she died. It was located 2 miles from Hartsville." Letter from Nellie Mobley Collins says she was a McFalls, citing information from Milton C. Mobley. They had the following children:
1130	i.	Jesse (1841 - before 1864)
1131	ii.	Elijah B. (1844-1923)
1132	iii.	Thomas G. (1848-)
1133	iv.	Ruth Ann (1850-)
1134	v.	Phillip (1852-)
1135	vi.	Daniel L. (1856-)
1136	vii.	Andrew Jackson (1859-1920)
1137	viii.	Jacob A. (1865-)
1138	ix.	Mahala (1867-)

760. Alameda MOBLEY, 10G Granddaughter, born on 5 Apr 1820 in Whitely, Clark Co. IN. Alameda died on 19 May 1893; she was 73. Source; Warren.

In 1836 Alameda married John TAYLOR, in Whitely, Clark Co. IN.

761. Lucretia MOBLEY, 10G Granddaughter, born on 17 Nov 1821 in Whitely, Clark Co. IN.

On 24 Sep 1847 when Lucretia was 25, she married Thomas Green LEE, in Bartholomew Co. IN, born on 11 Feb 1831 in Hartsville, Bartholomew Co. IN. Thomas Green died in Scott IN, on 23 Oct 1898; he was 67. They had the following children:
1139	i.	William (1848-1925)
1140	ii.	Margarete A. "Maggie" (1849-)
1141	iii.	Henry (1851-1917)
1142	iv.	Jay (1853-1927)
1143	v.	Sarah Isabelle "Belle" (1855-1883)

762. John Henry MOBLEY, 10G Grandson, born on 19 Oct 1823 in Whitely, Clark Co. IN. John Henry died in Hartsville, Bartholomew Co. IN, on 8 Aug 1897; he was 73. Ref.: Warren. He owned the original Mobley farm. Farmed and raised livestock. 1870 Census Clifty, Bartholomew IN, p. 19.

On 28 Feb 1854 when John Henry was 30, he married Mary Ann BURKE, in Fairfield, Franklin Co. IN, born on 9 Nov

1831 in Lancaster Co. PA. Mary Ann died in Hartsville, Bartholomew Co. IN, on 13 Oct 1916; she was 84. *Death Certificate Book 2H-1*, p. 4. They had the following children:

1144	i.	William R. (1849-)
1145	ii.	Lyman (1854-1945)
1146	iii.	Emma (1856-1950)
1147	iv.	Fasine or Rosina (1857-)
1148	v.	Randolph "Randy" (1858-1942)
1149	vi.	Theodore T. "Dory" (1860-1937)
1150	vii.	Margaret A. "Maggie" (about 1862-1949)
1151	viii.	--- (1865-1865)
1152	ix.	Ella P. (1867-1897)
1153	x.	Loran (1868-1870)
1154	xi.	William Henry "Hen" (1871-1959)
1155	xii.	James Hunter "Hunt" (1873-1932)

763. Mahala MOBLEY, 10G Granddaughter, born on 19 Jan 1826 in Clark Co. IN. Mahala died in Kokomo, Howard Co. IN, on 25 May 1912; she was 86.

On 28 May 1848 when Mahala was 22, she married William FIX, born on 20 Sep 1825 or 6 in Jefferson, Clinton Co. IN. William died in Hartsville, Bartholomew Co. IN, on 9 Jul 1890; he was 64. Refs.: Warren; Hartsville, Bartholomew, IN 1880 Census p. 169. Farmer, Agent for Hartsville College, minister of the United Brethren Church, and teacher Hartsville College. They had the following children:

1156	i.	Sarah Catherine (1849-)
1157	ii.	John Wesley (about 1851-)
1158	iii.	Mary J. (about 1854-)
1159	iv.	Laura C. (1858-1868)
1160	v.	Leona (1862-)
1161	vi.	Josephine
1162	vii.	Genevra

764. Sarah MOBLEY, 10G Granddaughter, born on 21 Jan 1828 in Whitely, Clark Co. IN. Sarah died on 18 Feb 1909; she was 81. Warren listed husbands and children as below; also Census Hartsville, Bartholomew, p. 173.

On 9 Aug 1849 when Sarah was 21, she first married John FIX, in Bartholomew Co. IN, born in Aug 1827 in Jefferson, Clinton Co. IN. John died in Aug 1854 in Bartholomew Co. IN. They had the following children:

1163	i.	Mary M. (1850-1880)
1164	ii.	Cynthia Alice (1855-)

On 3 Sep 1857 when Sarah was 29, she second married Albert CRISLER, in Bartholomew Co. IN, born about 1832. They had the following children:

1165	i.	William (1858-)
1166	ii.	Letta or Meta (1860-)
1167	iii.	Sallie E. (1863-)

On 17 Feb 1863 when Sarah was 35, she third married John FLORAN, in Bartholomew Co. IN, born in 1808 in PA. John died about 1871 in Bartholomew Co. IN. They had the following children:

1168	i.	Phillip Beechers (1864-)
1169	ii.	Laura Jennie (1864-)
1170	iii.	William S. (1866-)
1171	iv.	Lewis H. (1871-)

765. Lewis MOBLEY, 10G Grandson, born on 19 Jan 1830 in Columbus, Bartholomew Co. IN. Lewis died in Columbus, Bartholomew Co. IN, on 23 Jan 1902; he was 72. Warren listed wife and children. Graduate of Hartsville College and later a professor of chemistry there. Death Certificate Bartholomew County IN, *Book HD-7*, p. 1. 1870 Census of Clifty, Bartholomew, IN, p. 12.

In 1854 Lewis married Julia Anna RHORER, in Whitely, Clark Co. IN, born on 19 Jun 1832 in Clermont Co. OH. Julia Anna died on 31 May 1911; she was 78. They had the following children:

1172	i.	Darius Arrelian (1855-1929)
1173	ii.	Laura Josephine (1857-1952)
1174	iii.	Luanna Jane (1859-)
1175	iv.	Alta Florence (1862-)
1176	v.	Ora (about 1863-)
1177	vi.	Minnie May (1865-)
1178	vii.	Jacob A. (1865 - before 1870)
1179	viii.	John Orion (1868-)
1180	ix.	Rita Florence (1869 - before 1870)
1181	x.	Mertie E (1871-)
1182	xi.	Lewis Dana (1874-)
1183	xii.	Lyda Blanche (1879-)
1184	xiii.	John Orion (- before 1880)

766. Reason D. MOBLEY, 10G Grandson, born on 11 Dec 1831 in Hartsville, Bartholomew Co. IN. Reason D. died in Clifty Twp., Bartholomew Co. IN, on 20 Sep 1903; he was 71. Refs.: Warren; 1850 Census Cliffty Township; Bartholomew Co. IN, death certificate Bartholomew County *HD-7*, p. 23. Marriage #1 *Certificate Book C5*, Marriage #2; *Certificate Book C-11*, p. 459. 1870 Census Clifty, Bartholomew Co. IN, p. 19.

On 4 Dec 1853 when Reason D. was 21, he first married Frances E. PATTON, born in 1837 in IN. Frances E. died on 18 Mar 1884. They had the following children:

1185	i.	Marietta (1857-)
1186	ii.	Viola (1859-)
1187	iii.	Columbus (1861-)
1188	iv.	Anne Almy (about 1863-)
1189	v.	William (1866-)
1190	vi.	Allen (1869-)

On 10 Dec 1884 when Reason D. was 52, he second married Mary Gant ISGREGG, born in 1845 in IN. They had the following children:

1191	i.	Orville (1873-1892)
1192	ii.	John W. (1877-)
1193	iii.	Rilla (1880 - about 1881)

767. Catherine Minerva MOBLEY, 10G Granddaughter, born on 15 Nov 1833 in Whitely, Clark Co. IN. Catherine Minerva died on 15 Mar 1906; she was 72. Refs.: Warren, 1850 Census Cliffty Township, Bartholomew Co. IN, p. 24.

Catherine Minerva married Robert GILLILANT. They had the following children:

1194	i.	Irwin (1851-)
1195	ii.	George W. (1853-)
1196	iii.	Margaret (1855-)
1197	iv.	Robert J. (1857-)
1198	v.	Eliza Jane (1859 - before 1870)
1199	vi.	William E. (1861-)
1200	vii.	John L. (1863-)
1201	viii.	Edward C. (1866-)
1202	ix.	Cora A. (1870-)

768. William MOBLEY, 10G Grandson, born on 29 Aug 1835 in Bartholomew Co. IN. William died on 7 Jan 1865; he was 29. 1850 Census Cliffty Township, Bartholomew Co. IN. Warren listed wife and children's names. Marriage Certificate listed wife Mary Jane Coover (*Marriage Certificate Book C-6*, p. 398). 1870 Census Hartsville, p. 173. In the latter, William is not listed, only wife and family.

On 4 Dec 1859 when William was 24, he married Mary Jane COOVERT, in Bartholomew Co. IN, born on 17 Jun 1837 in Preble Co. OH. Mary Jane died in Newton Co. IN, on 22 Dec 1912; she was 75. They had the following children:

1203	i.	Alonzo (1861-)
1204	ii.	Monte Belle (1862-)
1205	iii.	Sara Willa (1865-)

769. Warren Wesley MOBLEY, 10G Grandson, born on 8 Jan 1838 in Whitely, Clark Co. IN. Warren Wesley died in Hartsville, Bartholomew Co. IN, on 9 Feb 1907; he was 69. Refs.: Warren; 1850 Census Cliffty Township; Bartholomew Co. IN. *Death Certificate Book 2H-1*, p. 2.; *Marriage Certificate Book C-9*, p. 245.

On 13 Aug 1874 when Warren Wesley was 36, he married Mary F. RYAN, in Bartholomew Co. IN, born in 1852 in IN. Mary F. died in 1928. They had the following children:
- **1206**   i.   Lewis F. (1875-)
- **1207**   ii.   Warren Wesley (about 1878-1893)
- **1208**   iii.   Elsie P. (1878-)
- **1209**   iv.   Nina A. (1883-)
- **1210**   v.   Otto W. (1886-)

Family of John W. BROWN (536) and Elizabeth ---

770. John W. BROWN, 10G Grandson, born in 1835.

771. Benjamin F. BROWN, 10G Grandson, born on 18 Aug 1839. Benjamin F. died on 2 Nov 1892; he was 53. Buried at Springfield Cemetery, Sykesville MD.

Benjamin F. first married Lavina ---, born on 18 Aug 1839. Lavina died on 8 May 1891; she was 51.

Benjamin F. second married Rachel ---, born on 27 Jun 1859. Rachel died on 23 Jan 1894; she was 34.

772. Margaret E. BROWN, 10G Granddaughter, born in 1843.

773. Mary Jane BROWN, 10G Granddaughter, born on 5 Aug 1845. Mary Jane died on 13 Jan 1894; she was 48. Buried at Wesley Freedom Methodist Church Cemetery, Carroll County MD.

774. Josiah BROWN, 10G Grandson, born on 8 Sep 1847. Josiah died on 3 Feb 1942; he was 94. Buried in Springfield Cemetery, Sykesville MD.

Josiah married Caroline R. ---, born on 20 Mar 1858. Caroline R. died on 17 Jan 1926; she was 67. They had one child:
- **1211**   i.   Annie B. (1886-1921)

Family of Cordelia BROWN (537) and Levi ELDER

775. Margaret E. ELDER, 10G Granddaughter.

776. Sarah E. ELDER, 10G Granddaughter.

777. Levi Marshall ELDER, 10G Grandson.

778. Emma E. ELDER, 10G Grandson.

779. James M. ELDER, 10G Grandson.

James M. married Ellen Roseanne SELBY.

780. William E. ELDER, 10G Grandson.

781. Alessa ELDER, 10G Grandson.

Family of Lloyd BROWN (538) and Mary E. WILLCOCK / WILCOX

782. Archibald BROWN, 10G Grandson, born on 4 May 1843. Archibald died in Marriottsville, MD, on 20 Oct 1917; he was 74. Resident of Howard County Maryland in 1875. Buried in the Springfield Cemetery, Sykesville Maryland.

Archibald married Melinda SELBY, daughter of Richard SELBY, born on 26 May 1843 in Carroll Co. MD. Melinda died on 6 Aug 1908; she was 65. Selby family and descendants information per Francis X. Sis Sr. They had the following children:
1212	i.	Hattie (1870-)
1213	ii.	Ernest Wade (1872-1960)

783. John T. BROWN, 10G Grandson, born in 1846. Resident of Baltimore in 1875.

784. Charles E. BROWN, 10G Grandson, born in 1847 in Carroll Co. MD. Charles E. died about 1923. Resident of Baltimore in 1875. Buried in the Springfield Cemetery, Sykesville Maryland.

Charles E. married Lucinda A. BROOKELY, born about 1846 in PA. Lucinda A. died about 1914. Buried in Springfield Cemetery, Sykesville MD. They had the following children:
1214	i.	Charles H. (about 1865 - about 1947)
1215	ii.	Margaret A. (about 1868 - about 1947)
1216	iii.	Lewis E. (about 1871 - about 1915)
1217	iv.	Susanna A. (about 1875 - about 1925)
1218	v.	Lucinda (about 1889 - about 1915)

785. Lewis E. BROWN, 10G Grandson, born in 1850 in New Windsor, Carroll Co. MD. Lewis E. died in Baltimore City MD. Lewis Brown family and descendants are here per Walter McPherson and 1880 Census, Catonsville, Baltimore County Maryland, p. 332B.

Lewis E. married Sarah C. HIGH, daughter of William HIGH and Emily KURTZ, born in Baltimore City MD. Sarah C. died in Baltimore City MD. They had the following children:
1219	i.	George E. (about 1874-)
1220	ii.	Emely C. (about 1877-)
1221	iii.	Mary C. (about 1888-)
1222	iv.	Laura Virginia

786. Georgianna BROWN, 10G Granddaughter.

Georgianna married John Alonza MARSH.

787. Lloyd A. BROWN, 10G Grandson, born on 1 Aug 1853 in Carroll Co. MD. He died in Sykesville MD, on 6 Jul 1921; he was 67. Buried in Springfield Presbyterian Church, Sykesville. Lloyd A. Brown family and descendants per William Shaffer.

Lloyd A. first married Rebecca ---, born on 17 Mar 1857. Rebecca died in Carroll Co. MD, on 25 Feb 1893; she was 35. They had the following children:
1223	i.	Mamie (1879-)
1224	ii.	Arthur C. (1885-1963)
1225	iii.	Harris
1226	iv.	Lucy
1227	v.	George A. (1893-1893)

In 1896 Lloyd A. second married Sarah E. FOGLE, in Carroll Co. MD, born on 25 Sep 1853. Sarah E. died in Carroll Co. MD, on 19 Aug 1925; she was 71. Buried in Springfield Presbyterian Church, Sykesville.

788. Amelia W. BROWN, 10G Granddaughter.

789. Saib D. BROWN, 10G Grandson, born on 1 Aug 1857 in Carroll Co. MD. Saib D. died in Carroll Co. MD, on 24

Feb 1926; he was 68. Buried at Springfield Cemetery, Sykesville Maryland.

Saib D. married Lucrecia ---, born on 19 Nov 1864 in Carroll Co. MD. Lucrecia died in Carroll Co. MD, on 22 Mar 1922; she was 57. They had the following children:
1228	i.	F.L. (about 1892 - about 1915)
1229	ii.	G.O. (about 1893 - about 1894)
1230	iii.	M.E. (about 1896 - about 1897)

790. Isaiah BROWN, 10G Grandson, born on 21 Oct 1860 in Carroll Co. MD. Isaiah died in Carroll Co. MD, on 28 May 1931; he was 70. Buried at Springfield Cemetery, Sykesville Maryland.

Isaiah married Florence T. G. ---, born on 25 Nov 1866. Florence T. G. died on 12 Apr 1895; she was 28. They had the following children:
1231	i.	Florence
1232	ii.	Frank D.
1233	iii.	Isabella

791. Jefferson J. BROWN, 10G Grandson, born about 1863.

Family of Vincent BROWN (540) and Adahzilah CARTER

792. Alice BROWN, 10G Granddaughter, born about 1858.

Alice married William MCQUANE. Resident of Philadelphia in 1877.

793. Granville BROWN, 10G Grandson, born about 1855. Resident of Philadelphia.

794. Clara Josephine BROWN, 10G Granddaughter, born on 24 Mar 1857 in MD. Clara Josephine died in Baltimore City, MD, on 29 Oct 1916; she was 59. Buried in the Greenmount Cemetery, Philadelphia Pennsylvania.

On 14 Oct 1875 when Clara Josephine was 18, she first married "Dr." Jabez SHIPLEY, in Centenary Methodist Episcopal Church, Westminster, Carroll Co, born on 13 Jul 1855 in Woolery District, Carroll Co. MD. Jabez died in Philadelphia PA, on 3 Dec 1914; he was 59. Buried in Greenmount Cemetery, Philadelphia. The "Doctor" was apparently a nickname, as he was so named in the 1870 Census at age 14. They had the following children:
1234	i.	Osko R. (1876-1910)
1235	ii.	Ada Waltz (1878-1881)
1236	iii.	Birdie Selvena (1880-1907)
1237	iv.	Walter Alaska (1882-1897)
1238	v.	Roy Leroy (1885-1904)
1239	vi.	Clara Josephine (1887-1905)
1240	vii.	Franklin F. (1889-1944)
1241	viii.	Florence (Edna May) (1890-1926)
1242	ix.	Charles Howard (1893-1952)

Clara Josephine second married --- HUNTER.

795. Vincent BROWN, 10G Grandson, born about 1860. Resident of Baltimore City.

Family of Vincent BROWN (540) and Matilda Ann ZENZ

796. Jerome N. BROWN, 10G Grandson, born about 1869.

Family of Hillary TWIST (543) and Martha Ann BURKS

797. Rebecca TWIST, 10G Granddaughter, born about 1830.

798. William H. TWIST, 10G Grandson, born about 1831.

799. John TWIST, 10G Grandson, born about 1832.

800. James TWIST, 10G Grandson, born about 1837.

801. Eliza E. TWIST, 10G Granddaughter, born about 1841.

802. Norbury G. TWIST, 10G Grandson, born about 1844.

803. Samuel TWIST, 10G Grandson, born about 1846.

804. Sarah TWIST, 10G Granddaughter, born about 1847.

Family of Margaret TWIST (544) and Ephraim (?) LOVETT

805. Margaret S. LOVETT, 10G Granddaughter, born about 1830.

806. William LOVETT, 10G Grandson, born about 1832. 1860 Census Baltimore County, Towsontown P.O. pp. 639-40. Carpenter.

William married Tabatha ---, born about 1836. They had the following children:
- 1243   i.   Elizabeth (1856-)
- 1244   ii.   Charles (1860-)

807. Samuel LOVETT, 10G Grandson, born about 1835. 1860 Census Baltimore County, Towsontown, p. 640. Carpenter.

Samuel married Mary Ann ---, born about 1834. They had the following children:
- 1245   i.   Joseph (about 1854-)
- 1246   ii.   Frances (about 1856-)
- 1247   iii.   Georgianna (about 1859-)

Family of Louis H. BROWN (545) and Susan HUDSON

808. Emma BROWN, 10G Granddaughter, born in 1846. Emma died on 9 Dec 1903 in Baltimore City MD. Buried in Greenmount Cemetery. Raised by her aunt Prudence Patterson. Marriage: Carroll Co. Marriages.

On 28 Oct 1868 Emma married J. Randolph MORDECAI, son of Moses Cohen MORDECAI and Mabel LYONS, in Carroll Co. MD, born in 1837. J. Randolph died in 1895 in Baltimore City MD. Buried in Greenmount Cemetery. Doug Mordecai wrote that "Moses Cohen Mordecai, Emma's Father-in-Law, was an unbelievable guy. State Senator of South Carolina for two terms. Millionaire. Newspaper owner. Shipping magnate, had ships running the Union blockades during the Civil War, was a staunch Confederate. Moved his shipping business Mordecai and Co. and his family to Baltimore in 1865. That was a tremendous feat for a Jew in those times (e-mail 6 Jun 2004)." They had the following children:
- 1248   i.   Randolph J. (1871-)
- 1249   ii.   Florence (1873-)
- 1250   iii.   Mary J. (1875-)
- 1251   iv.   George Patterson (1879-1955)
- 1252   v.   Louis

1253   vi.   Henry

809. Louisiana BROWN, 10G Granddaughter.

Louisiana married --- PAYNE.

810. Ruth BROWN, 10G Granddaughter. Ruth died in 1894 in Texas (Albert S. Brown).

811. George BROWN, 10G Grandson.

812. Louis BROWN, 10G Grandson.

813. Horatio BROWN, 10G Grandson.

Family of Prudence Ann BROWN (546) and George PATTERSON

814. George PATTERSON, 10G Grandson, born on 9 Sep 1844. George died on 21 Dec 1849; he was 5. Buried at the Springfield Presbyterian Church of Sykesville.

815. Florence PATTERSON, 10G Granddaughter, born on 13 Jun 1847 in Carroll Co. MD. Florence died in Carroll Co. MD, on 15 Oct 1878; she was 31. Buried at the Springfield Presbyterian Church of Sykesville. "Died in child-bed" (Albert S. Brown). An infant son is buried there with her.

On 6 Sep 1877 when Florence was 30, she married James CARROLL, son of Charles CARROLL, in Carroll Co. MD. Buried at the Springfield Presbyterian Church of Sykesville.

Family of Stephen Thomas Cockey BROWN (547) and Susan Ann BENNETT (564)

816. Mary Ridgely BROWN, 10G Granddaughter, born about 1844 in Baltimore Co. MD. Age 6 in 1850 Census, Steven T. Brown family Dist. 5, Carroll County, p. 221.

817. Gov. Francis (Frank) BROWN, 10G Grandson, born on 8 Aug 1846 in Carroll Co. MD. Francis (Frank) died in MD on 3 Feb 1920; he was 73. Buried in Greenmount Cemetery, Baltimore MD. Enumerated at age 3 in the 1850 Census, in the Steven T. Brown family of District 5, Carroll County Maryland, p. 221. Frank Brown was the 44th governor of Maryland from 1892 through 1896. His home, known as the Springfield Estate, was near Sykesville and purchased in 1880, and added to the tract Brown's Inheritance that he had inherited from his father. That estate was later made into the Springfield Hospital Center for the insane. The hospital's historian Bill Ebeling recalled that "Springfield was [previously] owned by Governor Frank Brown, a descendant of the William Patterson family, a wealthy colonial era farmer and merchant. William Patterson's daughter, Elizabeth, or 'Betsy', gained international fame and notoriety when she married Jerome Bonaparte, brother of Napoleon Bonaparte. This courtship, and the ill-fated marriage that followed has been the subject of numerous books and at least one movie" (see also Prudence Ann Brown, 546). His obituary was published in the *Baltimore Sun*, 4 Feb 1920.

Of the Governor it is recorded that "he was born at the plantation Brown's Inheritance, Carroll County, Maryland, son of Stephan Thomas Cockey Brown. His first American ancestor, Abel Brown, came from Dumfries, Scotland, [but see below and elsewhere] and settled near Annapolis, Md. Several of his sons served in the Revolutionary War and some of his grandsons in the, war of 1812-'14. Frank Brown was educated at Springfield Academy, and at private academies in Baltimore city. [His obituary stated that he left school when the Emancipation Proclamation resulted in the loss of his father's sixty slaves, and he returned home to help operate the family farm.] In 1870 he was appointed to a clerkship in one of the state tobacco warehouses, a position which he held for the ensuing six years. In 1875 he was elected a member of the House of Delegates from Carroll county, and was re-elected in 1877. He inherited large estates from his father and his uncle, George Patterson, to the care of which he devoted much of his time. He was president of the Maryland State Agricultural and Mechanical Association from 1880 to 1892. He took a prominent part in the presidential campaign of

1884, and in 1886 was appointed by President Cleveland postmaster of Baltimore city; during his term in this office he was instrumental in initiating various postal reforms. In the fall of 1887 he was a candidate for gubernatorial honors, and failed of nomination. In 1891 he was the unanimous nominee of the Democratic convention, and was elected governor by a majority of thirty thousand votes. In addition to his duties as the chief executive of the state, he was ex-officio president of the board of trustees of the Maryland Agricultural College; president of the Board of Trustees of the House of Correction; of the Board of Trustees of St. John's College, Annapolis, Md.; President of the State Board of Education, and of the Board of Public Works, 1892-96" (*Dumfries-Galloway Scots in America*, http://homepages.rootsweb.com/). His ancestor is there as elsewhere listed as a Dumfries Scot, but a major argument of the present study indicates otherwise.

Howard Smith wrote: "In about 1996, the State of Maryland transferred acreage from Springfield Mental Hospital to the Maryland State Police for a training facility. While excavating they found 14 graves. After several years of study it was decided they could not be members of the Brown family because the stress on the bones proved they were working people. I asked for a DNA test but it didn't happen" (letter to the author, 5 Jul 2005). He added that "most of the Brown family that stayed in the area were poor farmers" and he was rightfully dissatisfied with the State's finding.

On 22 Dec 1879 when Francis (Frank) was 33, he married Mary RIDGELY, daughter of David RIDGELY, in MD, born in 1847 in MD. Mary died on 11 May 1895 in MD. Buried in Greenmount Cemetery, Baltimore MD. The First Ladies Exhibit of the Maryland State Archives said of her: "Mary Ridgely Preston Brown was born on February 23, 1857 to David and Mary R. Ridgely of Baltimore. She was educated at private schools in Baltimore, and finished her education abroad in Wiesbaden. On June 12, 1877, she married Horatio Wyman Preston, but their marriage was short lived, as Mr. Preston died on October 13, 1878. On December 22, 1879, the young widow married Frank Brown of Carroll County. The Browns had two children, Mary (nicknamed May) and Frank Jr."

1254	i.	Mary Ridgley "Mamie" or "May"
1255	ii.	Francis Snowden (- before 1920)

Family of Ann Cockey BROWN (548) and Vachel W. BEASMAN

818. Elias Brown BEASMAN, 10G Grandson, born in Baltimore (later Carroll) Co. MD. Elias Brown died on 6 Jul 1857 in Carroll Co. MD. Died in infancy. Albert S. Brown wrote in 1897 that his headstone was situated next to his grandfather Elias's grave in the Brown Cemetery.

819. Aletha V. EBAUGH (adopted), 10G Granddaughter.

Family of Elias BROWN (549) and Catherine E. J. BARNETT

820. Elias BROWN, 10G Grandson, born on 24 Oct 1853 in Carroll Co. MD. Elias died in Nov 1855. Albert S. Brown gave his date of death as 18 Dec 1861.

821. William M. BROWN, 10G Grandson, born on 13 Aug 1855 in Carroll Co. MD. See 1900 Census of Howard County Maryland, p. 75.

In 1893 William M. married Ida Lee, born in 1864 in MD. They had the following children:

1256	i.	Eliza
1257	ii.	Jessie A.
1258	iii.	Corrie M.

822. Edward D. BROWN, 10G Grandson, born on 18 Jul 1859. Edward D. died on 3 Feb 1919 of the flu epidemic; he was 59. Buried Oakland United Methodist Cemetery, Carroll Co. MD. Wives and family per Eleanor Crissman, Ed Gamble and William Shaffer.

On 25 Oct 1883 when Edward D. was 24, he first married Susie E. THOMPSON, born in 1862. They had one child:

1259	i.	Elias (1885-1934)

Edward D. second married Susannah R. SHIPLEY, daughter of Henry Baskum SHIPLEY and Susan R. BIDDINGER, born on 1 Mar 1862. Susannah R. died in Carroll Co. MD, on 4 Apr 1938; she was 76. Buried in the Oakland United Methodist Cemetery, Carroll Co. MD. They had the following children:

1260	i.	Lula Catherine (1895-1923)
1261	ii.	Sara "Sadie" (twin, 1896-1966) Had a male twin who d. inf.
1262	iii.	Edward Lee (1899-1968)
1263	iv.	Bessie Susan (1900-1933)
1264	v.	William Henry (1904-1964)

823. Catherine E. BROWN, 10G Granddaughter, born on 16 Nov 1861. Catherine E. died on 30 Nov 1861; she was less than 1. Per Albert S. Brown.

824. Samuel Thomas BROWN, 10G Grandson, born on 12 Apr 1866 in Carroll Co. MD. Samuel Thomas died in Baltimore MD, on 6 Dec 1934; he was 68. In the 1900 Census of Howard County Maryland, p. 75, he was living with brother William.

Samuel Thomas first married Mary Jane CAVEY.

On 23 Feb 1892 when Samuel Thomas was 25, he second married Nancy "Nannie" MILLER, born on 15 Sep 1866 in Woodstock MD. Nancy "Nannie" died in Baltimore MD, on 7 Mar 1899; she was 32. His second wife claimed also to be Mollie Kimber (per Crissman). They had the following children:

1265	i.	Nancy Clara Etta (1892-)
1266	ii.	Minnie
1267	iii.	Bernice

825. Susannah Amelia BROWN, 10G Granddaughter, born on 11 Jul 1868.

Susannah Amelia married John L. "Acre" PEARCE. They had the following children:

1268	i.	Joseph
1269	ii.	John

Family of Benjamin Franklin BROWN (555) and Dorcas H. REICH

826. Florence BROWN, 10G Granddaughter, born on 22 Jul 1853.

On 21 Dec 1876 when Florence was 23, she married Edwin B. HAY. Lawyer, Washington D.C. They had the following children:

1270	i.	Edward B. (1879-)
1271	ii.	Jewel D. (1883-)
1272	iii.	Paul B. (1888-)

827. Fannie BROWN, 10G Granddaughter, born on 22 Mar 1857.

On 20 Nov 1879 when Fannie was 22, she married Richard K. EVANS, a lawyer, Washington D.C. They had the following children:

1273	i.	Albert S. (1863-)
1274	ii.	Mildred Lee (1865-1890)

828. Albert S. BROWN, 10G Grandson, born on 8 Sep 1863 in MD. Albert S. died after 1930. Attorney in Frederick MD and author of the Brown family manuscript held at the University of Maryland, College Park. Additional refs.: 1910 Census Frederick, Frederick County MD, p. 93; 1920 Census, p. 122; 1930 Census, p. 156.

On 18 Jun 1904 when Albert S. was 40, he married Emma POPE, born about 1868. Emma died after 1930. They had one child:

1275	i.	Mildred (about 1905-)

829. Mildred Lee BROWN, 10G Granddaughter, born on 29 May 1865 in MD. Mildred Lee died on 3 Feb 1890; she was 24.

On 25 Oct 1889 when Mildred Lee was 24, she married Harry S. TAYLOR.

830. Miriam E. BROWN, 10G Granddaughter.

Miriam E. married H. J. KEFAUVER. They had one child:
   1276   i.   Evans Brown

Family of Jemima Elizabeth BROWN (556) and John Gorsuch PEARCE

831. William Brown PEARCE, 10G Grandson, born on 20 Dec 1852 in Carroll Co. MD. Resident of Baltimore.

On 18 Aug 1888 when William Brown was 35, he married Lillie May COOK, in Baltimore Co. MD. They had the following children:
   1277   i.   Bertie Cook (1889-1891)
   1278   ii.   Mildred Elizabeth (1899-)

832. John Thomas PEARCE, 10G Grandson, born on 20 Apr 1854 in Carroll Co. MD. John Thomas died in Carroll Co. MD, on 3 Feb 1916; he was 61. Buried at Wesley Freedom Cemetery.

833. Elias Joseph PEARCE, 10G Grandson, born on 2 Feb 1856 in Carroll Co. MD. Elias Joseph died on 29 Aug 1876; he was 20. Buried at Wesley Freedom Cemetery.

834. George Marshall PEARCE, 10G Grandson, born on 4 Nov 1857 in Carroll Co. MD. Lawyer, Washington D.C.

On 29 Jul 1886 when George Marshall was 28, he married Mary Elizabeth "Mamie" PARRAN, in Baltimore Co. MD. They had the following children:
   1279   i.   Anna Elizabeth (1887-)
   1280   ii.   Mary Evelyn (1894-1900)

835. Mary Virginia PEARCE, 10G Granddaughter, born on 8 May 1859 in Carroll Co. MD.

On 7 Aug 1881 when Mary Virginia was 22, she married Hershey Simpson CUMMINGS, in Baltimore Co. MD. Resident of Baltimore. They had one child:
   1281   i.   John Pearce (1883-)

836. Charles Cockey PEARCE, 10G Grandson, born on 4 Mar 1861 in Carroll Co. MD. Charles Cockey died in Jan 1916 in Carroll Co. MD.

Charles Cockey married Mrs. Emma SHANKS.

Family of Lucinda Rachel Jackson BROWN (557) and William REICH

837. William John REICH, 10G Grandson, born on 9 Feb 1854 in Baltimore Co. MD.

838. Lucy Brown REICH, 10G Granddaughter, born on 7 Jun 1855 in Baltimore Co. MD.

On 30 Apr 1884 when Lucy Brown was 28, she married H. Gates SMITH, in Baltimore Co. MD. H. Gates died on 25 Nov 1922. Family lived in Georgia. They had the following children:
   1282   i.   Eleanor Frances (1887-)
   1283   ii.   Agnes (1889-)
   1284   iii.   Gordon (1893-)

839. Phillip Valentine REICH, 10G Grandson, born on 5 Jun 1857 in Baltimore Co. MD. Phillip Valentine died on 8 Nov 1912; he was 55.

840. Elenore REICH, 10G Granddaughter, born on 6 Feb 1859 in Baltimore Co. MD.

841. Benjamin Franklin REICH, 10G Grandson, born on 16 Jun 1861 in MD. Lawyer, resident of Frederick County.

Family of Rebecca Ann Worthington BROWN (558) and Christian SHRYOCK

842. William Brown SHRYOCK, 10G Grandson, born on 24 Sep 1853. This family resided in Everett MA (Albert S. Brown).

William Brown married Addie SCHROEDER.

843. Henrietta SHRYOCK, 10G Granddaughter, born about 1855. Henrietta died before 1897. This family had a son and a daughter (Albert S. Brown).

Henrietta married George CHAMBERLAIN.

844. Leonora P. "Lena" SHRYOCK, 10G Granddaughter, born in 1857.

In 1878 Leonora P. "Lena" married Samuel TREGALLAS, in Baltimore Co. MD. This family lived in Baltimore; he founded and headed Tregallas Hertel and Co., a large dry goods firm. They had one child:
    1285   i.   Samuel Staley (about 1881-)

Family of Mary Ann BROWN (559) and Alfred A. TILYARD

845. John S. TILYARD, 10G Grandson, born in 1855.

846. Charles H. TILYARD, 10G Grandson, born in 1859. Lived in Baltimore.

Charles H. married Nora GREENFIELD, in Baltimore Co. MD.

847. Mattie TILYARD, 10G Granddaughter. Died in infancy.

Family of Susannah Delila BROWN (560) and Charles Thomas COCKEY

848. Edward Augustus COCKEY, 10G Grandson, born on 3 Feb 1853 in Baltimore Co. MD. Edward Augustus died in Baltimore Co. MD, on 26 Apr 1922; he was 69.

On 18 Jun 1878 when Edward Augustus was 25, he married Alice Mitchell COUNCILMAN, in Baltimore Co. MD. They had the following children:
    1286   i.   Urath Cromwell (1879-1882)
    1287   ii.   Charles Thomas (1880-1882)
    1288   iii.   Edward Augustus (1882-)
    1289   iv.   John Councilman (1884-1918)
    1290   v.   Alexander Drummond (1886-)

849. Ann A. COCKEY, 10G Granddaughter, born on 26 Jan 1855 in Baltimore Co. MD.

On 18 Feb 1890 when Ann A. was 35, she married Dr. Cameron PIGGOT, son of Dr. Aaron PIGGOT and Margaret MOORE, in Baltimore Co. MD. Resident of Sewanee, TN. They had the following children:

 1291 i. Charles Snowden (1892-)
 1292 ii. William Cameron (1895-1895)

850. Thomas Beale COCKEY, 10G Grandson, born on 17 Nov 1857 in Baltimore Co. MD.

On 17 Nov 1885 when Thomas Beale was 28, he married Mary Thomas "Mamie" WARFIELD, daughter of Dr. Evan WARFIELD and Sallie Ann ---, in Baltimore Co. MD. They had the following children:

 1293 i. Eva (1886-)
 1294 ii. Sally Ann (1889-)
 1295 iii. Emma Shepherd (1891-)
 1296 iv. Charles Thomas (1893-)
 1297 v. Thomas Beale (1895-)

851. Urath Cromwell COCKEY, 10G Granddaughter, born on 23 Jul 1859 in Baltimore Co. MD.

On 15 Sep 1923 when Urath Cromwell was 64, she married Charles Butler ROGERS, son of Nathan ROGERS and Eunice BUTLER, in Baltimore Co. MD. McCallahan wrote "These two were married in their 60s at St. Thomas' Church, Garrison Forest" (p. 10).

852. William Brown COCKEY, 10G Grandson, born on 13 Aug 1861 in Baltimore Co. MD.

William Brown first married Dora HOLMES, daughter of Charles HOLMES and Virginia LEFEVRE, in Baltimore Co. MD.

William Brown second married Ida HOLMES, daughter of Charles HOLMES and Virginia LEFEVRE, in Baltimore Co. MD.

853. Charles Thomas COCKEY, 10G Grandson, born on 21 Jun 1863 in Baltimore Co. MD.

On 15 Oct 1902 when Charles Thomas was 39, he married Mary Clarke COOK, daughter of Capt. Adolphus COOK and Rachel CLARKE, in Baltimore Co. MD. They had the following children:

 1298 i. Charles Thomas (1905-)
 1299 ii. Mary (1906-1906)

Family of Ann Virginia BROWN (561) and Phillip H. TILYARD

854. Tyson TILYARD, 10G Grandson, born in Jul 1863 in Baltimore Co. MD. Died young.

855. Mattie Virginia TILYARD, 10G Granddaughter, born on 9 Sep 1866 in Baltimore Co. MD.

Mattie Virginia married William Chamberlain WATKINS, in Baltimore Co. MD.

856. Walter TILYARD, 10G Grandson, born on 20 Sep 1867 in Baltimore Co. MD.

Walter married Grace GIBSON, in Baltimore Co. MD. They had the following children:

 1300 i. Dorothy
 1301 ii. Walter Robert

857. Irene TILYARD, 10G Grandson, born on 28 Dec 1869 in Baltimore Co. MD. Unmarried.

858. Florence Patterson TILYARD, 10G Granddaughter, born on 9 Jun 1871 in Baltimore Co. MD. Unmarried.

Family of Mary Ellen BENNETT (563) and Elisha H. BENNETT

859. Laura Ella BENNETT, 10G Granddaughter, born on 11 Sep 1856 in Oakland MD. Laura Ella died in Baltimore MD, on 8 Nov 1946; she was 90.

On 23 Dec 1885 when Laura Ella was 29, she married Johnzie E. BEASMAN, son of Joshua BEASMAN and Nacissa Sara GORE, in MD, born on 16 Mar 1852 in Lewisville, Carroll Co. MD. Johnzie E. died in Baltimore Co. MD, on 25 Jan 1922; he was 69. They had the following children:
- **1302** i. Frank Bennett (1889-1960)
- **1303** ii. (Infant) (1888-1888)

Family of Miranda BENNETT (566) and Mordecai Cockey STOCKSDALE (604)

860. Florence STOCKSDALE, 10G Granddaughter.

Florence married --- BREEN.

861. Annie STOCKSDALE, 10G Granddaughter.

Annie married --- CONNOLLY.

Family of Comfort W. DORSEY (567) and Gilchrist PORTER

862. Mary Eleanor PORTER, 10G Granddaughter, born about 1841.

863. Julia PORTER, 10G Granddaughter, born about 1848.

864. Margaret D. PORTER, 10G Granddaughter, born in 1849.

Family of Mary Snowden DORSEY (568) and James Overton BROADHEAD

865. Edward BROADHEAD, 10G Grandson, born about 1849.

Family of Rebecca Ann LAWRENCE (579) and George Benton LAWRENCE

866. Hammond LAWRENCE, 10G Grandson, born on 6 Nov 1868 in ND. Hammond died on 2 Mar 1900; he was 31.

867. Ida Lee LAWRENCE, 10G Granddaughter, born on 15 May 1872 in ND.

On 28 Dec 1895 when Ida Lee was 23, she married John Oscar CARTER, born about 1868 in ND.

868. France Edward LAWRENCE, 10G Grandson, born on 11 Feb 1875 in ND.

On 13 Jul 1906 when France Edward was 31, he married Ida ARMOUR, born about 1879 in ND.

869. Claude LAWRENCE, 10G Grandson, born on 16 Sep 1878 in ND.

On 19 May 1901 when Claude was 22, he married Inez SHOEMAKER, born about 1882 in ND. They had one child:

1304   i.   Hazel Dell (1902-1954)

Family of Jennie Dorsey LAWRENCE (580) and John Henry MCCLINTOCK

870. Clemmie Irene MCCLINTOCK, 10G Granddaughter, born on 22 Sep 1874 in Pike Co. IL.

On 22 Aug 1900 when Clemmie Irene was 25, she married Chiles Lester KEITHLY.

871. James Henry MCCLINTOCK, 10G Grandson, born on 27 Jul 1876 in Lincoln Co. MO.

On 23 Nov 1898 when James Henry was 22, he married Amelia SCHULTZ, in MO.

872. George Edward MCCLINTOCK, 10G Grandson, born on 6 Sep 1879 in Pike Co. IL.

George Edward married Olive Ann LITTLE, daughter of William Henry "Bud" LITTLE and Josephine Ann DONNALLY, born on 25 Feb 1884 in Center, Ralls Co. MO. Olive Ann died in Fresno, Fresno Co. CA, on 25 Jun 1966; she was 82. They had one child:
    1305   i.   Alma Louise (1919-)

873. Robert Levin MCCLINTOCK, 10G Grandson, born on 9 Jun 1882 in Hatch, MO.

874. Nettie Myrtle MCCLINTOCK, 10G Granddaughter, born on 1 Dec 1884 in Hatch, MO.

875. Orie Lawrence MCCLINTOCK, 10G Grandson, born on 15 Feb 1888 in Hatch, MO.

Family of Levin LAWRENCE (582) and Florence MURPHEY

876. Musa LAWRENCE, 10G Granddaughter, born on 25 May 1877 in Lincoln Co. MO. Musa died in 1877 in Lincoln Co. MO.

877. Charles Larkin LAWRENCE, 10G Grandson, born on 12 May 1879 in Lincoln Co. MO. Charles Larkin died in Oakdale, Stanislaus Co. CA, on 12 Jun 1923; he was 44.

On 27 Dec 1902 when Charles Larkin was 23, he married Grace Darling BARNHART, born on 17 Jan 1884 in Columbus, Franklin Co. OH. They had one child:
    1306   i.   Hazel (1904-)

878. Verdie LAWRENCE, 10G Grandson, born on 15 Jul 1883 in MO. Died in Bowling Green, MO, on 25 Aug 1905.

879. Leone LAWRENCE, 10G Grandson, born on 4 Dec 1890 in MO.

880. Everett Curtis LAWRENCE, 10G Grandson, born on 17 Feb 1892 in MO.

881. Raymond Vance LAWRENCE, 10G Grandson, born on 29 Apr 1895 in MO.

Family of Florence Elizabeth STEELE (586) and --- MARTIN

882. Harry MARTIN.

Family of Annie Stansbury COCKEY (596) and Edward Dawes MCCONKY

883. Mary Grafton MCCONKY, 10G Granddaughter, born on 16 Aug 1867. Mary Grafton died about 1879.

884. Edward Dawes MCCONKY, 10G Grandson, born on 11 May 1877 in Baltimore Co. MD. Edward Dawes died in Baltimore Co. MD, on 3 Mar 1963; he was 85.

On 29 Nov 1904 when Edward Dawes was 27, he married Nellie Brown LASSITER, in Baltimore Co. MD. They had one child:
    1307   i.   Eleanor

Family of Mordecai Gist COCKEY (597) and Olivia "Ollie" SLADE

885. Mary Etta COCKEY, 10G Granddaughter, born on 17 Feb 1874. Mary Etta died on 5 Jul 1965; she was 91. Unmarried.

886. John Robert COCKEY, 10G Grandson, born on 1 Oct 1875 in Baltimore Co. MD. Lived in Roanoke VA.

John Robert married Eva JONES.

887. Edward Randolph COCKEY, 10G Grandson, born on 18 Jun 1877 in Baltimore Co. MD. Edward Randolph died in Baltimore Co. MD, on 11 Feb 1913; he was 35.

On 30 Nov 1908 when Edward Randolph was 31, he married Ellen LUCAS, in Baltimore Co. MD. They had one child:
    1308   i.   Randolph Lucas (1910-1967)

888. Anna Griselda COCKEY, 10G Granddaughter, born on 13 Apr 1879. Anna Griselda died on 7 Jan 1974; she was 94. Unmarried.

889. William Warfield COCKEY, 10G Grandson, born on 14 Oct 1880 in Baltimore Co. MD. William Warfield died in Baltimore Co. MD, on 22 Jun 1923; he was 42.

William Warfield married --- FIRESTINE, EVANS. No issue.

890. Mordecai Gist COCKEY, 10G Grandson, born on 4 Aug 1884.

891. Sally Montgomery COCKEY, 10G Granddaughter, born on 3 Jul 1892. Sally Montgomery died on 21 Feb 1969; she was 76. Unmarried.

892. James Powell COCKEY, 10G Granddaughter, born on 3 Jul 1892.

Family of Mary Elizabeth COCKEY (598) and William Henry BOSLEY

893. William Henry BOSLEY, 10G Grandson.

William Henry married Ellen SCOTT.

894. Capt. John Robert BOSLEY, 10G Grandson. Surgeon in the U.S. Army.

John Robert married Gertie DANIELTON of Norway.

895. Marie Elise BOSLEY, 10G Granddaughter, born in Baltimore Co. MD.

On 1 Apr 1913 Marie Elise married Dr. William MANGES, in Baltimore Co. MD. X-ray specialist. This couple lived in Philadelphia, had two sons.

896. Chauncey Brooks BOSLEY, 10G Grandson, born in Baltimore Co. MD.

Chauncey Brooks married Alice HELM, daughter of Wilbur Taylor HELM, in Baltimore Co. MD. They had the following children:
1309	i.	Jean
1310	ii.	Chauncy Brooks
1311	iii.	William Henry

897. Harrryman Gist BOSLEY, 10G Grandson, born on 16 Jan 1894.

Harrryman Gist married Helen BARR.

898. Mollie BOSLEY 10G Granddaughter.

Family of Ann Rebecca COCKEY (601) and Stephen Brown STOCKSDALE (612)

899. Harry Cockey STOCKSDALE, 10G Grandson, born on 21 Apr 1867. Harry Cockey died in Finksburg MD, on 19 Jan 1898; he was 30.

On 27 Nov 1895 when Harry Cockey was 28, he married Grace Irene HITCHENS, born on 26 May 1870. Grace Irene died on 15 Dec 1932; she was 62. They had one child:
1312 i. John Hitchens (1896-1929)

900. Georgia Virginia STOCKSDALE, 10G Granddaughter, born on 2 Jun 1871. Georgia Virginia died on 12 Mar 1872; she was less than 1.

901. Mordecai Bramwell STOCKSDALE, 10G Grandson, born on 25 Apr 1875. Mordecai Bramwell died on 10 Feb 1926; he was 50.

On 19 Apr 1915 when Mordecai Bramwell was 39, he married Dorothea Elizabeth RADER, born on 9 Jun 1888.

Family of Lewis Henry STOCKSDALE (605) and Catherine E. GARDNER

902. Emma R. STOCKSDALE, 10G Granddaughter, born on 4 Jan 1854. Emma R. died on 4 Sep 1854; she was less than 1.

903. Annie Ida STOCKSDALE, 10G Granddaughter, born on 15 Aug 1857. Annie Ida died on 2 May 1922; she was 64.

Annie Ida married N. Dorsey NORRIS, born on 31 Oct 1850. N. Dorsey died on 30 May 1930; he was 79. They had one child:
1313 i. Elizabeth

904. Louisianna STOCKSDALE, 10G Granddaughter, born about 1859.

905. William G. STOCKSDALE, 10G Grandson, born on 22 Aug 1865. William G. died on 16 Jun 1902; he was 36.

906. Harry Cockey STOCKSDALE, 10G Grandson, born on 23 Mar 1868. Harry Cockey died on 18 Apr 1869; he was 1.

Family of John Thomas Cockey STOCKSDALE (608) and Eliza COOK

907. George Tevis STOCKSDALE, 10G Grandson, born on 25 Mar 1854. George Tevis died on 26 Apr 1938; he was 84.

George Tevis married Annie YOX. Annie died in Nov 1917. They had one child:
    1314   i.   Elizabeth Jane (1891-)

908. Dolly Maud STOCKSDALE, 10G Granddaughter, born on 4 Dec 1855. Dolly Maud died on 5 Jun 1943; she was 87.

909. Clara May STOCKSDALE, 10G Granddaughter, born on 5 May 1858. Clara May died on 17 Mar 1941; she was 82.

On 21 Jun 1892 when Clara May was 34, she married William Oliver BOLDEN, born on 22 Jan 1854. William Oliver died on 21 Jan 1932; he was 77. They had the following children:
    1315   i.   William (1893-)
    1316   ii.   Olie Mazie (1894-)
    1317   iii.   Lulu Lee (1899-1901)

910. Annie Howard STOCKSDALE, 10G Granddaughter, born on 28 Dec 1859. Annie Howard died on 27 Aug 1930; she was 70.

On 12 Apr 1888 when Annie Howard was 28, she married Harold Randolph MORGAN. Harold Randolph died on 1 Jul 1891. They had one child:
    1318   i.   Harold Randolph (1890-)

911. John Thomas Cockey STOCKSDALE, 10G Grandson, born on 12 Mar 1862. John Thomas Cockey died on 12 Jun 1913; he was 51.

912. Lillie Eliza STOCKSDALE, 10G Granddaughter, born on 10 May 1864.

On 28 Sep 1892 when Lillie Eliza was 28, she married William Butler DOWNES, born on 12 Aug 1860. William Butler died on 17 Jan 1917; he was 56. They had one child:
    1319   i.   William Beryl (1896-)

913. Gertrude STOCKSDALE, 10G Granddaughter, born on 13 Feb 1866. Gertrude died on 7 Apr 1950; she was 84.

914. Arthur Lee STOCKSDALE, 10G Grandson, born on 3 Feb 1870. Arthur Lee died on 22 Dec 1922; he was 52.

915. Howard Hewett STOCKSDALE, 10G Grandson, born on 25 May 1875.

On 22 Jun 1905 when Howard Hewett was 30, he married Katherine A. K. CARL, born on 30 Apr 1879. Katherine died on 29 Dec 1945; she was 66.

Family of Elias Cockey STOCKSDALE (609) and Martha WHALEN

916. William Vinton STOCKSDALE, 10G Grandson, born on 17 May 1850. William Vinton died on 7 Oct 1855; he was 5.

917. Rebecca Jane STOCKSDALE, 10G Granddaughter, born on 6 Sep 1852. Rebecca Jane died on 1 Jul 1938; she was 85.

918. Susannah STOCKSDALE, 10G Granddaughter, born on 2 Mar 1857. Susannah died on 12 Mar 1868; she was 11.

919. Elias Cockey STOCKSDALE, 10G Grandson, born on 2 Mar 1857. Elias Cockey died on 10 Jul 1912; he was 55.

Family of Stephen Brown STOCKSDALE (612) and Mary Jane "Jennie" PATTERSON

920. Rebecca Jane STOCKSDALE, 10G Granddaughter, born on 26 Mar 1899.

On 26 Apr 1930 when Rebecca Jane was 31, she married Leroy L. STUMP, born on 17 Mar 1900. Leroy L. died on 9 Feb 1951; he was 50.

Family of Ruth Ann Elizabeth STOCKSDALE (613) and Theodore Wesley BASEMAN

921. Emma Dolly BASEMAN, 10G Granddaughter, born on 12 Aug 1858 in Baltimore Co. MD. Emma Dolly died in MD on 7 Oct 1924; she was 66.

In Jul 1887 Emma Dolly married Irving GOSNELL, in MD. They had the following children:
- 1320   i.   Bernard
- 1321   ii. Edna (-1919)

922. Fannie Howard BASEMAN, 10G Granddaughter, born on 5 Feb 1860 in Baltimore Co. MD. Fannie Howard died in Finksburg MD, on 20 May 1941; she was 81.

On 25 Jan 1881 when Fannie Howard was 20, she married Thomas N. IRELAND, in Carroll Co. MD, born on 8 Oct 1858. Thomas N. died on 17 Oct 1939; he was 81. Obituaries for both per Field. They had the following children:
- 1322   i.   Thomas Moale (1882-1961)
- 1323   ii.   Jack
- 1324   iii. Norris Ireland (1885-)
- 1325   iv.   Frank Howard (1891-)
- 1326   v.   Deborah "Fannie" (1891-1983)
- 1327   vi.   Julia
- 1328   vii. Campbell Charles (about 1903 - about 1975)

923. Julie Ann BASEMAN, 10G Granddaughter, born on 30 Jun 1862 in Baltimore Co. MD. Julie Ann died in Baltimore Co. MD, on 20 Nov 1925; she was 63. Buried Lutheran Cemetery Reisterstown MD.

924. Ellen Bedford BASEMAN, 10G Granddaughter, born on 28 Jun 1864 in Baltimore Co. MD.

925. Dora Florence BASEMAN, 10G Granddaughter, born on 24 Oct 1866 in Baltimore Co. MD.

926. Grant T. BASEMAN, 10G Grandson, born on 15 Dec 1868 in Baltimore Co. MD. Additional source: *Carroll County Times* obituary dated 26 Jan 1986 per Field.

Grant T. married Rosse YOX. They had one child:
- 1329   i.   Grant A. (about 1918-1986)

927. Littlewood Alfred BASEMAN, 10G Grandson, born on 15 Feb 1872 in Baltimore Co. MD. Littlewood died in Baltimore Co. MD, on 20 Oct 1878; he was 6.

928. Rosa Estella BASEMAN, 10G Granddaughter, born on 1 Sep 1874 in Baltimore Co. MD. Rosa Estella died in Baltimore Co. MD, on 18 Oct 1878; she was 4.

929. Grace Ruth Ann BASEMAN, 10G Granddaughter, born on 28 Dec 1876 in Baltimore Co. MD.

930. Ray F. BASEMAN, 10G Grandson, born on 1 May 1879. Ray F. died on 7 Feb 1882; he was 2.

931. May Pauline BASEMAN, 10G Granddaughter, born on 1 May 1879 in Baltimore Co. MD. May Pauline died in Baltimore Co. MD, on 7 Feb 1882; she was 2.

Family of Joseph OSBORN (616) and Nancy PENNINGTON

932. Solomon OSBORN, 10G Grandson, born on 21 Dec 1804 in NC. Solomon died in McDonough Co. IL, on 9 Sep 1878; he was 73.

On 15 May 1824 when Solomon was 19, he first married Dicey SMITH, in Hamilton Co. IL, born on 3 Apr 1808 in NC. Dicey died in Industry, McDonough Co. IL, on 15 Nov 1861; she was 53. They had the following children:

1330	i.	Joseph (1825-)
1331	ii.	William M. (1827-)
1332	iii.	Elizabeth (1829-)
1333	iv.	Lydia (1830-)
1334	v.	Isaac (1832 - before 1878)
1335	vi.	Nancy (1835-)
1336	vii.	Mary Smith (1836-1880)
1337	viii.	Francis Marion (1838-1901)
1338	ix.	Elijah S. (1841-1901)
1339	x.	Louisa (1842-1913)
1340	xi.	M. Jane (1844-)
1341	xii.	Aurena (1847-)
1342	xiii.	Dicy Ann (1850-1919)
1343	xiv.	Alfria (1851 - before 1878)
1344	xv.	Lucinda (1851-)

On 14 Jun 1866 when Solomon was 61, he second married Elsa JOHNSON, in McDonough Co. IL, born in 1835 in IN. They had the following children:

1345	i.	Ada Louella (1866-)
1346	ii.	Sarah Almeda (1868-)
1347	iii.	Lorina (1871-1949)
1348	iv.	Dora Alice (1873-1947)
1349	v.	John (1874-)
1350	vi.	Noah Webster (1876-1943)
1351	vii.	Henry C. (1877-)

933. Lydia OSBORN, 10G Granddaughter, born in 1809 in IL. Lydia died in 1859 in Adair Co. KY.

On 27 May 1826 Lydia married Ephraim OSBORNE, son of John OSBORNE and Sarah "Sally" STEWART, in Vermillion Co. IL, born in 1804 in NC. Ephraim died in 1880 in Harrison Co. MO. They had the following children:

1352	i.	Mary Jane (1828-)
1353	ii.	John (1833-)
1354	iii.	Eliza (1835-)
1355	iv.	Joseph (1838-)
1356	v.	Andrew Jackson (1847-)
1357	vi.	Daniel Boone (1850 - about 1920)
1358	vii.	Francis (1852-)

934. John OSBORN, 10G Grandson, born in 1810 in NC.

On 21 Jan 1830 John married Frances HACKWORTH, in Vermillion Co. IL, born in 1810 in IN. They had the following children:

1359	i.	Susannah (1830-)
1360	ii.	Sarah (1833-)
1361	iii.	Andrew J. (1835-)
1362	iv.	Daniel (1836-)

1363	v.	Hiram (1838-)
1364	vi.	James (1840-)
1365	vii.	Martha (1843-)
1366	viii.	Robert (1846-)
1367	ix.	Isaac (1851-)
1368	x.	John (1853-)

935. Stephen Jones OSBORN, 10G Grandson, born in 1812 in NC.

On 8 Sep 1852 Stephen Jones married Julian SIMPSON. They had the following children:
| 1369 | i. | Jasper (about 1854-) |
| 1370 | ii. | Lydia (1856-) |

936. Sabrina OSBORN, 10G Granddaughter, born in 1818 in IL.

On 9 Jan 1837 Sabrina married John MAYFIELD, in McDonough Co. IL, born in 1812 in TN. They had the following children:
1371	i.	Joseph (1842-)
1372	ii.	James (1845-)
1373	iii.	Nancy (1848-)

937. Andrew Jackson OSBORN, 10G Grandson, born in 1825 in IL. Andrew Jackson died after 1880.

On 11 Mar 1841 Andrew Jackson married Elizabeth COCKERHAM, daughter of Stephen COCKERHAM and Rachel OSBORN, in McDonough Co. IL, born on 8 Jul 1823. Elizabeth died before 1880 in McDonough Co. IL. They had the following children:
1374	i.	Louisa (1844-)
1375	ii.	Abner (1846-)
1376	iii.	Rachel A. (1849-)
1377	iv.	Stephen (1855-1944)
1378	v.	Finis (1858-)
1379	vi.	Joseph (1863-)

Family of James OSBORN (617) and Ruth OSBORN (627)

938. Solomon OSBORN, 10G Grandson, born about 1816 in IN.

939. Amalthea OSBORN, 10G Granddaughter, born in 1821 in IN.

In Sep 1844 Amalthea married Peter CRABTREE, in Champaign Co. IL.

940. Robert Patient OSBORN, 10G Grandson, born about 1825 in IL.

Robert Patient married Esther ---, born about 1830 in OH.

941. Elizabeth OSBORN, 10G Granddaughter, born in 1827 in IL.

On 29 Jan 1844 Elizabeth married Fielding W. STEWART, in Champaign Co. IL.

942. Clarissa OSBORN, 10G Granddaughter, born about 1830 in IL.

On 7 Sep 1854 Clarissa married Joseph S. MARTIN, in Champaign Co. IL, born about 1830.

943. Noah OSBORN, 10G Grandson, born about 1832 in IL.

944. Julia Ann OSBORN, 10G Granddaughter, born about 1834 in IL.

On 12 Feb 1852 Julia Ann married Joseph WRIGHT, in Champaign Co. IL, born in 1830.

945. Jonathan B. OSBORN, 10G Grandson, born about 1837 in IL.

946. Martha C. OSBORN, 10G Granddaughter, born about 1839 in IL.

947. Elmira OSBORN, 10G Granddaughter, born about 1841 in IL.

Family of Doddridge ALLEY (626) and Jane PHILLIPS

948. William W. ALLEY, 10G Grandson, born on 1 Nov 1810 in KY.

William W. married Angeline MARTIN, born in 1815 in KY. They had one child:
   1380   i.   Emily Savannah (1843-)

Family of Joseph OSBORN (628) and Lydia COPELAND

949. Cynthia OSBORN, 10G Granddaughter, born about 1822 in IL.

Cynthia married Philip STANFORD.

950. Serena OSBORN, 10G Granddaughter, born about 1825 in IL.

On 10 Dec 1849 Serena married McDonald OSBORN, born about 1814 in KY.

951. Angeline OSBORN, 10G Granddaughter, born about 1828 in IL.

Angeline married Nathaniel H. TOWNER.

952. Green OSBORN, 10G Grandson, born about 1828 in IL.

953. Mary OSBORN, 10G Granddaughter, born about 1831 in IL.

Mary married Charles W. TRIMM, born about 1828 in TN.

954. Malinda OSBORN, 10G Granddaughter, born about 1832 in IL.

955. Lurilla OSBORN, 10G Granddaughter, born about 1834 in IL.

956. Joseph OSBORN, 10G Grandson, born about 1842 in IL.

Family of James OSBORN (631) and Christianna "Ann" SOUDER

957. Mary A. OSBORN, 10G Granddaughter, born about 1833 in IL.

958. Adelaide OSBORN, 10G Granddaughter, born about 1835 in IL.

959. Phillip OSBORN, 10G Grandson, born about 1839 in MO.

Family of James OSBORN (631) and Mary WRIGHT

960. George OSBORN, 10G Grandson, born about 1847 in MO. George died before 1883.

961. Lewis OSBORN, 10G Grandson, born about 1848.

962. Martha OSBORN, 10G Granddaughter, born about 1849.

Martha married W.J. COX.

963. Byron W. OSBORN, 10G Grandson, born about 1850.

Family of Joanna OSBORN (632) and George Washington WAKEFIELD

964. William WAKEFIELD, 10G Grandson, born in 1827.

965. John Allen WAKEFIELD, 10G Grandson, born in 1831.

966. Susan WAKEFIELD, 10G Granddaughter, born in 1833.

967. Almeda WAKEFIELD, 10G Granddaughter, born in 1834. Almeda died on 27 Nov 1878.

968. Martha Adeline WAKEFIELD, 10G Granddaughter, born on 15 Aug 1838. Martha Adeline died on 16 Dec 1911; she was 73.

969. Dianna WAKEFIELD, 10G Granddaughter, born in 1843.

970. Ruth Emma WAKEFIELD, 10G Granddaughter, born on 18 Sep 1846.

971. George Washington WAKEFIELD, 10G Grandson, born in 1849. George Washington died on 11 Oct 1931.

Family of Comfort OSBORNE (641) and Solomon DRACE

972. Mary Elizabeth DRACE, 10G Granddaughter.

On 26 Dec 1837 Mary Elizabeth married Martin JOHNSON.

Family of Sarah "Sally" OSBORNE (642) and Silas DRACE

973. William Thomas "W.T." DRACE, 10G Grandson, born on 16 Mar 1839 in Franklin Co. MO. William Thomas "W.T." died after 1900. Physician.

William Thomas "W.T." married Francesca CHILES.

974. Annie Rebecca DRACE, 10G Granddaughter. Annie Rebecca died in Montgomery Co. MO.

On 18 Dec 1860 Annie Rebecca married Archibald WHITE.

975. Minerva DRACE, 10G Granddaughter. Minerva died in Franklin Co. MO.

On 15 Dec 1870 Minerva married James GIERSA.

976. Scott DRACE, 10G Grandson. Scott died in Phoenix AZ.

977. Mary Francis "Polly" DRACE, 10G Granddaughter, born on 7 May 1843 in Franklin Co. MO. Mary Francis "Polly" died in Lockwood, Dade Co. MO, on 7 Dec 1922; she was 79.

On 8 Nov 1865 when Mary Francis "Polly" was 22, she married David Campbell MALONEY, son of Campbell MALONEY and Eliza POLLARD, in Washington, Franklin Co. MO, born on 27 Apr 1836 in Aspinwall, Charlotte Co. VA. David Campbell died in Lockwood, Dade Co. MO, on 6 Nov 1923; he was 87. "David Campbell Maloney was a blacksmith near St. Louis Mo. His cordwood was delivered by a local farmer named U.S. Grant. Served in the Confederate Army under Gen. Sterling Price" (Pj Sessick citing James Maloney and her aunt Mary Dean). They had the following children:

1381	i.	Sara Eliza "Sadie" (1866-1956)
1382	ii.	William Archibald (1868-1935)
1383	iii.	Amanda Lee (1869-)
1384	iv.	Eda Lurene (1872-)
1385	v.	Eugene Pollard (1874-1953)
1386	vi.	David Crocket (1880-)
1387	vii.	Frank Sterling (1885-)

978. James A. DRACE, 10G Grandson. James A. died in Lafayette MO.

979. S.S. "Donnie" DRACE, 10G Grandson. S.S. "Donnie" died in Fayette MO.

On 22 Nov 1876 S.S. "Donnie" married E.W. BUSH.

980. Emma Laura DRACE, 10G Granddaughter. Emma Laura died in Fayette MO.

On 8 Jan 1876 Emma Laura married Alburn CHILES.

981. Charles P. DRACE, 10G Grandson. Charles P. died in Aurora MO.

Family of Annis DOLLARHIDE (648) and Jonathan COMPTON

982. Margaret Susan COMPTON, 10G Granddaughter.

Margaret Susan married Hugh Bell SMITH. They had one child:
1388	i.	Sally

Family of Franklin LANHAM (668) and Mrs. Margaret JORDAN

983. Unity LANHAM, 10G Granddaughter, born in 1840 in MS.

On 28 Feb 1860 Unity married James O. WILLIAMS, in Bienville Parish, LA.

984. Abel LANHAM, 10G Grandson, born in 1843 in LA.

985. Elizabeth LANHAM, 10G Granddaughter, born on 10 Jan 1846 in Bienville Parish, LA. Elizabeth died in Post, Garza Co. TX, on 14 Mar 1929; she was 83.

On 16 Aug 1870 when Elizabeth was 24, she married John Thomas JAMES, in Coryell Co. TX, born on 6 Sep 1848 in Limestone Co. TX. John Thomas died in Post, Garza Co. TX, on 28 Nov 1913; he was 65. Their children were:

1389	i.	John Wesley (1873-1917)
1390	ii.	Mittie (1876-)
1391	iii.	Allan

986. Sophenia LANHAM, 10G Granddaughter, born in 1849 in LA.

Family of Franklin LANHAM (668) and Elizabeth SANDERS

987. Solomon J. LANHAM, 10G Grandson, born in 1864 in AL.

988. Nancy J. LANHAM, 10G Granddaughter, born in 1865 in AL.

Family of Jane LANHAM (669) and Ira J. MITCHELL

989. Frank L. MITCHELL, 10G Grandson.

Family of Lucinda LANHAM (670) and Angus DAWKINS

990. Mary DAWKINS, 10G Granddaughter, born in Bienville Parish, LA.

991. Jackson DAWKINS, 10G Grandson, born in Bienville Parish, LA.

992. Abigail DAWKINS, 10G Granddaughter.

993. Ophelia DAWKINS, 10G Granddaughter.

Family of Lucinda LANHAM (670) and Daniel N. DAVIS

994. William L. DAVIS, 10G Grandson.

995. Christian DAVIS, 10G Grandson.

996. Cynthia DAVIS, 10G Granddaughter.

997. James DAVIS, 10G Grandson.

Family of Randolph LANHAM (672) and Jalie Wood ROBERTS

998. Solomon Thomas LANHAM, 10G Grandson, born on 23 Aug 1835 in MS.

On 20 Apr 1856 when Solomon Thomas was 20, he married Sara MASON, in Smith Co. TX, born on 19 Jan 1835 in IN. Sara died in Hunt Co. TX, on 5 Jun 1873; she was 38. They had the following children:

1392	i.	Elizabeth
1393	ii.	Matilda
1394	iii.	Randolph

1395	iv.	Frank
1396	v.	Abe
1397	vi.	Mary

999. Mary A. LANHAM, 10G Granddaughter, born on 22 Dec 1837. Mary A. died on 8 Sep 1838; she was less than 1.

1000. Cynthia Elizabeth LANHAM, 10G Granddaughter, born on 28 Nov 1839 in Nashoba Co. MS. Cynthia Elizabeth died in Jack Co. TX, on 18 Aug 1905; she was 65. Buried in Cundiff Cemetery, Jack Co. TX.

On 12 Jan 1860 when Cynthia Elizabeth was 20, she married Josiah Washington EVANS, in Smith Co. TX, born on 28 Jan 1835 in Newton Co. GA. Josiah Washington died in Jack Co. TX, on 24 Dec 1901; he was 66. Buried in Cundiff Cemetery, Jack Co. TX. They had the following children:

1398	i.	Emma Abigail (1861-1939)
1399	ii.	William Randolph (1863-1864)
1400	iii.	Ora Lee (1865-1950)
1401	iv.	Joe Boomer (1868-1954)
1402	v.	John Benton (1870-1957)
1403	vi.	Susan James (1872-1873)
1404	vii.	George Washington (1874-1874)
1405	viii.	Erby Doyle (1874-1947)
1406	ix.	Cintha Theodisia (1877-1878)
1407	x.	Josiah Theodore (1877-1894)

1001. Abel LANHAM, 10G Grandson, born on 12 Nov 1841. Abel died on 9 Dec 1841; he was less than 1.

1002. Joseph B. LANHAM, 10G Grandson, born on 22 Dec 1842.

Joseph B. married Mary POWELL. They had the following children:

1408	i.	Jodie
1409	ii.	Annie
1410	iii.	Lizzie

1003. John Castleton LANHAM, 10G Grandson, born on 4 Nov 1844.

On 2 Jan 1868 when John Castleton was 23, he married R. Josephine ---, in Hunt Co. TX. They had the following children:

1411	i.	Benton
1412	ii.	Jim
1413	iii.	Docia
1414	iv.	Mary Elizabeth (1876-1967)
1415	v.	Jaley
1416	vi.	Myrtle
1417	vii.	Lela
1418	viii.	Charlie
1419	ix.	Jodie
1420	x.	Bonnie

1004. Sarah Jane LANHAM, 10G Granddaughter, born on 17 Jul 1847 in Bienville Parish, LA. Sarah Jane died in Kaufman Co. TX, on 2 Sep 1926; she was 79. Buried in Wilson Chapel Cemetery, Kaufman Co. TX.

On 26 Jul 1865 when Sarah Jane was 18, she married Shadrack James CONNER, son of Thomas CONNER and Ruth DENSON, in Navarro Co. TX, born in 1836 in Bond Co. IL. Shadrack died on 11 Aug 1911 in Kaufman Co. TX. Buried in Wilson Chapel Cemetery, Kaufman Co. TX. They had the following children:

1421	i.	Mary Angelina (1866-)
1422	ii.	Lucy (1869-1940)
1423	iii.	Jaley (1870-1913)
1424	iv.	Ruth (1872-1945)
1425	v.	Thomas Randolph (1875-1937)

1426	vi.	Emma (1877-1913)
1427	vii.	Elizabeth (1878-)
1428	viii.	Theodicia (1881-1948)
1429	ix.	Edwin Joseph (1881-1949)
1430	x.	Charlie B. (1887-1953)

1005. Jailie Ann LANHAM, 10G Granddaughter, born on 25 Aug 1849. Jailie Ann died in Coleman Co. TX, on 24 Jan 1931; she was 81.

On 6 Dec 1866 when Jailie Ann was 17, she first married James Rufus EVANS, born on 24 Dec 1839 in Troup Co. GA. James Rufus died in Coleman Co. TX, on 11 Jan 1922; he was 82. They had the following children:

1431	i.	Cora Lee (1868-)
1432	ii.	Charlie Randolph (1869-1933)
1433	iii.	James Bunyan (1872-1880)
1434	iv.	Susan Exer (1874-)
1435	v.	William Walter (1879-1944)
1436	vi.	Joseph Walter (1882-1943)
1437	vii.	Claude Max (1884-)

Aft 1889 Jailie Ann second married --- PAYNE.

1006. Rachel Lucinda LANHAM, 10G Granddaughter, born on 16 Mar 1851.

Rachel Lucinda married Sam PAYNE.

1007. Margaret Narcissa LANHAM, 10G Granddaughter, born on 11 Feb 1853.

Margaret Narcissa first married Columbus G. EVANS, born on 7 Feb 1847 in Smith Co. TX. Columbus G. died in Parker Co. TX. They had the following children:

1438	i.	John E.
1439	ii.	Mary O.
1440	iii.	Albert M.
1441	iv.	William G.

On 13 Mar 1873 when Margaret Narcissa was 20, she second married Joseph W. JOLLY, in Hunt Co. TX. They had one child:

1442	i.	May

1008. Samuel LANHAM, 10G Grandson, born on 17 Jun 1854. Samuel died on 17 Jun 1854; he was less than 1.

1009. Hannah Theodicia LANHAM, 10G Granddaughter, born on 22 Jul 1856.

On 28 Mar 1886 when Hannah Theodicia was 29, she married Robert HEROLD, in Hunt Co. TX. They had the following children:

1443	i.	Sadie
1444	ii.	James
1445	iii.	Joe
1446	iv.	Evelyn
1447	v.	Johnson

Family of Minerva Ann LANHAM (673) and Charles GILLEY

1010. Mary A. GILLEY, 10G Granddaughter.

Mary A. married Robert REYNOLDS.

1011. Thomas Newton GILLEY, 10G Grandson.

1012. John Solomon GILLEY, 10G Grandson.

1013. William Robert GILLEY, 10G Grandson.

1014. Susan Margaret GILLEY, 10G Granddaughter.

Susan Margaret married William M. CARR.

1015. Eula GILLEY, 10G Granddaughter.

Family of Bedford LANHAM (674) and Georgia Louisiana FRIEND

1016. Maria Jane Curtis LANHAM, 10G Granddaughter, born on 14 Sep 1851 in Troup, Smith Co. TX. Maria Jane Curtis died in El Paso, Hudspeth Co. TX, on 19 Oct 1923; she was 72. Buried in Pauls Valley OK.

On 30 Aug 1870 when Maria Jane Curtis was 18, she married Holland Coffey RANDOLPH, son of James Mayberry RANDOLPH and Tabitha Jerucha SHELTON, in Smith Co. TX, born on 10 Sep 1845 in Sherman, Grayson Co. TX. Holland died in Pauls Valley, Garvin Co. OK, on 6 Jun 1921; he was 75. Buried in Mt. Olivet Cemetery, Garvin Co. OK. They had the following children:

1448	i.	Olive Louisa (1873-1943)
1449	ii.	Laura Alice (1875-)
1450	iii.	Ella Mae (1878-1879)
1451	iv.	Joseph Edwin (1880-)
1452	v.	Ora Vivian (1882-)
1453	vi.	Cora Belle (1885-)
1454	vii.	Eula Tobitha (1888-)
1455	viii.	Raymond Coffee (1890-)
1456	ix.	James Bedford (1894-)
1457	x.	William Wirt (1896-1973)

1017. Samuel LANHAM, 10G Grandson, born on 11 Nov 1853 in Troup, Smith Co. TX. Samuel died in TX on 26 Jun 1854; he was less than 1.

1018. Mary Margaret LANHAM, 10G Granddaughter, born on 4 May 1855 in Troup, Smith Co. TX. Mary Margaret died in Dallas, Dallas Co. TX, on 13 Nov 1938; she was 83. Buried in Fairmont Cemetery, San Angelo TX.

On 31 Aug 1873 when Mary Margaret was 18, she married Reuben Thomas BATES, son of William BATES and Rosa C. KEITH, in Gatesville, Coryell Co. TX, born on 27 Sep 1847 in Murray Co. GA. Reuben died in San Angelo, Tom Green Co. TX, on 4 Mar 1935; he was 87. Buried in Fairmont Cemetery, San Angelo TX. They had the following children:

1458	i.	Beulah Ann (1874-1973)
1459	ii.	Luther Edwin (1876-1930)
1460	iii.	Flora Alice (1880-1956)
1461	iv.	James Carroll (1882-1946)
1462	v.	Doctor Kiefer (1885-1887)
1463	vi.	Isaac Whitt (1887-1919)
1464	vii.	Mary Elizabeth (1891-1984)
1465	viii.	Fannie Mae (1894-1984)
1466	ix.	Harriett Lanham (1898-1984)

1019. James Millard LANHAM, 10G Grandson, born on 17 May 1858 in Coryell Co. TX. James Millard died in Fort Worth, Tarrant Co. TX. Buried in Rosehill Cemetery, Fort Worth, Tarrant Co. TX.

In 1886 James Millard married Fannie L. BISHOP, in TX, born in 1868 in TX. Three additional children reported but not named below. They had the following children:

1467	i.	Anna
1468	ii.	Bedford
1469	iii.	Carolyn Bethal
1470	iv.	Inez
1471	v.	James B.
1472	vi.	Samuel
1473	vii.	Frank Millard (1900-1968)

1020. Georgia Alice LANHAM, 10G Granddaughter, born on 5 May 1861 in Coryell Co. TX. Georgia Alice died on 24 Aug 1889; she was 28.

Georgia Alice married Sam LANDIS. They had the following children:

1474	i.	John M.
1475	ii.	Robert
1476	iii.	Frank

1021. Robert Edward Lee LANHAM, 10G Grandson, born on 9 Feb 1864 in Coryell Co. TX. Robert Edward Lee died in Coryell Co. TX, on 20 Nov 1884; he was 20.

1022. Franklin LANHAM, 10G Grandson, born on 19 Feb 1865 in Coryell Co. TX. Franklin died in Coryell Co. TX, on 23 Apr 1865; he was less than 1.

1023. Monroe LANHAM, 10G Grandson, born on 4 Mar 1868.

Monroe married Dovie THOMPSON.

1024. Annie Maud LANHAM, 10G Granddaughter, born on 5 Jan 1872 in Coryell Co. TX. Annie Maud died on 14 May 1962; she was 90.

On 19 Feb 1891 when Annie Maud was 19, she married Benjamin Thomas CROWLEY, in Gatesville, Coryell Co. TX, born on 27 Aug 1862. They had one child:

1477	i.	Joseph Lanham (1894-)

1025. Edwin Friend LANHAM, 10G Grandson, born on 11 Aug 1874 in Coryell Co. TX. Edwin Friend died in TX on 20 Aug 1933; he was 59. Buried in Hillcrest Cemetery, Bell Co. TX.

In 1901 Edwin Friend married Josephine MULLINS, in TX, born in 1879 in TX. Josephine died in 1944 in TX. Buried in Hillcrest Cemetery, Bell Co. TX. They had two children. One child reported but not named.

1478	i.	Edwin Friend (1905-1976)

Family of Samuel LANHAM (676) and Elizabeth ---

1026. William S. LANHAM, 10G Grandson, born in 1851 in Smith Co. TX.

William S. married Celie BARRON. They had one child:

1479	i.	Frank H. (1883-1973)

1027. Franklin C. LANHAM, 10G Grandson, born on 9 Oct 1854 in TX. Franklin C. died in Smith Co. TX, on 7 Jul 1936; he was 81. Buried in Salem Cemetery, Smith Co. TX.

In 1874 Franklin C. married Eliza Jane WILSON, in TX, born on 18 Aug 1857 in TX. Eliza Jane died in TX on 14 Jul 1935; she was 77. Buried in Salem Cemetery, Smith Co. TX. They had the following children:

1480	i.	Beatrice (1875-)
1481	ii.	William S. (1878-1926)

1482	iii.	John H. (1886-1961)
1483	iv.	Cynthia (1887-)
1484	v.	Jefferson David (1890-1980)
1485	vi.	James Carroll (1898-1990)

Family of Cynthia LANHAM (677) and Aaron W. WEEKS

1028. Samuel WEEKS, 10G Grandson, born in 1849. Child:
1486	i.	Lula

Family of Cynthia LANHAM (677) and Ezequiel BARRON

1029. Ophelia BARRON, 10G Granddaughter, born on 20 Aug 1856. Ophelia died in Smith Co. TX, on 2 Jun 1928; she was 71.

Ophelia married P.M. WILSON.

1030. Caleb Ezekiel BARRON, 10G Grandson, born on 12 Oct 1858 in Smith Co. TX. Caleb Ezekiel died in Smith Co. TX, on 21 Sep 1946; he was 87. Buried in Ebenezer Cemetery, Smith Co. TX.

Caleb Ezekiel married Mary A. ---, born on 9 Oct 1862. Mary A. died in Smith Co. TX, on 25 Mar 1916; she was 53. Buried in Ebenezer Cemetery, Smith Co. TX. They had one child:
1487	i.	Hattie (1884-1885)

1031. Solomon BARRON, 10G Grandson, born on 5 Dec 1861 in Smith Co. TX. Solomon died in Smith Co. TX, on 14 Jan 1934; he was 72.

Family of Cynthia LANHAM (677) and E. JARVIS

1032. Ada JARVIS, 10G Granddaughter, born on 12 Sep 1868. Ada died in Smith Co. TX, on 2 Dec 1947; she was 79.

Ada married J.H. MURPH, born in Jul 1857. J.H. died on 7 Dec 1920 in Smith Co. TX.

1033. Rob JARVIS, 10G Grandson, born in Jan 1872.

Family of Louisa Worthington BROWN (683) and Caleb Dorsey DAVIS

1034. John Brown DAVIS, 10G Grandson, born on 11 Dec 1819. John Brown died on 11 Feb 1889; he was 69.

John Brown married Betty BARLIN.

1035. Elizabeth DAVIS, 10G Granddaughter, born in Oct 1821. Elizabeth died in 1827.

1036. Hon. Henry Gassaway DAVIS, 10G Grandson, born on 16 Nov 1823 in Howard Co. MD. Worked with the Baltimore and Ohio Railroad for several years, then moved to Piedmont WV where he became involved in banking and mining, rose to presidency of the Piedmont National Bank and there constructed a large brick school building as a gift to the town. Founder and President of the West Virginia Railroad, later the Piedmont and Cumberland Railroad, President of the Davis Coal and Coke Company, held interests in the lumber business as well. Elected 1865 to the WV House of Delegates and in 1868 as a state senator. In 1871 he became U.S. Senator and was re-elected in 1877.

On 22 Feb 1853 when Henry Gassaway was 29, he married Katherine A. S. BANTZ, born in Frederick MD. They had the following children:

1488	i.	Hallie Louise (1854-)
1489	ii.	Kate Bantz (1856-)
1490	iii.	Anderson Cord (1859-)
1491	iv.	Ada Kate (1865-)
1492	v.	Grace Thomas (1869-)
1493	vi.	Henry Gassaway (1871-1894)
1494	vii.	John Thomas (1874-)

1037. Eliza Ann DAVIS, 10G Granddaughter, born on 10 Dec 1825.

Eliza Ann married Upton BUXTON. They had the following children:

1495	i.	Fannie Brown
1496	ii.	Mollie
1497	iii.	Henry Gassaway
1498	iv.	Blanche

1038. Hon. Thomas Beale DAVIS, 10G Grandson, born on 25 Apr 1828.

1039. William R. DAVIS, 10G Grandson, born on 27 Aug 1832. William R. died in 1879.

William R. married Mollie TILLSON. They had the following children:

1499	i.	Mary Tillson
1500	ii.	Matilda
1501	iii.	William R.
1502	iv.	Thomas Beale (1875-)

Family of Elizabeth A. BROWN (688) and Peter GORMAN

1040. Honorable Arthur Pue GORMAN, 10G Grandson. U.S. Senator.

Family of Samuel BROWN (689) and Elizabeth JENKINS

1041. Henry BROWN, 10G Grandson.

1042. Samuel Thomas BROWN, 10G Grandson, born in 1847. "... formerly of Woodstock, Howard County, Md., held many offices of trust and emolument in his native county prior to 1878, when he removed to Baltimore City, to enter into its commercial life. Is a prominent Democrat and frequently takes part in the councils of his party" (Mackenzie, Vol. I, p. 46).

In 1883 Samuel Thomas married Lydia BROME, daughter of Nathaniel Wilson BROME and Anne Harriet BROOKE, born on 7 Nov 1858 in Calvert Co. MD. They had one child:

1503	i.	Florence (1885-)

1043. Charles BROWN, 10G Grandson.

1044. Frank D. BROWN, 10G Grandson, born in 1853.

Frank D. married Louise DAVIS, daughter of William DAVIS and Sarah GORSUCH. They had the following children:

1504	i.	Samuel
1505	ii.	Ruth Davis
1506	iii.	Francis Louise

1045. Josephine BROWN, 10G Granddaughter.

Family of Janet TODD (704) and Jacob JOHNSON

1046. Benjamin H. JOHNSON, 10G Grandson.

Family of Elizabeth TODD (707) and William JOHNSON

1047. Tom M. JOHNSON, 10G Grandson, born about 1848 in OH.

1048. Emma E. JOHNSON, 10G Granddaughter, born about 1849 in OH.

Family of Alexander TODD (709) and Elizabeth WITHROW

1049. David Withrow TODD, 10G Grandson, born on 4 Apr 1839 in Columbiana Co. OH. David Withrow died in Cleveland, Cuyahoga Co. OH, on 15 Aug 1893; he was 54.

On 11 Dec 1866 when David Withrow was 27, he married Rachel CURREN, in Columbiana Co. OH, born on 16 Sep 1846 in Columbiana Co. OH. Rachel died in Cleveland, Cuyahoga Co. OH, on 19 Jun 1893; she was 46.

Family of Edna TODD (711) and Peter STALEY

1050. Warfield D. STALEY, 10G Grandson, born on 7 May 1815 in Baltimore Co. MD. Warfield D. died in Springfield, Sangamon Co. IL, on 15 Sep 1898; he was 83.

On 19 Nov 1835 when Warfield D. was 20, he married Mary A. HORN, in Washington Co. MD, born on 4 Sep 1817 in Harrisburg, Dauphin Co. PA. Mary A. died on 8 Apr 1880; she was 62. They had the following children:
1507	i.	Louisa C. (about 1836-)
1508	ii.	William H. (1838-)
1509	iii.	Margaret I. (about 1842-)
1510	iv.	Charles E. (about 1844-)
1511	v.	John W. (1850-)

Family of Alexander TODD (722) and Eliza RAMSOWER

1051. Mary Ellen TODD, 10G Granddaughter, born on 12 Sep 1833 in Frederick Co. MD. Mary Ellen died in Carroll Co. MD, on 28 Feb 1916; she was 82.

Mary Ellen married Peter DAVIS, born on 9 Nov 1822 in Frederick Co. MD. Peter died in Carroll Co. MD, on 25 Jan 1900; he was 77. They had the following children:
1512	i.	Sarah E. (1854-)
1513	ii.	Upton L. (1858-)
1514	iii.	Virginia H.R. (1859-)
1515	iv.	Ira Rodney (1861-1933)
1516	v.	Lucy (1862-)
1517	vi.	Splientientiom (1865-)
1518	vii.	Tirzah (1867-1943)

1519	viii.	Henry W. (1868-)
1520	ix.	Walter F. (1871-)
1521	x.	Leanna (1872-)
1522	xi.	William (1874-)

1052. Ira A. TODD, 10G Grandson, born about 1833 in MD. Ira A. died before 1920.

1053. Rachel Ruth TODD, 10G Granddaughter, born on 8 Dec 1835 in MD. Rachel Ruth died in Hopeville, Clark Co. IA, on 30 Aug 1881; she was 45.

Rachel Ruth married Jepthah Entler TUCKER, born on 6 Dec 1828 in VA. Jepthah Entler died in Hopeville, Clark Co. IA, on 31 Dec 1886; he was 58. They had the following children, plus one not listed who died in infancy

1523	i.	Arthur B. (about 1857-)
1524	ii.	Lee Forest (1860-)
1525	iii.	Effie Kate (1862-1948)
1526	iv.	Jesse (about 1863-)
1527	v.	Margaret (about 1873-)
1528	vi.	Dewit (about 1876-)

1054. Janet TODD, 10G Granddaughter, born about 1837 in MD. Janet died before 1920.

1055. --- TODD, 10G Grandson, born about 1839 in MD. --- died before 1850 in MD.

1056. Margaret A. TODD, 10G Granddaughter, born about 1840 in MD. Margaret A. died after 1920.

Margaret A. married James F. THOMSON, born on 24 Jun 1831 in Franklin Co. VT. James F. died in 1895 in IL. They had the following children:

1529	i.	Cora A. (about 1860-)
1530	ii.	Ethel (about 1864 - about 1870)
1531	iii.	John C. (about 1867-)
1532	iv.	Susan E. (1870-)
1533	v.	Mary Edna (about 1871-)
1534	vi.	Kate A. (about 1874-)
1535	vii.	Maud (about 1883-)

1057. Susannah Cevelah TODD, 10G Granddaughter, born on 8 Mar 1843 in Carroll Co. MD. Susannah Cevelah died in Prescott, Linn Co. KS, on 12 Sep 1920; she was 77.

Susannah Cevelah married Harry Charles JOHNSON, born on 14 Sep 1834 in Cortland Co. NY. Harry Charles died in Kansas City, Wyandotte Co. KS, on 13 Feb 1913; he was 78. They had the following children:

1536	i.	Lewis Wallace (1862 - before 1930)
1537	ii.	Eliza May (about 1864 - about 1864)
1538	iii.	Laclede Todd (1868-1938)
1539	iv.	Nettie Maude (1876-1918)
1540	v.	Ernest V. (1879-1956)
1541	vi.	Essie P. (1882-)
1542	vii.	Gladys Ethel (1890-1967)

1058. Benjamin Warfield TODD, 10G Grandson, born on 13 Oct 1846 in Carroll Co. MD. Benjamin Warfield died in Edmond, Oklahoma Co. OK, on 19 Apr 1928; he was 81.

On 1 Aug 1876 when Benjamin Warfield was 29, he married Henrietta BEVIER, in Toulon, Stark Co. IL, born on 23 Oct 1857 in Stark Co. IL. Henrietta died in Edmond, Oklahoma Co. OK, on 19 Sep 1930; she was 72. They had the following children:

1543	i.	Adie (1879-)
1544	ii.	Jesse Lee (1889-1939)

1059. Martha Alice TODD, 10G Granddaughter, born on 24 Jul 1847 in Baltimore City, Baltimore Co. MD. Martha

Alice died in Linn Co. KS, on 16 Jan 1923; she was 75.

Martha Alice married William L. CROWL, born on 8 Jan 1843 in Wheeling, Ohio Co. (W)VA. William L. died in Linn Co. KS, on 19 Jan 1920; he was 77. They had the following children:
- 1545   i.   Frank Wilson (1867-1929)
- 1546   ii.   Harry L. (1874-1970)
- 1547   iii.   Alice May (1880-1954)
- 1548   iv.   Bessie Mabel (1885-1886)

1060. Cachel TODD, 10G Granddaughter, born in Aug 1850. Cachel died before 1920.

Family of Charles Warfield TODD (723) and Marcelliar W. BONHAM

1061. Benjamin TODD, 10G Grandson, born on 20 Dec 1830 in Rodgeville, Carroll Co. MD. Benjamin died in Peoria, Peoria Co. IL, on 28 Apr 1905; he was 74.

On 5 May 1853 when Benjamin was 22, he married Frances D. JONES, in La Fayette, Stark Co. IL, born on 6 Jun 1830 in Greene Co. PA. Frances D. died in Peoria, Peoria Co. IL, on 1 Apr 1911; she was 80. They had the following children:
- 1549   i.   Ellen M. (about 1855-)
- 1550   ii.   Charles W. (about 1859-)
- 1551   iii.   Frank B. (about 1861-)
- 1552   iv.   Anna M. (about 1865-)
- 1553   v.   James F. (about 1867-)
- 1554   vi.   John W. (about 1870-)
- 1555   vii.   Josefa Frye (1875-1936)

1062. Sydney Jane TODD, 10G Granddaughter, born about 1832 in MD.

1063. Mary Elizabeth TODD, 10G Granddaughter, born about 1835 in MD. Mary Elizabeth died before 1850.

1064. Ellen Warfield TODD, 10G Granddaughter, born about 1839 in MD.

1065. James Forrest TODD, 10G Grandson, born about 1840 in IL.

Family of Charles Warfield TODD (723) and Abian Ann JACKSON

1066. Henrietta Jackson TODD, 10G Granddaughter, born on 23 Mar 1848 in IL.

Henrietta Jackson married --- ELLSWORTH. They had one child:
- 1556   i.   Emmitt A. (1861-)

Family of Vachel B. TODD (724) and Susan Brown

1067. Warfield Benjamin TODD, 10G Grandson, born on 23 Feb 1837 in Frederick Co. MD. Warfield Benjamin died in Lynn Twp., Knox Co. IL, on 20 Sep 1907; he was 70.

In Feb 1862 Warfield Benjamin married Euphemia LAFFERTY, in Lynn Twp., Knox Co. IL, born on 28 Oct 1838 in Lynn Twp., Knox Co. IL. Euphemia died in Lynn Twp., Knox Co. IL, on 21 Dec 1923; she was 85. They had the following children:
- 1557   i.   John (1863-)
- 1558   ii.   Susan (about 1863-)
- 1559   iii.   Anna R. (about 1866-)

1560	iv.	Nellie (1869-1937)
1561	v.	Jennie (about 1870-)
1562	vi.	Emma (1873-1896)
1563	vii.	Charles (1875-1943)
1564	viii.	Ben Ive (1877-)
1565	ix.	Upton B. (1884-)
1566	x.	Wilson (about 1885-)

1068. Vachel H. TODD, 10G Grandson, born on 16 Jul 1839 in MD. Vachel H. died in Lynn Twp., Knox Co. IL, on 25 Feb 1904; he was 64.

On 8 Nov 1860 when Vachel H. was 21, he married Margaret BRANGLE, in Stark Co. IL, born on 18 Feb 1839 in PA. Margaret died in Lynn Twp., Knox Co. IL, on 25 May 1891; she was 52.

1069. Henrietta TODD, 10G Granddaughter, born about 1841 in MD.

1070. Sarah TODD, 10G Granddaughter, born about 1852 in IL.

Family of Robert B. BROWN (727) and Hannah R. SULLIVAN

1071. Thomas J. BROWN, 10G Grandson, born on 30 Aug 1859 in MD. Thomas J. died in MD on 19 Oct 1924; he was 65.

Thomas J. married Maggie E. ---, born on 12 Mar 1862 in MD. Maggie E. died in MD on 27 Jan 1912; she was 49. They had the following children:

1567	i.	John W. (1899-1924)
1568	ii.	Francis M. (1905-1906)

1072. Edward B. BROWN, 10G Grandson, born on 10 Apr 1861 in MD. Edward B. died in 1905 in MD. Records of this family were prepared and kept by Dewey Octavius Brown, verified and augmented by Marshall Brown, here courtesy of Gregory S. Priebe.

In Jan 1883 Edward B. married Annie M. PHOEBUS, daughter of Charles Edward PHOEBUS and Martha J. LEAKINS, in Montgomery Co. MD, born about 1864 in Sykesville MD. Annie M. died after 1920. They had the following children:

1569	i.	Noland (1882-)
1570	ii.	Martha Thomas (1884-1970)
1571	iii.	Carrie Virginia (1885-1900)
1572	iv.	Ruby (1887-1970)
1573	v.	Edgar (1890-)
1574	vi.	Russell (1891-)
1575	vii.	Marshall A. (1894-)
1576	viii.	Dewey Octavius (1898-1981)
1577	ix.	Robert B. (-1905)
1578	x.	Carlton P. (1902-)
1579	xi.	Edward B. (-1905)

1073. Benjamin R. BROWN, 10G Grandson, born in 1864.

1074. Annie E. BROWN, 10G Granddaughter, born in 1867.

Family of Cilinda LANE (728) and Cornelius PETERSON

1075. Lydia PETERSON, 10G Granddaughter, born in 1827 in Athens Co. OH. Lydia died in Vermilion Co. IL.

On 9 Mar 1851 Lydia married Joseph PHIPPS, in Vermilion Co. IL.

1076. John L. PETERSON, 10G Grandson, born on 18 May 1828 in Deer Creek Prairie, Tippecanoe Co. IN. John L. died in Champaign Co. IL, on 2 Apr 1894; he was 65. Buried Dodson Cemetery, Vermilion Co. IL.

On 21 Jul 1854 when John L. was 26, he married Martha S. PHIPPS, in Vermilion Co. IL.

1077. Elmira PETERSON, 10G Granddaughter, born on 8 Aug 1832 in Athens Co. OH. Elmira died in Champaign Co. IL, on 2 Jun 1907; she was 74. Buried at the Armstrong Cemetery, Vermilion Co. IL.

Elmira married Johnson GAW.

1078. Sarah PETERSON, 10G Granddaughter, born in 1834 in OH.

On 4 May 1852 Sarah married William RODERICK, in Vermilion Co. IL.

1079. Benjamin PETERSON, 10G Grandson, born on 1 May 1836 in OH. Benjamin died in Vermilion Co. IL, on 12 Nov 1916; he was 80. Buried Wallace Chapel Cemetery, Vermilion Co. IL.

On 28 Oct 1860 when Benjamin was 24, he first married Lydia PILKINGTON, in Vermilion Co. IL.

On 1 Aug 1889 when Benjamin was 53, he second married Margaret A. GARLAND.

1080. Lucy PETERSON, 10G Granddaughter, born in 1837 in Dayton, Montgomery Co. OH. Lucy died on 21 Feb 1883 in Bixby, Vermilion Co. IL. Buried in Marysville, Vermilion Co. IL. Sources: death certificate, census, marriage records.

On 25 Apr 1855 Lucy first married Solomon RODERICK.

On 11 Jan 1873 Lucy second married Thomas Reed DOYLE (a.k.a. Francis REED), in Vermilion Co. IL. Thomas Reed died in 1916. Alice Marie Beard wrote: "One of Cornelius and Cilinda's grandsons was my grandfather. He was an unschooled, poor, illiterate, frequently moving tenant farmer, born to a remarried widow woman and a Civil War deserter who hid under a bogus name. My grandfather had no illusions of grandeur and used an outhouse most of his life. He was an old man with beautiful blue eyes who called me 'Morning Glory' and let me comb his hair over his bald spot." He enlisted as Frank Reed as a private in Co. K, 8th Regiment, Illinois Volunteers, an infantry unit, but re-emerged later as Tom Doyle and kept his former life a secret for many years (Source: "Itha Elmer Doyle, 1874-1958, Mary Louise Payne, 1883-1953," http://members.aol.com/alicebeard/ithamary.html by permission from Alice Beard). The continuing story, and that of the Doyle descendants, is Ms. Beard's own, and I am happy to leave it to her to tell in her own publication.

1081. Eli PETERSON, 10G Grandson, born in 1840 in IL. Eli died on 7 Apr 1887 in Vermilion Co. IL.

On 6 Sep 1861 Eli married Susan Elizabeth WRIGHT, in Vermilion Co. IL.

1082. Mary Jane PETERSON, 10G Granddaughter, born in 1842 in Vermilion Co. IL.

On 8 Aug 1861 Mary Jane first married Hiram GEARHART, in Vermilion Co. IL.

In about 1865 Mary Jane second married Durbin GAW.

1083. Charlotte PETERSON, 10G Granddaughter, born on 14 Dec 1844 in Vermilion Co. IL. Charlotte died in IL on 20 Sep 1873; she was 28. Buried Fairchild Cemetery, Vermilion Co. IL.

On 3 Jan 1868 when Charlotte was 23, she married Jacob WILLIAMS, in Champaign Co. IL.

1084. Selinda PETERSON, 10G Granddaughter, born in 1847 in Vermilion Co. IL. Selinda died on 3 Apr 1882 in Vermilion Co. IL. Buried Marysville, Vermilion Co. IL.

Selinda married Alfred F. BAKER.

FOURTEENTH GENERATION

Family of Benjamin Franklin BROWN (730) and Lavina ROBB

1085. George Alan BROWN, 11G Grandson, born on 9 Mar 1869. George Alan died in Sykesville MD, on 23 Dec 1920; he was 51. Buried at Springfield Cemetery, Sykesville MD.

On 6 Nov 1895 when George Alan was 26, he married Ella May ALLEN, daughter of Charles W. ALLEN and Caroline LINDSAY, in Sykesville MD, born on 18 May 1874 in Gist MD. Ella May died in Sykesville MD, on 13 Jul 1938; she was 64. Buried at Springfield Cemetery, Sykesville MD. They had the following children:
- **1580** i. Edna May (1899-1969)
- **1581** ii. George W.
- **1582** iii. Henry Allen

1086. Francis W. BROWN, 11G Grandson, born on 25 Jul 1870. Francis W. died on 18 Apr 1921; he was 50.

Francis W. married Mary ---.

1087. Walter C. BROWN, 11G Grandson, born on 5 May 1874. Walter C. died on 25 Oct 1910; he was 36.

1088. Benjamin Franklin BROWN, 11G Grandson, born in 1872. Benjamin Franklin died in 1942.

On 26 Mar 1896 Benjamin Franklin married Minnie HOBBS.

1089. Mary E. BROWN, 11G Granddaughter.

Mary E. married George STROEBEL.

Family of Eli BROWN (734) and Lavina ---

1090. --- BROWN, 11G Grandson, born in 1854 in Madison Co. IN.

1091. Peter BROWN, 11G Grandson, born in 1859 in Madison Co. IN.

Family of Obadiah BROWN (736) and Sarah WYSONG

1092. Alvina BROWN, 11G Granddaughter, born about 1858 in Anderson IN.

1093. James D. BROWN, 11G Grandson, born about 1861 in Anderson IN. James D. died after 1880. Heading factory laborer, Anderson IN

1094. Francis BROWN, 11G Grandson, born on 3 Mar 1865. Francis died in Anderson IN, on 5 Sep 1865; he was less than 1. Buried in Moss Cemetery, Anderson.

Family of Elijah BROWN (737) and Mary Jane COLLIS

1095. --- **BROWN**, 11G Grandchild, born in 1855 in Anderson IN. Died in 1855 in Anderson.

Family of Elijah BROWN (737) and Lydia C. EVANS

1096. Ralph Clark BROWN, 11G Grandson, born on 19 Nov 1857 in Anderson IN. Ralph Clark died in Plattsmouth NE, on 13 Jul 1941; he was 83. Known as "Rafe," married 11 Dec 1878 to Emma F. Raines, Ralph died 13 July 1941 in Plattsmouth Nebraska (untitled obituary clipping courtesy of Christine A. Kreick, who was the major source for this family). Moved as a young man to work on the farm of James Raines in Madison County, married Emma Raines and went to Nebraska when the Raines left Indiana for that state.

On 11 Dec 1878 when Ralph Clark was 21, he married Emma F. RAINS, born on 16 Dec 1858 in Anderson IN. Emma F. died in Nemaha City NE, on 1 Feb 1925; she was 66. They had the following children:
1583	i.	Effie Olive (1879-1952)
1584	ii.	Wade
1585	iii.	Bessie (1885-1940)
1586	iv.	Charles
1587	v.	Flossie (1895-1967)
1588	vi.	Floyd LeRoy (1897-1977)

1097. William Lloyd BROWN, 11G Grandson, born on 25 Dec 1859 in Bloomington IL. William Lloyd died in Mooreland IN, on 15 Sep 1950; he was 90. Resident in later life of Lakeland FL.

William Lloyd first married Rhoda RINARD, born on 31 Jan 1865. Rhoda died on 23 Jan 1890; she was 24. They had the following children:
1589	i.	Ida Belle (1886-1965)
1590	ii.	Nola Edith (1889-1985)
1591	iii.	Orville (1886-1887)

William Lloyd second married Sarah Malinda DOWNING. They had one child:
1592	i.	Edna Lillian (1901-1990)

1098. Nettie BROWN, 11G Granddaughter, born in 1861 in Bloomington IL. Nettie died about 1872 in IN.

1099. Ida BROWN, 11G Granddaughter, born on 24 Jun 1864 in Bloomington IL. Ida died in Perkinsville IN, on 13 Dec 1937; she was 73.

On 1 Mar 1882 when Ida was 17, she married Robert HOUSE, born on 20 Apr 1861. Robert died in Perkinsville IN, on 10 Dec 1932; he was 71. They had the following children:
1593	i.	Charles O. (1885-)
1594	ii.	Fern (1886-)
1595	iii.	Lucy Donald (1889-1917)
1596	iv.	Lacey A. (1891-1981)
1597	v.	Theodore "Tad" (1895-1970)
1598	vi.	William Kenneth "Bill" (1898-)
1599	vii.	Mary (1900-)
1600	viii.	Clifton G. (1906-)
1601	ix.	William K.

1100. Alonzo Grant BROWN, 11G Grandson, born on 29 Nov 1866 in McLean Co. IL. Alonzo "Lon" died in Anderson IN, on 28 Aug 1953; he was 86. Buried in W Maplewood Cemetery, Anderson. Agricultural and Industrial Laborer. Refs.: Madison County Indiana Marriages; Death Records; Censuses of 1850, 1860, 1870, 1880, 1900, 1910, 1920, and 1930; Anderson City Directories; family informants, including himself.

On 21 Nov 1891 when Alonzo was 24, he first married Julia Margaret LAWHORN, daughter of John H LAWHORN and Elizabeth F. EAST, in Anderson IN, born on 1 Sep 1871 in Pike Co. OH. Julia Margaret died in N Anderson IN, on 11 Sep 1902; she was 31. Buried in W Maplewood Cemetery Anderson IN. Refs.: Censuses of 1880, 1900; death certificate Madison County Indiana; Marriage Certificate Madison County, buried at West Maplewood Cemetery, Anderson Indiana. They had the following children:

1602	i.	Ethel (1893-1893)
1603	ii.	James Willard (1894-1978)
1604	iii.	Walter Ray (1897-1992)
1605	iv.	Elsie May (1901-1905)

On 14 Apr 1909 when Alonzo was 42, he second married Bertha Etta WAITMAN JARRETT, daughter of Solomon WAITMAN and Mary Ann WHISLER, in Anderson IN, born on 5 Oct 1877 in OH. Bertha Etta died in Anderson IN, on 23 Sep 1930; she was 52. They had the following children:

1606	i.	Katherine Christine (1910-2005)
1607	ii.	Cora Elmay (1913-2003)
1608	iii.	Leatha JARRETT (Adopted) (1894 - after 1968)
1609	iv.	Ralph Nelson JARRETT (Adopted) (1900-1985)

1101. Clara BROWN, 11G Granddaughter, born in 1869 in IL. Clara died before 1872 in IN.

1102. James Anderson BROWN, 11G Grandson, born on 10 Apr 1872 in Indiana. James Anderson died in Indianapolis IN, on 16 Sep 1928; he was 56. Buried in Memorial Park, Indianapolis IN. Sources on Anderson-Delph families: Zelma Fern Brown, much correspondence with the author in the 1970s; Katy Blume, e-mail 14 Feb 2004.

On 12 Sep 1895 when James Anderson was 23, he married Hattie Ellen DELPH, daughter of Larken DELPH and Sarah WAMPLER, in North Anderson IN, born on 22 May 1876 in Madison Co. IN. Hattie Ellen died in Indianapolis, IN, on 24 Aug 1938; she was 62. Buried in Memorial Park, Indianapolis IN. They had the following children:

1610	i.	Nellie May (1896-1957)
1611	ii.	Earl Jennings (1897-1977)
1612	iii.	Zelma Fern (1899-1989)
1613	iv.	Myrtle Marie (1902-1933)
1614	v.	Opal R. (1903-2002)
1615	vi.	Manvil F. (1908-1950)
1616	vii.	Lawrence Lewis (1910-1962)
1617	viii.	Ruth Adair (1913-1975)
1618	ix.	Harold Edward (1914-1989)
1619	x.	Stanley H. (1917-1991)

Family of Elijah BROWN (737) and Malissa Ellen WHITE

1103. Elmer E. BROWN, 11G Grandson, born on 13 Jun 1874 in IN. Elmer E. died in Madison Co. IN, on 27 Jun 1939; he was 65. Refs.: Elijah Brown Civil War Disabled Veteran's Pension application; Perkinsville IN United Methodist Episcopal Church Records; Censuses of 1880, 1900, 1910; Madison County Death Records; Ruby Tate Rynearson copy of family Bible page.

On 23 May 1897 when Elmer E. was 22, he married Sara A. McCORD, in Perkinsville IN United Methodist Episcopal Ch, born in 1877. They had the following children:

1620	i.	Evelyn (1900-)
1621	ii.	Estell Elmer (1903-)
1622	iii.	William Thurman (1906-)
1623	iv.	Ernest (1908-)

1104. Rosa B. BROWN, 11G Granddaughter, born on 8 Feb 1877 in IN. Rosa B. died in IN on 24 Jul 1900; she was 23. Refs.: Madison County Marriage Records; 1880 Census; Gerald Closser, Ruby Tate Rynearson copy of a family Bible page.

On 28 Mar 1897 when Rosa B. was 20, she married John Albert CLOSSER, in Madison Co. IN, born in 1876 in Madison Co. IN. John Albert died on 21 Nov 1943 in Frankton IN.

1105. John Scherer BROWN, 11G Grandson, born on 6 Jul 1880 in Hamilton Co. IN. John Scherer died in Anderson IN, on 13 Feb 1963; he was 82. Refs.: lengthy correspondence in the 1970s from Katherine York his step-daughter; Ruby Tate Rynearson's copy of Brown family Bible page. Served in the US Army 1901-4, Philippine Insurrection. Worked at the Delco-Remy GM Plant, Anderson Indiana.

On 12 Oct 1904 when John Scherer was 24, he first married Carrie B. McCLINTOCK, born about 1880. They had the following children:
1624	i.	Edward (1905-1989)
1625	ii.	Harold H. (1908-1980)
1626	iii.	Glenn (1908-1970)

In Jul 1952 John Scherer second married Emma Belle McDUFFEE, in Newcastle, IN, born on 14 Aug 1890 in Fairfield IN. Emma Belle died in Anderson IN, on 12 Sep 1985; she was 95. They had the following children:
1627	i.	George (Adopted)
1628	ii.	Katherine (Adopted)

1106. Mary C. BROWN, 11G Granddaughter, born on 28 Aug 1883. Mary C. died in 1939. Refs.: Perkinsville United Methodist Church archives; Elijah Brown Civil War Disabled Veteran's Pension application; Ruby Tate Rynearson copy of family Bible page.

On 15 Sep 1902 when Mary C. was 19, she married Curtis L. TATE, in Perkinsville IN United Methodist Episcopal Church Records, born on 17 Jan 1872 in Connersville IN. His second marriage. They had the following children:
1629	i.	Ruby Thelma (1903-1977)
1630	ii.	Garnet Zelma (1909-1993)
1631	iii.	Catherine Curtis
1632	iv.	Orlia Arthur (1916-1984)

1107. Bessie M. BROWN, 11G Granddaughter, born on 22 Mar 1890. Bessie M. died in Perkinsville on 9 Dec 1942; she was 52. Refs.: Elijah Brown Civil War Disabled Veteran's Pension application, Ruby Tate Rynearson copy of family Bible page.

On 4 Sep 1910 when Bessie M. was 20, she married Lucien LEWIS. Resided in the rural Lapel IN area.

1108. Elijah BROWN Jr., 11G Grandson, born on 11 Oct 1893 in Madison Co. IN. Elijah died in Frankton IN, on 12 Mar 1948; he was 54. Buried in 100F Cemetery Lafayette Twp. Served in WW I. Refs.: Elijah Brown Civil War Disabled Veteran's Pension application; Ruby Tate Rynearson copy of family Bible page; Madison County Marriage Records; Death Records; Ed Brown, family informant. Lived for a time in Michigan where he may have married Margaret. Laborer, painter, farmer.

On 20 Dec 1919 when Elijah was 26, he first married Ida (---) CONDON, URRY OR RIGSBY, in Madison Co. IN, born about 1883. She, Elijah and her children Alfred, Paul, Charles Condon enumerated in the 1920 Census Anderson p. 210, also Brother-in-law James Rigsby in the household.

On 9 Sep 1922 when Elijah was 28, he second married Margaret WILKINSON, born on 24 Aug 1883 in MI. Margaret died in Madison Co. IN, on 25 Oct 1968; she was 85. Buried in 100F Cemetery Lafayette Twp.

1109. Sherman BROWN, 11G Grandson, born on 20 Jul 1896. Sherman died on 29 Dec 1898; he was 2. Refs.: father's Civil War Disabled Veteran's Pension application; Ruby Tate Rynearson copy of family Bible page; obituary newspaper clipping; Gerald Closser, family informant.

Family of Catherine BROWN (740) and Abraham ELLIOTT

1110. Montreville ELLIOTT, 11G Grandson, born about 1864 in Anderson IN.

1111. Jennette ELLIOTT, 11G Granddaughter, born about 1865 in Anderson IN. Jennette died on 6 Feb 1948 in Kokomo IN. Buried in Crown Point Cemetery, Kokomo.

Jennette married Rudolph H. BROWN.

1112. William Lankford ELLIOTT, 11G Grandson, born on 27 Mar 1870. William Lankford died in Danville, Vermillion Co. IL, on 22 Sep 1929; he was 59. These Elliott Descendants of William are courtesy of Eugene Elliott.

William Lankford first married --- ---. Had a child that died in infancy, probably in childbirth (Eugene Elliott).

On 27 Jan 1897 when William Lankford was 26, he second married Minnie Jane FIFER, daughter of William FIFER and Martha NEFF, in Delaware Co. IN, born on 27 Oct 1870 in Anderson, Madison Co. IN. Minnie Jane died in Danville, Vermillion Co. IL, on 12 Oct 1952; she was 81. They had the following children:

1633	i.	Clarence William (1900-1934)
1634	ii.	Charles (1906-1969)
1635	iii.	Walter Winslow (1909-1992)
1636	iv.	Donald (1913-)

1113. Frank ELLIOTT, 11G Grandson, born about 1874 in Anderson IN.

1114. Daisy M. ELLIOTT, 11G Granddaughter, born about 1878 in Anderson IN.

1115. Leroy "Roy" ELLIOTT, 11G Grandson, born on 3 Jul 1885. Leroy "Roy" died in Kokomo IN, on 11 Jan 1962; he was 76.

Family of Mary Ann or Lydia BROWN (750) and Francis M. HOPPES

1116. Emma Frances HOPPES, 11G Granddaughter.

1117. Cary A. HOPPES, 11G Granddaughter.

1118. Minnie J. HOPPES, 11G Granddaughter.

1119. Ollie G. HOPPES, 11G Grandson.

1120. Charles C. HOPPES, 11G Grandson.

1121. Thomas G. HOPPES, 11G Grandson.

1122. Myrtle M. HOPPES, 11G Granddaughter.

1123. Asa R. HOPPES, 11G Grandson.

1124. Elizabeth HOPPES, 11G Granddaughter.

1125. Edward HOPPES., 11G Grandson

1126. Flossie HOPPES, 11G Granddaughter.

1127. Hazel HOPPES, 11G Granddaughter.

Family of Elizabeth A. MOBLEY (758) and Retus DUNN

1128. Mary DUNN, 11G Granddaughter.

1129. Nannie DUNN, 11G Granddaughter.

Family of Jesse Ralph MOBLEY (759) and Nellie or Ellen LAWS or MCFALLS

1130. Jesse MOBLEY, 11G Grandson, born in 1841 in IL. Jesse died before 1864. Refs.: 1850, 1860 Census, Bartholomew Co. IN. Killed in the Civil War. Letter from Alta to Lillian Thompson in 1961. Refs.: Warren; marriage certificate which gave his name as James (*Marriage Certificate Book C-6*, p. 515).

On 18 Mar 1861 Jesse married Sarah Ann ANDERSON, in Bartholomew Co. IN, born in 1843 in IN. They had one child:
    1637   i.   Elizabeth (1862-)

1131. Elijah B. MOBLEY, 11G Grandson, born in 1844 in IL. Elijah B. died in 1923 in MO. Letter from his granddaughter Ellen Thompson in 1961 states that Elijah was often called E.B. or Lige. He married his brother Jesse's widow Sarah. Refs.: 1850, 1860, 1870, 1880 Census, Bartholomew Co. IN, Letter from Nellie Mobley Collins.

Elijah B. married Sarah Ann ANDERSON, born in 1843 in IN. They had the following children:
    1638   i.   William (1866-1930)
    1639   ii.   John W. (1867-)
    1640   iii.   Elsworth (1869-)
    1641   iv.   Isaac (1871-)
    1642   v.   Jesse (1874-)
    1643   vi.   Lettie (1876-)
    1644   vii.   Mary (1878-)

1132. Thomas G. MOBLEY, 11G Grandson, born in 1848 in IN. A letter from Don Mobley to Bertha Mobley stated that Tom Mobley married his mother after his [Tom's] brother Daniel died (Warren). Possible first marriage to Rebecca J. Darnell 20 Jan 1870 (*Certificate Book C-8*, p. 187). Also a letter from her daughter Nellie stated that he was said to have had brothers named Lon and John. That letter, to Lillian Mobley Thompson, says she lived in MO and knew Mary Jane Galentine's two sons and John as they lived close by. Mary Jane died at daughter Nellie's home (letter from Downy Mobley to Lillian Thompson Mobley). Daniel brother's Thomas Mobley married after the death of her husband. 1880 Census p. 11, Springhill, Greene, PA shows Galentine family living near Mary and her. They are Wm. Galentine age 60 yrs Farmer, Hester 60 yrs Keeping house, Elmore 14 yrs, Leora 12 yrs. 1920 Census of Kiowa, Harper Co. OK, p. 2A shows Thomas living with Ellie and family.

On 20 Jan 1870 Thomas G. first married Rebecca J. DARNELL, in Bartholomew Co. IN.

Thomas G. second married Mary Jane GALENTINE, daughter of William GALENTINE and Hester CHAMBERS, born on 1 Jan 1848 in Greene Co. PA. Mary Jane died in Gate, Harper Co. OK, on 19 Jan 1920; she was 72. A letter to Lillian Mobley Thompson stated she lived in MO and knew Mary Jane Galentine's two brothers Lonn and John as they lived close by. Mary Jane died at daughter Nellie's home. A letter from Downy Mobley to Lillian Thompson Mobley claimed that Daniel's brother Thomas Mobley married her after the death of her husband. The 1880 Census of Springhill, Greene Co. PA shows the Galentine family living near Mary and her. In the family are Wm. Galentine age 60 yrs Farmer, Hester 60 yrs, Elmore and Leora. Additional ref.: 1920 Census, Kiowa, Harper Co. OK, p. 2A.

Thomas G. third married Susie ---, born in 1847 in IN.

1133. Ruth Ann MOBLEY, 11G Granddaughter, born in 1850 in IN. Refs.: 1850, 1860, 1870, 1880 Census, Bartholomew Co. IN. 1870 Census Hartsville, Bartholomew Co. IN, p. 170.

After 26 May 1870 Ruth Ann married Noah BETTS, in Bartholomew Co. IN.

1134. Phillip MOBLEY, 11G Grandson, born in 1852 in IN. Refs.: 1870 Census Clifty, Bartholomew Co. IN, p. 18; 1880 Census, Bartholomew Co. IN; Warren.

1135. Daniel L. MOBLEY, 11G Grandson, born in 1856 in IN. Ref.: verbal Information of Lillian Mobley Thompson, who stated that he traveled much and his wife was left with the raising of the children. He supposedly fell from the top of a church and was killed, but another family story claimed that he died of typhoid fever. Additional refs.: *The Mobley Family* by Mildred Mobley; Marriage Certificate C-9, p. 421; 1870 Census Clifty Township p. 16; 1880 Census Springhill, Greene PA, p. 366A.

Daniel L. married Mary Jane GALENTINE, daughter of William GALENTINE and Hester CHAMBERS, born on 1 Jan 1848 in Greene Co. PA. Mary Jane died in Gate, Harper Co. OK, on 19 Jan 1920; she was 72. A letter to Lillian Mobley Thompson stated she lived in MO and knew Mary Jane Galentine's two brothers Lonn and John as they lived close by. Mary Jane died at daughter Nellie's home. A letter from Downy Mobley to Lillian Thompson Mobley claimed that Daniel's brother Thomas Mobley married her after the death of her husband. The 1880 Census of Springhill, Greene Co. PA shows the Galentine family living near Mary and her. In the family are Wm. Galentine age 60 yrs Farmer, Hester 60 yrs, Elmore and Leora. Additional ref; 1920 Census, Kiowa, Harper Co. OK, p. 2A. They had the following children:

1645	i.	William Terriel (1876-1961)
1646	ii.	Hester Ellen (1878-1964)
1647	iii.	Jesse Ralph (1880-1964)
1648	iv.	Nellie (1882-)
1649	v.	Alonzo Downy (1885-1963)

1136. Andrew Jackson MOBLEY, 11G Grandson, born in Aug 1859. Andrew Jackson died in 1920. 1870 Census Clifty, Bartholomew Co. IN, p. 18. 1880 Census, Bartholomew Co. IN. Family chart sent to Hazel Mobley Ketron includes wife and children. Barbara McReynolds and Jesse Crisler. *Marriage Record Book C-12*, p. 9.

On 10 Aug 1890 Andrew Jackson married Isabell V. COLLINS, in Bartholomew Co. IN, born on 7 Apr 1872 in IN. Isabell V. died on 8 Dec 1951; she was 79. They had the following children:

1650	i.	John H. (1891-)
1651	ii.	Bertha M. (1892-1970)
1652	iii.	Loretti Laverne (1896-1897)
1653	iv.	Blanch

1137. Jacob A. MOBLEY, 11G Grandson, born in Aug 1865 in IN. 1870 Census Clifty, Bartholomew Co. IN, p. 18. 1880 Census, Bartolomew, Indiana. Letter from Don Mobley to Bertha Mobley stated that Jacob Mobley was a brickmason. Bartholomew Co. IN *Marriage Record Book C-12*, p. 9.

On 8 Apr 1886 Jacob A. married Jennie F. BOTTORF, in Bartholomew Co. IN, born in Sep 1867 in IN. They had the following children:

1654	i.	Ozalla P. (1887-)
1655	ii.	Ethel M. (1889-)
1656	iii.	Elsie Ferne (1891-)
1657	iv.	Leroy (1893-1963)
1658	v.	Delbert R. (1896-1978)
1659	vi.	Irwin E.
1660	vii.	Albert E. (1899-1981)

1138. Mahala MOBLEY, 11G Granddaughter, born in 1867 in IN. 1870 Census Clifty, Bartholomew Co. IN, p. 18. 1880 Census, Bartholomew Co. IN. Barbara McReynold and Jesse Crisler.

Family of Lucretia MOBLEY (761) and Thomas Green LEE

1139. William LEE, 11G Grandson, born in 1848. William died in 1925.

1140. Margarete A. "Maggie" LEE, 11G Granddaughter, born in 1849.

On 18 Oct 1869 Margarete A. "Maggie" married Ralph MOODY, in Dry Creek. Walla Walla Co. WA.

1141. Henry LEE, 11G Grandson, born in 1851. Henry died in 1917.

1142. Jay LEE, 11G Grandson, born in 1853. Jay died in 1927.

Jay married Nancy Ann POINTER.

1143. Sarah Isabelle "Belle" LEE, 11G Granddaughter, born in 1855. Sarah Isabelle "Belle" died in 1883.

On 18 Feb 1872 Sarah Isabelle married Henry HART. They had the following children:
- **1661**   i.   Nellie (1872-1876)
- **1662**   ii.   Charles Henry (1875-1950)

Family of John Henry MOBLEY (762) and Mary Ann BURKE

1144. William R. MOBLEY, 11G Grandson, born in 1849.

1145. Lyman MOBLEY, 11G Grandson, born in 1854. Lyman died in 1945.

Lyman married Nanny DOGGETT, in Decatur IN. They had one child:
- **1663**   i.   Clio (1881 - after 1984)

1146. Emma MOBLEY, 11G Granddaughter, born on 21 Nov 1856 in Hartsville, Bartholomew Co. IN. Emma died in 1950.

On 3 Oct 1876 when Emma was 19, she married John G. WILSON, in Bartholomew Co. IN.

1147. Fasine or Rosina MOBLEY, 11G Granddaughter, born in 1857. 1860, 1870 Census.

1148. Randolph "Randy" MOBLEY, 11G Grandson, born in 1858. Randolph died in 1942. They had one unnamed child born in 1885.

Randolph married Rilla RISINGER.

1149. Theodore T. "Dory" MOBLEY, 11G Grandson, born on 16 Nov 1860 in Hartsville, Bartholomew Co. IN. Theodore died in 1937 in Mitchell IN.

Theodore T. "Dory" married Phoebe Alberta Bertha YOST. Phoebe Alberta Bertha died in 1937. They had the following children:
- **1664**   i.   Jim (1891-)
- **1665**   ii.   Vivian P.

1150. Margaret A. "Maggie" MOBLEY, 11G Granddaughter, born about 1862 in Hartsville, Bartholomew Co. IN. Margaret died in 1949.

On 22 Dec 1882 Margaret married J. Taylor WRIGHT, in Bartholomew Co. IN. They had the following children:
- **1666**   i.   Chester
- **1667**   ii.   Mabel
- **1668**   iii.   LaVern
- **1669**   iv.   Lorene

1151. --- MOBLEY, 11G Grandson, born on 13 Feb 1865 in Hartsville, Bartholomew Co. IN. --- died in Hartsville, Bartholomew Co. IN, on 7 Mar 1865; he was less than 1.

1152. Ella P. MOBLEY, 11G Granddaughter, born on 4 Feb 1867 in Hartsville, Bartholomew Co. IN. Ella P. died in 1897.

On 22 Aug 1894 when Ella P. was 27, she married Floyd F. LOOSE, in Bartholomew Co. IN. They had one child:
    1670   i.   Corinna Clare

1153. Loran MOBLEY, 11G Grandson, born on 4 Jan 1868 or 1869 in Hartsville, Bartholomew Co. IN. Loran died in 1870 in Hartsville, Bartholomew Co. IN.

1154. William Henry "Hen" MOBLEY, 11G Grandson, born on 19 Feb 1871 in Hartsville, Bartholomew Co. IN. William Henry died in Hartsville, Bartholomew Co. IN, on 7 May 1959; he was 88.

On 28 Jan 1903 when William Henry was 31, he married Grace MYERS, born in 1880. Grace died on 16 Feb 1962. They had the following children:
    1671   i.   Mary
    1672   ii.   Wayne

1155. James Hunter "Hunt" MOBLEY, 11G Grandson, born on 4 Sep 1873 in Hartsville, Bartholomew Co. IN. James Hunter "Hunt" died in Columbus, Bartholomew Co. IN, on 13 Apr 1932; he was 58. 1880 Census, WWI draft registration.

On 26 Mar 1898 when James Hunter "Hunt" was 24, he first married Cora B. WHITE, in Bartholomew Co. IN. They had the following children:
    1673   i.   Virgil (1899-1959)
    1674   ii.   Beatrice (1900-1975)

James Hunter "Hunt" second married India ROSCOE, born on 23 Apr 1881 in Monroe Co. IN. India died in Bartholomew Co. IN, on 11 Dec 1955; she was 74. They had one child:
    1675   i.   Clarence Edward (1919-1991)

Family of Mahala MOBLEY (763) and William FIX

1156. Sarah Catherine FIX, 11G Granddaughter, born in 1849.

Sarah Catherine married John CARTER, born in 1845.

1157. John Wesley FIX, 11G Grandson, born about 1851 in Decatur, Adams Co. IN.

1158. Mary J. FIX, 11G Granddaughter, born about 1854 in Decatur, Adams Co. IN.

1159. Laura C. FIX, 11G Granddaughter, born on 1 Dec 1858 in Decatur, Adams Co. IN. Laura C. died in Decatur, Adams Co. IN, on 15 Sep 1868; she was 9.

1160. Leona FIX, 11G Granddaughter, born in 1862 in Decatur, Adams Co. IN.

On 25 Sep 1883 Leona married Henry S. MURPHY.

1161. Josephine FIX, 11G Granddaughter.

1162. Genevra FIX, 11G Granddaughter.

Family of Sarah MOBLEY (764) and John FIX

1163. Mary M. FIX, 11G Granddaughter, born in 1850 in IN. Mary M. died in Dec 1880.

In 1880 Mary M. married John B. PHILLIPS.

1164. Cynthia Alice FIX, 11G Granddaughter, born in 1855.

Family of Sarah MOBLEY (764) and Albert CRISLER

1165. William CRISLER, 11G Grandson, born in 1858 in Bartholomew Co. IN.

1166. Letta or Meta CRISLER, 11G Granddaughter, born in 1860 in Whitely, Clark Co. IN.

1167. Sallie E. CRISLER, 11G Granddaughter, born in 1863 in Bartholomew Co. IN.

Family of Sarah MOBLEY (764) and John FLORAN

1168. Phillip Beechers FLORAN, 11G Grandson, born in 1864 in Bartholomew Co. IN.

1169. Laura Jennie FLORAN, 11G Granddaughter, born in 1864 in Whitely, Clark Co. IN.

1170. William S. FLORAN, 11G Grandson, born in 1866 in Whitely, Clark Co. IN.

1171. Lewis H. FLORAN, 11G Grandson, born in 1871 in Bartholomew Co. IN.

Family of Lewis MOBLEY (765) and Julia Anna RHORER

1172. Rev. Darius Arrelian MOBLEY, 11G Grandson, born on 2 Apr 1855 in Columbus, Bartholomew Co. IN. Darius Arrelian died on 10 Dec 1929; he was 74.

On 18 May 1876 when Darius was 21, he first married Harriett Ann HESSEY, in Whitely, Clark Co. IN. They had the following children:
1676	i.	Gertrude Iris (1877-)
1677	ii.	Mary Catherine "Lota" (1878-)
1678	iii.	Blanche Julia (1879-)
1679	iv.	Harriett Ethel (1881-)
1680	v.	William Lewis (1882-1904)
1681	vi.	Philo Darius (1885-)
1682	vii.	Hadassah Belle (1886-)
1683	viii.	Edith K. (1889-1980)
1684	ix.	Harry S. (1894-1965)

On 6 Jul 1899 when Darius was 44, he second married Mabel F. BURROWS, in Bartholomew Co. IN, born on 6 Nov 1865. They had one child:
1685	i.	Rosamond Ruth

1173. Laura Josephine MOBLEY, 11G Granddaughter, born on 6 Aug 1857 in Columbus, Bartholomew Co. IN. Laura Josephine died on 20 Feb 1952; she was 94.

On 6 Nov 1879 when Laura Josephine was 22, she married Rev. Hugh C. FUNKHOUSER, in Bartholomew Co. IN.

1174. Luanna Jane MOBLEY, 11G Granddaughter, born on 25 Mar 1859 in Columbus, Bartholomew Co. IN.

1175. Alta Florence MOBLEY, 11G Granddaughter, born on 7 Sep 1862 in Columbus, Bartholomew Co. IN.

On 13 Jul 1881 when Alta Florence was 18, she married Albert W. WRIGHT, in Bartholomew Co. IN.

1176. Ora MOBLEY, 11G Granddaughter, born about 1863.

1177. Minnie May MOBLEY, 11G Granddaughter, born on 13 Oct 1865 in Whitely, Clark Co. IN.

On 1 Sep 1892 when Minnie May was 26, she married Edward M. HOWARD, in Bartholomew Co. IN.

1178. Jacob A. MOBLEY, 11G Grandson, born on 13 Oct 1865. Jacob A. died before 1870.

1179. John Orion MOBLEY, 11G Grandson, born on 22 Apr 1868 in Whitely, Clark Co. IN.

1180. Rita Florence MOBLEY, 11G Granddaughter, born on 7 Sep 1869. Rita Florence died before 1870.

1181. Mertie E MOBLEY, 11G Granddaughter, born on 14 Jul 1871 in Whitely, Clark Co. IN.

1182. Lewis Dana MOBLEY, 11G Grandson, born on 3 Mar 1874 in Whitely, Clark Co. IN.

1183. Lyda Blanche MOBLEY, 11G Granddaughter, born on 1 Dec 1879.

1184. John Orion MOBLEY, 11G Grandson. John Orion died before 1880.

Family of Reason D. MOBLEY (766) and Frances E. PATTON

1185. Marietta MOBLEY, 11G Granddaughter, born in 1857 in IN.

1186. Viola MOBLEY, 11G Granddaughter, born in 1859 in IN.

On 27 Sep 1877 Viola married A.J. RUTHERFORD, in Bartholomew Co. IN.

1187. Columbus MOBLEY, 11G Grandson, born in 1861 in IN.

1188. Anne Almy MOBLEY, 11G Granddaughter, born about 1863 in IN.

On 22 Dec 1888 Anne Almy married Lincoln JACKSON, in Bartholomew Co. IN.

1189. William MOBLEY, 11G Grandson, born in 1866 in IN.

1190. Allen MOBLEY, 11G Grandson, born in 1869 in IN.

On 4 Sep 1898 Allen married Martha SMITH.

Family of Reason D. MOBLEY (766) and Mary Gant ISGREGG

1191. Orville MOBLEY, 11G Grandson, born in 1873 in IN. Orville died on 20 Apr 1892 in Clifty Twp., Bartholomew Co. IN. 1880 Census. Death Record Bartholomew Co. IN *Book HD-3*, p. 28.

1192. John W. MOBLEY, 11G Grandson, born in 1877 in IN. Had two unnamed children.

On 28 Nov 1900 John W. married Emaline Anna GREEN, in Bartholomew Co. IN.

1193. Rilla MOBLEY, 11G Granddaughter, born in 1880 in IN. Rilla died about 1881.

Family of Catherine Minerva MOBLEY (767) and Robert GILLILANT

1194. Irwin GILLILANT, 11G Grandson, born in 1851.

1195. George W. GILLILANT, 11G Grandson, born in 1853.

1196. Margaret GILLILANT, 11G Granddaughter, born in 1855.

1197. Robert J. GILLILANT, 11G Grandson, born in 1857.

1198. Eliza Jane GILLILANT, 11G Granddaughter, born in 1859. Eliza Jane died before 1870.

1199. William E. GILLILANT, 11G Grandson, born in 1861.

1200. John L. GILLILANT, 11G Grandson, born in 1863.

1201. Edward C. GILLILANT, 11G Grandson, born in 1866.

1202. Cora A. GILLILANT, 11G Granddaughter, born in 1870.

Family of William MOBLEY (768) and Mary Jane COOVERT

1203. Alonzo MOBLEY, 11G Grandson, born in 1861 in IN.

1204. Monte Belle MOBLEY, 11G Granddaughter, born in 1862.

On 17 May 1879 Monte Belle married Charles L. DILLMAN, in Bartholomew Co. IN.

1205. Sara Willa MOBLEY, 11G Granddaughter, born in 1865 in IN.

Family of Warren Wesley MOBLEY (769) and Mary F. RYAN

1206. Dr. Lewis F. MOBLEY, 11G Grandson, born in 1875 in IN. Ref.: 1880 Census.

On 31 Dec 1902 Lewis F. married Louise E. TAYLOR, in Bartholomew Co. IN.

1207. Warren Wesley MOBLEY, 11G Grandson, born about 1878. Warren Wesley died on 27 Jan 1893 in Bartholomew Co. IN. Ref.: Family records of Hazel Mobley Ketron; Bartholomew Co. IN death records.

1208. Elsie P. MOBLEY, 11G Granddaughter, born in 1878 in IN. Ref.: 1880 Census.

On 12 Jun 1903 Elsie P. married Anthon M. DAY, in Bartholomew Co. IN.

1209. Nina A. MOBLEY, 11G Granddaughter, born on 9 Oct 1883 in Bartholomew Co. IN. Ref.: Family records of Hazel Mobley Ketron; Bartholomew IN Birth *Record Book H-1*.

1210. Otto W. MOBLEY, 11G Grandson, born on 15 Apr 1886 in Bartholomew Co. IN. Ref.: Family records of Hazel Mobley Ketron. Bartholomew, IN *Birth Record Book H-2*.

Family of Josiah BROWN (774) and Caroline R. ---

1211. Annie B. BROWN, 11G Granddaughter, born on 14 Oct 1886 in MD. Annie B. died in Carroll Co. MD, on 21 Oct 1921; she was 35. Buried at Springfield Cemetery, Sykesville Maryland.

Family of Archibald BROWN (782) and Melinda SELBY

1212. Hattie BROWN, 11G Granddaughter, born on 13 Feb 1870 in Carroll Co. MD.

Hattie married Charles THOMPSON, born on 15 Aug 1880 in Baltimore MD. Charles died on 24 Apr 1950; he was 69.

1213. Ernest Wade BROWN, 11G Grandson, born on 16 Apr 1872 in Howard Co. MD. Ernest Wade died on 24 Apr 1960; he was 88.

Ernest Wade married Catherine MURRY.

Family of Charles E. BROWN (784) and Lucinda A. BROOKELY

1214. Charles H. BROWN, 11G Grandson, born about 1865 in Carroll Co. MD. Charles H. died about 1947. Buried in Springfield Cemetery, Sykesville MD, near the ancestral grounds. Howard Smith wrote (7 Jul 2005) to say that Charles H. Brown "was one of the last Browns to leave the area. In the early 1940's he sold his 100 plus acre farm on Ridge Road to William Haydel. Charles moved to his smaller farm on Marriottsville Road. The only thing I remember about Mr. Brown is that he never owned a car and you would see him riding in his horse and buggy on Marriottsville Road."

Charles H. married Margaret A. ---, born about 1868. Margaret A. died about 1947.

1215. Margaret A. BROWN, 11G Granddaughter, born about 1868. Margaret A. died about 1947. Buried in Springfield Cemetery, Sykesville MD.

1216. Lewis E. BROWN, 11G Grandson, born about 1871. Lewis E. died about 1915. Buried in Springfield Cemetery, Sykesville MD.

1217. Susanna A. BROWN, 11G Granddaughter, born about 1875 in MD. Susanna A. died about 1925 in Carroll Co. MD. Buried in Springfield Cemetery, Sykesville MD.

1218. Lucinda BROWN, 11G Granddaughter, born about 1889. Lucinda died about 1915. Buried in Springfield Cemetery, Sykesville MD.

Family of Lewis E. BROWN (785) and Sarah C. HIGH

1219. George E. BROWN, 11G Grandson, born about 1874 in MD.

1220. Emely C. BROWN, 11G Granddaughter, born about 1877 in MD.

1221. Mary C. BROWN, 11G Granddaughter, born about 1888 in MD.

1222. Laura Virginia BROWN, 11G Granddaughter. Laura Virginia died in Baltimore City MD.

Laura Virginia married Harry Cornelius MUSGROVE, son of Hezekiah MUSGROVE and Rebecca STINEHAGEN, born in Baltimore City MD. Harry Cornelius died in Baltimore City MD. Chief Gardener at Four Farms. They had the following children:

1686	i.	Margaret Hazel (1910-1966)
1687	ii.	Harry
1688	iii.	Brady
1689	iv.	Loyd
1690	v.	Eleanor
1691	vi.	Esther
1692	vii.	Ellsworth
1693	viii.	Pinckney
1694	ix.	Bernard
1695	x.	Sarah

Family of Lloyd A. BROWN (787) and Rebecca ---

1223. Mamie BROWN, 11G Granddaughter, born in 1879 in Howard Co. MD.

1224. Arthur C. BROWN, 11G Grandson, born on 4 Mar 1885 in Carroll Co. MD. Arthur C. died in Carroll Co. MD, on 16 May 1963; he was 78. Buried in Springfield Cemetery, Sykesville MD.

Arthur C. married Virginia ---, born on 22 Feb 1883. Virginia died on 12 Nov 1951; she was 68. Young says her given names were Tirzah Virginia. They had the following children:

1696	i.	Celius L. (1907-1994)
1697	ii.	Arthur Allen (1911-1934)

1225. Harris BROWN, 11G Grandson.

1226. Lucy BROWN, 11G Granddaughter.

1227. George A. BROWN, 11G Grandson, born in Feb 1893. George A. died on 27 Jul 1893 in Carroll Co. MD. Buried in Springfield Cemetery, Sykesville MD.

Family of Saib D. BROWN (789) and Lucrecia ---

1228. F.L. BROWN, 11G Grandson, born about 1892. F.L. died about 1915. Buried at Springfield Cemetery, Sykesville Maryland.

1229. G.O. BROWN, 11G Grandson, born about 1893. G.O. died about 1894. Buried at Springfield Cemetery, Sykesville Maryland.

1230. M.E. BROWN, 11G Grandson, born about 1896. M.E. died about 1897. Buried at Springfield Cemetery, Sykesville Maryland.

Family of Isaiah BROWN (790) and Florence T. G. ---

1231. Florence BROWN, 11G Granddaughter.

1232. Frank D. BROWN, 11G Grandson.

1233. Isabella BROWN, 11G Granddaughter.

Family of Clara Josephine BROWN (794) and "Dr." Jabez SHIPLEY

1234. Osko R. SHIPLEY, 11G Grandson, born on 21 May 1876. Osko R. died on 15 Dec 1910; he was 34.

On 27 Sep 1897 when Osko R. was 21, he married Francis ---. Francis died on 17 Feb 1920. They had the following children:
1698	i.	Walter J. (-1943)
1699	ii.	Osko R. (-1901)
1700	iii.	Ethel
1701	iv.	Viola R. (1909-1988)

1235. Ada Waltz SHIPLEY, 11G Granddaughter, born on 7 Aug 1878. Ada Waltz died on 6 Sep 1881; she was 3.

1236. Birdie Selvena SHIPLEY, 11G Granddaughter, born on 3 Oct 1880 in Mechanicsville, St. Marys Co. MD. Birdie Selvena died in Philadelphia PA, on 29 May 1907; she was 26. Buried on 29 May 1907 in Greenmount Cemetery Philadelphia PA.

On 19 Jul 1899 when Birdie Selvena was 18, she married Lawrence Manogue BOSLER, born on 6 Mar 1878 in Philadelphia PA. Lawrence Manogue died in Philadelphia PA, on 7 Apr 1944; he was 66. They had the following children:
1702	i.	Katherine Selvena (1900-1983)
1703	ii.	Lawrence Manogue (1901-1964)
1704	iii.	Louise Frances "Lulu" (1904-1985)
1705	iv.	Clara Josephine (1906-)

1237. Walter Alaska SHIPLEY, 11G Grandson, born on 27 Sep 1882. Walter Alaska died in Philadelphia PA, on 17 Jan 1897; he was 14. Buried on 19 Jan 1897 in Fernwood Cemetery, Lansdowne, Delaware Co. PA.

1238. Roy Leroy SHIPLEY, 11G Grandson, born on 23 Mar 1885. Roy Leroy died on 4 Mar 1904; he was 18. Buried in Greenmount Cemetery Philadelphia PA.

1239. Clara Josephine SHIPLEY, 11G Granddaughter, born on 21 Apr 1887. Clara Josephine died on 5 Jul 1905; she was 18. Buried in Greenmount Cemetery Philadelphia PA.

1240. Franklin F. SHIPLEY, 11G Grandson, born on 13 Jun 1889. Franklin F. died in Philadelphia PA, on 21 Feb 1944; he was 54. Buried at Lawnview Cemetery, Rockledge, Montgomery County, Pennsylvania.

On 30 Aug 1908 when Franklin F. was 19, he married Rose M. GUYTON, born on 10 Oct 1886. Rose M. died in Sep 1966. They had the following children:
1706	i.	Mabel C. (1909-1965)
1707	ii.	Franklin F. (1911-1969)
1708	iii.	Leroy (1921-)
1709	iv.	Kenneth H. (1928-1928)
1710	v.	Dolores May (1929-)

1241. Florence (Edna May) SHIPLEY, 11G Granddaughter, born on 21 Oct 1890. Florence (Edna May) died on 29 Oct 1926; she was 36.

On 12 Dec 1906 when Florence (Edna May) was 16, she married --- BISHOP. They had the following children:
1711	i.	Alma May (1917-)
1712	ii.	Mildred (1912-)

1242. Charles Howard SHIPLEY, 11G Grandson, born on 26 Jan 1893. Charles Howard died in Philadelphia PA, on 23 Jun 1952; he was 59.

On 27 Aug 1913 when Charles Howard was 20, he married Emily M. STEVENSON. They had the following children:
- 1713   i.   Thelma May (1913-1913)
- 1714   ii.   Charles H. (1916-)
- 1715   iii.   Mildred (1919-)

Family of William LOVETT (806) and Tabatha ---

1243. Elizabeth LOVETT, 11G Granddaughter, born in 1856.

1244. Charles LOVETT, 11G Grandson, born in 1860.

Family of Samuel LOVETT (807) and Mary Ann ---

1245. Joseph LOVETT, 11G Grandson, born about 1854.

1246. Frances LOVETT, 11G Granddaughter, born about 1856.

1247. Georgianna LOVETT, 11G Granddaughter, born about 1859.

Family of Emma BROWN (808) and J. Randolph MORDECAI

1248. Randolph J. MORDECAI, 11G Grandson, born in 1871 in MD.

1249. Florence MORDECAI, 11G Granddaughter, born in 1873 in MD.

Florence married George HARRISON. They had one child:
- 1716   i.   Florence Patterson

1250. Mary J. MORDECAI, 11G Granddaughter, born in 1875 in MD.

1251. George Patterson MORDECAI, 11G Grandson, born on 15 May 1879 in Baltimore MD. George Patterson died in Baltimore MD, on 28 Nov 1955; he was 76. Family and descendants per Doug Mordecai.

George Patterson married Champe Moncure ROBINSON, born on 4 Oct 1874. Champe Moncure died in Baltimore MD, on 13 Nov 1953; she was 79. Buried in Greenmount Cemetery. They had one child:
- 1717   i.   John Robinson (1907-1982)

1252. Louis MORDECAI, 11G Grandson.

1253. Henry MORDECAI, 11G Grandson.

Family of Gov. Francis (Frank) BROWN (817) and Mary RIDGELY

1254. Mary Ridgley "Mamie" or "May" BROWN, 11G Granddaughter **born** in Howard Co. MD. At Frank Brown's death, May Dietrich of New York was the only family member to be present among many Maryland notables who attended the deathbed (Frank Brown obituary, *Baltimore Sun*, 4 Feb 1920).

Mary Ridgley "Mamie" or "May" first married Gordon Hughes. They were divorced.

Mary Ridgley "Mamie" or "May" second married Alfred E. DIETRICH. They were divorced.

Mary Ridgley "Mamie" or "May" third married --- LEE.

1255. Francis Snowden BROWN, 11G Grandson. Francis Snowden died before 1920.

Francis Snowden first married --- ---. They were divorced.

Francis Snowden second married --- ---. They had one child:
    1718   i.   Frank

Family of William M. BROWN (821) and Ida Lee

1256. Eliza BROWN, 11G Granddaughter.

1257. Jessie A. BROWN, 11G Grandson.

1258. Corrie M. BROWN, 11G Granddaughter.

Family of Edward D. BROWN (822) and Susie E. THOMPSON

1259. Elias BROWN, 11G Grandson, born on 9 Jan 1885. Elias died on 7 Jan 1934; he was 48.

Elias married Blanche TROTT, born on 15 Mar 1886. Blanche died on 7 Aug 1968; she was 82. They had one child:
    1719   i.   Albert

Family of Edward D. BROWN (822) and Susannah R. SHIPLEY

1260. Lula Catherine BROWN, 11G Granddaughter, born on 2 Oct 1895. Lula Catherine died in 1923. She died on the birth of a son, who also died. Buried at the Wesley Freedom Cemetery, Eldersburg MD.

Lula Catherine married Roger DAY.

1261. Sara "Sadie" BROWN, 11G Granddaughter, born on 23 May 1896. Sara "Sadie" died on 16 Dec 1966; she was 70. .

On 15 Mar 1916 when Sara "Sadie" was 19, she married William Julius MIELKE, born on 10 Mar 1885. William Julius died on 28 Mar 1977; he was 92. Both buried in Ward's Chapel Cemetery, Randallstown MD. Their children:
    1720   i.   William August (1917-)
    1721   ii.   Julius Edward (1919-)
    1722   iii.   Carl Arthur (1920-)
    1723   iv.   Lula Eleanor (1922-)
    1724   v.   Vernon Walter (1926-)

1262. Edward Lee BROWN, 11G Grandson, born on 9 Sep 1899. Edward Lee died in 1968.

On 2 Oct 1930 when Edward Lee was 31, he married Cornelia JOHNSON. This couple had no issue.

1263. Bessie Susan BROWN, 11G Granddaughter, born on 15 Oct 1900. Bessie Susan died on 16 May 1934..

On 22 Jun 1924 when Bessie Susan was 23, she married Lawrence Joseph GAMBLE, born in 1893. Lawrence Joseph died in 1961. They had the following children:
- 1725   i.   William Robert BEALEFIELD (1921- 1995) Adopted. Reassumed birth surname on coming of age.
- 1726   ii.   Charles Lawrence (1928-)
- 1727   iii.   Edward Bernard (1932-)

1264. William Henry BROWN, 11G Grandson, born on 25 Sep 1904. William Henry died on 20 Oct 1964; he was 60. Buried at the New Oakland Cemetery.

Family of Samuel Thomas BROWN (824) and Nancy "Nannie" MILLER

1265. Nancy Clara Etta BROWN, 11G Granddaughter, born on 24 Dec 1892 in Woodstock, Howard Co., MD. In DAR # 572628 recorded as descendant of Abel Brown.

On 18 Jun 1913 when Nancy Clara Etta was 20, she first married --- KAUFFMANN, who died before 1918.

On 25 Dec 1918 when Nancy Clara Etta was 26, she second married William Wilson SOUTHARD, in Baltimore Co. MD, born on 10 May 1890. William Wilson died on 14 Jan 1965; he was 74. They had one child:
- 1728   i.   William W. (1923-)

1266. Minnie BROWN, 11G Granddaughter.

1267. Bernice BROWN 11G Granddaughter.

Family of Susannah Amelia BROWN (825) and John L. "Acre" PEARCE

1268. Joseph BROWN 11G Grandson.

1269. John BROWN 11G Grandson.

Family of Florence BROWN (826) and Edwin B. HAY

1270. Edward B. HAY, 11G Grandson, born on 19 Aug 1879 in Baltimore Co. MD.

1271. Jewel D. HAY, 11G Granddaughter, born on 9 Nov 1883 in Baltimore Co. MD.

Jewel D. married George NASH, in Baltimore Co. MD. They had one child:
- 1729   i.   George

1272. Paul B. HAY, 11G Grandson, born on 30 Sep 1888 in Baltimore Co. MD.

Family of Fannie BROWN (827) and Richard K. EVANS

1273. Albert S. EVANS, 11G Grandson, born on 8 Sep 1863.

1274. Mildred Lee EVANS, 11G Granddaughter. born on 29 May 1865. Mildred Lee died on 3 Feb 1890; she was 24. On 25 Oct 1889 when Mildred Lee was 24, she married Harry S. TAYLOR.

Family of Albert S. BROWN (828) and Emma POPE

1275. Mildred BROWN, 11G Granddaaughter **born** about 1905.

Family of Miriam E. BROWN (830) and H. J. KEFAUVER

1276. Evans Brown KEFAUVER, 11G Grandson.

Family of William Brown PEARCE (831) and Lillie May COOK

1277. Bertie Cook PEARCE, 11G Granddaughter, born on 17 Jul 1889 in Baltimore Co. MD. Bertie Cook died in 1891.

1278. Mildred Elizabeth PEARCE, 11G Granddaughter, born on 7 Dec 1899 in Baltimore Co. MD.

On 1 Dec 1923 when Mildred Elizabeth was 23, she married Henry Barramore TODD, in Baltimore Co. MD. They had one child:
    1730   i.   Nancy PEARCE (1924-)

Family of George Marshall PEARCE (834) and Mary Elizabeth "Mamie" PARRAN

1279. Anna Elizabeth PEARCE, 11G Granddaughter, born on 19 Jul 1887.

In Mar 1907 Anna Elizabeth married Arthur S. STIVERS, in Baltimore Co. MD. They had one child:
    1731   i.   Elizabeth Jeannie (1908-)

1280. Mary Evelyn PEARCE, 11G Granddaughter, born on 9 Sep 1894 in Baltimore Co. MD. Mary Evelyn died in Baltimore Co. MD, on 2 Aug 1900; she was 5.

Family of Mary Virginia PEARCE (835) and Hershey Simpson CUMMINGS

1281. John Pearce CUMMING, 11G Grandson, born on 9 Apr 1883 in Baltimore Co. MD.

On 10 May 1917 when John Pearce was 34, he married Charlotte Miriam FOSSETT, in Baltimore Co. MD. They had the following children:
    1732   i.   Jeanne Miriam (1918-)
    1733   ii.   Gordon Fossett (1920-)

Family of Lucy Brown REICH (838) and H. Gates SMITH

1282. Eleanor Frances SMITH, 11G Granddaughter, born on 22 Sep 1887 in Baltimore Co. MD.

On 20 Mar 1906 when Eleanor Frances was 18, she married Robert O. WATERS, in Baltimore Co. MD. Children:
- 1734   i.   Eleanor Mildred (1908-)
- 1735   ii.   Robert O. (1908-)
- 1736   iii.   Agnes (1924-)

1283. Agnes SMITH, 11G Granddaughter, born on 27 Jul 1889 in Baltimore Co. MD.

On 25 Aug 1913 when Agnes was 24, she married Alvin H. GRAY, in Baltimore Co. MD.

1284. Gordon SMITH, 11G Grandson, born on 2 Mar 1893 in Baltimore Co. MD.

On 24 Dec 1914 when Gordon was 21, he married Drusilla KILLEBREW, in Baltimore Co. MD.

Family of Leonora P. "Lena" SHRYOCK (844) and Samuel TREGALLAS

1285. Samuel Staley TREGALLAS, 11G Grandson, born about 1881.

Samuel Staley married Helen A. PAGENSTECHER. This family had one son (McCallahan).

Family of Edward Augustus COCKEY (848) and Alice Mitchell COUNCILMAN

1286. Urath Cromwell COCKEY, 11G Granddaughter, born on 10 Oct 1879 in Baltimore Co. MD. Urath Cromwell died on 13 Feb 1882; she was 2.

1287. Charles Thomas COCKEY, 11G Grandson, born on 19 Oct 1880 in Baltimore Co. MD. Charles Thomas died on 2 Feb 1882; he was 1.

1288. Edward Augustus COCKEY, 11G Grandson, born on 6 Jun 1882 in Baltimore Co. MD.

On 9 Nov 1909 when Edward Augustus was 27, he married Nannie Strother MOORE, daughter of Alexander Compton MOORE and Nannie BUTLER, in Baltimore Co. MD. They had the following children:
- 1737   i.   Urath Cromwell (1911-)
- 1738   ii.   Edward Augustus (1913-)
- 1739   iii.   Alexander Moore (1915-)
- 1740   iv.   Alice Councilman (1917-)

1289. John Councilman COCKEY, 11G Grandson, born on 5 Jun 1884 in Baltimore Co. MD. John Councilman died in Baltimore Co. MD, on 30 Oct 1918; he was 34.

On 10 Nov 1908 when John was 24, he married Florence Lydia SOTHORON, daughter of Rev. Levin SOTHORON and Lydia CASTOR. Florence died on 30 Oct 1918. They died from the influenza epidemic on the same day. They had the following children:
- 1741   i.   Lydia Sothoron (1912-)
- 1742   ii.   John Sothoron (1916-)

1290. Alexander Drummond COCKEY, 11G Grandson, born on 23 Jun 1886 in Baltimore Co. MD.

On 6 Nov 1915 when Alexander Drummond was 29, he first married Frances BURLEY, in Baltimore Co. MD. Frances died before 1921. They had one child:
- 1743   i.   Alice Councilman "Frances" (1917-)

On 15 Oct 1921 when Alexander Drummond was 35, he second married Ellen Rebecca MOORE, daughter of Charles H. MOORE and Alice GARDINER, in Baltimore Co. MD. They had one child:
- 1744   i.   Alexander (1922-)

Family of Ann A. COCKEY (849) and Dr. Cameron PIGGOT

1291. Charles Snowden PIGGOT, 11G Grandson, born on 5 Jun 1892 in Baltimore Co. MD.

1292. William Cameron PIGGOT, 11G Grandson, born on 3 Feb 1895 in Baltimore Co. MD. William Cameron died in Baltimore Co. MD, on 3 Mar 1895; he was less than 1.

Family of Thomas Beale COCKEY (850) and Mary Thomas "Mamie" WARFIELD

1293. Eva COCKEY, 11G Granddaughter, born in 1886 in Baltimore Co. MD.

Eva married Henry REGISTER, in Baltimore Co. MD.

1294. Sally Ann COCKEY, 11G Granddaughter, born in 1889 in Baltimore Co. MD.

Sally Ann married William Maury WERTH, in Baltimore Co. MD. They had the following children:
- 1745   i.   Virginia Lee
- 1746   ii.   Sally Ann

1295. Emma Shepherd COCKEY, 11G Granddaughter, born in 1891 in Baltimore Co. MD.

Emma Shepherd married Bruce H. HELFRICH, in Baltimore Co. MD. They had the following children:
- 1747   i.   Emma Shepherd
- 1748   ii.   Robert Bruce
- 1749   iii.   Thomas Cockey
- 1750   iv.   Samuel Cockey

1296. Charles Thomas COCKEY, 11G Grandson, born in 1893 in Baltimore Co. MD.

1297. Thomas Beale COCKEY, 11G Grandson, born in 1895 in Baltimore Co. MD.

Thomas Beale married Sarah Davis BRADLEY, in Baltimore Co. MD.

Family of Charles Thomas COCKEY (853) and Mary Clarke COOK

1298. Charles Thomas COCKEY, 11G Grandson, born on 13 Aug 1905.

1299. Mary COCKEY, 11G Granddaughter, born on 7 Sep 1906. Mary died in 1906.

Family of Walter TILYARD (856) and Grace GIBSON

1300. Dorothy TILYARD, 11G Granddaughter.

Dorothy married Col. Edward M. HOSHALL.

1301. Walter Robert TILYARD, 11G Grandson.

Family of Laura Ella BENNETT (859) and Johnzie E. BEASMAN

1302. Frank Bennett BEASMAN, 11G Grandson, born on 10 May 1889 in Sykesville MD. Frank Bennett died in Baltimore MD, on 10 Jul 1960; he was 71.

On 12 Dec 1923 when Frank Bennett was 34, he married Viola Jeanette RITTER, in MD.

1303. (Infant) BEASMAN, 11G Grandson, born on 2 Jun 1888. (Infant) died on 2 Jun 1888; he was less than 1.

Family of Claude LAWRENCE (869) and Inez SHOEMAKER

1304. Hazel Dell LAWRENCE, 11G Granddaughter, born on 5 Mar 1902 in ND. Hazel Dell died in Hansboro, Towner Co. ND, on 19 May 1954; she was 52.

On 26 Jun 1923 when Hazel Dell was 21, she married Carl JOHNSON, born on 20 Sep 1900 in Rolla, Rolette Co. ND.

Family of George Edward MCCLINTOCK (872) and Olive Ann LITTLE

1305. Alma Louise MCCLINTOCK, 11G Granddaughter, born in 1919 in Fresno, Fresno Co. CA.

Family of Charles Larkin LAWRENCE (877) and Grace Darling BARNHART

1306. Hazel LAWRENCE, 11G Granddaughter, born on 25 Mar 1904 in MO.

Family of Edward Dawes MCCONKY (884) and Nellie Brown LASSITER

1307. Eleanor MCCONKY, 11G Granddaughter.

Eleanor married --- MCCALLAHAN.

Family of Edward Randolph COCKEY (887) and Ellen LUCAS

1308. Randolph Lucas COCKEY, 11G Grandson, born on 26 Aug 1910 in Baltimore Co. MD. Randolph Lucas died in Baltimore Co. MD, on 14 Dec 1967; he was 57.

On 31 May 1941 when Randolph Lucas was 30, he married Louise Dilworth KEYSER, in Baltimore Co. MD. They had the following children:
1751	i.	Randolph Lucas (1942-)
1752	ii.	Robert Fielding (1944-)
1753	iii.	Louise Randall (1947-)
1754	iv.	Christopher Slade (1957-)

Family of Chauncey Brooks BOSLEY (896) and Alice HELM

1309. Jean BOSLEY, 11G Granddaughter

1310. Chauncy Brooks BOSLEY, 11G Grandson.

1311. William Henry BOSLEY, 11G Grandson.

Family of Harry Cockey STOCKSDALE (899) and Grace Irene HITCHENS

1312. John Hitchens STOCKSDALE, 11G Grandson, born on 21 Aug 1896. John Hitchens died on 10 Apr 1929; he was 32.

Family of Annie Ida STOCKSDALE (903) and N. Dorsey NORRIS

1313. Elizabeth NORRIS, 11G Granddaughter.

Family of George Tevis STOCKSDALE (907) and Annie YOX

1314. Elizabeth Jane STOCKSDALE, 11G Granddaughter, born on 23 Mar 1891.

Family of Clara May STOCKSDALE (909) and William Oliver BOLDEN

1315. William BOLDEN, 11G Grandson, born on 5 Aug 1893.

1316. Olie Mazie BOLDEN, 11G Granddaughter, born on 20 Jul 1894.

1317. Lulu Lee BOLDEN, 11G Granddaughter, born on 25 Aug 1899. Lulu Lee died on 17 Feb 1901; she was 1.

Family of Annie Howard STOCKSDALE (910) and Harold Randolph MORGAN

1318. Harold Randolph MORGAN, 11G Grandson, born on 20 Nov 1890.

Family of Lillie Eliza STOCKSDALE (912) and William Butler DOWNES

1319. William Beryl DOWNES, 11G Grandson, born on 5 Aug 1896.

Family of Emma Dolly BASEMAN (921) and Irving GOSNELL

1320. Bernard GOSNELL, 11G Grandson.

Bernard married Ivy BRIGHTWELL.

1321. Edna GOSNELL, 11G Granddaughter. Edna died in May 1919.

Family of Fannie Howard BASEMAN (922) and Thomas N. IRELAND

1322. Thomas Moale IRELAND, 11G Grandson, born on 9 May 1882 in Carroll Co. MD. Thomas Moale died in Carroll Co. MD, on 23 Sep 1961; he was 79. Buried Finksburg Cemetery.

1323. Jack IRELAND, 11G Grandson.

1324. Norris Ireland IRELAND, 11G Grandson, born on 7 Feb 1885.

1325. Frank Howard IRELAND, 11G Grandson, born on 3 Jul 1891.

1326. Deborah "Fannie" IRELAND, 11G Granddaughter, born on 3 Jul 1891 in Carroll Co. MD. Deborah "Fannie" died in Carroll Co. MD, on 28 Nov 1983; she was 92. Buried at Finksburg Cemetery.

Deborah "Fannie" married Fred Reed MUSE. They had the following children:
1755	i.	Helen M.
1756	ii.	Julia A.
1757	iii.	Fred R.
1758	iv.	John M.
1759	v.	C. Thomas
1760	vi.	William F.

1327. Julia IRELAND, 11G Granddaughter.

1328. Campbell Charles IRELAND, 11G Grandson, born about 1903 in Carroll Co. MD. Campbell Charles died about 1975 in Carroll Co. MD. Buried at Finksburg Cemetery.

Campbell Charles married Inez B. ---.

Family of Grant T. BASEMAN (926) and Rosse YOX

1329. Grant A. BASEMAN, 11G Grandson, born about 1918 in MD. Grant A. died on 27 Jan 1986 in Baltimore Co. MD. *Carroll County Times* obituary of 28 Jan 1986 per Field.

Grant A. married Mamie MYERS. They had the following children:
1761	i.	Grant A.
1762	ii.	Earl G.
1763	iii.	Vincent
1764	iv.	Frances
1765	v.	Joan

Family of Solomon OSBORN (932) and Dicey SMITH

1330. Joseph OSBORN, 11G Grandson, born in 1825 in IL.

On 6 Dec 1848 Joseph married Mary C. ELKINS, in Franklin Co. IL, born in 1832 in IL. They had one child:
1766	i.	W. T. (1849-)

1331. William M. OSBORN, 11G Grandson, born in 1827.

William M. married Sarah M. HARRIS, daughter of Benjamin HARRIS and Abigail BROOKS, born in 1830 in NY. They had the following children:
1767	i.	Emmett A. (1854 - before 1920)

1768	ii.	Aevlia? (1858-)
1769	iii.	Caroline M. (1863-)
1770	iv.	William R. (1865-)
1771	v.	Milton N. (1868-)
1772	vi.	Malona S. (1869-)
1773	vii.	Xanthus L. (1871-)

1332. Elizabeth OSBORN, 11G Granddaughter, born in 1829 in Vermillion Co. IL.

Elizabeth married John WEBB, born in 1829.

1333. Lydia OSBORN, 11G Granddaughter, born in 1830 in Vermillion Co. IL.

On 31 Aug 1850 Lydia married William Raleigh SMITH, in Franklin Co. IL, born about 1827 in IA. They had one child:
| 1774 | i. | Solomon (1860-1934) |

1334. Isaac OSBORN, 11G Grandson, born in 1832 in 1832. Isaac died before 1878.

On 26 Feb 1854 Isaac married Sarah ---, in McDonough Co. IL, born about 1836 in IN.

1335. Nancy OSBORN, 11G Granddaughter, born in 1835 in IA.

On 19 Nov 1859 Nancy married John GRIFFITH, in McDonough Co. IL, born about 1831 in IA.

1336. Mary Smith OSBORN, 11G Granddaughter, born on 2 Oct 1836 in Ithaca, Tompkins Co. NY. Mary Smith died in Rochester, Monroe Co. NY, on 12 Sep 1880; she was 43.

On 10 Jan 1856 when Mary Smith was 19, she first married Samuel P. WILHEIMS, in McDonough Co. IL, who was born about 1833 in IA.

On 20 Sep 1858 when Mary Smith was 21, she second married Samuel H. WILLIAMS, in Ithaca, Tompkins Co. NY, born on 22 Jan 1822 in Crookhaven, County Cork, Ireland. Samuel H. died in Rochester, Monroe Co. NY, on 27 Mar 1890; he was 68. They had the following children:
1775	i.	John Samuel (1859-1861)
1776	ii.	Samuel Kingston (1861-1864)
1777	iii.	Ida (1864-1878)
1778	iv.	William Mead (1867-1956)
1779	v.	Minnie (1868-1936)

1337. Francis Marion OSBORN, 11G Grandson, born on 16 Sep 1838 in Franklin Co. IL. Francis Marion died in Stillwater, Payne Co. OK, on 18 Mar 1901; he was 62. Buried in Osborn Family Cemetery, Stillwater OK.

On 3 Mar 1861 when Francis Marion was 22, he married Catherine HUSTED, in McDonough Co. IL, who was born in 1842 in McDonough Co. IL. Catherine died in May 1873 in Cowley Co. KS. They had the following children:
1780	i.	Louisa (1863-)
1781	ii.	Eva Augusta (1865-1914)
1782	iii.	Albert A. (1867-)
1783	iv.	Dudley E. (1870-)
1784	v.	Josephine (1872-1943)

1338. Elijah S. OSBORN, 11G Grandson, born on 16 Aug 1841 in IL. Elijah S. died in Lebanon, Linn Co. OR, on 30 Sep 1901; he was 60.

On 29 Dec 1862 when Elijah S. was 21, he married Lucinda DRISKELL, in McDonough Co. IL, who was born on 24 Sep 1844 in IL. Lucinda died in 1918 in OR. They had the following children:
1785	i.	Nellie Filena (1863-1934)
1786	ii.	Parthena A. (1866-1939)
1787	iii.	Roena Evaline or Estaline (1868 - about 1945)

1788	iv.	Francis N. (1870-1872)
1789	v.	Teressa Emaline (1873-1950)
1790	vi.	Homer M. (1875-1955)
1791	vii.	Lulu E. (1878-1963)
1792	viii.	Charles A. (1881-1968)

1339. Louisa OSBORN, 11G Granddaughter, born on 13 Apr 1842 in Franklin Co. IL. Louisa died in Industry, McDonough Co. IL, on 8 Aug 1913; she was 71.

On 18 Mar 1860 when Louisa was 17, she married John Wesley FLACK, in McDonough Co. IL, who was born on 30 Dec 1840 in Schuyler, IL. John Wesley died in Kansas City, Jackson Co. MO, on 13 Nov 1932; he was 91. They had the following children:

1793	i.	Elijah Alexander (1860-1955)
1794	ii.	Alice B. (1862-1945)
1795	iii.	Charles Wesley (1865-1950)
1796	iv.	Willis Edgar (1868-1940)
1797	v.	Lucy E. (1870-)
1798	vi.	Louis E. (1870-1946)

1340. M. Jane OSBORN, 11G Granddaughter, born in 1844 in IL.

On 8 Mar 1866 M. Jane married William MCHALEY, in Schuyler, IL, born about 1840 in IL.

1341. Aurena OSBORN, 11G Granddaughter, born in 1847 in IL.

On 8 Nov 1866 Aurena married Elisha A. FRISBIE, in McDonough Co. IL, born about 1843 in IL.

1342. Dicy Ann OSBORN, 11G Granddaughter, born on 22 May 1850 in McDonough Co. IL. Dicy Ann died on 1 Mar 1919; she was 68.

On 1 Aug 1867 when Dicy Ann was 17, she married Peter E. SMITH, in McDonough Co. IL, born about 1846 in McDonough Co. IL.

1343. Alfria OSBORN, 11G Granddaughter, born in 1851 in McDonough Co. IL. Alfria died before 1878.

1344. Lucinda OSBORN, 11G Granddaughter, born in 1851.

On 1 Aug 1868 Lucinda first married John S. WEBB, in Franklin Co. IL, born in 1847 in McDonough Co. IL.

Lucinda second married Elsa JOHNSON, born in 1835.

Family of Solomon OSBORN (932) and Elsa JOHNSON

1345. Ada Louella OSBORN, 11G Granddaughter, born in 1866 in IL.

1346. Sarah Almeda OSBORN, 11G Granddaughter, born on 23 Sep 1868 in IL.

Sarah Almeda married Harry TINKER, born about 1865.

1347. Lorina OSBORN, 11G Granddaughter, born on 6 Sep 1871. Lorina died on 10 Apr 1949; she was 77.

Lorina married John HILTY.

1348. Dora Alice OSBORN, 11G Granddaughter, born on 24 Mar 1873. Dora Alice died on 7 Jun 1947; she was 74.

Dora Alice married Eddy D. HILTY.

1349. John OSBORN, 11G Grandson, born in 1874.

1350. Noah Webster OSBORN, 11G Grandson, born on 9 Nov 1876. Noah Webster died on 8 Dec 1943; he was 67.

1351. Henry C. OSBORN, 11G Grandson, born in 1877.

Family of Lydia OSBORN (933) and Ephraim OSBORNE

1352. Mary Jane OSBORN, 11G Granddaughter, born in 1828 in IL.

1353. John OSBORN, 11G Grandson, born on 12 Feb 1833 in IL.

1354. Eliza OSBORN, 11G Granddaughter, born in 1835 in IL.

1355. Joseph OSBORN, 11G Grandson, born in 1838 in IL.

1356. Andrew Jackson OSBORNE, 11G Grandson, born on 2 Jan 1847 in IL.

In about 1863 Andrew Jackson first married Mary SALLADE, in MO. Mary died on 2 Dec 1869. They had the following children:
1799	i.	Margaret (1864-)
1800	ii.	Angeline (1865-)
1801	iii.	Andrew Jackson (1869-1870)

Andrew Jackson second married Sarah A. VERMILLION, born on 2 Feb 1858 in MO. They had one child:
1802	i.	Dewey (1898-)

On 29 Jan 1870 when Andrew Jackson was 23, he third married Jane LAININGER, in Adair Co. MO, born in 1844 in PA. Surname also given as Lanzier. They had the following children:
1803	i.	Lydia Adella (1871-)
1804	ii.	Arthur Selvester (1873-1945)
1805	iii.	Mary Alfretta (1875-1954)
1806	iv.	Addie Ella (1877-1893)
1807	v.	Joseph William (1878-)
1808	vi.	Armina (1880-)
1809	vii.	John Albert (1886-1945)
1810	viii.	Albert A. (1885-)
1811	ix.	Viola (1893-)
1812	x.	Violet (1893-)

1357. Daniel Boone OSBORN, 11G Grandson, born in Jul 1850 in IL. Daniel Boone died about 1920.

1358. Francis OSBORN, 11G Grandson, born in 1852.

Family of John OSBORN (934) and Frances HACKWORTH

1359. Susannah OSBORN, 11G Granddaughter, born in 1830 in IL.

1360. Sarah OSBORN, 11G Granddaughter, born in 1833 in IL.

1361. Andrew J. OSBORN, 11G Grandson, born in 1835 in IL.

1362. Daniel OSBORN, 11G Grandson, born in 1836 in IL.

1363. Hiram OSBORN, 11G Grandson, born on 25 Nov 1838 in IL.

On 4 Oct 1860 when Hiram was 21, he married Lucy Mahala HUNTLY, in Putnam Co. MO. They had the following children:
1813	i.	Willis P. (1866-)
1814	ii.	Albert W. (1868-)

1364. James OSBORN, 11G Grandson, born in 1840 in IL.

James married Mary A. WATTS. They had the following children:
1815	i.	Sarah (1863-)
1816	ii.	Emma (1865-)
1817	iii.	Annette (1867-)
1818	iv.	James (1869-)

1365. Martha OSBORN, 11G Granddaughter, born in 1843 in IL.

1366. Robert OSBORN, 11G Grandson, born in 1846 in IL.

On 2 Oct 1870 Robert married Mary Elizabeth J. FRAKES, in McDonough Co. IL. They had the following children:
1819	i.	William (1872-)
1820	ii.	Isaac (1873-)
1821	iii.	Emmasiah (1875-)
1822	iv.	Susannah (1876-)
1823	v.	Brice (1879-)

1367. Isaac OSBORN, 11G Grandson, born in 1851.

1368. John OSBORN, 11G Grandson, born in 1853.

Family of Stephen Jones OSBORN (935) and Julian SIMPSON

1369. Jasper OSBORN, 11G Grandson, born about 1854.

1370. Lydia OSBORN, 11G Granddaughter, born in 1856.

Family of Sabrina OSBORN (936) and John MAYFIELD

1371. Joseph MAYFIELD, 11G Grandson, born in 1842.

1372. James MAYFIELD, 11G Grandson, born in 1845.

1373. Nancy MAYFIELD, 11G Granddaughter, born in 1848.

Family of Andrew Jackson OSBORN (937) and Elizabeth COCKERHAM

1374. Louisa OSBORN, 11G Granddaughter, born in 1844 in McDonough Co. IL.

1375. Abner OSBORN, 11G Grandson, born in 1846 in McDonough Co. IL.

1376. Rachel A. OSBORN, 11G Granddaughter, born on 15 Dec 1849 in McDonough Co. IL.

1377. Stephen OSBORN, 11G Grandson, born on 10 Oct 1855 in Industry, McDonough Co. IL. Stephen died in Orange Co. CA, on 21 Feb 1944; he was 88.

1378. Finis OSBORN, 11G Grandson, born in 1858 in Industry, McDonough Co. IL.

1379. Joseph OSBORN, 11G Grandson, born in 1863 in Industry, McDonough Co. IL.

Family of William W. ALLEY (948) and Angeline MARTIN

1380. Emily Savannah ALLEY, 11G Granddaughter, born in 1843 in KY.

Emily Savannah married Jacob ROSIER, born after 4 Jul 1835 in Wildcat, Tipton Co. IN. They had one child:
 1824 i. Minora Angeline (1869-)

Family of Mary Francis "Polly" DRACE (977) and David Campbell MALONEY

1381. Sara Eliza "Sadie" MALONEY, 11G Granddaughter, born on 9 Aug 1866 in Washington, Franklin Co. MO. Sara Eliza "Sadie" died in Brunswick, Chariton Co. MO, on 19 Aug 1956; she was 90.

On 11 Apr 1888 when Sara Eliza "Sadie" was 21, she married George Washington STAUBUS, son of Christian Wilhelm STAUBUS and Nancy Jane CORMAN, in Brunswick, Charlton Co. MO, born in Jun 1860 in Bristol, Sullivan Co. TN. George Washington died on 18 May 1918 in Brunswick, Charlton Co. MO. "[The couple] met when he applied for a teaching position at Allega School. Interview was with school board member, David Campbell Maloney" (Sisseck, citing her aunt Mary Dean). They had the following children:
 1825 i. Clara Mae (1889-1979)
 1826 ii. Mary Etta "Dolly" (1891 - after 1916)
 1827 iii. George Washington (1893-1983)
 1828 iv. Alma Virginia (1896-)
 1829 v. John Henry (1898-)

1382. William Archibald MALONEY, 11G Grandson, born in Feb 1868 in Franklin Co. MO. William Archibald died in 1935 in Lockwood, Dade Co. MO.

1383. Amanda Lee MALONEY, 11G Granddaughter, born on 5 Oct 1869 in Franklin Co. MO.

Amanda Lee married William A. STAUBUS, son of Christian Wilhelm STAUBUS and Nancy Jane CORMAN.

1384. Eda Lurene MALONEY, 11G Granddaughter, born on 16 Apr 1872 in Franklin Co. MO.

Eda Lurene married --- SHELTON.

1385. Eugene Pollard MALONEY, 11G Grandson, born on 5 May 1874 in Franklin Co. MO. Eugene Pollard died on 22 Apr 1953; he was 78.

In 1903 Eugene Pollard married Lula Dell KENNEDY.

1386. David Crocket MALONEY, 11G Grandson, born on 16 Jun 1880 in perhaps Charlton Co. MO.

1387. Frank Sterling MALONEY, 11G Grandson, born on 11 Apr 1885 in Brunswick, Charlton Co. MO.

Family of Margaret Susan COMPTON (982) and Hugh Bell SMITH

1388. Sally SMITH, 11G Granddaughter.

Sally married John Ace EYE.

Family of Elizabeth LANHAM (985) and John Thomas JAMES

1389. John Wesley JAMES, 11G Grandson, born on 28 May 1873 in Erath Co. TX. John Wesley died in Post, Garza Co. TX, on 2 Oct 1917; he was 44.

1390. Mittie JAMES, 11G Granddaughter, born on 6 Feb 1876.

1391. Allan JAMES, 11G Grandson.

Family of Solomon Thomas LANHAM (998) and Sara MASON

1392. Elizabeth LANHAM, 11G Granddaughter.

1393. Matilda LANHAM, 11G Granddaughter.

1394. Randolph LANHAM, 11G Grandson.

1395. Frank LANHAM, 11G Grandson.

1396. Abe LANHAM, 11G Grandson.

1397. Mary LANHAM, 11G Granddaughter.

Family of Cynthia Elizabeth LANHAM (1000) and Josiah Washington EVANS

1398. Emma Abigail EVANS, 11G Granddaughter, born on 1 Jan 1861. Emma Abigail died on 30 May 1939; she was 78.

1399. William Randolph EVANS, 11G Grandson, born on 19 Feb 1863. William Randolph died on 13 Jun 1864; he was 1.

1400. Ora Lee EVANS, 11G Granddaughter, born on 29 Dec 1865 in Collinsville TX. Ora Lee died in Moore, MT, on 7 May 1950; she was 84.

1401. Joe Boomer EVANS, 11G Grandson, born on 17 Jan 1868 in Parke Co. TX. Joe Boomer died in Jacksboro, Jack Co. TX, on 29 Jul 1954; he was 86.

1402. John Benton EVANS, 11G Grandson, born on 20 Feb 1870 in Collinsville TX. John Benton died in Mountainair, NM, on 4 Dec 1957; he was 87.

1403. Susan James EVANS, 11G Granddaughter, born on 7 Mar 1872. Susan James died on 9 Oct 1873; she was 1.

1404. George Washington EVANS, 11G Grandson, born on 12 Jan 1874. George Washington died on 12 Jan 1874; he was less than 1.

1405. Erby Doyle EVANS, 11G Grandson, born on 28 Nov 1874 in Collinsville TX. Erby Doyle died in Olney, TX, on 30 May 1947; he was 72.

1406. Cintha Theodisia EVANS, 11G Granddaughter, born on 26 Jan 1877. Cintha Theodisia died on 8 Oct 1878; she was 1.

1407. Josiah Theodore EVANS, 11G Grandson, born on 26 Jan 1877. Josiah Theodore died in Cundiff Cemetery, Jack Co. TX, on 12 May 1894; he was 17.

Family of Joseph B. LANHAM (1002) and Mary POWELL

1408. Jodie LANHAM, 11G Granddaughter.

1409. Annie LANHAM, 11G Granddaughter.

1410. Lizzie LANHAM, 11G Granddaughter.

Family of John Castleton LANHAM (1003) and R. Josephine ---

1411. Benton LANHAM, 11G Grandson.

1412. Jim LANHAM, 11G Grandson.

1413. Docia LANHAM, 11G Granddaughter.

1414. Mary Elizabeth LANHAM, 11G Granddaughter, born on 1 Dec 1876. Mary Elizabeth died in Taylor Co. TX, on 17 Jan 1967; she was 90.

1415. Jaley LANHAM, 11G Granddaughter.

1416. Myrtle LANHAM, 11G Granddaughter.

1417. Lela LANHAM, 11G Granddaughter.

1418. Charlie LANHAM, 11G Grandson.

1419. Jodie LANHAM, 11G Granddaughter.

1420. Bonnie LANHAM, 11G Granddaughter.

Family of Sarah Jane LANHAM (1004) and Shadrack James CONNER

1421. Mary Angelina CONNER, 11G Granddaughter, born on 11 Jun 1866 in Navarro Co. TX. Mary Angelina died in Kaufman Co. TX.

1422. Lucy CONNER, 11G Granddaughter, born on 28 Jul 1869 in TX. Lucy died on 3 Jun 1940; she was 70.

1423. Jaley CONNER, 11G Granddaughter, born on 2 Jun 1870 in Navarro Co. TX. Jaley died in Hunt Co. TX, on 1 Oct 1913; she was 43.

1424. Ruth CONNER, 11G Granddaughter, born in 1872 in Navarro Co. TX. Ruth died on 21 Dec 1945 in Dallas, Dallas Co. TX.

1425. Thomas Randolph CONNER, 11G Grandson, born on 11 Jun 1875. Died in Kaufman Co. TX, on 24 Feb 1937.

1426. Emma CONNER, 11G Granddaughter, born on 2 Mar 1877 in TX. Emma died in Kaufman Co. TX, on 2 Nov 1913; she was 36.

1427. Elizabeth CONNER, 11G Granddaughter, born in 1878.

1428. Theodicia CONNER, 11G Granddaughter, born on 15 Sep 1881. Theodicia died in Dallas, Dallas Co. TX, on 15 Aug 1948; she was 66.

1429. Edwin Joseph CONNER, 11G Grandson, born in Jan 1881 in Corsicana, Navarro Co. TX. Edwin Joseph died on 17 Apr 1949 in Shamrock TX.

1430. Charlie B. CONNER, 11G Grandson, born in Nov 1887 in TX. Charlie B. died in 1953 in Kaufman Co. TX.

Family of Jailie Ann LANHAM (1005) and James Rufus EVANS

1431. Cora Lee EVANS, 11G Granddaughter, born on 13 Jul 1868.

1432. Charlie Randolph EVANS, 11G Grandson, born on 26 Nov 1869. Charlie Randolph died in 1933.

1433. James Bunyan EVANS, 11G Grandson, born on 17 Mar 1872. James Bunyan died on 10 Nov 1880; he was 8.

1434. Susan Exer EVANS, 11G Granddaughter, born on 28 Aug 1874.

1435. William Walter EVANS, 11G Grandson, born on 20 Apr 1879. William Walter died on 4 Feb 1944; he was 64.

1436. Joseph Walter EVANS, 11G Grandson, born on 20 Jun 1882. Joseph Walter died on 4 Jun 1943; he was 60.

1437. Claude Max EVANS, 11G Grandson, born on 27 Apr 1884.

Claude Max first married Minnie Mae VEASY.

Claude Max second married Mary Ann RAY.

Family of Margaret Narcissa LANHAM (1007) and Columbus G. EVANS

1438. John E. EVANS, 11G Grandson.

1439. Mary O. EVANS, 11G Granddaughter.

1440. Albert M. EVANS, 11G Grandson.

1441. William G. EVANS, 11G Grandson.

Family of Margaret Narcissa LANHAM (1007) and Joseph W. JOLLY

1442. May JOLLY, 11G Granddaughter.

Family of Hannah Theodicia LANHAM (1009) and Robert HEROLD

1443. Sadie HEROLD, 11G Granddaughter.

1444. James HEROLD, 11G Grandson.

1445. Joe HEROLD, 11G Grandson.

1446. Evelyn HEROLD, 11G Granddaughter.

1447. Johnson HEROLD, 11G Grandson.

Family of Maria Jane Curtis LANHAM (1016) and Holland Coffey RANDOLPH

1448. Olive Louisa RANDOLPH, 11G Granddaughter, born on 18 Apr 1873 in Grayson Co. TX. Olive Louisa died in Marietta, OK, on 9 Sep 1943; she was 70.

1449. Laura Alice RANDOLPH, 11G Granddaughter, born on 11 Aug 1875.

1450. Ella Mae RANDOLPH, 11G Granddaughter, born on 23 Apr 1878. Ella Mae died in Garvin Co. OK, on 2 Jul 1879; she was 1.

1451. Joseph Edwin RANDOLPH, 11G Grandson, born on 1 Apr 1880.

1452. Ora Vivian RANDOLPH, 11G Granddaughter, born on 22 Sep 1882.

1453. Cora Belle RANDOLPH, 11G Granddaughter, born on 23 Jan 1885.

1454. Eula Tobitha RANDOLPH, 11G Granddaughter, born on 13 Jul 1888.

1455. Raymond Coffee RANDOLPH, 11G Grandson, born on 18 Aug 1890.

1456. James Bedford RANDOLPH, 11G Grandson, born on 2 Mar 1894.

1457. William Wirt RANDOLPH, 11G Grandson, born on 17 Apr 1896. William Wirt died in Aug 1973 in VA.

Family of Mary Margaret LANHAM (1018) and Reuben Thomas BATES

1458. Beulah Ann BATES, 11G Granddaughter, born on 4 Aug 1874 in Gatesville, Coryell Co. TX. Beulah Ann died in Eastland Co. TX, on 31 Jul 1973; she was 98.

1459. Luther Edwin BATES, 11G Grandson, born on 16 Dec 1876 in Levita, Coryville Co. TX. Luther Edwin died in Fort Worth, Tarrant Co. TX, on 19 Dec 1930; he was 54.

1460. Flora Alice BATES, 11G Granddaughter, born on 31 Jan 1880 in Comanche Co. TX. Flora Alice died in San Angelo, Tom Green Co. TX, on 14 Jan 1956; she was 75.

1461. James Carroll BATES, 11G Grandson, born on 12 Mar 1882 in Comanche Co. TX. James Carroll died in Brown Co. TX, on 8 Jun 1946; he was 64.

On 5 Oct 1930 when James Carroll was 48, he married Mary NEWBY, daughter of Charles NEWBY and Belle TERRY, in San Angelo, Tom Green Co. TX, born in 1893 in TX. Mary died after 1961.

1462. Doctor Kiefer BATES, 11G Grandson, born on 13 Apr 1885 in Comanche Co. TX. Doctor Kiefer died in Comanche Co. TX, on 30 Sep 1887; he was 2.

1463. Isaac Whitt BATES, 11G Grandson, born on 28 Nov 1887 in Comanche Co. TX. Isaac Whitt died in El Paso, Hudspeth Co. TX, on 14 Oct 1919; he was 31.

On 24 Aug 1915 when Isaac Whitt was 27, he married Mabel Cora POWELL, daughter of Lee POWELL and Lannie HICKMAN, in Fort Stockton TX, born in 1896 in TX.

1464. Mary Elizabeth BATES, 11G Granddaughter, born on 5 Jul 1891 in Comanche Co. TX. Mary Elizabeth died in San Angelo, Tom Green Co. TX, on 20 Feb 1984; she was 92.

1465. Fannie Mae BATES, 11G Granddaughter, born on 11 Jul 1894 in Comanche Co. TX. Fannie Mae died in San Angelo, Tom Green Co. TX, on 20 Feb 1984; she was 89.

On 14 Jan 1924 when Fannie Mae was 29, she married Charles Watson BILLINGS, son of George Henry BILLINGS and Eliza Tennessee DRAPER, in Dallas, Dallas Co. TX, born on 5 Jul 1882 in Pike Co. AR. Charles Watson died in Dallas Co. TX, on 17 Sep 1978; he was 96.

1466. Harriett Lanham BATES, 11G Granddaughter, born on 15 Aug 1898 in Comanche Co. TX. Harriett Lanham died in Downey, Los Angeles Co. CA, on 15 Jul 1984; she was 85.

Family of James Millard LANHAM (1019) and Fannie L. BISHOP

1467. Anna LANHAM, 11G Granddaughter.

1468. Bedford LANHAM, 11G Grandson.

1469. Carolyn Bethal LANHAM, 11G Granddaughter.

1470. Inez LANHAM, 11G Granddaughter.

1471. James B. LANHAM, 11G Grandson.

1472. Samuel LANHAM, 11G Grandson.

1473. Frank Millard LANHAM, 11G Grandson, born on 22 Sep 1900 in TX. Frank Millard died in Tarrant Co. TX, on 20 Oct 1968; he was 68.

Family of Georgia Alice LANHAM (1020) and Sam LANDIS

1474. John M. LANDIS, 11G Grandson.

1475. Robert LANDIS, 11G Grandson.

1476. Frank LANDIS, 11G Grandson.

Family of Annie Maud LANHAM (1024) and Benjamin Thomas CROWLEY

1477. Joseph Lanham CROWLEY, 11G Grandson, born on 28 Oct 1894.

Family of Edwin Friend LANHAM (1025) and Josephine MULLINS

1478. Edwin Friend LANHAM Jr., 11G Grandson, born in 1905 in TX. Edwin Friend died on 7 Jul 1976 in Victoria TX.

Family of William S. LANHAM (1026) and Celie BARRON

1479. Frank H. LANHAM, 11G Grandson, born in Nov 1883 in TX. Frank H. died in Mar 1973 in Midland, Midland Co. TX.

Family of Franklin C. LANHAM (1027) and Eliza Jane WILSON

1480. Beatrice LANHAM, 11G Granddaughter, born in 1875 in TX.

In 1894 Beatrice married Robert L. BRADFORD, in Smith Co. TX, born in 1873 in TX.

1481. William S. LANHAM, 11G Grandson, born on 15 May 1878. William S. died on 11 Oct 1926; he was 48.

1482. John H. LANHAM, 11G Grandson, born in Apr 1886 in Smith Co. TX. John H. died in 1961.

1483. Cynthia LANHAM, 11G Granddaughter, born in 1887.

1484. Jefferson David LANHAM, 11G Grandson, born on 1 Apr 1890. Jefferson David died in Troup, Smith Co. TX, on 15 Jan 1980; he was 89.

1485. James Carroll LANHAM, 11G Grandson, born in 1898 in TX. James Carroll died in 1990 in Smith Co. TX.

Family of Samuel WEEKS (1028)

1486. Lula WEEKS, 11G Granddaughter.

Family of Caleb Ezekiel BARRON (1030) and Mary A. ---

1487. Hattie BARRON, 11G Granddaughter, born on 14 Jun 1884 in Smith Co. TX. Hattie died in Smith Co. TX, on 26 Aug 1885; she was 1.

Family of Hon. Henry Gassaway DAVIS (1036) and Kateherine A. S. BANTZ

1488. Hallie Louise DAVIS, 11G Granddaughter **born** on 19 Dec 1854 in Frederick MD.

On 14 Apr 1875 when Hallie Louise was 20, she married Hon. Stephen Benton ELKINS, born on 20 Sep 1841 in Perry

Co. OH. He had a B.A. Columbia, George Washington University M.A. in Law, admitted to the bar in 1864, served as Attorney General of New Mexico in 1867, in 1868 appointed U.S. Attorney General by President Johnson. In 1869 he became President of the Bank of Santa Fe. Married when he was U.S. Congressman from New Mexico, to which he was elected in 1873 and 1875. Member of many civic and social organizations. They had the following children:

1830	i.	Davis (1876-)
1831	ii.	Stephen Benton (1877-)
1832	iii.	Richard (1879-)
1833	iv.	Elaine (1881-)
1834	v.	Katherine Hallie (1886-)

1489. Kate Bantz DAVIS, 11G Granddaughter, born on 1 Dec 1856.

Kate Bantz married Robert M. G. BROWN. U.S. Navy. They had one child:
1835	i.	Katherine Grace Davis

1490. Anderson Cord 11G Grandson, born on 4 Nov 1859.

1491. Ada Kate DAVIS, 11G Granddaughter, born on 14 Jan 1865.

1492. Grace Thomas DAVIS, 11G Granddaughter, born on 19 Oct 1869.

In Sep 1898 Grace Thomas married Arthur LEE. They had the following children:
1836	i.	George
1837	ii.	Ellen Bruce

1493. Henry Gassaway DAVIS, 11G Grandson, born in May 1871. Henry Gassaway died in May 1894.

1494. John Thomas DAVIS, 11G Grandson, born on 1 Mar 1874.

In Sep 1897 John Thomas married Elizabeth ARMSTEAD. They had one child:
1838	i.	Hallie Elkins

Family of Eliza Ann DAVIS (1037) and Upton BUXTON

1495. Fannie Brown BUXTON, 11G Granddaughter.

Fannie Brown married Frederick GERSTILL.

1496. Mollie BUXTON, 11G Granddaughter.

Mollie married Rev. William WORF.

1497. Henry Gassaway BUXTON, 11G Grandson.

1498. Blanche BUXTON, 11G Granddaughter.

Blanche married Ernest PRICE.

Family of William R. DAVIS (1039) and Mollie TILLSON

1499. Mary Tillson DAVIS, 11G Granddaughter.

Mary Tillson married Fairfax LANDSREET.

1500. Matilda DAVIS, 11G Granddaughter.

Matilda married Maj. George DOWNEY.

1501. William R. DAVIS, 11G Grandson.

William R. married --- GODFREY.

1502. Thomas Beale DAVIS, 11G Grandson, born on 6 Nov 1875.

Family of Samuel Thomas BROWN (1042) and Lydia BROME

1503. Florence BROWN, 11G Granddaughter, born on 25 Jan 1885.

Family of Frank D. BROWN (1044) and Louise DAVIS

1504. Samuel BROWN, 11G Grandson.

1505. Ruth Davis BROWN, 11G Granddaughter.

1506. Francis Louise BROWN, 11G Granddaughter.

Family of Warfield D. STALEY (1050) and Mary A. HORN

1507. Louisa C. STALEY, 11G Granddaughter, born about 1836 in MD.

1508. William H. STALEY, 11G Grandson, born in Aug 1838 in MD.

1509. Margaret I. STALEY, 11G Granddaughter, born about 1842 in MD.

1510. Charles E. STALEY, 11G Grandson, born about 1844 in MD.

1511. John W. STALEY, 11G Grandson, born in Aug 1850 in MD.

Family of Mary Ellen TODD (1051) and Peter DAVIS

1512. Sarah E. DAVIS, 11G Granddaughter, born in 1854.

1513. Upton L. DAVIS, 11G Grandson, born in 1858.

1514. Virginia H.R. DAVIS, 11G Granddaughter, born on 3 Jul 1859 in Carroll Co. MD. Virginia H.R. died on 21 Jun in Carroll Co. MD.

1515. Ira Rodney DAVIS, 11G Grandson, born on 20 Sep 1861 in Carroll Co. MD. Ira Rodney died in Winfield, Carroll Co. MD, on 6 Feb 1933; he was 71.

1516. Lucy DAVIS, 11G Granddaughter, born in 1862.

1517. Spliententiom DAVIS, 11G Grandson, born in 1865 in Carroll Co. MD.

1518. Tirzah DAVIS, 11G Granddaughter, born on 29 Jan 1867 in Carroll Co. MD. Tirzah died in Carroll Co. MD, on 26 Jul 1943; she was 76.

1519. Henry W. DAVIS, 11G Grandson, born in Jan 1868 in MD.

1520. Walter F. DAVIS, 11G Grandson, born in Aug 1871 in Carroll Co. MD.

1521. Leanna DAVIS, 11G Granddaughter, born in Apr 1872.

1522. William DAVIS, 11G Grandson, born in 1874.

Family of Rachel Ruth TODD (1053) and Jepthah Entler TUCKER

1523. Arthur B. TUCKER, 11G Grandson, born about 1857 in IL.

1524. Lee Forest TUCKER, 11G Grandson, born in Jan 1860 in IL.

1525. Effie Kate TUCKER, 11G Granddaughter, born on 4 Feb 1862 in Henry Co. IL. Effie Kate died in Des Moines Twp., Van Buren Co. IA, on 12 Dec 1948; she was 86.

1526. Jesse TUCKER, 11G Grandson, born about 1863 in IL.

1527. Margaret TUCKER, 11G Granddaughter, born about 1873 in IA.

1528. Dewit TUCKER, 11G Grandson, born about 1876 in IA.

Family of Margaret A. TODD (1056) and James F. THOMSON

1529. Cora A. THOMSON, 11G Granddaughter, born about 1860.

1530. Ethel THOMSON, 11G Granddaughter, born about 1864 in IL. Ethel died about 1870 in IL.

1531. John C. THOMSON, 11G Grandson, born about 1867 in IL.

1532. Susan E. THOMSON, 11G Granddaughter, born in Apr 1870 in IL.

1533. Mary Edna THOMSON, 11G Granddaughter, born about 1871 in IL.

1534. Kate A. THOMSON, 11G Granddaughter, born about 1874 in IL.

1535. Maud THOMSON, 11G Granddaughter, born about 1883 in IL.

Family of Susanah Cevelah TODD (1057) and Harry Charles JOHNSON

1536. Lewis Wallace JOHNSON, 11G Grandson, born on 2 Jul 1862 in IL. Lewis Wallace died before 1930.

1537. Eliza May JOHNSON, 11G Granddaughter, born about 1864. Eliza May died about 1864 in KS.

1538. Laclede Todd JOHNSON, 11G Grandson, born on 9 May 1868 in Pleasanton, Linn Co. KS. Laclede Todd died in Ashland, Clark Co. KS, on 6 Mar 1938; he was 69.

1539. Nettie Maude JOHNSON, 11G Granddaughter, born on 10 Feb 1876 in KS. Nettie Maude died in Enid, Garfield Co. OK, on 11 Nov 1918; she was 42.

1540. Ernest V. JOHNSON, 11G Grandson, born on 9 Aug 1879 in KS. Ernest V. died in 1956.

1541. Essie P. JOHNSON, 11G Granddaughter, born on 1 Aug 1882 in KS.

Essie P. married --- CARPENTER.

1542. Gladys Ethel JOHNSON, 11G Granddaughter, born on 8 Dec 1890 in KS. Gladys Ethel died in Fulton, Bourbon Co. KS, on 15 Oct 1967; she was 76.

Family of Benjamin Warfield TODD (1058) and Henrietta BEVIER

1543. Adie TODD, 11G Granddaughter, born in Nov 1879 in IN.

1544. Jesse Lee TODD, 11G Grandson, born on 20 May 1889 in Ida Co. IA. Jesse Lee died on 12 Feb 1939; he was 49.

Jesse Lee married Zee GILLILAND, born about 1893.

Family of Martha Alice TODD (1059) and William L. CROWL

1545. Frank Wilsom CROWL, 11G Grandson, born on 29 Mar 1867 in Kewanne, Henry Co. IL. Frank Wilsom died on 4 Jul 1929; he was 62.

1546. Harry L. CROWL, 11G Grandson, born on 11 Jan 1874 in Kewanne, Henry Co. IL. Harry L. died on 20 Nov 1970; he was 96.

On 28 Nov 1900 when Harry L. was 26, he married Margaret Elizabeth STARK, in Fulton, Bourbon Co. KS, born on 6 Dec 1868 in IL. Margaret Elizabeth died on 26 Aug 1962; she was 93.

1547. Alice May CROWL, 11G Granddaughter, born on 20 May 1880 in Kewanne, Henry Co. IL. Alice May died on 14 Jan 1954; she was 73.

1548. Bessie Mabel CROWL, 11G Granddaughter, born on 8 Aug 1885 in Linn Co. KS. Bessie Mabel died in Linn Co. KS, on 25 Oct 1886; she was 1.

Family of Benjamin TODD (1061) and Frances D. JONES

1549. Ellen M. TODD, 11G Granddaughter, born about 1855 in IL.

1550. Charles W. TODD, 11G Grandson, born about 1859 in IL.

1551. Frank B. TODD, 11G Grandson, born about 1861 in IL.

1552. Anna M. TODD, 11G Granddaughter, born about 1865 in IL.

1553. James F. TODD, 11G Grandson, born about 1867 in IL.

1554. John W. TODD, 11G Grandson, born about 1870 in IL.

1555. Josefa Frye TODD, 11G Granddaughter, born on 15 Dec 1875 in Peoria, Peoria Co. IL. Josefa Frye died in Alhambra, Los Angeles Co. CA, on 15 Apr 1936; she was 60.

Family of Henrietta Jackson TODD (1066) and --- ELLSWORTH

1556. Emmitt A. ELLSWORTH, 11G Grandson, born on 12 Nov 1861 in IL.

Family of Warfield Benjamin TODD (1067) and Euphemia LAFFERTY

1557. John TODD, 11G Grandson, born in Feb 1863 in Knox Co. IL.

1558. Susan TODD, 11G Granddaughter, born about 1863 in Knox Co. IL.

On 6 Dec 1882 Susan married Frank L. HILLIARD, in Henry Co. IL.

1559. Anna R. TODD, 11G Granddaughter, born about 1866 in Knox Co. IL.

On 22 Dec 1885 Anna R. married John G. DRYDEN, in Stark Co. IL.

1560. Nellie TODD, 11G Granddaughter, born in Sep 1869 in Knox Co. IL. Nellie died on 25 Jul 1937.

1561. Jennie TODD, 11G Granddaughter, born about 1870 in Knox Co. IL.

1562. Emma TODD, 11G Granddaughter, born on 15 Oct 1873 in Knox Co. IL. Died in Knox Co. IL, on 22 Jan 1896.

On 6 Mar 1893 when Emma was 19, she married Nicholas GIBBS, in Knox Co. IL.

1563. Charles TODD, 11G Grandson, born in Oct 1875 in Knox Co. IL. Charles died in 1943 in IL.

1564. Ben Ive TODD, 11G Grandson, born in May 1877 in Knox Co. IL.

On 26 Jul 1900 Ben Ive married Ida M. THURSTON, in Knox Co. IL.

1565. Upton B. TODD, 11G Grandson, born in Aug 1884 in Knox Co. IL.

1566. Wilson TODD, 11G Grandson, born about 1885 in IL.

Wilson married Edna ---.

Family of Thomas J. BROWN (1071) and Maggie E. ---

1567. John W. BROWN, 11G Grandson, born on 30 Sep 1899 in MD. John W. died in MD on 22 Nov 1924; he was 25.

1568. Francis M. BROWN, 11G Grandson, born on 10 Sep 1905 in MD. Francis M. died in Aug 1906 in MD.

Family of Edward B. BROWN (1072) and Annie M. PHOEBUS

1569. Noland BROWN, 11G Grandson, born in 1882.

Noland married Mary V. ---.

1570. Martha Thomas BROWN, 11G Granddaughter, born on 13 Jul 1884 in Sunshine, Montgomery Co. MD. Martha Thomas died in 1970 in Unity, Montgomery Co. MD.

Martha Thomas married August William PRIEBE, son of Herman C. PRIEBE and Bertha Louise FIEBELKORN, born on 15 Sep 1882 in Brighton MD. August William died in 1967 in Unity, Montgomery Co. MD. Their farm was named Pleasant Fields, later known as Sundown Farm. They had the following children:
1839	i.	Annie Mary (1909-)
1840	ii.	Sylvan Augustus (1911-1986)
1841	iii.	Russell (1919-)
1842	iv.	William Courtney (1921-)

1571. Carrie Virginia BROWN, 11G Granddaughter, born on 2 May 1885 in MD. Carrie Virginia died in MD on 4 Oct 1900; she was 15.

1572. Ruby BROWN, 11G Granddaughter, born on 23 Jun 1887 in Sunshine, Montgomery Co. MD. Ruby died near Unity MD, on 15 Mar 1970; she was 82.

Ruby married Herman H. PRIEBE, son of Herman C. PRIEBE and Bertha Louise FIEBELKORN, born on 16 Jan 1885 in Brighton MD. Herman H. died in MD on 6 Jan 1962; he was 76. They had the following children:
1843	i.	Louise (1909-)
1844	ii.	Lillian May (1910-1997)
1845	iii.	Rosalie (1910-)
1846	iv.	Herman Brown (1914-1992)
1847	v.	Margaret (1915-)
1848	vi.	Henry (1917-)
1849	vii.	Elsie (1920-)
1850	viii.	Freddie (1924-)

1573. Edgar BROWN, 11G Grandson, born in 1890. Edgar Brown became his brother Edgar's guardian on the father's death. He served with the American Expeditionary Force in WWI. Resident of Balston Virginia.

Edgar married Elsie BURROUGHS, born in 1899. They had the following children:
1851	i.	Joyce (1929-)
1852	ii.	Shirley (1929-)
1853	iii.	Leland (1933-)

1574. Russell BROWN, 11G Grandson, born in 1891. Served with the American Expeditionary Force in WWI. Resident of Washington D.C.

Russell married Myrtle ---.

1575. Marshall A. BROWN, 11G Grandson, born in 1894. Resident of Howard County Maryland, Oxford Pennsylvania, Newark and Irvington New Jersey, and Washington D.C.

Marshall A. married Catherine O. ---. They had the following children:
1854	i.	Catherine Eugenie (1920-)
1855	ii.	Marshall John (1922-)

1576. Dewey Octavius BROWN, 11G Grandson, born on 6 Jan 1898 in Montgomery Co. MD. Dewey Octavius died in Lisbon MD, on 3 Jan 1981; he was 82. Resident of Washington D.C.

Dewey Octavius first married Mignonette Anne RUSSELL, born in 1894 in St. Mary's Co. MD. Mignonette Anne died on 21 Aug 1929. They had one child:
    1856   i.   James Russell (1917-)

On 21 Jun 1934 when Dewey Octavius was 36, he second married Emily Jones PICKETT, born in Howard Co. MD.

1577. Robert B. BROWN, 11G Grandson. Robert B. died in 1905.

1578. Carlton P. BROWN, 11G Grandson, born in 1902. Resident of Washington D.C. and Arlington Virginia.

Carlton P. married Beulah ---.

1579. Edward B. BROWN, 11G Grandson. Edward B. died in 1905.

FIFTEENTH GENERATION

Family of George Alan BROWN (1085) and Ella May ALLEN

1580. Edna May BROWN, 12G Granddaughter, born on 22 Jul 1899 in Sykesville MD. Edna May died in Baltimore Co. MD, on 15 May 1969; she was 69. Buried Mt. View Cemetery.

On 24 Nov 1923 when Edna May was 24, she married Howard Arrington SMITH, son of Phillip F. SMITH and Sarah J. ARRINGTON, in Carroll Co. MD, born on 31 May 1895 in Woodsboro MD. Howard Arrington died in Baltimore MD, on 12 Aug 1967; he was 72. Worshipful Master of Freedom Lodge A. F. and A. M. in 1941, Sykesville. Buried Mt. View Cemetery. They had the following children:
    i.   Betty Jean (1929-)
    ii.   Howard Arrington (1932-)

1581. George W. BROWN, 12G Grandson, born in Sykesville MD. George W. died in TX.

George W. married Margaret HOBBS. They had the following children:
    i.   Donald
    ii.   Betty Lou

1582. Henry Allen BROWN, 12G Grandson, born in Sykesville MD. Henry Allen died in Baltimore Co. MD.

Henry Allen married Loney YOUNG. They had one child:
    i.   Catherine

Family of Ralph Clark BROWN (1096) and Emma F. RAINS

1583. Effie Olive BROWN, 12G Granddaughter, born on 14 Nov 1879 in Anderson IN. Effie Olive died in Humboldt NE, on 9 Dec 1952; she was 73.

On 7 Mar 1900 when Effie Olive was 20, she married William Grant HELMICK, in Auburn NE, born on 18 Jan 1879. William Grant died in Feb 1971 in Stella NE. They had one child:
    i.   Wayne E. (1921-1972)

1584. Wade BROWN, 12G Grandson. Died in infancy.

1585. Bessie BROWN, 12G Granddaughter, born on 15 Dec 1885 in Nemaha City NE. Bessie died in Los Angeles CA, on 3 Aug 1940; she was 54.

In Dec 1904 Bessie married Edward O'DONNELL, in Falls City NE, born on 4 Feb 1882. Edward died in Apr 1967 in Los Angeles CA. They had the following children:
    i.   Irene (1906-1985)
    ii.   Dale (1908-)
    iii.   Floyd (1911-1983)

1586. Charles BROWN, 12G Grandson. Died in infancy.

1587. Flossie BROWN, 12G Granddaughter, born on 13 Feb 1895 in Stella NE. Flossie died in Omaha NE, on 2 Mar 1967; she was 72.

Flossie married Will ADAMS. They had the following children:
- i. Leila (1912-1982)
- ii. Clark (1913-1992)
- iii. Glen (1916-1982)
- iv. John (1921-1984)
- v. Emma Maxine (1930-)

1588. Floyd LeRoy BROWN, 12G Grandson, born on 23 Sep 1897. Floyd LeRoy died in Auburn NE, on 16 Mar 1977; he was 79.

On 18 May 1915 when Floyd LeRoy was 17, he married Fern Alverdia McDOWELL, in Salem NE, born on 1 Oct 1897. Fern Alverdia died on 16 Oct 1976; she was 79. They had the following children:
- i. Thelma Mae (1915-)
- ii. Marie Fern (1917-1989)
- iii. Cleon LeRoy
- iv. Betty Ilene
- v. Faye Edward (1926-1990)

Family of William Lloyd BROWN (1097) and Rhoda RINARD

1589. Ida Belle BROWN, 12G Granddaughter, born on 14 Jan 1886. Ida Belle died in Lakeland FL, on 25 Oct 1965; she was 79.

On 29 Oct 1909 when Ida Belle was 23, she married Francis Edward TAYLOR, in Mooreland IN, born on 7 May 1879. Francis Edward died in Orlando FL on 22 Mar 1942; he was 62. Carpenter. Moved his family from Indiana to Lakeland Florida in 1933. They had the following children:
- i. Sarah Eloise (1911-1993)
- ii. Aubrey Brown (1913-1966)
- iii. Faith (1918-1983)
- iv. Alton Edward (1919-1983)
- v. Grace Belle (1926-)

1590. Nola Edith BROWN, 12G Granddaughter, born on 3 Nov 1889. Nola Edith died in May 1985 in Madison County IL. Resident of Godfrey IL.

Nola Edith married Felix PECKINPAUGH, born on 11 Jan 1884 in IN. Felix died in Aug 1977 in Orlando FL. They had the following children:
- i. Mary Kathryn
- ii. William Edward (1909-1974)

1591. Orville BROWN, 12G Grandson, born on 18 Oct 1886. Orville died on 17 Oct 1887; he was less than 1.

Family of William Lloyd BROWN (1097) and Sarah Malinda DOWNING

1592. Edna Lillian BROWN, 12G Granddaughter, born on 26 Feb 1901. Edna Lillian died in Dec 1990 in Madison Co. IN. She was 99.

Edna Lillian married Ernest HALL. They had the following children:
- i. Patricia (1925-)

  ii. Brian (1928-)
  iii. Carter Lyle (1932-)

Family of Ida BROWN (1099) and Robert HOUSE

1593. Charles O. HOUSE, 12G Grandson, born on 20 Feb 1885 in IN. Resided in the Cicero IN area.

Charles O. married Nellie HAWKINS, born in 1888. They had the following children:
  i. Glen (1910-)
  ii. Lucile (1912-)
  iii. Robert (1916-)
  iv. Janet (1917-)
  v. Edna (1919-)

1594. Fern HOUSE, 12G Granddaughter, born on 17 Nov 1886.

Fern married Edgar A. COPPLE, born in 1885. Resident of the Upland IN area.

1595. Lucy Donald HOUSE, 12G Grandson, born on 28 Jan 1889. Lucy Donald died in 1917. Unmarried.

1596. Lacey A. HOUSE, 12G Grandson, born on 4 May 1891 in IN. Lacey A. died in Cicero IN, on 19 Jan 1981; he was 89. He lived in the Cicero IN area.

Lacey A. married Muriel MC CORD, born in 1892. They had the following children:
  i. Thelma (1912-)
  ii. Mildred (1919-)

1597. Theodore "Tad" HOUSE, 12G Grandson, born on 7 Jun 1895 in IN. Theodore "Tad" died in IN on 13 May 1970; he was 74. He lived in the Cicero IN area.

Theodore "Tad" married Geneva L. WOODWARD. They had the following children:
  i. Joan
  ii. Laverne
  iii. Terrel

1598. William Kenneth "Bill" HOUSE, 12G Grandson, born on 6 Aug 1898 in IN.

1599. Mary HOUSE, 12G Granddaughter, born in 1900-1901 in IN.

Mary married W. G. HOLLIDAY. Resident of the Arcadia IN area.

1600. Clifton G. HOUSE, 12G Grandson, born on 9 Jan 1906 in Hamilton County IN. Resident in the Elwood IN area.

1601. William K. HOUSE, 12G Grandson. Resident of the Cicero IN area.

Family of Alonzo Grant BROWN (1100) and Julia Margaret LAWHORN

1602. Ethel BROWN, 12G Granddaughter, born on 1 Mar 1893 in N Anderson IN. Ethel died in N Anderson IN, on 5 Sep 1893; she was less than 1. Buried in Maplewood Cemetery, Anderson.

1603. James Willard BROWN, 12G Grandson, born on 14 Aug 1894 in Richland Twp., N. Anderson IN. James Willard died in Anderson IN, on 2 Apr 1978; he was 83. Buried in Anderson Memorial Cemetery. Attended College Corner Elementary School, North Anderson Indiana and completed later studies in electronics. Owner Brown Electric Company, Anderson Indiana; served in US Army WW I. Refs.: Madison County Marriages; birth, death, marriage certificates;

military discharge; Netterville, *Centennial History of Madison County*, Vol. II, p. 250; Censuses of 1900, 1910, 1920, 1930; Anderson City Directories of 1910 through 1925; various family informants including himself.

On 29 Dec 1921 when James Willard was 27, he married Bertha Alice THOMPSON, in Anderson IN, born on 26 Jan 1897 in Hancock Co. IN. Bertha Alice died in Largo FL, on 4 Feb 1987; she was 90. Buried in Anderson Memorial Cemetery. Refs.: Hancock County Indiana Births; Madison County Indiana Marriages; Marriage Certificate; Censuses of 1900, 1910, 20, 30; death certificate; numerous family informants including herself. They had the following children:
    i.   Donna Marie (1922-2004)
    ii.   Betty Jean (1925-)
    iii.   James Willard (1934-)

1604. Walter Ray BROWN, 12G Grandson, born on 27 Nov 1897 in Richland Twp. (North Anderson) IN. Walter Ray died in Centerville OH, on 11 Jan 1992; he was 94. Buried in Memorial Park, Centerville OH. US Army 1918, France. Engineer, Wright-Patterson Air Force Base, Dayton Ohio. Refs.: autobiography written at the author's request; Madison County Marriages; Censuses of 1900, 1910, 1920; Anderson City Directories of 1910 through 1925; various family informants including himself

On 26 Nov 1921 when Walter Ray was 23, he married Mary Pauline MERRICK, born on 4 Aug 1898. Mary Pauline died in May 1980 in Centerville OH. Buried in Memorial Park, Centerville OH. They had one child:
    i.   Mary Alice (1925-1925)

1605. Elsie May BROWN, 12G Granddaughter, born in 1901 in N Anderson IN. Elsie May died on 26 Sep 1905 in Perkinsville IN, typhoid. Buried in Maplewood Cemetery, Anderson.

Family of Alonzo Grant BROWN (1100) and Bertha Etta WAITMAN JARRETT

1606. Katherine Christine BROWN, 12G Granddaughter, born on 12 Aug 1910 in Anderson IN, died 17 Aug 2005. She was 95. Family ref.: Barbara Sue Kreigh.

On 20 Jun 1931 when Katherine Christine was 20, she married Perry Oliver BANGLE, in Anderson IN, who was born on 17 Dec 1904 in Hamilton Co. IN. Perry Oliver died in Anderson IN, on 10 Jun 1978; he was 73. Buried in Anderson Memorial Park Cemetery. Foreman at Delco Remy, Anderson. They had the following children:
    i.   Barbara Sue (1934-)
    ii.   Ralph Thomas (Adopted) (1942-1999)

1607. Cora Elmay BROWN, 12G Granddaughter, born on 29 Jun 1913 in North Anderson IN. Cora Elmay died in Seminole FL, on 31 Oct 2003; she was 90. Buried in Anderson IN. Secretary-bookkeeper, Anderson IN and Philadelphia PA.

On 3 Jan 1946 when Cora Elmay was 32, she married Jack Dale HOWES, in Anderson IN, born on 1 May 1909 in Charleroi PA. Jack Dale died in Seminole FL on 4 May 1986; he was 77. US Army WW II, N. Africa and Italy; Salesman. The couple had no issue.

1608. Leatha JARRETT, 12G Granddaughter, born on 17 Nov 1894. Leatha died after 1968.

On 30 Jun 1914 when Leatha was 19, she married Earl WILKINSON, born on 21 Mar 1890. Earl died in Henry County IN, auto accident., on 22 Oct 1968; he was 78. Railroad employee and electrician. They had the following children:
    i.   Helen Delmaya (1916-1947)
    ii.   Darlene

1609. Ralph Nelson JARRETT, 12G Grandson, born on 17 Feb 1900 in Anderson IN. Ralph Nelson died in Desoto IN, on 4 Jul 1985; he was 85. Served in US Army 1920-3, resident of Desoto IN. Employed at Warner Gear of Muncie IN.

On 15 May 1926 when Ralph Nelson was 26, he married Madonna NEEDLER, born on 24 Feb 1904. Madonna died on

26 Oct 1994; she was 90. She had siblings Martha, Nelda, Delbert, Christine Needler. They had the following children:
- i. Jacqueline (1929-)
- ii. Frank Nelson (1933-)
- iii. Leonard L. (1937-)

Family of James Anderson BROWN (1102) and Hattie Ellen DELPH

1610. Nellie May BROWN, 12G Granddaughter, born on 7 Jul 1896 in Anderson, Madison Co. IN. Nellie May died in Indianapolis, Marion Co. IN, on 9 Nov 1957; she was 61.

Nellie May married James Fred DAVIS, born on 1 Jan 1895. James Fred died about 1970. They had the following children:
- i. Paul Howard (1918-)
- ii. James Howard (1919-)
- iii. Wilma May (1923-)

1611. Earl Jennings BROWN, 12G Grandson, born on 9 Aug 1897 in Anderson, Madison Co. IN. Earl Jennings died in Silver Springs MD, on 17 Nov 1977; he was 80. Graduated from the Georgetown University Law School, served in the US Marine Corps during WW I, employed as a Veterans Administration attorney in Washington for 35 years. Member New Jerusalem Masonic Lodge, Silver Spring Maryland, member of the Presbyterian Church of Bethesda Maryland (per K. Blume). Additional source: 1900 Census, Madison Co., Lafayette Township, Indiana.

On 31 Dec 1935 when Earl Jennings was 38, he married Edith TRAYLOR. Edith died in 1974. They had one child:
- i. James Jennings

1612. Zelma Fern BROWN, 12G Granddaughter, born on 26 Jul 1899 in Madison Co. IN. Zelma Fern died on 30 Apr 1989; she was 89. Buried in Memorial Park, Indianapolis IN. Resided in Silver Springs MD. She was source of much information regarding James Anderson Brown family and descendants.

1613. Myrtle Marie BROWN, 12G Granddaughter, born on 16 Jun 1902 in Anderson, Madison Co. IN. Myrtle Marie died in Indianapolis IN, on 21 Feb 1933; she was 30. Buried in Memorial Park, Indianapolis IN.

Myrtle Marie married Theodore P. JETT. They had the following children, plus three unreported:
- i. Caroline M. (1926-1926)
- ii. Bernice (1932-1932)

1614. Opal R. BROWN, 12G Granddaughter, born on 5 Nov 1903. Opal R. died on 17 Mar 2002; she was 98.

Opal R. married --- KELLY. They had one child:
- i. Marjorie

1615. Manvil F. BROWN, 12G Grandson, born on 21 Jun 1908 in Anderson, Madison Co. IN. Manvil F. died in Indianapolis, Marion Co. IN, on 17 Dec 1950; he was 42. Buried in Memorial Park, Indianapolis IN.

Manvil F. married Gwynith ---. They had the following children:
- i. Lois R.
- ii. Ellen K.
- iii. Durward L.
- iv. Robert A.

1616. Lawrence Lewis BROWN, 12G Grandson, born on 18 Jun 1910 in Westport IN. Lawrence Lewis died in Indianapolis IN, on 19 Apr 1962; he was 51. Buried in Memorial Park, Indianapolis IN. Died in an auto accident.

Lawrence Lewis married Marjorie Elizabeth WINKLER, daughter of Fred WINKLER and Rae HORN, born on 23 Jul 1915. Marjorie Elizabeth died in Indianapolis, Marion Co. IN, on 15 Sep 1994; she was 79. They had the following children:

i.	Marilyn Marie (1932-)
ii.	Virginia Ann (1934-)
iii.	Janice June (1937-1988)
iv.	David Lawrence (1944-1991)
v.	Margaret Ellen (about 1946-)
vi.	Theresa Jean (about 1949-)

1617. Ruth Adair BROWN, 12G Granddaughter, born on 2 Oct 1913 in Westport IN. Ruth Adair died in Indiana, Marion Co. IN, on 24 Oct 1975; she was 62. Buried in Memorial Park, Indianapolis IN.

1618. Harold Edward BROWN, 12G Grandson, born on 22 Mar 1914 in Indianapolis IN. Harold Edward died in Indianapolis IN, on 12 Sep 1989; he was 75. Buried in Memorial Park, Indianapolis IN.

1619. Stanley H. BROWN, 12G Grandson, born on 16 Aug 1917. Stanley H. died in Marion County IN, on 12 Jun 1991; he was 73. Buried in Memorial Park, Indianapolis IN.

Family of Elmer E. BROWN (1103) and Sara A. McCORD

1620. Evelyn BROWN, 12G Granddaughter, born in 1900 in Madison Co. IN.

1621. Estell Elmer BROWN, 12G Grandson, born in 1903 in Madison Co. IN.

1622. William Thurman BROWN, 12G Grandson, born in 1906 in Madison Co. IN.

1623. Ernest BROWN, 12G Grandson, born in 1908 in Madison Co. IN.

Family of John Scherer BROWN (1105) and Carrie B. McCLINTOCK

1624. Edward BROWN, 12G Grandson, born on 30 Jul 1905 in Madison Co. IN. Edward died in Anderson IN, on 28 Jan 1989; he was 83. Ref.: author's interviews during the 1970s.

Edward married Lavinia BONER. Lavinia died in Anderson IN.

1625. Harold H. BROWN, 12G Grandson, born on 3 Mar 1908 in Madison Co. IN. Harold H. died in Apr 1980 in Sodus NY.

1626. Glenn BROWN, 12G Grandson, born on 10 Nov 1908 in Madison Co. IN. Glenn died in Jun 1970 in Madison Co. IN.

Glenn married Mabel ---. They had one child:
    i.   Beverly Jo

Family of John Scherer BROWN (1105) and Emma Belle McDUFFEE

1627. George FLEEMAN, 12G Grandson.

1628. Katherine FLEEMAN, 12G Granddaughter.

Katherine married Henry A. YORK.

Family of Mary C. BROWN (1106) and Curtis L. TATE

1629. Ruby Thelma TATE, 12G Granddaughter, born on 17 Jul 1903. Ruby Thelma died in Jan 1977 in Fayette County IN.

Ruby Thelma married Robert RYNEARSON, born on 5 Aug 1906. Robert died in Nov 1963 in Fayette County IN.

1630. Garnet Zelma TATE, 12G Granddaughter, born on 20 Nov 1909. Garnet Zelma died in Sarasota FL, on 21 Jun 1993; she was 83.

1631. Catherine Curtis TATE, 12G Granddaughter.

1632. Orlia Arthur TATE, 12G Grandson, born on 25 Dec 1916. Orlia Arthur died in Jan 1984 in Fayette County IN.

Family of William Lankford ELLIOTT (1112) and Minnie Jane FIFER

1633. Clarence William ELLIOTT, 12G Grandson, born in Sep 1900 in IN. Clarence William died in 1934 in Danville, Vermillion Co. IL.

1634. Charles ELLIOTT, 12G Grandson, born on 24 Jun 1906 in IN. Charles died in Sacramento CA, on 24 Jun 1969; he was 63. Buried in Danville, Vermillion Co. IL.

1635. Walter Winslow ELLIOTT, 12G Grandson, born on 10 Feb 1909 in Danville, Vermillion Co. IL. Walter Winslow died in Danville, Vermillion Co. IL, on 10 Apr 1992; he was 83.

Walter Winslow married Dorothy Wyoma BOUCIER, born on 20 Jul 1913 in Danville, Vermillion Co. IL. Dorothy Wyoma died in Danville, Vermillion Co. IL, on 19 May 1998; she was 84. They had one child:
     i.   Eugene (1931-)

1636. Donald ELLIOTT, 12G Grandson, born on 23 Feb 1913 in Danville, Vermillion Co. IL. Donald died in Newark OH.

Family of Jesse MOBLEY (1130) and Sarah Ann ANDERSON

1637. Elizabeth MOBLEY, 12G Granddaughter, born in 1862 in IN. Letter from Alta to Lillian Thompson in 1961.

Family of Elijah B. MOBLEY (1131) and Sarah Ann ANDERSON

1638. William MOBLEY, 12G Grandson, born in 1866 in IN. William died in 1930. 1870 Census.

1639. John W. MOBLEY, 12G Grandson, born in 1867. 1870 Census.

1640. Elsworth MOBLEY, 12G Grandson, born in 1869 in IN. 1870 Census.

1641. Isaac MOBLEY, 12G Grandson, born in 1871 in IN. 1880 Census.

1642. Jesse MOBLEY, 12G Grandson, born in 1874 in IN. 1880 Census.

1643. Lettie MOBLEY, 12G Granddaughter, born in 1876 in IN. 1880 Census.

1644. Mary MOBLEY, 12G Granddaughter, born in 1878 in IN. 1880 Census.

Family of Daniel L. MOBLEY (1135) and Mary Jane GALENTINE

1645. William Terriel MOBLEY, 12G Grandson, born on 7 Nov 1876 in PA. William Terriel died in Aug 1961. 1880 Census Springhill, Greene Co. PA p. 366A; 1930 Census Buffalo, Harper Co. OK p. 11A; Letter from Nellie Mobley Collins; Obituary of son Charles Mobley; WWI draft registration which had him then living in Oklahoma,.

In about 1900 William Terriel married Ida Bell CALLAUGH, born in 1866. Ida Bell died in 1926. They had the following children:
       i.   Charles Henry Raymond (1907-1979)
      ii.   Virgil (- before 1979)
     iii.   Roy Edward

1646. Hester Ellen MOBLEY, 12G Granddaughter, born in 1878 in IN. Hester Ellen died on 11 Nov 1964 in CA. 1880 Census Springhill; Green Co. PA, p. 366A; Letter from Nellie Mobley Collins; Interviews with Lillian Thompson Mobley.

Hester Ellen married William WALKER, born in 1870. William died in 1946. They had one child:
       i.   Frances (1899-1962)

1647. Jesse Ralph MOBLEY, 12G Grandson, born on 16 Apr 1880 in Springhill, Greene Co. PA. Jesse Ralph died in Dinuba, Tulare Co. CA, on 7 Feb 1964; he was 83. Interview with Lillian Thompson, who related that Jesse Ralph left Indiana with three friends the summer of 1875. He was to have entered medical school. Jesse took his medicine kit with him in case he needed it. His uncle John was a doctor and had encouraged him in that area. He went along on a cattle drive in which some of the cowboys became sick with smallpox. He had been vaccinated so he took care of the sick cowboys. On the way back from the cattle drive they stopped at Ft. Supply to rest. There Jesse met the Hopper family and fell in love with their pretty daughter. They were married and settled in OK. He then practiced veterinary medicine. Other sources: Letter from Nellie Mobley Collins; WWI Draft record which states his birth date as 17 Apr 1887 in Paint Mine, PA. He worked in a lumber yard and in a dray business. He was tall, stout, blue eyes, brown hair. Other refs.: 1880 Census Springhill, Greenhille Co. PA p. 366A; 1920 Census Penn, Woods Co. OK, p. 3A; 1930 Census, Doby, Harper Co. OK, p. 2A; marriage certificate.

On 17 Feb 1903 when Jesse Ralph was 22, he first married Luritta "Lula" May HOPPER, daughter of Marion Meridith HOPPER and Mary Catherine LAWS, in Woodward, Woodward Co. OK, born on 4 May 1886 in Aurora, Lawrence Co. MO. Luritta "Lula" May died in Laverne, Harper Co. OK, on 23 Oct 1918; she was 32. Verbal information from Lillian Mobley Thompson stated she was only 16 yrs old when she married so her father had to write a note of permission, she died in the great flu epidemic of 1918, and was a loving mother who gathered her children around to say goodbye to them. Other refs.: 1900, 1910 census; marriage certificate; father Marion Hopper's Civil War pension record.; gravestone. They had the following children:
       i.   Jesse Ralph (1903-1985)
      ii.   Gladys Hazel (1905-1999)
     iii.   William Eldon (1906-1968)
     iv.   Daharell (1908-1919)
      v.   Hester Ellen (1909-1914)
     vi.   Mary Frances (1911-1990)
    vii.   Lillian Juanita (1913-2000)
   viii.   Lawrence Alonzo (1916-1916)
     ix.   Victoria Ellen (1917-1917)

In Mar 1920 Jesse Ralph second married Ollie May TURNER. Ollie May died in 1950. History from Hazel Mobley Ketron. They had the following children:
       i.   Charley Lee (1921-1970)
      ii.   Nina Fay
     iii.   Ollie Jean (1927-1931)

In Sep 1954 Jesse Ralph third married Lula Elizabeth ANDERSON, in Las Vegas, Clark Co. NV, born on 24 Sep 1889. Lula Elizabeth died in Aug 1976 in Fresno, Fresno Co. CA (Social Security Death Index). Ref.; interview with Lillian Mobley Thompson on marriage of Lula to Jesse Ralph Mobley.

1648. Nellie MOBLEY, 12G Granddaughter, born in 1882 in Cameron, Cameron Co. PA. Refs.: 1920 Census Kiowa, Harper, OK, p. 2A; 1930 Census Kiowa, Harper, OK, p. 4A; Letter from Nellie Mobley Collins; *Marriage Certificate Book C-14*, p. 273.

On 23 Feb 1898 Nellie married Charles H. COLLINS, in Bartholomew Co. IN, born on 28 Jun 1869. Charles H. died on 7 Nov 1957; he was 88. They had the following children:
        i.   Anna
        ii.   Ariatla
        iii.   Ray
        iv.   Fran

1649. Alonzo Downy MOBLEY, 12G Grandson, born on 18 Mar 1885 in Elizabethtown, Bartholomew Co. IN. Alonzo Downy died on 1 Jan 1963; he was 77. Alonzo Downy Mobely was known as "Don." He served in the U.S. Army during World War One, and claimed that he was fighting at 11 AM on 11 Nov 1918 when the war ended. Ref.: letter from Nellie Mobley Collins.

Alonzo Downy married Hazel PARRITT.

Family of Andrew Jackson MOBLEY (1136) and Isabell V. COLLINS

1650. John H. MOBLEY, 12G Grandson, born on 1 May 1891 in Bartholomew Co. IN. *Birth Record Book H-4*, p. 14.

1651. Bertha M. MOBLEY, 12G Granddaughter, born on 28 Jun 1892 in IN. Bertha M. died in Jun 1970 in Wolcottville IN. Bartholomew Co. IN *Birth Record Book H-4*, p. 39.

On 16 May 1908 when Bertha M. was 15, she married Clayton BERKANSTOCK, in Bartholomew Co. IN. They had the following children:
        i.   Raymond (1908-1967)
        ii.   Virgil (1914-1991)

1652. Loretti Laverne MOBLEY, 12G Granddaughter, born on 27 May 1896 in Bartholomew Co. IN. Loretti Laverne died in Bartholomew Co. IN, on 10 Feb 1897; she was less than 1. Refs.: Bartholomew Co. IN *Birth Record Book H-5*, p. 29, *Death Records Book HD-5*, p. 18.

1653. Blanch MOBLEY, 12G Granddaughter.

Blanch married --- TORMAS.

Family of Jacob A. MOBLEY (1137) and Jennie F. BOTTORF

1654. Ozalla P. MOBLEY, 12G Granddaughter, born on 13 Apr 1887 in Bartholomew Co. IN. Ref.: Bartholomew Co. IN *Birth Record Book H2*, p. 54.

1655. Ethel M. MOBLEY, 12G Granddaughter, born on 8 Nov 1889 in Bartholomew Co. IN. Ref.: Bartholomew Co. IN *Birth Record Book H3*, p. 17.

1656. Elsie Ferne MOBLEY, 12G Granddaughter, born on 14 Feb 1891 in Bartholomew Co. IN. Ref.: Bartholomew Co. IN *Birth Record Book H4*, p. 8.

On 9 May 1908 when Elsie Ferne was 17, she married Edwin J. GILLILAND, in Bartholomew Co. IN.

1657. Leroy MOBLEY, 12G Grandson, born on 21 Nov 1893 in Bartholomew Co. IN. Leroy died in Aug 1963. Ref.: Bartholomew Co. IN *Birth Record Book H4*, p. 71.

1658. Delbert R. MOBLEY, 12G Grandson, born on 16 Apr 1896 in Bartholomew Co. IN. Delbert R. died in Jan 1978 in Poteau, LeFlore Co. OK. Ref.: Bartholomew Co. IN *Birth Record Book H5*, p. 28.

1659. Irwin E. MOBLEY, 12G Grandson.

1660. Albert E. MOBLEY, 12G Grandson, born on 5 Dec 1899 in Bartholomew Co. IN. Albert E. died in Apr 1981 in Garfield CO. Bartholomew Co. IN *Birth Record Book H7*, p. 7.

Family of Sarah Isabelle "Belle" LEE (1143) and Henry HART

1661. Nellie HART, 12G Granddaughter, born in 1872 in Walla Walla WA. Nellie died in 1876.

1662. Charles Henry HART Jr., 12G Grandson, born on 23 May 1875 in Walla Walla WA. Charles Henry died in Spokane WA, on 24 Aug 1950; he was 75.

On 1 Nov 1899 when Charles Henry was 24, he married Cornelia Luella "Nellie" STILSON, born on 18 Jan 1881 in Diamond WA. Cornelia Luella "Nellie" died in Thornton WA, on 18 Feb 1920; she was 39. They had the following children:
      i.   Ray Newell (1901-1974)
     ii.   Charles Leroy (1902-1980)
    iii.   Ralph Murral (1903-1970)
    iv.   Lewis Clarke (1905-1949)
     v.   Ira Winfield (1907-1995)

Family of Lyman MOBLEY (1145) and Nanny DOGGETT

1663. Clio MOBLEY, 12G Grandson, born on 9 Feb 1881. Clio died after 1984.

Family of Theodore T. "Dory" MOBLEY (1149) and Phoebe Alberta Bertha YOST

1664. Jim MOBLEY, 12G Grandson, born on 25 Apr 1891 in Bartholomew Co. IN.

1665. Vivian P. MOBLEY, 12G Granddaughter.

Vivian P. married Lora W. JOLIFF.

Family of Margaret A. "Maggie" MOBLEY (1150) and J. Taylor WRIGHT

1666. Chester WRIGHT, 12G Grandson.

1667. Mabel WRIGHT, 12G Granddaughter.

1668. LaVern WRIGHT, 12G Granddaughter.

1669. Lorene WRIGHT, 12G Granddaughter.

Family of Ella P. MOBLEY (1152) and Floyd F. LOOSE

1670. Corinna Clare LOOSE, 12G Granddaughter.

Family of William Henry "Hen" MOBLEY (1154) and Grace MYERS

1671. Mary MOBLEY, 12G Granddaughter.

1672. Wayne MOBLEY, 12G Grandson.

Family of James Hunter "Hunt" MOBLEY (1155) and Cora B. WHITE

1673. Virgil MOBLEY, 12G Grandson, born on 4 Jan 1899 in Bartholomew Co. IN. Virgil died in Westport IN, on 7 May 1959; he was 60.

1674. Beatrice MOBLEY, 12G Granddaughter, born on 22 Mar 1900 in Bartholomew Co. IN. Beatrice died in CA on 27 Jun 1975; she was 75.

Family of James Hunter "Hunt" MOBLEY (1155) and India ROSCOE

1675. Clarence Edward MOBLEY, 12G Grandson, born on 5 Jun 1919 in Bartholomew Co. IN. Clarence Edward died in Columbus, Bartholomew Co. IN, on 20 Dec 1991; he was 72.

Family of Rev. Darius Arrelian MOBLEY (1172) and Harriett Ann HESSEY

1676. Gertrude Iris MOBLEY, 12G Granddaughter, born on 4 Feb 1877 in Bartholomew Co. IN.

1677. Mary Catherine "Lota" MOBLEY, 12G Granddaughter, born on 18 Oct 1878 in Montgomery Co. OH.

1678. Blanche Julia MOBLEY, 12G Granddaughter, born on 5 Dec 1879.

1679. Harriett Ethel MOBLEY, 12G Granddaughter, born on 28 Jul 1881 in Napa CA.

1680. William Lewis MOBLEY, 12G Grandson, born on 6 Aug 1882 in Napa CA. William Lewis died on 27 Aug 1904; he was 22.

1681. Philo Darius MOBLEY, 12G Grandson, born on 22 May 1885 in Napa CA.

1682. Hadassah Belle MOBLEY, 12G Granddaughter, born on 20 Dec 1886.

1683. Edith K. MOBLEY, 12G Granddaughter, born on 1 Sep 1889. Edith K. died in May 1980 in Alameda, Alameda Co. CA.

1684. Harry S. MOBLEY, 12G Grandson, born on 5 Apr 1894. Harry S. died in Feb 1965.

Family of Rev. Darius Arrelian MOBLEY (1172) and Mabel F. BURROWS

1685. Rosamond Ruth MOBLEY, 12G Granddaughter.

Family of Laura Virginia BROWN (1222) and Harry Cornelius MUSGROVE

1686. Margaret Hazel MUSGROVE, 12G Granddaughter, born on 27 May 1910 in Baltimore City MD. Margaret Hazel died in Hampton VA, on 31 May 1966; she was 56. Master seamstress.

Margaret Hazel married Walter Elmer SCHAEFER, son of Walter SCHAEFER and Bazie Antonia BELL, born on 29 May 1911 in Baltimore City MD. Walter Elmer died in Baltimore City MD, on 29 Jan 1992; he was 80. Housepainter and home improvement business owner. They had nine children, names unreported.

1687. Harry MUSGROVE, 12G Grandson.

1688. Brady MUSGROVE, 12G Grandson.

1689. Loyd MUSGROVE, 12G Grandson.

1690. Eleanor MUSGROVE, 12G Granddaughter.

1691. Esther MUSGROVE, 12G Granddaughter.

1692. Ellsworth MUSGROVE, 12G Grandson.

1693. Pinckney MUSGROVE, 12G Grandson.

1694. Bernard MUSGROVE, 12G Grandson.

1695. Sarah MUSGROVE, 12G Granddaughter.

Family of Arthur C. BROWN (1224) and Virginia ---

1696. Celius L. BROWN, 12G Grandson, born on 21 Mar 1907 in Carroll Co. MD. Celius L. died on 3 Feb 1994; he was 86.

Celius L. married Mildred FLOHR.

1697. Arthur Allen BROWN, 12G Grandson, born on 19 Jun 1911. Arthur Allen died on 5 Sep 1934; he was 23. Buried in Springfield Cemetery, Sykesville MD.

Family of Osko R. SHIPLEY (1234) and Francis ---

1698. Walter J. SHIPLEY, 12G Grandson. Walter J. died on 26 Oct 1943.

1699. Osko R. SHIPLEY, 12G Grandson. Osko R. died on 15 Feb 1901.

1700. Ethel SHIPLEY, 12G Granddaughter.

1701. Viola R. SHIPLEY, 12G Granddaughter, born on 25 Jun 1909. Viola R. died in Carroll Co. MD, on 16 Apr 1988;

she was 78. Buried at Deer Park Methodist Church Cemetery, Smallwood, Carroll County, Maryland.

Family of Birdie Selvena SHIPLEY (1236) and Lawrence Manogue BOSLER

1702. Katherine Selvena BOSLER, 12G Granddaughter, born on 20 Feb 1900 in Philadelphia PA. Katherine Selvena died in Philadelphia PA, on 4 Jul 1983; she was 83. Buried at Greenmount Cemetery, Philadelphia PA.

1703. Lawrence Manogue BOSLER, 12G Grandson, born on 15 Dec 1901 in Philadelphia PA. Lawrence Manogue died in Warminster, Bucks Co., PA, on 10 Sep 1964; he was 62. Buried at Sunset Memorial Park, Feasterville, Bucks County PA.

On 27 Apr 1935 when Lawrence Manogue was 33, he married Emma Amelia WEBBER, in the Nazareth Evangelical Lutheran Church, Philadelphia PA, born on 27 Oct 1906 in Philadelphia PA. Emma Amelia died in Bristol, Bucks Co. PA, on 3 Sep 1975; she was 68. They had the following children:
    i.   Mary Ann (1936-1992)
    ii.   Lawrence M. "Bucky" (1940-)

1704. Louise Frances "Lulu" BOSLER, 12G Granddaughter, born on 23 May 1904 in Philadelphia PA. Louise Frances "Lulu" died in Ridley Park, Delaware Co., PA, on 2 Oct 1985; she was 81. Buried at Greenmount Cemetery, Philadelphia PA.

In 1926 Louise Frances "Lulu" married Jacob G. BECKER, born in 1906 in Philadelphia PA. Jacob G. died in 1972 in Philadelphia PA. They had one child:
    i.   Jacob G.

1705. Clara Josephine BOSLER, 12G Granddaughter, born on 25 Aug 1906 in Philadelphia PA.

On 24 Sep 1925 when Clara Josephine was 19, she married Elmer Sergeant HOLDEN, in Elkton, Cecil Co., MD, born on 17 Feb 1904 in Philadelphia PA. Elmer Sergeant died in Audubon, Camden Co., NJ, on 16 Feb 1980; he was 75. They had the following children:
    i.   Clara "Clair" (1927-)
    ii.   Elmer Sergeant "Bubby" (1930-)
    iii.   Katherine Frances "Kay" (1935-)

Family of Franklin F. SHIPLEY (1240) and Rose M. GUYTON

1706. Mabel C. SHIPLEY, 12G Granddaughter, born on 16 Nov 1909. Mabel C. died on 8 Nov 1965; she was 55.

On 7 Jun 1926 when Mabel C. was 16, she married Thomas BROOKS.

1707. Franklin F. SHIPLEY Jr., 12G Grandson, born on 28 Nov 1911. Franklin F. died on 6 Jul 1969; he was 57.

Franklin first married Ada ---, born on 3 Nov 1918. They had one child:
    i.   Ronald (1950-)

In 1928 Franklin second married Rachel ---. They had the following children:
    i.   Franklin (1930-)
    ii.   Dorothy (1933-1936)
    iii.   William (1934-)
    iv.   Patricia (1939-)

1708. Leroy SHIPLEY, 12G Grandson, born on 20 Nov 1921.

On 23 Jan 1943 when Leroy was 21, he married Constance STEVENS, born on 21 Dec 1922. They had the following children:
    i.   Kenneth (1947-)
    ii.   Lee (1948-)
    iii.   Connie (1956-)

1709. Kenneth H. SHIPLEY, 12G Grandson, born on 4 May 1928. Kenneth H. died on 15 Jun 1928; he was less than 1.

1710. Dolores May SHIPLEY, 12G Granddaughter, born on 27 Jul 1929.

In 1947 Dolores May first married Ernest WICHTERMAN, born on 22 Jan 1925. They had the following children:
    i.   Richard (1949-)
    ii.   Denny (1951-)
    iii.   David

In 1972 Dolores May second married Jacob ROLLER.

Aft 1973 Dolores May third married Anthony DESANTIS.

Family of Florence (Edna May) SHIPLEY (1241) and --- BISHOP

1711. Alma May BISHOP, 12G Granddaughter, born on 5 Feb 1917.

1712. Mildred BISHOP, 12G Granddaughter, born on 17 Dec 1912.

Family of Charles Howard SHIPLEY (1242) and Emily M. STEVENSON

1713. Thelma May SHIPLEY, 12G Granddaughter, born on 15 Sep 1913. Thelma May died on 14 Dec 1913; she was less than 1. Buried in Greenmount Cemetery Philadelphia PA.

1714. Charles H. SHIPLEY Jr., 12G Grandson, born on 16 Apr 1916.

1715. Mildred SHIPLEY, 12G Granddaughter, born on 20 Aug 1919.

Family of Florence MORDECAI (1249) and George HARRISON

1716. Florence Patterson HARRISON, 12G Granddaughter.

Family of George Patterson MORDECAI (1251) and Champe Moncure ROBINSON

1717. John Robinson MORDECAI, 12G Grandson, born on 22 May 1907. John Robinson died in Feb 1982.

John Robinson married Mary Mercer FORSYTHE, born on 7 Sep 1912 in 15 May 1981. They had one child:
    i.   Monte

Family of Francis Snowden BROWN (1255) and --- ---

1718. Frank BROWN III, 12G Grandson.

Family of Elias BROWN (1259) and Blanche TROTT

1719. Albert BROWN, 12G Grandson.

Albert married Elizabeth POHLMAN. This couple had two daughters.

Family of Sara "Sadie" BROWN (1261) and William Julius MIELKE

1720. William August MIELKE, 12G Grandson, born on 25 Mar 1917.

On 10 Jan 1940 when William August was 22, he married Nellie OURSLER. Nellie died on 18 Jan 1994. This couple had no issue.

1721. Julius Edward MIELKE, 12G Grandson, born on 5 Apr 1919. Died in World War II. Buried in Ward's Chapel Cemetery.

On 6 Sep 1940 when Julius Edward was 21, he married Blanche TRIPLETT, born on 26 May 1923. This couple had no issue.

1722. Carl Arthur MIELKE, 12G Grandson, born on 23 Nov 1920.

On 12 Dec 1941 when Carl Arthur was 21, he married Theresa HUSH, born on 26 May 1923. They had the following children:
- i. William Samuel "Butch" (1943-)
- ii. Linda Jane (1945-)
- iii. Carl Arthur (1949-)
- iv. Joy Anne (1961-)

1723. Lula Eleanor MIELKE, 12G Granddaughter, born on 10 Apr 1922.

On 2 Oct 1942 when Lula Eleanor was 20, she first married Robert Eugene KNAUFF, born on 4 Mar 1923. Died in Belgium, World War II. They had one child:
- i. Robert Eugene Jr. (1944-)

On 14 Aug 1949 when Lula Eleanor was 27, she second married Jessie Odell CRISSMAN. They had one child:
- i. Barbara Jean (1952-)

1724. Vernon Walter MIELKE, 12G Grandson, born on 19 Aug 1926.

On 17 Feb 1950 when Vernon Walter was 23, he married Marian Louise WHALEN, born on 15 Jul 1934. They had the following children:
- i. Dennis Richard (1952-)
- ii. Douglas Edward (1957-)
- iii. Karen Anne (1965-)

Family of Bessie Susan BROWN (1263) and Lawrence Joseph GAMBLE

1725. William Robert BEALEFIELD, 12G Grandson. Adopted as Gamble but later reassumed his birth surname. Married Sarah May ---; children: William Robert, Theresa Ann, Edward Joseph, Patricia Ann, Paul L. Bealefield.

1726. Charles Lawrence GAMBLE, 12G Grandson, born in 1928.

Charles Lawrence married Elizabeth M. ---. They had:
- i. Lawrence William
- ii. Bessie M.
- iii. Charles Lawrence Jr.

1727. Edward Bernard GAMBLE, 12G Grandson, born in 1932

Edward Bernard married Mary Virginia DELUCA, born in 1931. They had:
- i. Elaine Susan (died at birth)
- ii. Edward Bernard Jr.
- iii. Robert Bruce
- iv. Gloria Marie

Family of Nancy Clara Etta BROWN (1265) and William Wilson SOUTHARD

1728. William W. SOUTHARD Jr., 12G Grandson, born on 5 Dec 1923 in Woodlawn, MD. Ref.: He is in Sons of the American Revolution No. 102209 identified as a descendant of Abel Brown, Revolutionary War patriot.

On 15 Jul 1952 when William W. was 28, he married Arlene R. CRAWFORD, in Las Vegas NE, born on 5 Sep 1927 in Carmen OK. They had one child:
- i. James Carson (1958-)

Family of Jewel D. HAY (1271) and George NASH

1729. George NASH Jr., 12G Grandson.

Family of Mildred Elizabeth PEARCE (1278) and Henry Barramore TODD

1730. Nancy PEARCE TODD, 12G Granddaughter, born on 30 Sep 1924.

Family of Anna Elizabeth PEARCE (1279) and Arthur S. STIVERS

1731. Elizabeth Jeannie STIVERS, 12G Granddaughter, born on 19 Apr 1908.

Family of John Pearce CUMMING (1281) and Charlotte Miriam FOSSETT

1732. Jeanne Miriam CUMMING, 12G Granddaughter, born on 10 Mar 1918 in Baltimore Co. MD.

1733. Gordon Fossett CUMMING, 12G Grandson, born on 10 Feb 1920 in Baltimore Co. MD.

Family of Eleanor Frances SMITH (1282) and Robert O. WATERS

1734. Eleanor Mildred WATERS, 12G Granddaughter, born on 3 Sep 1908.

1735. Robert O. WATERS, 12G Grandson, born on 3 Sep 1908. Date of birth 1 Aug 1910 per McCallahan.

1736. Agnes WATERS, 12G Granddaughter, born on 2 Sep 1924.

Family of Edward Augustus COCKEY (1288) and Nannie Strother MOORE

1737. Urath Cromwell COCKEY, 12G Granddaughter, born on 21 Jul 1911.

1738. Edward Augustus COCKEY, 12G Grandson, born on 27 May 1913.

1739. Alexander Moore COCKEY, 12G Grandson, born on 13 Jul 1915.

1740. Alice Councilman COCKEY, 12G Granddaughter, born on 1 Jan 1917.

Family of John Councilman COCKEY (1289) and Florence Lydia SOTHORON

1741. Lydia Sothoron COCKEY, 12G Granddaughter, born on 24 Jan 1912.

1742. John Sothoron COCKEY, 12G Grandson, born on 21 Sep 1916.

Family of Alexander Drummond COCKEY (1290) and Frances BURLEY

1743. Alice Councilman "Frances" COCKEY, 12G Granddaughter, born on 10 Jul 1917 in Baltimore Co. MD.

Family of Alexander Drummond COCKEY (1290) and Ellen Rebecca MOORE

1744. Alexander COCKEY, 12G Grandson, born on 2 Sep 1922 in Baltimore Co. MD.

Family of Sally Ann COCKEY (1294) and William Maury WERTH

1745. Virginia Lee WERTH, 12G Granddaughter.

1746. Sally Ann WERTH, 12G Granddaughter.

Family of Emma Shepherd COCKEY (1295) and Bruce H. HELFRICH

1747. Emma Shepherd HELFRICH, 12G Granddaughter.

1748. Robert Bruce HELFRICH, 12G Grandson.

1749. **Thomas Cockey HELFRICH**, 12G Grandson.

1750. **Samuel Cockey HELFRICH**, 12G Grandson.

Family of Randolph Lucas COCKEY (1308) and Louise Dilworth KEYSER

1751. **Randolph Lucas COCKEY**, 12G Grandson, born on 13 Aug 1942.

1752. **Robert Fielding COCKEY**, 12G Grandson, born on 2 Oct 1944.

1753. **Louise Randall COCKEY**, 12G Granddaughter, born on 22 Oct 1947.

1754. **Christopher Slade COCKEY**, 12G Grandson, born on 31 May 1957.

Family of Deborah "Fannie" IRELAND (1326) and Fred Reed MUSE

1755. **Helen M. MUSE**, 12G Granddaughter.

Helen M. married --- VOGT.

1756. **Julia A. MUSE**, 12G Granddaughter.

Julia A. married --- NAILL.

1757. **Fred R. MUSE**, 12G Grandson.

1758. **John M. MUSE**, 12G Grandson.

1759. **C. Thomas MUSE**, 12G Grandson.

1760. **William F. MUSE**, 12G Grandson.

Family of Grant A. BASEMAN (1329) and Mamie MYERS

1761. **Grant A. BEASMAN**, 12G Grandson. See note with No. 613 regarding surname spelling.

1762. **Earl G. BEASMAN**, 12G Grandson.

1763. **Vincent BEASMAN**, 12G Grandson.

1764. **Frances BASEMAN**, 12G Granddaughter.

Frances married --- WESTIN.

1765. **Joan BASEMAN**, 12G Granddaughter.

Joan married --- CROOKS.

Family of Joseph OSBORN (1330) and Mary C. ELKINS

1766. W. T. OSBORN, 12G Grandson, born in 1849 in Franklin Co. IL.

Family of William M. OSBORN (1331) and Sarah M. HARRIS

1767. Emmett A. OSBORN, 12G Grandson, born in Nov 1854 in MI. Emmett A. died before 1920.

On 28 Dec 1893 Emmett A. married Ellen T. KELLY, daughter of Cornelius KELLY and Eliza ---, in Cook Co. IL, born in Dec 1862 in MI. Ellen T. died before 1920. They had one child:
    i.   Albert Emmett (1895-1953)

1768. Aevlia? OSBORN, 12G Granddaughter, born in 1858.

1769. Caroline M. OSBORN, 12G Granddaughter, born in 1863.

1770. William R. OSBORN, 12G Grandson, born in 1865.

On 26 Dec 1888 William R. married Alice ALBERT, in Vermillion Co. IL.

1771. Milton N. OSBORN, 12G Grandson, born in 1868.

1772. Malona S. OSBORN, 12G Granddaughter, born in 1869.

1773. Xanthus L. OSBORN, 12G Grandson, born in 1871.

Family of Lydia OSBORN (1333) and William Raleigh SMITH

1774. Solomon SMITH, 12G Grandson, born on 14 Oct 1860 in Macomb, McDonough Co. IL. Solomon died in Carthage MO, on 31 Jul 1934; he was 73.

Solomon married Frances Rosetta WILFONG, born on 28 Jun 1857 in IL. Frances Rosetta died in Carthage MO, on 11 Jul 1924; she was 67. They had one child:
    i.   Marion Francis (1882-1969)

Family of Mary Smith OSBORN (1336) and Samuel H. WILLIAMS

1775. John Samuel WILLIAMS, 12G Grandson, born on 18 Jul 1859 in Rochester, Monroe Co. NY. Died 23 May 1861; he was 1.

1776. Samuel Kingston WILLIAMS, 12G Grandson, born on 8 Jul 1861 in Rochester, Monroe Co. NY. Samuel Kingston died on 2 Mar 1864; he was 2.

1777. Ida WILLIAMS, 12G Granddaughter, born on 30 Oct 1864 in Rochester, Monroe Co. NY. Ida died on 1 Aug 1878; she was 13.

1778. William Mead WILLIAMS, 12G Grandson, born on 7 Jan 1867 in Rochester, Monroe Co. NY. William Mead died on 22 Aug 1956; he was 89.

1779. Minnie WILLIAMS, 12G Granddaughter, born on 28 Mar 1868 in Rochester, Monroe Co. NY. Minnie died on 2 Mar 1936; she was 67.

Family of Francis Marion OSBORN (1337) and Catherine HUSTED

1780. Louisa OSBORN, 12G Granddaughter, born on 18 Jun 1863 in McDonough Co. IL.

1781. Eva Augusta OSBORN, 12G Granddaughter, born on 16 Jan 1865 in McDonough Co. IL. Eva Augusta died on 28 Apr 1914; she was 49.

1782. Albert A. OSBORN, 12G Grandson, born on 28 Mar 1867 in Cowley Co. KS.

1783. Dudley E. OSBORN, 12G Grandson, born on 25 Mar 1870 in Cowley Co. KS.

1784. Josephine OSBORN, 12G Granddaughter, born on 11 Aug 1872 in Cowley Co. KS. Josephine died in Wendell, Gooding Co. ID, on 4 Mar 1943; she was 70. Buried in Twin Falls ID.

Family of Elijah S. OSBORN (1338) and Lucinda DRISKELL

1785. Nellie Filena OSBORN, 12G Granddaughter, born on 29 Nov 1863/64 in IL. Nellie Filena died in Declo, Cassia Co. ID, on 15 Sep 1934; she was 70.

On 23 Dec 1883 when Nellie Filena was 20, she married Oscar COX, in Shelton NE, born in Mar 1866 in NE. Oscar died on 5 Aug 1934 in Rupert, Minidoka Co. ID. They had the following children:
- i. William Clarence (1884-1966)
- ii. Eva Viola (1887-1953)
- iii. Arthur Franklin (1890-1948)
- iv. Donivan Elijah (1892-1980)
- v. Lucinda Ethel (1895-1964)
- vi. Edelia Etta (1897-1993)
- vii. Olive Leota (1898-1926)
- viii. Alta Florence (1903-1986)
- ix. Ralph Edgar (1905-1982)

1786. Parthena A. OSBORN, 12G Granddaughter, born on 27 Mar 1866 in IL. Parthena A. died in OR on 22 Sep 1939; she was 73.

On 20 May 1888 when Parthena A. was 22, she married Arthur E. HENDRYX.

1787. Roena Evaline or Estaline OSBORN, 12G Granddaughter, born on 8 May 1868 in IL. Roena Evaline or Estaline died about 1945 in CA.

On 1 Mar 1885 when Roena Evaline or Estaline was 16, she married Grant BARRETT.

1788. Francis N. OSBORN, 12G Grandson, born on 19 Nov 1870. Francis N. died on 15 Aug 1872; he was 1.

1789. Teressa Emaline OSBORN, 12G Granddaughter, born on 9 Jan 1873. Teressa Emaline died on 3 Nov 1950; she was 77.

On 18 Nov 1888 when Teressa Emaline was 15, she married William J. TURNIDGE, born in Dec 1866 in MO. William J. died in 1950.

1790. Homer M. OSBORN, 12G Grandson, born on 4 Dec 1875/76. Homer M. died in Lebanon, Linn Co. OR, on 19 Mar 1955; he was 79.

On 13 Nov 1899 when Homer M. was 23, he married Salome BLAND, born in 1873 in OR. Salome died in 1912 in OR.

1791. Lulu E. OSBORN, 12G Granddaughter, born on 11 Dec 1878. Lulu E. died in Aug 1963 in Santa Cruz CA.

On 14 Mar 1897 when Lulu E. was 18, she married James W. KELLER, born in Dec 1864 in IN.

1792. Charles A. OSBORN, 12G Grandson, born on 27 Aug 1881 in MO. Charles A. died in Ocala FL, on 27 Jan 1968; he was 86.

On 25 Nov 1911 when Charles A. was 30, he married Bessie ---, in Multomah Co. OR.

Family of Louisa OSBORN (1339) and John Wesley FLACK

1793. Elijah Alexander FLACK, 12G Grandson, born on 27 Dec 1860 in Schuyler, IL. Elijah Alexander died in Pesoria, IL, on 2 Jul 1955; he was 94.

On 26 Dec 1880 when Elijah Alexander was 19, he married Anna Catherine WILSON, in McDonough Co. IL, born on 2 Feb 1859 in Colchester, McDonough Co. IL. Anna Catherine died in Industry, McDonough Co. IL, on 8 Feb 1916; she was 57.

1794. Alice B. FLACK, 12G Granddaughter, born on 20 Jun 1862. Alice B. died in 1945.

On 22 Apr 1884 when Alice B. was 21, she married William CORDELL, born in 1859 in OH. William died in 1940 in IL.

1795. Charles Wesley FLACK, 12G Grandson, born on 2 Jun 1865 in Freemont, IA. Charles Wesley died in Macomb, McDonough Co. IL, on 20 Jul 1950; he was 85.

On 18 Aug 1887 when Charles Wesley was 22, he married Ura KEE, born on 3 Jan 1865 in Industry, McDonough Co. IL. Ura died in Macomb, McDonough Co. IL, on 2 Jan 1950; she was 84.

1796. Willis Edgar FLACK, 12G Grandson, born on 24 Apr 1868 in Industry, McDonough Co. IL. Willis Edgar died in Kansas City, Jackson Co. MO, on 7 Dec 1940; he was 72.

On 24 Oct 1889 when Willis Edgar was 21, he married Margaret INGLES, born on 31 Dec 1874 in Schuyler, IL. Margaret died in Denver, Arapahoe Co. CO, on 21 Jul 1953; she was 78.

1797. Lucy E. FLACK, 12G Granddaughter, born on 20 Oct 1870 in Industry, McDonough Co. IL.

On 27 May 1895 when Lucy E. was 24, she married William G. EVANS.

1798. Louis E. FLACK, 12G Grandson, born on 20 Oct 1870 in Industry, McDonough Co. IL. Louis E. died in Industry, McDonough Co. IL, on 22 Dec 1946; he was 76.

On 2 Oct 1895 when Louis E. was 24, he married Loucinda F. BRANDON, born on 1 Jul 1873 in Industry, McDonough Co. IL. Loucinda F. died in Chicago, Cook Co. IL, on 28 Mar 1948; she was 74.

Family of Andrew Jackson OSBORNE (1356) and Mary SALLADE

1799. Margaret OSBORN, 12G Granddaughter, born in 1864 in MO.

1800. Angeline OSBORN, 12G Granddaughter, born in 1865 in MO.

1801. Andrew Jackson OSBORN, 12G Grandson, born on 2 Dec 1869 in Adair Co. KY. Andrew Jackson died in Adair Co. KY, on 15 Sep 1870; he was less than 1.

Family of Andrew Jackson OSBORNE (1356) and Sarah A. VERMILLION

1802. Dewey OSBORN, 12G Grandson, born on 2 Apr 1898 in Saline Co. MO.

Family of Andrew Jackson OSBORNE (1356) and Jane LAININGER

1803. Lydia Adella OSBORNE, 12G Granddaughter, born on 8 Oct 1871 in Adair Co. MO.

Lydia Adella married James Sanders ADKINS, born in 1869. They had the following children:
- i. Laura (1891-)
- ii. Jacob Samuel (1893-)
- iii. Roy Earl (1898-)
- iv. Opal Leona

1804. Arthur Selvester OSBORNE, 12G Grandson, born on 30 Sep 1873 in Adair Co. MO. Arthur Selvester died on 25 Aug 1945; he was 71.

Arthur Selvester married Permelia WEBSTER. They had the following children:
- i. Myrtle
- ii. Archie
- iii. Marvin
- iv. Elsie

1805. Mary Alfretta OSBORNE, 12G Granddaughter, born on 17 Aug 1875 in Adair Co. MO. Mary Alfretta died on 31 Jul 1954; she was 78.

Mary Alfretta married William LAWSON, born in 1873. They had the following children:
- i. Nettie (1893-)
- ii. Noah E. (1894-)
- iii. Thelma
- iv. Edwin Burl

1806. Addie Ella OSBORNE, 12G Granddaughter, born in 1877. Addie Ella died on 1 Jan 1893 in MO.

Addie Ella married Charles MAY, born about 1875.

1807. Joseph William OSBORNE, 12G Grandson, born on 12 Apr 1878 in IL.

In 1898 Joseph William married Mary Virginia PERCIVAL, in Saline Co. MO, born in Dec 1883 in KY. They had the following children:
- i. Ada Lucrecia (1899-)
- ii. Oscar Sylvester (about 1900-)
- iii. Joseph Merle (about 1901-)
- iv. Robert Lee (about 1902-)
- v. Rosebud Jane (about 1904-)
- vi. James Percival (about 1905-)
- vii. John Ernest (about 1907-)

1808. Armina OSBORNE, 12G Granddaughter, born in Sep 1880 in MO.

1809. John Albert OSBORNE, 12G Grandson, born on 11 Jan 1886. John Albert died in 1945.

John Albert married Addit GOULDEN.

1810. Albert A. OSBORNE, 12G Grandson, born in Jan 1885 in MO.

1811. Viola OSBORNE, 12G Granddaughter, born in Oct 1893.

1812. Violet OSBORNE, 12G Granddaughter, born in Oct 1893.

Family of Hiram OSBORN (1363) and Lucy Mahala HUNTLY

1813. Willis P. OSBORN, 12G Grandson, born on 3 May 1866.

1814. Albert W. OSBORN, 12G Grandson, born on 29 Apr 1868.

Family of James OSBORN (1364) and Mary A. WATTS

1815. Sarah OSBORN, 12G Granddaughter, born in 1863.

1816. Emma OSBORN, 12G Granddaughter, born in 1865.

1817. Annette OSBORN, 12G Granddaughter, born in 1867.

1818. James OSBORN, 12G Grandson, born in 1869.

Family of Robert OSBORN (1366) and Mary Elizabeth J. FRAKES

1819. William OSBORN, 12G Grandson, born in 1872.

1820. Isaac OSBORN, 12G Grandson, born in 1873.

1821. Emmasiah OSBORN, 12G Grandson, born in 1875.

1822. Susannah OSBORN, 12G Granddaughter, born in 1876.

1823. Brice OSBORN, 12G Grandson, born in 1879.

Family of Emily Savannah ALLEY (1380) and Jacob ROSIER

1824. Minora Angeline ROSIER, 12G Granddaughter, born on 20 Sep 1869 near Windfall, Tipton Co. IN.

Minora Angeline married Charles Henry PREVOST, born on 4 Aug 1869 in Dunkirk, Jay Co. IN. They had one child:
    i.   Eva Josephine (1897-)

Family of Sara Eliza "Sadie" MALONEY (1381) and George Washington STAUBUS

1825. Clara Mae STAUBUS, 12G Granddaughter, born on 1 Mar 1889 in Brunswick, Charlton Co. MO. Clara Mae died in May 1979 in Brunswick, Charlton Co. MO.

On 11 Jun 1911 when Clara Mae was 22, she married Clyde Nathaniel ELLIOTT, son of Asa Wilson ELLIOTT and Viola Ruth TURNER, in Brunswick, Charlton Co. MO, born on 12 Jun 1890 in Brunswick, Charlton Co. MO. Clyde Nathaniel died in Brunswick, Charlton Co. MO, on 28 Jan 1969; he was 78. They had the following children:

    i.   --- (1913-)
    ii.   George Wilson (1914-1970)
    iii.   Clyde Russell (1917-1997)
    iv.   James LeRoy (1919-)
    v.   Robie Joe (1921-)
    vi.   Mary Dean (1927-)
    vii.   Paul Edward (1930-)

1826. Mary Etta "Dolly" STAUBUS, 12G Granddaughter, born in Dec 1891 in Brunswick, Charlton Co. MO. Mary Etta "Dolly" died after 1916.

Mary Etta "Dolly" married Samuel WILKERSON.

1827. George Washington STAUBUS Jr., 12G Grandson, born on 23 May 1893 in Brunswick, Charlton Co. MO. George Washington died in May 1983 in Brunswick, Charlton Co. MO.

George Washington married Florence PITTMAN.

1828. Alma Virginia STAUBUS, 12G Granddaughter, born in Apr 1896 in Brunswick, Charlton Co. MO.

Alma Virginia married Dewey PROCTOR.

1829. John Henry STAUBUS, 12G Grandson, born in Sep 1898 in Brunswick, Charlton Co. MO.

John Henry married Olive Irene SMITH.

Family of Hallie Louise DAVIS (1488) and Hon. Stephen Benton ELKINS

1830. Davis ELKINS, 12G Grandson, born on 24 Jan 1876 in Washington D.C. Began study at Harvard but left to accept a position as Assistant Adjutant General of Volunteers in the Spanish-American War, where he was stationed in Puerto Rico.

1831. Stephen Benton ELKINS Jr, 12G Grandson, born on 19 Sep 1877 in Washington D.C. Graduated with honors from Yale in 1900. Lieutenant in the Signal Corps on General F.D. Grant's staff in Puerto Rico until Nov. 1898.

1832. Richard ELKINS, 12G Grandson, born on 6 Mar 1879 in New York. Studied science at Princeton.

1833. Elaine ELKINS, 12G Granddaughter, born on 14 Sep 1881 in New York. Studied at Princeton University.

1834. Katherine Hallie ELKINS, 12G Granddaughter, born on 14 Jan 1886 in New York.

Family of Kate Bantz DAVIS (1489) and Robert M. G. BROWN

1835. Katherine Grace Davis BROWN, 12G Granddaughter.

Family of Grace Thomas DAVIS (1492) and Arthur LEE

1836. George LEE, 12G Grandson.

1837. Ellen Bruce LEE, 12G Grandson.

Family of John Thomas DAVIS (1494) and Elizabeth ARMSTEAD

1838. Hallie Elkins DAVIS, 12G Granddaughter.

Family of Martha Thomas BROWN (1570) and August William PRIEBE

1839. Annie Mary PRIEBE, 12G Granddaughter, born on 29 Jan 1909 in Unity, Montgomery Co. MD.

On 11 Apr 1936 when Annie Mary was 27, she married Gillis C. OWINGS, son of Thomas OWINGS and Elizabeth A. ROYER, born on 4 Nov 1908 in Etchison MD.

1840. Sylvan Augustus PRIEBE, 12G Grandson, born on 11 Aug 1911 in Unity, Montgomery Co. MD. Sylvan Augustus died in Apr 1986.

Sylvan Augustus married Elva SETTLERS, in Washington D.C, born on 2 Jul 1918. Elva died in Oct 1981 in Baltimore MD. They had the following children:
      i.   Judith Ann (1943-)
      ii.   Nancy Lee (1944-)
      iii. Annie Mary (1953-)

1841. Russell PRIEBE, 12G Grandson, born on 1 Jul 1919 in Glenelg, Howard Co. MD.

Russell married Christine KING. They had the following children:
      i.   Sandra Faye (1945-)
      ii.   Gayle (1947-)

1842. William Courtney PRIEBE, 12G Grandson, born on 16 Sep 1921 in Glenelg, Howard Co. MD.

On 6 Oct 1945 when William Courtney was 24, he married Doris Elizabeth BECKMANN, daughter of Henry Randolph BECKMANN and Barbara DEHNE, in Baltimore MD. They had the following children:
      i.   Lawrence William (1946-)
      ii.   Ronald Steven (1948-)
      iii. Susan Lorraine (1953-)
      iv. Kevin Arthur (1955-)

Family of Ruby BROWN (1572) and Herman H. PRIEBE

1843. Louise PRIEBE, 12G Granddaughter, born in 1909.

1844. Lillian May PRIEBE, 12G Granddaughter, born on 10 Nov 1910 in MD. Lillian May died in Jan 1997 in MD.

1845. Rosalie PRIEBE, 12G Granddaughter, born in 1910.

1846. Herman Brown PRIEBE, 12G Grandson, born in 1914 in MD. Herman Brown died in 1992 in MD.

1847. Margaret PRIEBE, 12G Granddaughter, born in 1915.

1848. Henry PRIEBE, 12G Grandson, born in 1917.

1849. Elsie PRIEBE, 12G Granddaughter, born in 1920.

1850. Freddie PRIEBE, 12G Grandson, born in 1924.

Family of Edgar BROWN (1573) and Elsie BURROUGHS

1851. Joyce BROWN, 12G Granddaughter, born in 1929.

1852. Shirley BROWN, 12G Granddaughter, born in 1929.

1853. Leland BROWN, 12G Grandson, born in 1933.

Family of Marshall A. BROWN (1575) and Catherine O. ---

1854. Catherine Eugenie BROWN, 12G Granddaughter, born on 27 Nov 1920 in Philadelphia PA.

In Sep 1942 Catherine Eugenie married Jesse ROWLAND.

1855. Marshall John BROWN Jr., 12G Grandson, born on 18 Aug 1922 in Passaic NJ. Electrical engineer, resident of Ft. Walton Beach Florida.

Marshall John married Margaret Virginia SMITH, born in Pensacola FL. They had the following children:
- i. Marshall H.
- ii. Patrick D.
- iii. Carolyn M.
- iv. Russell A.
- v. Christopher C.
- vi. Jeffrey P.

Family of Dewey Octavius BROWN (1576) and Mignonette Anne RUSSELL

1856. James Russell BROWN, 12G Grandson, born on 8 Feb 1917 in Washington D.C. Served in WW II, U.S. Army. Resident of Brooklyn New York, Falls Church Washington D.C., employee of the U.S. Maritime Commission, Birmingham Alabama with Ingalls Iron Works and Ingalls Shipbuilding in Pascagoula Mississippi, then Washington D.C.

On 7 Dec 1939 when James Russell was 22, he married Margaret Virginia SMITH, daughter of Jared Dunklin SMITH, in Washington D.C, born in 1918. Worked at the Department of Commerce. They had one child:
- i. Roger Allen (1943-)

SOURCES

These are secondary sources and valued informants. Primary citations from church and governmental records, etc. are cited in the text.

Barnes, R. *Marriages and Deaths from Baltimore Newspapers 1796-1816*. Baltimore: Genealogical Pub. Co., 1978.
_____, and B. S. Carothers. *1783 Tax List of Baltimore County*. Westminster MD: Family Line Pubs., (1978) 1998.
Beard, Alice Marie, "Itha Elmer Doyle, 1874-1958, Mary Louise Payne, 1883-1953." http://members.aol.com/.
Beckman, Vern.
Block, Virginia Brown.
Blocker, Martha.
Blume, Katy.
Bosler, Lawrence.
Brenneman, Sara Eloise Taylor.
Brown, Albert S., "An Imperfect Chronological Record of the House of Brown." Manuscript at the University of Maryland, College Park, 1897.
[Brown Family in Sykesville]. *Sykesville Herald*. 14 May 1936.
"Brown Family." Manuscript at the Maryland Historical Society Archives, Baltimore. Filing Case A.
Brown. James W., "Anne Arundel's Abell Browne and Descendants: Review, Critique, Addenda." *Maryland Genealogical Society Bulletin*. 45, 3 (Spring 2004): 241-258.
_____, "Anne Arundel's Abell Browne, Part II." *Maryland Genealogical Society Bulletin*. 46, 1 (Winter 2005): 3-13.
Brown, Lloyd W. *The Browns of the Patuxent River*. Silver Spring, MD, 1991.
Brown, Marshall. *The Robert Brown Family of Maryland*. Undated manuscript provided by his great-grand nephew Gregory S. Priebe.
Brown, Samuel. Family Bible dated 14 August 1780 and inscribed by Samuel Brown 2 Dec 1817 saying that "my grandson Samuel Ray Brown should inherit this Bible after the death of his father Elisha." Photocopy at the Maryland Historical Society. Cabinet A.
Brown, Walter Ray.
Brown, Zelma Fern.
Browne, Sir William *et al.* "Browne Letters." Collection, index and synopses of correspondence archived at the Centre for Kentish studies on behalf of the Viscount De L'Isle, Maidstone, Kent, 1596-1610.
Carlson, Deana. Brown family.
Carroll County Maryland Historical Society. *Carroll County Maryland Cemeteries Volume I, Southeast*. Westminster MD, 1989.
Channing, Adrian.
Colket, M.B. *Founders of Early American Families: Emigrants from Europe 1607-1657*. Rev. ed. Washington D. C.: Foundersand Patriots, 1985.
Collins, Arthur, ed. *Letters and Memorials of State*. Sydney family papers. 2 vols. London: Osborne, (1746), 1973.
Crissman, Lula Eleanor
Descendants of John Bristow. Bermuda Website. http://www.rootsweb.com/~bmuwgw/.
Descendants of John Darrell. Bermuda Website. http://www.rootsweb.com/~bmuwgw/.
Doliante, S. J. *Maryland and Virginia Colonials: Genealogies of Some Colonial Families*. Baltimore: Genealogical Publishing Co., 1991.
Dunn, R. S., J. Savage and L. Yeadle, eds. *The Journal of John Winthrop 1630-1649*. Cambridge MA: Harvard UP, 1996.
Elliott, Eugene.
Field, Kathleen.
Fischer, D.H. *Albion's Seed: Four British Folkways in America*. New York: Oxford UP, 1989.
Ford, Harold. Brown – Osborne families.
Gamble, Edward.

Granger, D.S. *The Shipleys of Maryland*. 3rd. ed. Baltimore: Gateway Press, ca 2002.

Griffith, Lori.

Hahn, Patricia. *Moss Cemetery*. Typescript at the Anderson Indiana Public Library. 1977.

Harden, S. *The Pioneer. History and Genealogy of Hancock and Madison County*. Knightstown IN: Bookmark, (1895) 1977.

_____, *History of Madison County Indiana 1820-1874*. [s.n.], 1874.

Hodges, M.R. *Unpublished Revolutionary Records of Maryland*. 6 vols. Typescript at the Maryland Historical Society Archives, Baltimore.

Horvath, George J. *1838 Tax List of Baltimore County, Maryland*. Westminster MD: Family Line Pubs., 1995.

_____. *The Particular Assessment Lists for Baltimore and Carroll Counties, 1798*. Westminster MD: Family Line Pubs., 1986.

Hollis Hallett, A. C. *Early Bermuda Records 1619-1826*. Bermuda: Juniperhill Press, 1991.

Hotten, John C., ed. *The Original Lists of Persons of Quality*. Baltimore: Genealogical Pub. Co., 1976.

Ives, V.A., ed. *The Rich Papers: Letters from Bermuda 1615-1646*. Bermuda: Bermuda National Trust, 1984.

Jacobus, D. L. "The House of Rich." *The American Genealogist*, 21 (1944): 234-8; 22 (1945): 27-37. 157-165. 240-8; 23 (1946): 101-9.

Jones, Wendy.

Jourdan, E. G. *Early Families of Southern Maryland*.10 vols. Westminster MD: Family Line Pubs., 1992-.

Kupperman, K.O., comp. *Papers Relating to the Providence Island Company and Colony, 1630-1641*. 2 microfilm reels. Wakefield W. Yorkshire: Microform Academic Publishers, 1989.

_____. *Providence Island, 1630-1641: The Other Puritan Colony*. Cambridge: Cambridge UP, 1993.

_____. "Errand to the Indies." *The William and Mary Quarterly*, 45 (1988): 70 – 99.

Lawrence, Dawson. "Historical Sketch of Anne Arundel, MD.," *Atlas of Anne Arundel County Maryland*. Glen Burnie MD: Greater Glen Burnie Jaycees, (1878) 1991.

Lefroy, J. H. *Memorials of the Discovery and Early Settlement of the Bermudas or Somers Islands 1515-1685*. 2 vols. Hamilton: Bermuda Historical Soc., (1877) 1981.

Lesure, Nancy.

Love, William.

Mackenzie, G.N. *Colonial Families of the United States of America*. 7 vols. New York: Grafton Pess, 1907 -.

Mallick and Wright. *Frederick County Militia in the War of 1812*. Westminster MD: Family Line Pubs., 1992.

Marks, L. B. "Moses Brown 1768 – 1817." Typescript held by the Historical Society of Carroll County, Maryland., 1982.

Marriage Records of Madison County. WPA typescript, n.d. Anderson IN Public Library

Mayer, Micki.

McCallahan, Eleanor. "A Brown Family of Maryland." *Maryland Genealogical Society Bulletin*, 19, 1 (1978): 1-16.

McFadden, Marlys.

McPherson, Walter.

Mercer, J.E. *Bermuda Settlers of the 17th Century*. Baltimore: Genealogical Pub. Co., 1982.

Mordecai, Douglas.

Mueller, Dianne.

Myhre, Colleen.

Netterville, J. J., ed. *Centennial History of Madison County, Indiana, 1823-1923*. Anderson IN: Historian's Association, Vol. I, 1923; Vol. II, 1925.

Newman, H. *Anne Arundel Gentry*. Baltimore: Lord Baltimore Press, 1933.

Peden, H.C. *Bastardy Cases in Baltimore County, Maryland 1673-1783*. Westminster MD, Willow Bend, c2001.

_____. *Revolutionary Patriots of Baltimore Town and Baltimore County Maryland 1775 – 1783*. Westminster MD: Family Line Pubs., 1988.

Priebe, Gregory S.

Richards and Jay. *Roots and Fruits: Family Records of Tobias Stocksdale*. n.p.

Richardson, H.D. *Side-Lights on Maryland History*. 2 vols. Baltimore: Genealogical Pub. Co., (1913) 1967.

Roberts, G. B. *The Royal Descents of 500 Immigrants to the American Colonies or the United States*. Baltimore: Genealogical Pub. Co., 1993.

Roth, Marylin.

Rynearson, Ruby Tate.

Sanders, Doris.

Scharf, J.T. *History of Western Maryland*. 2 vols. Baltimore: Regional Pub. Co., (1882) 1968.

Scull, G. D. *Sir William Browne, Knight, 1556-1610; and Sir Nathaniel Rich, Knight, 1636*. Manuscript archived at the New England Historical and Genealogical Society's R. Stanton Avery Special Collections Department, Boston, 1882.

Shaffer, William.

Shaw, W. A. *The Knights of England*. 2 vols. London: Central Chancery of the Orders of Knighthood, 1906.

Shelton, A. L. *Lawrence & Related Families: Browne, Dorsey, Hammond, Howard, Ridgley, Talbott*, 1990.

Shirk, I.M.M. *Descendants of Richard and Elizabeth (Ewen) Talbott*. [?]: Day Printing Co., 1927.

Sis, Francis X., Jr.

Sisseck, Pj.

Smith, Captaine John. *The Generall Historie of Virginia, New-England and the Summer Isles. Book 5*. Cleveland: World Pub. Co, (1624) 1966.

Smith, Howard.

Spear, Elmer C., ed., *Four Generation Charts from the Members of the Florida Chapter OGS*. (s.l., s.n.) 1996 - .

Stenley, V.D., ed. *Chancery Books of Carroll County Maryland Volumes 21-40 1873-1889*. Abstracts. Westminster MD: Family Line - Willow Bend, 1996.

Suggs, Donna.

Virkus, F. The Abridged *Compendium of American Genealogy*. 7 vols. Baltimore: Genealogical Pub. Co., (1935-42) 1987.

Warfield, J.D. *Founders of Anne Arundel and Howard Counties*. Baltimore: Regional Pub. Co., (1905) 1980.

Waters, H.F. "Sir Nathaniel Rich." In the series "Genealogical Gleanings in England," *New England Historical and Genealogical Register*, 48 (April 1894): 267-70. Reprinted in Genealogical *Gleanings in England*. Vol. II. (1981): 871-874.

White, Virgil. *Index of Old Wars Pension Files 1815-1926*. Rev. ed. National Historical Pub. Co., 1993.

_____. *Index of War of 1812 Pension Files*. 2 vols. Rev. ed. National Historical Pub. Co., 1992.

_____. *Index to Revolutionary War Service Records*. 4 vols. National Historical Pub. Co., 1995

Yeatman, J. P. *The Brownes of Bechworth Castle*. [London]: Published by the author, 1903.

_____. "The Brownes of Snelston." Vol. 4, Sect. 7, of *The Feudal History of the County of Derby*, 6 Vols. London: Bemrose, ca 1886-1908.

INDEX

---, Ada spouse of 1707
---, Annie spouse of 756
---, Bessie spouse of 1792
---, Beulah spouse of 1578
---, Caroline R. spouse of 774
---, Catherine spouse of 46
---, Catherine parent of spouse of 165
---, Catherine O. spouse of 1575
---, Edna spouse of 1566
---, Eliza parent of spouse of 1767
---, Elizabeth spouse of 536
---, Elizabeth spouse of 676
---, Elizabeth spouse of 79
---, Elizabeth spouse of 42
---, Elizabeth spouse of 1726
---, Elizabeth spouse of 90
---, Elizabeth spouse of 517
---, Elliner parent of spouse of 46
---, Esther spouse of 940
---, Florence T. G. spouse of 790
---, Francis spouse of 1234
---, Gwynith spouse of 1615
---, Hannah spouse of 103
---, Harriett spouse of 525
---, Inez B. spouse of 1328
---, Lavina spouse of 771
---, Lavina spouse of 734
---, Lucinda spouse of 376
---, Lucrecia spouse of 789
---, Lucy spouse of 104
---, Mabel spouse of 1626
---, Magdalen spouse of 403
---, Maggie E. spouse of 1071
---, Margaret parent of spouse of 523
---, Margaret A. spouse of 1214
---, Mary spouse of 636
---, Mary spouse of 45
---, Mary parent of spouse of 499
---, Mary parent of spouse of 35
---, Mary spouse of 151
---, Mary parent of spouse of 730
---, Mary spouse of 1086
---, Mary A. spouse of 1030
---, Mary Ann spouse of 526
---, Mary Ann spouse of 807
---, Mary Catherine spouse of 166
---, Mary V. spouse of 1569
---, Myrtle spouse of 1574

---, Patience spouse of 185
---, Phebe parent of spouse of 557
---, Providence spouse of 446
---, R. Josephine spouse of 1003
---, Rachel spouse of 771
---, Rachel spouse of 1707
---, Rebecca spouse of 787
---, Rebecca parent of spouse of 555
---, Sabra spouse of 355
---, Sallie Ann parent of spouse of 850
---, Sarah spouse of 23
---, Sarah parent of spouse of 410
---, Sarah parent of spouse of 416
---, Sarah spouse of 1334
---, Sarah spouse of 40
---, Sarah parent of spouse of 673
---, Sarah parent of spouse of 563
---, Sarah H. spouse of 407
---, Susanna spouse of 333
---, Susannah parent of spouse of 728
---, Susie spouse of 1132
---, Tabatha spouse of 806
---, Virginia spouse of 1224
ADAMS: Clark child of 1587, Emma Maxine child of 1587, Glen child of 1587, John child of 1587, Leila child of 1587, Will spouse of 1587
ADELAIDE see 5
ADELAIDE OF LORRAINE see 5
ADKINS: Elisha spouse of 302, Elisha 324, Elizabeth (twin) 325, Jacob Samuel child of 1803, James Sanders spouse of 1803, Joel spouse of 125, Joel parent of spouse of 302, Joel 327, Laura child of 1803, Mary (twin) 326, Olive 328, Opal Leona child of 1803, Roy Earl child of 1803
ALBERT: Alice spouse of 1770
ALBERT I: see 5
ALBERT II: see 5
ALBERT III: see 5
ALKIRE: Elizabeth parent of spouse of 641, Elizabeth parent of spouse of 642
ALLEN: Anna spouse of 56, Charles W. parent of spouse of 1085, Ella May spouse of 1085, Francis spouse of 519, Sarah spouse of 369
ALLEY: Doddridge 626, Emily Savannah 1380, Samuel Jay spouse of 465, William W. 948
ANDERSON: Lula Elizabeth spouse of 1647, Sarah Ann spouse of 1130, Sarah Ann spouse of 1131

ARMOUR: Ida spouse of 868
ARMSTEAD: Elizabeth spouse of 1494
ARRINGTON: Caroline R. spouse of 731, Sarah J. parent of spouse of 1580
BACON: --- spouse of 357, Anna spouse of 127, Hannah spouse of 121, Hannah parent of spouse of 324, Hannah parent of spouse of 337, Jeremiah spouse of 299, Josiah spouse of 226, Sarah spouse of 66
BAIRD: Mira parent of spouse of 586
BAKER: --- 275, Alfred F. spouse of 1084, Anna 273, Bayzie 313, Comfort 272, Daniel 265, Eleanor 317, Elijah spouse of 117, Elijah 271, Elijah 274, Ephraim spouse of 116, Ephraim 268, Hannah 316, Jeremiah 318, John spouse of 169, Mary 267, Mehitabel 269, Mercy spouse of 246, Morris spouse of 409, Nathan 264, Samuel 263, Sarah 266, Susanna 314, Thankful 270, Thankful 312, Timothy spouse of 123, Timothy 311, Timothy 315, William 319
BALCAM: Mary spouse of 228
BALL: Eleanor spouse of 509
BANGLE: Barbara Sue child of 1606, Perry Oliver spouse of 1606, Ralph Thomas child of 1606
BANTZ: Kateherine A. S. spouse of 1036
BARLIN: Betty spouse of 1034, Mary spouse of 689
BARNARD: Ebenezer spouse of 347
BARNETT: Catherine E. J. spouse of 549, Eliza spouse of 449
BARNHART: Grace Darling spouse of 877
BARR: Helen spouse of 897
BARRETT: Grant spouse of 1787
BARRINGTON: Henry spouse of 504
BARRON: Caleb Ezekiel 1030, Celie spouse of 1026, Ezequiel spouse of 677, Hattie 1487, Ophelia 1029, Solomon 1031
BASEMAN: Dora Florence 925, Ellen Bedford 924, Emma Dolly 921, Fannie Howard 922, Grace Ruth Ann 929, Grant A. 1329, Grant T. 926, Joan 1765, Julie Ann 923, Littlewood Alfred 927, May Pauline 931, Ray F. 930, Rosa Estella 928, Sylvester Wesley parent of spouse of 613, Theodore Wesley spouse of 613
BASSET, Joan Basset see 5
BATES: Beulah Ann 1458, Doctor Kiefer 1462, Fannie Mae 1465, Flora Alice 1460, Harriett Lanham 1466, Isaac Whitt 1463, James Carroll 1461, Luther Edwin 1459, Mary Elizabeth 1464, Reuben Thomas spouse of 1018, William parent of spouse of 1018
BEALEFIELD: William 1725
BEASMAN: Earl G. 1762, Elias Brown 818, Frances 1764, Frank Bennett 1302, Grant A. 1761, (Infant) 1303, John parent of spouse of 548, Johnzie E. spouse of 859, Joshua parent of spouse of 859, Vachel W. spouse of 548, Vincent 1763
BECKER: Jacob G. spouse of 1704, Jacob G. child of 1704
BECKMANN: Doris Elizabeth spouse of 1842, Henry Randolph parent of spouse of 1842
BECKWITH: Baruch 380, Barzillai 376, Rev. George spouse of 140, George 379, Nathaniel Brown 377, Penelope 378, Rebecca 374, Sarah 375
BEDFORD: Ellen Ann parent of spouse of 613
BEECHER: Obedience spouse of 234
BELL: Bazie Antonia parent of spouse of 1686
BENHAM: John spouse of 236
BENNETT: Caroline 565, Elisha parent of spouse of 439, Elisha H. spouse of 563, Col. Jesse parent of spouse of 563, Laura Ella 859, Mary Ellen 563, Miranda 566, Miranda spouse of 604, Susan Ann spouse of 547, Susan Ann 564, Wesley spouse of 439, Wesley parent of spouse of 547, Wesley parent of spouse of 604
BENTON: Josiah spouse of 220
BERKANSTOCK: Clayton spouse of 1651, Raymond child of 1651, Virgil child of 1651
BERRY: Ann spouse of 481, Elizabeth Ann spouse of 499, Jeremiah parent of spouse of 499
BETTS: Noah spouse of 1133
BEVIER: Henrietta spouse of 1058
BIDDINGER: Susan R. parent of spouse of 822
BIDDLE: Jacob spouse of 508
BIDWELL: Benjamin spouse of 329, Hannah spouse of 102, Ozias spouse of 378
BIGELOW: Alvin spouse of 216
BILLINGS: Charles Watson spouse of 1465, George Henry parent of spouse of 1465
BINGLEY: Hannah 223, John spouse of 105, William 222
BISHOP: --- spouse of 1241, Abigail parent of spouse of 672, Alma May 1711, Fannie L. spouse of 1019, Mildred 1712
BLAKESLEE: --- 279, Abraham 281, Anna 282, Anna 284, Dan 250, David 253, Ebenezer 252, Eleanor 251, Eleanor 287, Isaac 283, James 286, Jonathan 247, Joseph 285, Justus 248, Mary 245, Miriam 115, Miriam 280, Rebecca 278, Ruth 277, Sabra 288, Samuel spouse of 49, Samuel 118, Samuel 276, Sarah 249, Sarah 116, Thankful 117, Tilley spouse of 114, Tilley 246
BLAND: Salome spouse of 1790
BOLDEN: Lulu Lee 1317, Olie Mazie 1316, William 1315, William Oliver spouse of 909
BOND: Jane spouse of 512
BONER: Lavinia spouse of 1624
BONHAM: Marcelliar W. spouse of 723
BOONE: Hannah parent of spouse of 464
BORING: --- spouse of 409
BOSLER: Clara Josephine 1705, Katherine Selvena 1702, Lawrence M. "Bucky" child of 1703, Lawrence Manogue spouse of 1236, Lawrence Manogue 1703, Louise Frances "Lulu" 1704, Mary Ann child of 1703
BOSLEY: Chauncey Brooks 896, Chauncy Brooks 1310, Harrryman Gist 897, Jean 1309, John parent of spouse of 598, Capt. John Robert 894, Marie Elise

895, Mollie 898, William Henry 1311, William Henry spouse of 598, William Henry 893

BOTTORF: Jennie F. spouse of 1137

BOUCIER: Dorothy Wyoma spouse of 1635

BOWEN: Elizabeth A. spouse of 609

BOWLIN: James spouse of 664

BRADFORD: Robert L. spouse of 1480

BRADLEY: Sarah Davis spouse of 1297

BRAMWELL: Urath spouse of 453, Urath parent of spouse of 612

BRANDON: Loucinda F. spouse of 1798

BRANGLE: Margaret spouse of 1068

BREEN: --- spouse of 860

BRIGHTWELL: Ivy spouse of 1320

BRISTOW: John spouse of 29, John Jr. 43, Judith 44, Katherine 84, Sarah 83

BROADHEAD: Edward 865, James Overton spouse of 568

BROME: Lydia spouse of 1042, Nathaniel Wilson parent of spouse of 1042

BROOKE: Anne Harriet parent of spouse of 1042

BROOKELY: Lucinda A. spouse of 784

BROOKS: Abigail parent of spouse of 1331, Clara spouse of 594, Thomas spouse of 1706

BROWN: --- 1090, Abel 415, Abel 411, Abel 403, Abel Sr. 90, Abel Jr. 163, Achsah 687, Achsah Riggs 501, Adam 170, Albert 1719, Albert S. 828, Alice 792, Alonzo Grant 1100, Alvina 1092, Amelia W. 788, Amos 742, Anderson 735, Ann Alexis 445, Ann Cockey 548, Ann Elizabeth 696, Ann Virginia 561, Annie 732, Annie B. 1211, Annie E. 1074, Archibald 422, Archibald 782, Archibald 541, Arthur Allen 1697, Arthur C. 1224, Basil Perry 551, Benjamin 192, Benjamin 96, Benjamin F. 771, Benjamin Franklin 555, Benjamin Franklin 730, Benjamin Franklin 1088, Benjamin R. 1073, Bernice 1267, Bessie 1585, Bessie M. 1107, Bessie Susan 1263, Betty Ilene child of 1588, Betty Jean child of 1603, Betty Lou child of 1581, Beverly Jo child of 1626, Brice 405, Carlton P. 1578, Caroline 746, Caroline 518, Carolyn M. child of 1855, Carrie Virginia 1571, Catherine 740, Catherine child of 1582, Catherine E. 823, Catherine Eugenie 1854, Celius L. 1696, Charles 1586, Charles 744, Charles 189, Charles 1043, Charles E. 784, Charles H. 1214, Chrisopher C. child of 1855, Clara 1101, Clara 743, Clara Josephine 794, Cleon LeRoy child of 1588, Cora Elmay 1607, Cordelia 537, Corrie M. 1258, David 164, David Jr. 410, David 404, David Lawrence child of 1616, Dewey Octavius 1576, Donald child of 1581, Donna Marie child of 1603, Durward L. child of 1615, Earl Jennings 1611, Ebenezer spouse of 49, Ebenezer 112, Edgar 1573, Edna Lillian 1592, Edna May 1580, Edward 1624, Edward 412, Edward B. 1072, Edward B. 1579, Edward D. 822, Edward Lee 1262, Effie Olive 1583, Eleanor 111, Eleanor 519, Eleanor Elizabeth "Ellen" 440, Eli 734, Elias 171, Elias parent of spouse of 437, Elias 549, Elias 526, Elias 1259, Honorable Elias Jr. 433, Honorable Elias Jr. spouse of 437, Elias 820, Elias Joseph 443, Elijah 737, Elijah Jr. 1108, Elijah 524, Elijah 747, Elijah 193, Elisha 494, Eliza 1256, Eliza 533, Eliza 686, Elizabeh Ann 682, Elizabeth 417, Elizabeth 413, Elizabeth A. 688, Elizabeth Ann 552, Elizabeth Ann 521, Ellen K. child of 1615, Elmer E. 1103, Elsie May 1605, Emely C. 1220, Emma 808, Ephraim 190, Ernest 1623, Ernest Wade 1213, Estell Elmer 1621, Ethel 1602, Evelyn 1620, F.L. 1228, Fannie 827, Faye Edward child of 1588, Florence 1503, Florence 826, Florence 1231, Flossie 1587, Floyd LeRoy 1588, Francis 1094, Gov. Francis (Frank) 817, Francis Louise 1506, Francis M. 755, Francis M. 1568, Francis Snowden 436, Francis Snowden 1255, Francis W. 1086, Frank III 1718, Frank D. 1232, Frank D. 1044, Frederick 194, G.O. 1229, George 811, George 726, George A. 1227, George Alan 1085, George E. 1219, George W. 757, George W. 1581, Georgianna 786, Glenn 1626, Granville 793, Hannah 110, Harold Edward 1618, Harold H. 1625, Harriet Elizabeth or Eliza 542, Harriot 522, Harris 1225, Hattie 1212, Henry 527, Henry 1041, Henry Allen 1582, Henry Gassaway 685, Horatio 813, Ida 1099, Ida Belle 1589, (Infant) 1095, Isabella 1233, Isaiah 539, Isaiah 790, Isaiah 420, Isaiah M. 756, Jacob 165, James 100, James 725, James 167, James Anderson 1102, James D. 1093, James Jennings child of 1611, James R. 681, James Russell 1856, James Willard Jr child of 1603, James Willard 1603, Janice June child of 1616, Jefferson J. 791, Jeffrey P. child of 1855, Jemima Elizabeth 556, Jerome N. 796, Jesse 423, Jessie A. 1257, John 166, John 414, John 511, John 1269, John Henry 729, Major John Riggs 495, John Riggs Jr. 691, John Scherer 1105, John T. 783, John W. 536, John W. 770, John W. 1567, John Wesley 517, Jonathan spouse of 237, Jonathan "John" 692, Joseph 500, Joseph 1268, Josephine 1045, Joshua 534, Joshua 185, Joshua D. 514, Josiah 774, Josiah 408, Josiah 731, Joyce 1851, Julia Ann 520, Katherine Ann Warfield "Kitty" 690, Katherine Christine 1606, Katherine Grace Davis 1835, Laura Virginia 1222, Lawrence Lewis 1616, Leland 1853, Lewis E. 1216, Lewis E. 785, Lloyd 538, Lloyd 523, Lloyd 515, Lloyd A. 787, Lois R. child of 1615, Louis 812, Louis H. 545, Louisa Worthington 683, Louisiana 809, Lucinda 1218, Lucinda Rachel Jackson 557, Lucracia 679, Lucy 745, Lucy 1226, Lula Catherine 1260, M.E. 1230, Mamie 1223, Manvil F. 1615, Margaret 741, Margaret A. 1215, Margaret E. 772, Margaret Ellen child of 1616, Marie Fern child of 1588, Marilyn Marie child of 1616, Marshall A. 1575, Marshall H. child of 1855, Marshall John Jr. 1855, Martha 748, Martha Thomas 1570, Mary 752, Mary 496, Mary 114, Mary Alice child of 1604, Mary Ann 439, Mary Ann parent of spouse of 547, Mary Ann parent of spouse of 604, Mary Ann 684, Mary Ann 559, Mary Ann or Lydia 750, Mary C. 1106, Mary C. 1221, Mary E. 1089, Mary Jane 773, Mary Jane 733, Mary Ridgely 816, Mary Ridgley "Mamie" or "May" 1254, Mildred 1275, Mildred Lee 829, Minnie 1266, Miriam E. 830, Major Moses 172, Major Moses parent of spouse of 433, Moses 562, Moses 438, Myrtle Marie 1613, Nancy 169, Nancy Ann 409, Nancy Clara Etta 1265, Nellie May 1610, Nettie 1098, Nola Edith 1590, Noland 1569, Obadiah 736, Opal R. 1614, Orville 1591, Patrick D. child of 1855, Peter 1091, Prudence Ann 546, Prudence Ann 435, Rachel 421, Rachel 183, Rachel 406, Ralph Clark 1096, Rebecca 99, Rebecca 442, Rebecca 191, Rebecca 113, Rebecca 175, Rebecca A. 738, Rebecca Ann Worthington 558, Richard 188, Richard 693, Robert 95, Robert 416, Robert 753, Robert 512, Robert A. child of 1615, Robert B. 727, Robert B. 1577, Robert M. G. spouse of 1489, Roger Allen child of 1856, Rosa 754, Rosa B. 1104, Rosanna 418, Ruby 1572, Rudolph H. spouse of 1111, Russell 1574, Russell A. child of 1855, Ruth 810, Ruth 184, Ruth Adair 1617, Ruth Ann 173, Ruth Ann 441, Ruth Ann 550, Ruth Davis 1505, Saib D. 789, Samuel 101, Samuel 168, Samuel 680, Samuel 689, Samuel 1504, General Samuel 182, Samuel 498, Samuel L. 697, Samuel Thomas 824, Samuel Thomas 1042, Sara "Sadie" 1261, Sarah 97, Sarah 419, Sarah 749, Sarah I. 739, Sarah Rebecca 535, Sherman 1109, Shirley 1852, Stanley H. 1619, Stephen Cockey 432, Stephen Thomas Cockey 547, Stephen Thomas Cockey spouse of 564, Susan spouse of 724, Susanna A. 1217, Susannah 174, Susannah 497, Susannah 187, Susannah Amelia 825, Susannah Delila 560, Susannah Eleanor spouse of 433, Susannah Eleanor 437, Thelma Mae child of 1588, Theresa Jean child of 1616, Theresia Josephine 444, Thomas Alexander 698, Thomas Cockey 431, Thomas Cockey parent of spouse of 564, Thomas Cockey 553, Thomas J. 1071, Vachel 499, Vachel 695, Vachel 186, Vincent 540, Vincent 795, Virginia Ann child of 1616, Wade 1584, Walter C. 1087, Walter Ray 1604, William 525, William 751, William 694, William 98, William 434, William Andrew Jackson 554, William Henry 1264, William Lloyd 1097, William M. 821, William Thurman 1622, Zachariah 407, Zachariah 516, Zelma Fern 1612

BROWNE: Abel 87, Abell 30, Abigail 75, Ann 17, Barbara 18, Benoni 37, Bristow 81, Comfort 93, Dorothy 143, Edmund 14, Edward 8, Eleanor 65, Elizabeth 88, Elizabeth 27, Elizabeth 142, Gertrude 10, Hannah 33, Hannah 69, Hannah 144, Hester 94, James 86, James 28, James 41, John 160, John 40, John 82, John 36, John 70, John 147, John 11, Joshua 162, Katherine 29, Katherine 39, Lydia 146, Margaret 3, Martha 64, Martha 74, Mary 89, Mary 20, Mary 63, Mary 71, Mary 148, Nathaniel see 5, Nathaniel 24, Nathaniel 32, Nathaniel 34, Nathaniel 66, Nathaniel 72, Nathaniel 145, Nicholas see 5, Nicolas Esquire 5, Percy see 5, Percy 19, Priscilla 92, Ralf 4, Robert 46, Robert 91, Rev. Robert 23, Robert 79, Robert 38, Robert 7, Samuel 45, Samuel 159, Samuel 42, Samuel 25, Samuel 67, Samuell 141, Sarah 77, Sarah 80, Sarah 140, Sir William 9, Sir William see 5, Solomon 78, Thomas 2, Thomas 85, Thomas 6, Thomas 35, Thomas 68, Thomas 73, Vachel 161, Walter 13, William 1, William 15, William 16, William 12

BUNNELL: Isaac spouse of 224
BURKE: Mary Ann spouse of 762
BURKS: Martha Ann spouse of 543
BURLESON: Mary Margaret spouse of 478
BURLEY: Frances spouse of 1290
BURROUGHS: Elsie spouse of 1573
BURROWS: Mabel F. spouse of 1172
BUSH: E.W. spouse of 979
BUSSARD: David spouse of 716, Henry spouse of 712
BUTLER: Eunice parent of spouse of 851, Nannie parent of spouse of 1288
BUXTON: Blanche 1498, Fannie Brown 1495, Henry Gassaway 1497, Mollie 1496, Upton spouse of 1037
CALLAUGH: Ida Bell spouse of 1645
CAMP CORNELL: Ann spouse of 121
CANDEE: Abigail 124, Abigail 302, Abigail spouse of 324, Abigail spouse of 337, Desire 290, Dinah 289, Hannah 123, Hannah 297, Hannah 299, Isaac 120, Isaac 300, John 301, Mary 125, Mary parent of spouse of 302, Mary 294, Rebecca 295, Rhoda 296, Samuel 298, Sarah 122, Sarah 292, Capt. Theophilus 121, Capt. Theophilus parent of spouse of 324, Capt. Theophilus parent of spouse of 337, Theophilus 291, Zaccheus spouse of 54, Zaccheus 119, Zaccheus 293
CARL: Katherine A. K. spouse of 915
CARPENTER: --- spouse of 1541
CARR: William M. spouse of 1014
CARROLL: Charles parent of spouse of 815, James spouse of 815
CARTER: Adahzilah spouse of 540, John spouse of 1156, John Oscar spouse of 867
CASSIDY: Thomas spouse of 666
CASTLE: William spouse of 270
CASTOR: Lydia parent of spouse of 1289
CATLIN: Esther spouse of 234
CAVEY: Mary Jane spouse of 824
CHAMBERLAIN: George spouse of 843
CHAMBERS: Hester parent of spouse of 1132, Hester parent of spouse of 1135
CHARLEMAGNE see 5
CHARLES THE BALD see 5
CHENEY: Richard parent of spouse of 46
CHENEY PARNELL: Katherine spouse of 46
CHETHAM: Margaret spouse of 2
CHEW: Ann parent of spouse of 96
CHILES: Alburn spouse of 980, Francesca spouse of 973

CHITTENDEN: --- spouse of 362, Benjamin spouse of 273

CHURCHILL: --- spouse of 296, Rebecca spouse of 291

CLARK: --- spouse of 267, Abigail spouse of 102, Benjamin 229, Elizabeth 230, Hannah 105, Joseph spouse of 48, Joseph 106, Joseph 227, Joseph 228, Mehitabel 108, Miriam 225, Sarah 107, Silence 109, Sybil 226, Timothy 231

CLARKE: Rachel parent of spouse of 853

CLARY: Charlotte spouse of 502

CLINTON: Levi spouse of 235

CLOSSER: John Albert spouse of 1104

COCKERHAM: Elizabeth spouse of 937, Stephen parent of spouse of 937

COCKEY: Alexander 1744, Alexander Drummond 1290, Alexander Moore 1739, Alice Councilman 1740, Alice Councilman "Frances" 1743, Andrew Rodney 447, Ann spouse of 171, Ann parent of spouse of 437, Ann A. 849, Ann Rebecca 601, Ann Rebecca spouse of 612, Anna Griselda 888, Annie Stansbury 596, Charles C. 456, Charles Thomas 1287, Charles Thomas 1296, Charles Thomas 853, Charles Thomas 1298, Charles Thomas spouse of 560, Christopher Slade 1754, Dolly Brown 455, Dolly Brown parent of spouse of 601, Edward 592, Edward Augustus 848, Edward Augustus 1288, Edward Augustus parent of spouse of 560, Edward Augustus 1738, Edward Randolph 887, Elias Brown 449, Elizabeth 599, Emma Shepherd 1295, Eva 1293, Georgius Rex 451, James Powell 892, John Councilman 1289, John Powell 595, John Robert 452, John Robert 886, John Sothoron 1742, Louise Randall 1753, Lydia Sothoron 1741, Mary 1299, Mary Elizabeth 598, Mary Etta 885, Mordecai Gist 453, Mordecai Gist parent of spouse of 612, Mordecai Gist 597, Mordecai Gist 890, Randolph Lucas 1308, Randolph Lucas 1751, Robert Fielding 1752, Ruth Brown 454, Ruth Brown parent of spouse of 566, Sally Ann 1294, Sally Montgomery 891, Samuel 591, Susanna Brown 450, Susannah 593, Thomas spouse of 173, Thomas parent of spouse of 171, Thomas parent of spouse of 173, Thomas Beale 850, Thomas Beale 1297, Thomas John 448, Thomas Robert 594, Urath 602, Urath Cromwell 1286, Urath Cromwell 851, Urath Cromwell 1737, Virginia 600, William 590, William Brown 852, William Henry 446, William Henry 615, William Warfield 889

COCKRELL: Celia "Sealy" spouse of 472

COLE: Daniel 395, Elisha 392, Elizabeth 393, Jonathan spouse of 148, Jonathan 394, Rachel Harryman parent of spouse of 598

COLLIER: Preston Hamilton spouse of 663

COLLINS: Ann 224, Anna child of 1648, Ariatla child of 1648, Charles H. spouse of 1648, Edward spouse of 277, Elizabeth spouse of 67, Fran child of 1648, Isabell V. spouse of 1136, Joseph spouse of 105, Ray child of 1648

COLLIS: Mary Jane spouse of 737

COMPTON: Jonathan spouse of 648, Margaret Susan 982

CONDON: Verlinda spouse of 505, Zachariah spouse of 510

CONDON, URRY OR RIGSBY: Ida (---) spouse of 1108

CONNER: Charlie B. 1430, Edwin Joseph 1429, Elizabeth 1427, Emma 1426, Jaley 1423, Lucy 1422, Mary Angelina 1421, Ruth 1424, Shadrack James spouse of 1004, Theodicia 1428, Thomas parent of spouse of 1004, Thomas Randolph 1425

CONNOLLY: --- spouse of 861

COOK: Capt. Adolphus parent of spouse of 853, Eliza spouse of 608, Hannah spouse of 513, Lillie May spouse of 831, Mary Clarke spouse of 853

COOVERT: Mary Jane spouse of 768

COPELAND: Charles parent of spouse of 628, Lydia spouse of 628

COPPLE: Edgar A. spouse of 1594

CORD: Muriel (MC) spouse of 1596

CORDELL: William spouse of 1794

CORMAN: Nancy Jane parent of spouse of 1381, Nancy Jane parent of spouse of 1383

CORNWELL: Abigail 321, Abigail 343, Elizabeth spouse of 57, Elizabeth 322, Hannah spouse of 308, Isaac 342, Joseph spouse of 124, Joseph spouse of 130, Joseph 320, Mindwell 344, Miriam spouse of 106

COUNCILMAN: Alice Mitchell spouse of 848

COUSENS: Mary spouse of 291

COX: Alta Florence child of 1785, Arthur Franklin child of 1785, Donivan Elijah child of 1785, Edelia Etta child of 1785, Eva Viola child of 1785, Lucinda Ethel child of 1785, Olive Leota child of 1785, Oscar spouse of 1785, Ralph Edgar child of 1785, W.J. spouse of 962, William Clarence child of 1785

CRABTREE: Peter spouse of 939

CRAFTS: --- spouse of 92

CRAWFORD: Arlene R. spouse of 1728

CRISLER: Albert spouse of 764, Letta or Meta 1166, Sallie E. 1167, William 1165

CRISSMAN: Barbara Jean child of 1723, Jessie Odell spouse of 1723

CROOKS: --- spouse of 1765

CROUCH: Chloe parent of spouse of 417

CROWL: Alice May 1547, Bessie Mabel 1548, Frank Wilsom 1545, Harry L. 1546, William L. spouse of 1059

CROWLEY: Benjamin Thomas spouse of 1024, Joseph Lanham 1477

CUMMING: Gordon Fossett 1733, Jeanne Miriam 1732, John Pearce 1281

CUMMINGS: Hershey Simpson spouse of 835

CURREN: Rachel spouse of 1049

CURTIS: Maria Jane parent of spouse of 674

D'AUBIGNEY, Isabel see 5
DANIELTON: Gertie spouse of 894
DARNELL: Rebecca J. spouse of 1132
DAVIS: Ada Kate 1491, Anderson Cord 1490, Caleb Dorsey spouse of 683, Christian 995, Cynthia 996, Daniel N. spouse of 670, Eliza Ann 1037, Elizabeth 1035, Grace Thomas 1492, Hallie Elkins 1838, Hallie Louise 1488, Hon. Henry Gassaway 1036, Henry Gassaway 1493, Henry W. 1519, Ira Rodney 1515, James 997, James Fred spouse of 1610, James Howard child of 1610, John Brown 1034, John Thomas 1494, Kate Bantz 1489, Leanna 1521, Louise spouse of 1044, Lucy 1516, Mary parent of spouse of 182, Mary Tillson 1499, Matilda 1500, Paul Howard child of 1610, Peter spouse of 1051, Robert parent of spouse of 683, Sarah E. 1512, Splientendiom 1517, Hon. Thomas Beale 1038, Thomas Beale 1502, Tirzah 1518, Upton L. 1513, Virginia H.R. 1514, Walter F. 1520, William parent of spouse of 1044, William 1522, William L. 994, William R. 1039, William R. 1501, Wilma May child of 1610
DAWKINS: Abigail 992, Angus spouse of 670, Jackson 991, Mary 990, Ophelia 993
DAY: Anthon M. spouse of 1208, Roger spouse of 1260
DE BAVANT: Eleanor see 5
DE BEAUCHAMPE: Maude see 5
DE BEAUMONT: Ermengarde see 5
DE BRAOSE: Beatrix see 5, William see 5
DE CROMWELL: Joan see 5, Ralph see 5
DE FREVILLE: Alexander see 5, Baldwin see 5, Margaret see 5, Sir Baldwin see 5
DE KILPECK, Joan see 5
DE PERCY: Joan see 5
DE ROS: Mary see 5, Robert see 5, Sir Robert see 5, Sir William see 5
DEAN: --- spouse of 178
DEHNE: Barbara parent of spouse of 1842
DELPH: Hattie Ellen spouse of 1102, Larken parent of spouse of 1102
DELUCA: Mary Virginia spouse of 1727
DENSON: Ruth parent of spouse of 1004
DESANTIS: Anthony spouse of 1710
DICKENSON: Mary spouse of 655
DIETRICH: Alfred E. spouse of 1254
DILLMAN: Charles L. spouse of 1204
DOGGETT: Nanny spouse of 1145
DOLLARHIDE: Annis 648, John spouse of 473
DONNALLY: Josephine Ann parent of spouse of 872
DOOLITTLE: Abigail spouse of 364, Abisha spouse of 341
DORSEY: Achsah Riggs 700, Ann parent of spouse of 422, Ann 574, Ann Worthington 701, Caleb 573, Comfort W. 567, Edward A. 576, Edward W. 570, Edward Worthington spouse of 440, Eleanor Elizabeth 572, Hammond spouse of 679, John Worthington 569, John Worthington parent of spouse of 440, Mary Snowden 568, Rebecca parent of spouse of 444, Reuben Meriwether spouse of 700, Sarah "Sally" 702, Susan 575, Thomas Beale Jr. spouse of 501, Judge Thomas Beale 699, Thomas Beale 571
DOWNES: William Beryl 1319, William Butler spouse of 912
DOWNEY: Maj. George spouse of 1500
DOWNING: Sarah Malinda spouse of 1097
DOWNS: Mehitabel 232, Nathaniel spouse of 242, Thomas spouse of 108
DOYLE: Thomas Reed (A.k.a. Francis REED) spouse of 1080
DRACE: Annie Rebecca 974, Charles P. 981, Emma Laura 980, James A. 978, Mary Elizabeth 972, Mary Francis "Polly" 977, Minerva 975, S.S. "Donnie" 979, Scott 976, Silas spouse of 642, Solomon spouse of 641, Thomas parent of spouse of 641, Thomas parent of spouse of 642, William Thomas "W.T." 973
DRAPER: Eliza Tennessee parent of spouse of 1465
DRISKELL: Lucinda spouse of 1338
DRYDEN: John G. spouse of 1559
DUKE CHARLES: see 5
DUNHAM: --- spouse of 292
DUNN: Mary 1128, Nannie 1129, Retus spouse of 758
DUPEE: Charles spouse of 135, Charles 348, Hannah 349, James (twin) 351, Nancy (twin) 352, Samuel 350, SARAH 353
DURHAM: --- spouse of 289
DYKE: Lydia spouse of 324
EADGIFU: see 5
EAST: Elizabeth F. parent of spouse of 1100
EASTON: Elizabeth spouse of 268, Joseph spouse of 269
EBAUGH: Aletha V. (adopted) 819
EDMONDSON: Lucinda Rebecca spouse of 436, Col. Robert parent of spouse of 436
EDMONDSTON: Dr. Benjamin spouse of 442
EGGLESTON: Ebenezer Jr. spouse of 128, Ebenezer Jr. parent of spouse of 302, Capt. Ebenezer spouse of 302, Capt. Ebenezer 337, Elihu 338, Elizabeth 336, Mary 335, Mindwell 339, Sybil 341, Thomas 340
EIKINS: Jerry spouse of 659
ELDER: Alessa 781, Emma E. 778, Harriet spouse of 422, James M. 779, Jemima spouse of 410, John Jr. parent of spouse of 410, John Jr. parent of spouse of 416, John Owen parent of spouse of 422, Levi spouse of 537, Levi Marshall 777, Margaret E. 775, Ruth spouse of 528, Sarah E. 776, Sarah Or Honor spouse of 416, William E. 780
ELIZABETH: see 5
ELIZABETH OF NAMUR: see 5
ELKINS: Davis 1830, Elaine 1833, Katherine Hallie 1834, Mary C. spouse of 1330, Richard 1832, Hon. Stephen Benton spouse of 1488, Stephen Benton Jr. 1831
ELLIOTT: --- child of 1825, Abraham spouse of 740, Asa Wilson parent of spouse of 1825, Charles 1634,

Clarence William 1633, Clyde Nathaniel spouse of 1825, Clyde Russell child of 1825, Daisy M. 1114, Donald 1636, Eugene child of 1635, Frank 1113, George Wilson child of 1825, James LeRoy child of 1825, Jennette 1111, Leroy "Roy" 1115, Mary Dean child of 1825, Montreville 1110, Paul Edward child of 1825, Robie Joe child of 1825, Walter Winslow 1635, William Lankford 1112

ELLIS: Mary spouse of 301

ELLSWORTH: --- spouse of 1066, Emmitt A. 1556

EMBREE: Isaac spouse of 629

ENGEL: Ara spouse of 721

ERMENTRUDE: see 5

EVANS: Albert M. 1440, Albert S. 1273, Ambrose parent of spouse of 737, Charlie Randolph 1432, Cintha Theodisia 1406, Claude Max 1437, Columbus G. spouse of 1007, Cora Lee 1431, Emma Abigail 1398, Erby Doyle 1405, George Washington 1404, James Bunyan 1433, James Rufus spouse of 1005, Joe Boomer 1401, John Benton 1402, John E. 1438, Joseph Walter 1436, Josiah Theodore 1407, Josiah Washington spouse of 1000, Lydia C. spouse of 737, Mary O. 1439, Mildred Lee 1274, Naomi parent of spouse of 454, Naomi parent of spouse of 455, Ora Lee 1400, Richard K. spouse of 827, Susan Exer 1434, Susan James 1403, William G. spouse of 1797, William G. 1441, William Randolph 1399, William Walter 1435

EVARTS: Eleanor 137, Elizabeth (twin) 139, Elizabeth 367, James spouse of 63, James 366, Jeremiah 368, John 370, Onner spouse of 138, Reuben Capt. 369, Rueben (twin) 138

EYE: John Ace spouse of 1388

FAITHFUL: --- spouse of 690

FELLOWS: David spouse of 314

FENTON: Lucinda spouse of 365

FIEBELKORN: Bertha Louise parent of spouse of 1570, Bertha Louise parent of spouse of 1572

FIFER: Minnie Jane spouse of 1112, William parent of spouse of 1112

FIRESTINE, EVANS: --- spouse of 889

FITZPIERS: Lucy see 5

FIX: Cynthia Alice 1164, Genevra 1162, John spouse of 764, John Wesley 1157, Josephine 1161, Laura C. 1159, Leona 1160, Mary J. 1158, Mary M. 1163, Sarah Catherine 1156, William spouse of 763

FLACK: Alice B. 1794, Charles Wesley 1795, Elijah Alexander 1793, John Wesley spouse of 1339, Louis E. 1798, Lucy E. 1797, Willis Edgar 1796

FLANNERY: Betty spouse of 472

FLEEMAN: George 1627, Katherine 1628

FLOHR: Mildred spouse of 1696

FLORAN: John spouse of 764, Laura Jennie 1169, Lewis H. 1171, Phillip Beechers 1168, William S. 1170

FLUHART: Mary Ann spouse of 718

FOGLE: Sarah E. spouse of 787

FOOTE: Aaron 262, David spouse of 115, David 255, Dorothy 259, Eleanor 261, Esther 258, Isaac 257, Mary 260, Miriam 254, Miriam 256

FORSYTHE: Mary Mercer spouse of 1717

FOSSETT: Charlotte Miriam spouse of 1281

FRAKES: Mary Elizabeth J. spouse of 1366

FRIEND: Georgia Louisiana spouse of 674, Samuel Edgar parent of spouse of 674

FRISBIE: Elisha A. spouse of 1341

FROST: Ann spouse of 685, Mary spouse of 691, William spouse of 686

FUNKHOUSER: Rev. Hugh C. spouse of 1173

GAITHER: Ruth parent of spouse of 683

GALENTINE: Mary Jane spouse of 1132, Mary Jane spouse of 1135, William parent of spouse of 1132, William parent of spouse of 1135

GAMBLE: Charles Lawrence 1726, Edward Bernard Sr. 1727, Lawrence Joseph spouse of 1263

GARDINER: Alice parent of spouse of 1290

GARDNER: Catherine E. spouse of 605

GARLAND: Margaret A. spouse of 1079

GARRIGAN: John spouse of 389

GASSAWAY: Brice John parent of spouse of 495, Sarah Griffith spouse of 495

GAW: Durbin spouse of 1082, Johnson spouse of 1077

GEARHART: Hiram spouse of 1082

GERBERGA: see 5

GERSTILL: Frederick spouse of 1495

GERVAISE: see 5

GIBBS: Nicholas spouse of 1562

GIBSON: Grace spouse of 856

GIERSA: James spouse of 975

GILBERT: Elizabeth spouse of 131, Hannah spouse of 301, Sarah spouse of 41

GILL: Prudence parent of spouse of 171, Prudence parent of spouse of 173

GILLEY: Charles spouse of 673, Eula 1015, John parent of spouse of 673, John Solomon 1012, Mary A. 1010, Susan Margaret 1014, Thomas Newton 1011, William Robert 1013

GILLILAND: Edwin J. spouse of 1656, Zee spouse of 1544

GILLILANT: Cora A. 1202, Edward C. 1201, Eliza Jane 1198, George W. 1195, Irwin 1194, John L. 1200, Margaret 1196, Robert spouse of 767, Robert J. 1197, William E. 1199

GODFREY: see 5

GODFREY: --- spouse of 1501

GOODRICH: Capt. Wait spouse of 207

GORE: Nacissa Sara parent of spouse of 859

GORMAN: Honorable Arthur Pue 1040, Peter spouse of 688

GORSUCH: Sarah parent of spouse of 1044

GOSNELL: Bernard 1320, Edna 1321, Irving spouse of 921, Peter parent of spouse of 163, Sarah spouse of 163

GOULDEN: Addit spouse of 1809

GRANNIS: Eldad spouse of 334, Esther spouse of 333
GRAVES: Joseph Jr. spouse of 307
GRAY: Alvin H. spouse of 1283, Martha "Mattie" spouse of 467
GREEN: Emaline Anna spouse of 1192
GREENE: Joane see 5
GREENFIELD: Nora spouse of 846
GRIFFEE: Rebecca parent of spouse of 548
GRIFFITH: Elizabeth spouse of 456, John spouse of 1335
GRIMES: Sarah spouse of 503
GUILD: Jeremiah spouse of 137, Jeremiah 365, Mary 363, Samuel 364
GUYTON: Rose M. spouse of 1240
HACKWORTH: Frances spouse of 934
HAGARTY: --- spouse of 177
HALE: Hannah spouse of 365
HALL: Abiah spouse of 229, Brian child of 1592, Carter Lyle child of 1592, Ernest spouse of 1592, Patricia child of 1592, Phebe spouse of 253
HAMILTON: Catherine parent of spouse of 90
HARPER: Henry spouse of 653
HARRIS: Benjamin parent of spouse of 1331, Joseph spouse of 343, Sarah M. spouse of 1331
Harrison: --- spouse of 99, Ann parent of spouse of 689, Florence Patterson 1716, George spouse of 1249
HARROLD: Jeremiah "Jerry" spouse of 471
HART: Charles Henry Jr. 1662, Charles Leroy child of 1662, Henry spouse of 1143, Ira Winfield child of 1662, Lewis Clarke child of 1662, Nellie 1661, Ralph Murral child of 1662, Ray Newell child of 1662
HAWKINS: Nellie spouse of 1593
HAY: Edward B. 1270, Edwin B. spouse of 826, Jewel D. 1271, Paul B. 1272
HELFRICH: Bruce H. spouse of 1295, Emma Shepherd 1747, Robert Bruce 1748, Samuel Cockey 1750, Thomas Cockey 1749
HELM: Alice spouse of 896, Wilbur Taylor parent of spouse of 896
HELMICK: Wayne E. child of 1583, William Grant spouse of 1583
HENDRYX: Arthur E. spouse of 1786
HEROLD: Evelyn 1446, James 1444, Joe 1445, Johnson 1447, Robert spouse of 1009, Sadie 1443
HESSEY: Harriett Ann spouse of 1172
HICKMAN: Lannie parent of spouse of 1463
HIGBY: Abigail 306, Amos 310, Ephraim 308, Jeduthan 309, John spouse of 122, John 303, Lois 307, Sarah 305, Zaccheus 304
HIGH: Sarah C. spouse of 785, William parent of spouse of 785
HILDEGARD: see 5
HILLIARD: Frank L. spouse of 1558
HILTY: Eddy D. spouse of 1348, John spouse of 1347
HITCHENS: Grace Irene spouse of 899
HOBBS: Margaret spouse of 1581, Minnie spouse of 1088

HODGE: Benjamin 240, Daniel spouse of 111, Daniel 239, Eleanor 241, Jesse 238, Martha 243, Mary 242, Rebecca 244, Sarah 237
HOLDEN: Clara "Clair" child of 1705, Elmer Sergeant spouse of 1705, Elmer Sergent "Bubby" child of 1705, Katherine Frances "Kay" child of 1705
HOLLIDAY: W. G. spouse of 1599
HOLLISTER: Damaris spouse of 197, Mabel spouse of 331, Ruth spouse of 198
HOLMES: Charles parent of spouse of 852, Charles parent of spouse of 852, Dora spouse of 852, Ida spouse of 852, Richard spouse of 461
HOOD: Henry spouse of 690, Letitia spouse of 719, General Thomas parent of spouse of 690
HOPPER: Luritta "Lula" May spouse of 1647, Marion Meridith parent of spouse of 1647
HOPPES: Asa R. 1123, Cary A. 1117, Charles C. 1120, Edward 1125, Elizabeth 1124, Emma Frances 1116, Flossie 1126, Francis M. spouse of 750, Hazel 1127, Minnie J. 1118, Myrtle M. 1122, Ollie G. 1119, Thomas G. 1121
HORN: Mary A. spouse of 1050, Rae parent of spouse of 1616
HORTON: Mary spouse of 656, William spouse of 665
HOSHALL: Col. Edward M. spouse of 1300
HOUSE: Charles O. 1593, Clifton G. 1600, Edna child of 1593, Fern 1594, Glen child of 1593, Janet child of 1593, Joan child of 1597, Lacey A. 1596, Laverne child of 1597, Lucile child of 1593, Lucy Donald 1595, Mary 1599, Mildred child of 1596, Robert spouse of 1099, Robert child of 1593, Terrel child of 1597, Thelma child of 1596, Theodore "Tad" 1597, William K. 1601, William Kenneth "Bill" 1598
HOW: Isaac spouse of 294
HOWARD: Edward M. spouse of 1177, Elizabeth Wells parent of spouse of 176, Henry spouse of 496
HOWELL: Letitia spouse of 127
HOWES: Jack Dale spouse of 1607
HUDSON: Susan spouse of 545
Hughes: Gordon spouse of 1254, Martha spouse of 34
HUMPHREYS: Elizabeth spouse of 624
HUNT: Ransom spouse of 288
HUNTER: --- spouse of 794
HUNTLY: Lucy Mahala spouse of 1363
HURD: Asahel spouse of 278, Content (---) spouse of 262, Jerusha spouse of 265, Ruth spouse of 118
HURLBUT: Anna spouse of 257, Ebenezer spouse of 272, Ebenezer spouse of 143, Ebenezer 383, Elizabeth 382, John 384, Martha 381, Mary 385
HUSH: Theresa spouse of 1722
HUSTED: Catherine spouse of 1337
HYATT: Sophia spouse of 506
IDA: see 5
INGLES: Margaret spouse of 1796
IRELAND: Campbell Charles 1328, Deborah "Fannie" 1326, Frank Howard 1325, Jack 1323, Julia 1327, Norris Ireland 1324, Thomas Moale 1322, Thomas N.

spouse of 922

ISABEL OF SCOTLAND: see 5

ISGREGG: Mary Gant spouse of 766

JACKSON: Abian Ann spouse of 723, Lincoln spouse of 1188

JAMES: Allan 1391, John Thomas spouse of 985, John Wesley 1389, Mittie 1390

JARRETT: Frank Nelson child of 1609, Jacqueline child of 1609, Leatha 1608, Leonard L. child of 1609, Ralph Nelson 1609

JARVIS: Ada 1032, E. spouse of 677, Rob 1033

JENKINS: Elizabeth spouse of 689, Henry parent of spouse of 689

JENOUR: Anthony spouse of 39

JETT: Bernice child of 1613, Caroline M. child of 1613, Theodore P. spouse of 1613

JOHNSON: Benjamin H. 1046, Carl spouse of 1304, Cornelia spouse of 1262, Eliza May 1537, Elsa spouse of 1344, Elsa spouse of 932, Emma E. 1048, Ernest V. 1540, Essie P. 1541, Gladys Ethel 1542, Harry Charles spouse of 1057, Jacob spouse of 704, Laclede Todd 1538, Lewis Wallace 1536, Martin spouse of 972, Nettie Maude 1539, Tom M. 1047, William spouse of 707

JOHNSON SPERRY: Mary spouse of 268

JOLIFF: Lora W. spouse of 1665

JOLLY: Joseph W. spouse of 1007, May 1442

JONES: Eva spouse of 886, Frances D. spouse of 1061

JORDAN: Mrs. Margaret spouse of 668

JOSE: Michael H. spouse of 634

JUDITH: see 5

JULIANE: see 5

KAUFFMANN: --- spouse of 1265

KEE: Ura spouse of 1795

KEFAUVER: Evans Brown 1276, H. J. spouse of 830

KEITH: Rosa C. parent of spouse of 1018

KEITHLY: Chiles Lester spouse of 870

KELLER: James W. spouse of 1791

KELLY: --- spouse of 1614, Cornelius parent of spouse of 1767, Ellen T. spouse of 1767, Marjorie child of 1614

KENNEDY: Lula Dell spouse of 1385

KENT: Priscilla spouse of 67

KEYSER: Louise Dilworth spouse of 1308

KILGORE: William spouse of 468

KILLEBREW: Drusilla spouse of 1284

KIMBERLY: Mary spouse of 103

KING: Christine spouse of 1841

KNAUFF: Robert spouse of 1723, Robert Eugene child of 1723

KURTZ: Emily parent of spouse of 785

KUYKENDAL: Jean spouse of 181

LAFFERTY: Euphemia spouse of 1067

LAININGER: Jane spouse of 1356

LANDIS: Frank 1476, John M. 1474, Robert 1475, Sam spouse of 1020

LANDSREET: Fairfax spouse of 1499

LANE: Abigail 61, Allen 333, Allen II 513, Anna 329, Ashbel 136, Ashbel 359, Benoni 58, Cilinda 728, Cornelius 133, Cornelius 360, Eleanor 49, Elizabeth 48, Elizabeth 346, Elizabeth 347, Elizabeth 362, Hannah 47, Hannah 135, Hannah 354, Isaac spouse of 33, Isaac (twin) 50, Isaac 57, Isaac 129, Isaac 331, Isaac 355, John (twin) 51, John (twin) 52, John 56, John 126, John 127, John 330, Letitia 332, Lydia 357, Martha "Mattie" 358, Mary 59, Mary 60, Mary 128, Mary parent of spouse of 302, Mindwell 130, Mindwell 356, Nathaniel 62, Capt. Nathaniel 131, Nathaniel 345, Nathaniel 361, Samuel 55, Samuel 132, Sarah (twin) 53, Sarah 54, Sarah 334, Zaccheus 134

LANHAM: Abe 1396, Abel Jr. 479, Abel Jr. 489, Abel 984, Abel 1001, Ann 482, Anna 1467, Annie 1409, Annie Maud 1024, August Abel 181, Beatrice 1480, Bedford 674, Bedford 1468, Benton 1411, Bonnie 1420, Carolyn Bethal 1469, Charlie 1418, Comfort Lana Renne 176, Cynthia 677, Cynthia 1483, Cynthia Elizabeth 1000, Docia 1413, Edwin Friend 1025, Edwin Friend Jr. 1478, Elizabeth 476, Elizabeth 985, Elizabeth 1392, Esther 178, Frank 1395, Frank H. 1479, Frank Millard 1473, Franklin 668, Franklin 1022, Franklin C. 1027, Georgia Alice 1020, Hannah Theodicia 1009, Inez 1470, Jailie Ann 1005, Jaley 1415, James B. 1471, James Carroll 1485, James Millard 1019, Jane 669, Jean 179, Jefferson David 1484, Jim 1412, Jodie 1408, Jodie 1419, John spouse of 93, John 484, John Castleton 1003, John H. 1482, Joseph 481, Joseph B. 1002, Lee 492, Lela 1417, Lizzie 1410, Lucinda 670, Luther 493, Malinda 487, Margaret 675, Margaret Narcissa 1007, Maria Jane Curtis 1016, Mary 671, Mary 1397, Mary A. 999, Mary Elizabeth 1414, Mary Margaret 1018, Matilda 491, Matilda 1393, Melissa Morgan 486, Minerva Ann 673, Monroe 1023, Myrtle 1416, Nancy J. 988, Rachel Lucinda 1006, Randal 485, Randolph 672, Randolph 1394, Robert 477, Robert Edward Lee 1021, Samivarnes 488, Samuel 483, Samuel 676, Samuel 1008, Samuel 1017, Samuel 1472, Sarah 177, Sarah 490, Sarah Jane 1004, Solomon 478, Solomon J. 987, Solomon Thomas 998, Sophenia 986, Unity 983, William 180, William parent of spouse of 93, William 480, William 678, William S. 1026, William S. 1481

LASSITER: Nellie Brown spouse of 884

LAWHORN: John H. parent of spouse of 1100, Julia Margaret spouse of 1100

LAWRENCE: Charles Larkin 877, Claude 869, Everett Curtis 880, France Edward 868, Francis 583, George Benton spouse of 579, Hammond 866, Hammond Dorsey parent of spouse of 579, Hazel 1306, Hazel Dell 1304, Ida Lee 867, Jennie Dorsey 580, Larkin spouse of 444, Larkin Dorsey 581, Leone 879, Levin 582, Levin parent of spouse of 444, Mary Elizabeth 577, Musa 876, Raymond Vance 881, Rebecca Ann

579, Sarah Ann 578, Verdie 878
LAWS: Mary Catherine parent of spouse of 1647
LAWS or MCFALLS: Nellie or Ellen spouse of 759
LAWSON: Edwin Burl child of 1805, Nettie child of 1805, Noah E. child of 1805, Thelma child of 1805, William spouse of 1805
LEAKINS: Martha J. parent of spouse of 1072
LEE: --- spouse of 1254, Arthur spouse of 1492, Ellen Bruce 1837, George 1836, Hannah spouse of 35, Henry 1141, Ida spouse of 821, Jay 1142, Margarete A. "Maggie" 1140, Sarah Isabelle "Belle" 1143, Thomas Green spouse of 761, Walter parent of spouse of 35, William 1139
LEEVER: G. spouse of 739
LEFEVRE: Virginia parent of spouse of 852, Virginia parent of spouse of 852
LEWIS: Hiram spouse of 652, Lucien spouse of 1107
LINDSAY: Caroline parent of spouse of 1085, Hannah spouse of 729, William G. spouse of 520
LITTLE: Olive Ann spouse of 872, William Henry "Bud" parent of spouse of 872
LOLLE: Amee parent of spouse of 5
LOOSE: Corinna Clare 1670, Floyd F. spouse of 1152
LOUIS II: see 5
LOUIS IV: see 5
LOUIS THE PIOUS: see 5
LOUIS THE SIMPLE: see 5
LOVETT: Charles 1244, Elizabeth 1243, Ephraim (?) spouse of 544, Frances 1246, Georgianna 1247, Joseph 1245, Margaret S. 805, Samuel 807, William 806
LUCAS: Ellen spouse of 887
LUM: John spouse of 109
LYONS: Mabel parent of spouse of 808
MACHELL: Jane Ann parent of spouse of 19
MAGRUDER: Susannah parent of spouse of 175
MAINS: Caroline M. spouse of 527, George parent of spouse of 527
MALONEY: Amanda Lee 1383, Campbell parent of spouse of 977, David Campbell spouse of 977, David Crocket 1386, Eda Lurene 1384, Eugene Pollard 1385, Frank Sterling 1387, Sara Eliza "Sadie" 1381, William Archibald 1382
MANGES: Dr. William spouse of 895
MARMION: Mazera see 5, Phillip see 5, Robert II see 5, Robert III see 5, Robert V see 5
MARSH: John Alonza spouse of 786, Rachel spouse of 379, William spouse of 312
MARSHALL: --- spouse of 363
MARTIN: --- spouse of 586, Angeline spouse of 948, Harry 882, Joseph S. spouse of 942
MASON: Sara spouse of 998
MASTERS: James spouse of 335
MAY: Charles spouse of 1806
MAYFIELD: James 1372, John spouse of 936, Joseph 1371, Nancy 1373
MCCALL: William spouse of 623

MCCALLAHAN: --- spouse of 1307
MCCARDIE: Washington Green spouse of 578
MCCLINTOCK: Alma Louise 1305, Carrie B. spouse of 1105, Clemmie Irene 870, George Edward 872, James Henry 871, John Henry spouse of 580, Nettie Myrtle 874, Orie Lawrence 875, Robert Levin 873, Robert Miller parent of spouse of 580
MCCONKY: Edward Dawes spouse of 596, Edward Dawes 884, Eleanor 1307, Mary Grafton 883
McCORD: Sara A. spouse of 1103
MCCOY: --- spouse of 179
MCCRARY: Vina spouse of 480
McDOWELL: Fern Alverdia spouse of 1588
McDUFFEE: Emma Belle spouse of 1105
MCFERRAN: Margaret parent of spouse of 445
MCGHEE: Louisa parent of spouse of 737
MCHALEY: William spouse of 1340
MCQUANE: William spouse of 792
MERRICK: Mary Pauline spouse of 1604
MERRY: Mindwell spouse of 57
MIELKE: Carl Arthur 1722, Carl Arthur child of 1722, Dennis Richard child of 1724, Douglas Edward child of 1724, Joy Anne child of 1722, Julius Edward 1721, Karen Anne child of 1724, Linda Jane child of 1722, Lula Eleanor 1723, Vernon Walter 1724, William August 1720, William Julius spouse of 1261, William Samuel "Butch" child of 1722
MILES: Eleanor parent of spouse of 172, Eleanor parent of spouse of 431, Jonathan spouse of 218, William spouse of 157
MILICENT OF RETHEL see 5
MILLER: Edward spouse of 715, Nancy "Nannie" spouse of 824
MING: James M. spouse of 645, William O. spouse of 643
MITCHELL: Frank L. 989, Ira J. spouse of 669
MOBLEY: --- 1151, Alameda 760, Albert E. 1660, Allen 1190, Alonzo 1203, Alonzo Downy 1649, Alta Florence 1175, Andrew Jackson 1136, Anne Almy 1188, Beatrice 1674, Bertha M. 1651, Blanch 1653, Blanche Julia 1678, Catherine Minerva 767, Charles Henry Raymond child of 1645, Charley Lee child of 1647, Clarence Edward 1675, Clio 1663, Columbus 1187, Daharell child of 1647, Daniel L. 1135, Rev. Darius Arrelian 1172, Delbert R. 1658, Edith K. 1683, Edward 529, Elias 530, Elijah B. 1131, Elizabeth 531, Elizabeth 1637, Elizabeth A. 758, Ella P. 1152, Elsie Ferne 1656, Elsie P. 1208, Elsworth 1640, Emma 1146, Ethel M. 1655, Fasine or Rosina 1147, Gertrude Iris 1676, Gladys Hazel child of 1647, Hadassah Belle 1682, Harriett Ethel 1679, Harry S. 1684, Hester Ellen 1646, Hester Ellen child of 1647, Irwin E. 1659, Isaac 1641, Jacob A. 1137, Jacob A. 1178, James Hunter "Hunt" 1155, Jesse 1130, Jesse 1642, Jesse Ralph 759, Jesse Ralph 1647, Jesse Ralph Jr. child of 1647, Jim 1664, John parent of spouse of 417, John H. 1650, John Henry 762, John Lewis 528,

John Orion 1179, John Orion 1184, John W. 1192, John W. 1639, Laura Josephine 1173, Lawrence Alonzo child of 1647, Leroy 1657, Lettie 1643, Lewis 765, Lewis Dana 1182, Dr. Lewis F. 1206, Lillian Juanita child of 1647, Loran 1153, Loretti Laverne 1652, Luanna Jane 1174, Lucretia 761, Lyda Blanche 1183, Lyman 1145, Mahala 763, Mahala 1138, Margaret A. "Maggie" 1150, Marietta 1185, Mary 1644, Mary 1671, Mary Catherine "Lota" 1677, Mary Frances child of 1647, Mertie E 1181, Minnie May 1177, Monte Belle 1204, Mordecai spouse of 417, Mordecai 532, Nellie 1648, Nina A. 1209, Nina Fay child of 1647, Ollie Jean child of 1647, Ora 1176, Orville 1191, Otto W. 1210, Ozalla P. 1654, Phillip 1134, Philo Darius 1681, Randolf "Randy" 1148, Reason D. 766, Rilla 1193, Rita Florence 1180, Rosamond Ruth 1685, Roy Edward child of 1645, Ruth Ann 1133, Sara Willa 1205, Sarah 764, Theodore T. "Dory" 1149, Thomas G. 1132, Victoria Ellen child of 1647, Viola 1186, Virgil 1673, Virgil child of 1645, Vivian P. 1665, Warren Wesley 769, Warren Wesley 1207, Wayne 1672, William 768, William 1189, William 1638, William Eldon child of 1647, William Henry "Hen" 1154, William Lewis 1680, William R. 1144, William Terriel 1645

MOODY: Ralph spouse of 1140
MOORE: Alexander Compton parent of spouse of 1288, Charles H. parent of spouse of 1290, Ellen Rebecca spouse of 1290, Margaret parent of spouse of 849, Nannie Strother spouse of 1288
MONTFORT: Elizabeth see 5
MORDECAI: Florence 1249, George Patterson 1251, Henry 1253, J. Randolph spouse of 808, John Robinson 1717, Louis 1252, Mary J. 1250, Monte child of 1717, Moses Cohen parent of spouse of 808, Randolph J. 1248
MORGAN: Harold Randolph spouse of 910, Harold Randolph 1318
MORTON: --- spouse of 358
MOSS: Catherine spouse of 526
MULLINS: Josephine spouse of 1025
MURPH: J.H. spouse of 1032
MURPHEY: Florence spouse of 582
MURPHY: Henry S. spouse of 1160
MURRY: Catherine spouse of 1213
MUSE: C. Thomas 1759, Fred R. 1757, Fred Reed spouse of 1326, Helen M. 1755, John M. 1758, Julia A. 1756, William F. 1760
MUSGROVE: Bernard 1694, Brady 1688, Eleanor 1690, Ellsworth 1692, Esther 1691, Harry 1687, Harry Cornelius spouse of 1222, Hezekiah parent of spouse of 1222, Loyd 1689, Margaret Hazel 1686, Pinckney 1693, Sarah 1695
MYERS: Grace spouse of 1154, Mamie spouse of 1329
NAILL: --- spouse of 1756
NASH: George spouse of 1271, George Jr. 1729
NEEDLER: Madonna spouse of 1609
NEFF: Martha parent of spouse of 1112
NEWBY: Charles parent of spouse of 1461, Mary spouse of 1461
NORRIS: Elizabeth 1313, N. Dorsey spouse of 903
NORTON: Aaron spouse of 344
NUNN: Sarah spouse of 181
ODONNELL: Dale child of 1585, Edward spouse of 1585, Floyd child of 1585, Irene child of 1585
OLCOTT: Margaret spouse of 210
ORAM: Joshua spouse of 542, Joshua spouse of 533
OSBORN: Abner 1375, Ada Louella 1345, Adelaide 958, Aevlia? 1768, Albert A. 1782, Albert Emmett child of 1767, Albert W. 1814, Alfria 1343, Amalthea 939, Andrew J. 1361, Andrew Jackson 1801, Andrew Jackson 937, Angeline 1800, Angeline 951, Anna parent of spouse of 616, Annette 1817, Aurena 1341, Brice 1823, Byron W. 963, Caroline M. 1769, Charles A. 1792, Clarissa 942, Comfort 651, Cynthia 949, Daniel 1362, Daniel Boone 1357, Dewey 1802, Dicy Ann 1342, Dora Alice 1348, Dudley E. 1783, Elijah S. 1338, Eliza 1354, Elizabeth 1332, Elizabeth 941, Elizabeth 650, Elmira 947, Emma 1816, Emmasiah 1821, Emmett A. 1767, Eva Augusta 1781, Finis 1378, Francis 1358, Francis Marion 1337, Francis N. 1788, George 960, Green 952, Hannah parent of spouse of 633, Henry C. 1351, Hester 652, Hiram 1363, Hiram spouse of 635, Homer M. 1790, Isaac 1334, Isaac 1820, Isaac 1367, James 1364, James 1818, James 617, James spouse of 627, James 631, James parent of spouse of 474, Jasper 1369, Joanna 632, John 1349, John 1353, John 934, John 1368, John 618, Jonathan spouse of 474, Jonathan B. 945, Joseph 628, Joseph 616, Joseph 1330, Joseph 1355, Joseph 1379, Joseph 956, Josephine 1784, Julia Ann 944, Lewis 961, Lorina 1347, Louisa 1780, Louisa 1339, Louisa 1374, Lucinda 1344, Lulu E. 1791, Lurilla 955, Lydia 1333, Lydia 933, Lydia 1370, M. Jane 1340, Mahala 623, Malinda 954, Malona S. 1772, Margaret 1799, Martha 1365, Martha 962, Martha 634, Martha C. 946, Mary 953, Mary A. 957, Mary A. 653, Mary Catherine 635, Mary Jane 1352, Mary Smith 1336, McDonald spouse of 950, Milton N. 1771, Nancy 1335, Naomi 629, Nellie Filena 1785, Noah 943, Noah 620, Noah Webster 1350, Parthena A. 1786, Phillip 959, Rachel parent of spouse of 937, Rachel A. 1376, Richard 621, Robert 1366, Robert Patient 940, Roena Evaline or Estaline 1787, Ruth spouse of 617, Ruth 627, Sabrina 936, Samuel M. 622, Sarah 1360, Sarah 1815, Sarah 619, Sarah Almeda 1346, Serena 950, Solomon 464, Solomon parent of spouse of 627, Solomon 932, Solomon 938, Stephen 1377, Stephen 649, Stephen Jones 935, Susannah 1359, Susannah 1822, Tabitha 625, Teressa Emaline 1789, Thomas 636, W. T. 1766, William 1819, William 624, William M. 1331, William R. 1770, Willis P. 1813, Xanthus L. 1773, Zachariah 630
OSBORNE: Ada Lucrecia child of 1807, Addie Ella

1806, Albert A. 1810, Andrew Jackson 1356, Archie child of 1804, Armina 1808, Arthur Selvester 1804, Comfort 641, Elizabeth 638, Elizabeth parent of spouse of 24, Elizabeth "Betsey" 474, Elsie child of 1804, Enoch 633, Ephraim spouse of 933, Gen. Ephraim Sr. parent of spouse of 176, Esther Louise 475, Hannah parent of spouse of 628, Hirum 639, James 469, James Percival child of 1807, Jane 637, Jemima 473, Jemima 645, John 472, John parent of spouse of 933, John 647, John Albert 1809, John Ernest child of 1807, Jonathan 467, Joseph Merle child of 1807, Joseph William 1807, Lucinda 646, Lydia Adella 1803, Malinda 644, Marvin child of 1804, Mary Alfretta 1805, Mary Ann "Polly" 643, Mary "Polly" 465, Myrtle child of 1804, Oscar Sylvester child of 1807, Robert 466, Robert parent of spouse of 617, Robert Lee child of 1807, Rosebud Jane child of 1807, Sarah "Sally" 471, Sarah "Sally" 642, Stephen spouse of 176, Stephen 640, Viola 1811, Violet 1812, Virginia Jane "Jenny" 468, William 470

OURSLER: Nellie spouse of 1720

OWINGS: Gillis C. spouse of 1839, Thomas parent of spouse of 1839, Urath Cromwell parent of spouse of 560

PAGENSTECHER: Helen A. spouse of 1285

PARGIN: James parent of spouse of 523, Sarah Ann spouse of 523

PARRAN: Mary Elizabeth "Mamie" spouse of 834

PARRITT: Hazel spouse of 1649

PATTERSON: Florence 815, George spouse of 546, George 814, Mary Jane "Jennie" spouse of 612, William "Billy" parent of spouse of 546

PATTON: Frances E. spouse of 766

PAUL: Isaac spouse of 496

PAYNE: --- spouse of 809, --- spouse of 1005, Sam spouse of 1006

PEARCE: Anna Elizabeth 1279, Bertie Cook 1277, Charles Cockey 836, Elias Joseph 833, George Marshall 834, John Gorsuch spouse of 556, John L. "Acre" spouse of 825, John Thomas 832, Mary Evelyn 1280, Mary Virginia 835, Mildred Elizabeth 1278, William Brown 831

PEASE: Dorothy spouse of 203, Noadiah spouse of 202

PECKINPAUGH: Felix spouse of 1590, Mary Kathryn child of 1590, William Edward child of 1590

PENNINGTON: Moses parent of spouse of 616, Nancy spouse of 616

PERCIVAL: Mary Virginia spouse of 1807

PERRY: Ann Waters spouse of 434, Basil Magruder parent of spouse of 434

PETERSON: Abraham Sr. parent of spouse of 728, Benjamin 1079, Charlotte 1083, Cornelius spouse of 728, Eli 1081, Elmira 1077, John L. 1076, Lucy 1080, Lydia 1075, Mary Jane 1082, Sarah 1078, Selinda 1084

PETTIT: --- spouse of 619

PHILLIPS: Elizabeth spouse of 30, Jane spouse of 626, John B. spouse of 1163, Commander Samuel parent of spouse of 30

PHIPPS: Joseph spouse of 1075, Martha S. spouse of 1076

PHOEBUS: Annie M. spouse of 1072, Charles Edward parent of spouse of 1072

PICKETT: Emily Jones spouse of 1576

PIGGOT: Dr. Aaron parent of spouse of 849, Dr. Cameron spouse of 849, Charles Snowden 1291, William Cameron 1292

PILKINGTON: Lydia spouse of 1079

PITTMAN: Florence spouse of 1827

PLATT: Sarah spouse of 239

POHLMAN: Elizabeth spouse of 1719

POINTER: Nancy Ann spouse of 1142

POLLARD: Eliza parent of spouse of 977

POPE: Emma spouse of 828

PORTER: Anna spouse of 36, Gilchrist spouse of 567, Julia 863, Margaret D. 864, Mary Eleanor 862

POWELL: Deborah Stansbury spouse of 452, Capt. John parent of spouse of 452, Lee parent of spouse of 1463, Mabel Cora spouse of 1463, Mary spouse of 1002

PREVOST: Charles Henry spouse of 1824, Eva Josephine child of 1824

PRICE: Ernest spouse of 1498, Mary Caroline spouse of 466, Mary Caroline parent of spouse of 617

PRIEBE: Annie Mary 1839, Annie Mary child of 1840, August William spouse of 1570, Elsie 1849, Freddie 1850, Gayle child of 1841, Henry 1848, Herman Brown 1846, Herman C. parent of spouse of 1570, Herman C. parent of spouse of 1572, Herman H. spouse of 1572, Judith Ann child of 1840, Kevin Arthur child of 1842, Lawrence William child of 1842, Lillian May 1844, Louise 1843, Margaret 1847, Nancy Lee child of 1840, Ronald Steven child of 1842, Rosalie 1845, Russell 1841, Sandra Faye child of 1841, Susan Lorraine child of 1842, Sylvan Augustus 1840, William Courtney 1842

PRIOR: John spouse of 332

PROCTOR: Dewey spouse of 1828

PUE: Dr. Arthur Jr. spouse of 702

PUMPHREY: Edward spouse of 708

RADER: Dorothea Elizabeth spouse of 901

RAINS: Emma F. spouse of 1096

RAMSOWER: Eliza spouse of 722

RANDALL: Christopher parent of spouse of 96, Susannah spouse of 96

RANDOLPH: Cora Belle 1453, Ella Mae 1450, Eula Tobitha 1454, Holland Coffey spouse of 1016, James Bedford 1456, James Mayberry parent of spouse of 1016, Joseph Edwin 1451, Laura Alice 1449, Olive Louisa 1448, Ora Vivian 1452, Raymond Coffee 1455, William Wirt 1457

RATHBURN: --- spouse of 305

RAY: Anne spouse of 494, Mary Ann spouse of 1437

REGINLINDE: see 5

REGISTER: Henry spouse of 1293
REICH: Benjamin Franklin 841, Dorcas H. spouse of 555, Elenore 840, John parent of spouse of 557, Lucy Brown 838, Phillip parent of spouse of 555, Phillip Valentine 839, William spouse of 557, William John 837
REISTER: Susannah parent of spouse of 609
REYNOLDS: Robert spouse of 1010
RHORER: Julia Anna spouse of 765
RIBBLE: Lorain parent of spouse of 580
RICH: Anne spouse of 19, Richard parent of spouse of 19
RICHMOND: Baby 667, Caroline Ann 661, Comfort 662, Elizabeth "Betsy" 657, Esther 659, Fanny 658, Isaac spouse of 475, Isaac 660, Jane 665, John Jr. parent of spouse of 470, Jonathan 655, Louisa 666, Matilda spouse of 469, Matilda "Fanny" spouse of 469, Polly Ann Sublett 664, Rebecca spouse of 470, Rebecca Sherrill 663, Sarah 654, William spouse of 654, William 656
RIDGELY: David parent of spouse of 817, Mary spouse of 817, Samuel spouse of 687
RIGGS: Achsah spouse of 182, Electa spouse of 388, John parent of spouse of 182
RINARD: Rhoda spouse of 1097
RISINGER: Rilla spouse of 1148
RITTER: Viola Jeanette spouse of 1302
ROBB: George parent of spouse of 730, Lavina spouse of 730
ROBERTS: Desire spouse of 119, Elisha spouse of 339, Hannah spouse of 342, Jalie Wood spouse of 672, Nathan parent of spouse of 672
ROBERTSON: John spouse of 625
ROBINSON: Champe Moncure spouse of 1251
RODERICK: Solomon spouse of 1080, William spouse of 1078
ROGERS: Charles Butler spouse of 851, Nathan parent of spouse of 851
ROLLER: Jacob spouse of 1710
ROOD: Joseph spouse of 261
ROOT: Ruth spouse of 286
ROSCOE: India spouse of 1155
ROSIER: Jacob spouse of 1380, Minora Angeline 1824
ROWLAND: Jesse spouse of 1854
ROWLINSON: Ira spouse of 354
ROYER: Elizabeth A. parent of spouse of 1839
RUSSELL: Joseph spouse of 230, Mignonette Anne spouse of 1576
RUTHERFORD: A.J. spouse of 1186
RYAN: Mary F. spouse of 769
RYNEARSON: Robert spouse of 1629
SALLADE: Mary spouse of 1356
SANDERS: Elizabeth spouse of 668
SAVAGE: Mary spouse of 9, see 5
SCHAEFER: Walter parent of spouse of 1686, Walter Elmer spouse of 1686
SCHROEDER: Addie spouse of 842

SCHULTZ: Amelia spouse of 871
SCOTT: Ellen spouse of 893
SCOVILLE: Stephen spouse of 336
SCRIVNOR: Nancy spouse of 408
SEARS: Charles spouse of 397
SELBY: Ellen Roseanne spouse of 779, Hannah parent of spouse of 527, Melinda spouse of 782, Richard parent of spouse of 782
SELLEW: Deacon John spouse of 221, Philip spouse of 212
SELLMAN: Rachel spouse of 730
SETTLERS: Elva spouse of 1840
SHANKS: Mrs. Emma spouse of 836
SHAW: Mary spouse of 621
SHELTON: --- spouse of 1384, Tabitha Jerucha parent of spouse of 1016
SHIPLEY: Ada Waltz 1235, Adam parent of spouse of 90, Birdie Selvena 1236, Charles H. Jr. 1714, Charles Howard 1242, Clara Josephine 1239, Connie child of 1708, Dolores May 1710, Dorothy child of 1707, Ethel 1700, Florence (Edna May) 1241, Franklin child of 1707, Franklin F. 1240, Franklin F. Jr. 1707, Henry Baskum parent of spouse of 822, "Dr." Jabez spouse of 794, Kenneth child of 1708, Kenneth H. 1709, Lee child of 1708, Leroy 1708, Louise parent of spouse of 579, Mabel C. 1706, Mildred 1715, Osko R. 1234, Osko R. 1699, Patricia child of 1707, Ronald child of 1707, Roy Leroy 1238, Samuel spouse of 714, Susannah spouse of 90, Susannah R. spouse of 822, Thelma May 1713, Viola R. 1701, Walter Alaska 1237, Walter J. 1698, William child of 1707
SHIPMAN: Asahel or Azel 388, Benjamin 387, Elizabeth 389, Lois 386, Phebe 390, Samuel spouse of 146, Stephen 391
SHIRLEY: Eleanor spouse of 5, John see 5, Ralph parent of spouse of 5, Robert see 5, Sir Robert see 5
SHOEMAKER: Inez spouse of 869
SHRYOCK: Christian spouse of 558, Henrietta 843, Leonora P. "Lena" 844, William Brown 842
SIMPSON: Julian spouse of 935
SIZAR?: Lucrecia spouse of 402
SLADE: Olivia "Ollie" spouse of 597
SMITH: Abraham 196, Abraham 197, Achsah 205, Agnes 1283, Anne 208, Anthony spouse of 684, Asaph 203, Bathsheba 209, Benjamin spouse of 47, Benjamin 195, Betty Jean child of 1580, Dicey spouse of 932, Dorothy 220, Eleanor Frances 1282, Elihu 200, Elizabeth spouse of 70, Elizabeth 212, Gordon 1284, H. Gates spouse of 838, Hannah 207, Howard Arrington spouse of 1580, Howard Arrington Jr. child of 1580, Hugh Bell spouse of 982, Irene 201, Isaac 198, Israel 199, Jared Dunklin parent of spouse of 1856, Jedidiah 217, Jeduthan 103, Jeduthan 211, Jemima 219, Lucy 218, Manoah 104, Margaret Virginia spouse of 1856, Margaret Virginia spouse of 1855, Marion Francis child of 1774, Martha spouse of 1190, Mary 206, Mercy 215, Nathan spouse of 233,

Olive Irene spouse of 1829, Peter E. spouse of 1342, Phillip F. parent of spouse of 1580, Prudence 214, Richard 102, Ruth 213, Sally 1388, Samuel 204, Sarah 221, Solomon 1774, Thankful 216, Thomas 210, Tirzah 202, William Raleigh spouse of 1333

SNOWDEN: Col. Francis parent of spouse of 172, Col. Francis parent of spouse of 431, Mary "Polly" spouse of 172, Mary "Polly" parent of spouse of 433, Susannah spouse of 431, Susannah parent of spouse of 564

SOTHORON: Florence Lydia spouse of 1289, Rev. Levin parent of spouse of 1289

SOUDER: Christianna "Ann" spouse of 631

SOUTHARD: James Carson child of 1728, William W. Jr. 1728, William Wilson spouse of 1265

SPEAR: Dorcas parent of spouse of 546

SPILLMAN: Rebecca Ann spouse of 524

STALEY: Charles E. 1510, John W. 1511, Louisa C. 1507, Margaret I. 1509, Peter spouse of 711, Warfield D. 1050, William H. 1508

STANFORD: Philip spouse of 949

STANSBURY: Ann parent of spouse of 452

STARK: Margaret Elizabeth spouse of 1546

STARR: Anna spouse of 633, John or James parent of spouse of 633

STAUBUS: Alma Virginia 1828, Christian Wilhelm parent of spouse of 1381, Christian Wilhelm parent of spouse of 1383, Clara Mae 1825, George Washington spouse of 1381, George Washington Jr. 1827, John Henry 1829, Mary Etta "Dolly" 1826, William A. spouse of 1383

STAUNTON: Margaret see 5

STEELE: Andrew parent of spouse of 445, Florence Elizabeth 586, Margaret 584, Samuel B. 587, Col. Samuel Bledsoe spouse of 445, Susannah 588, Teresa 585, Thomas 589

STEVENS: Aaron 149, Aaron 152, Aaron 402, Abigail 156, Abigail 400, Ann spouse of 318, Constance spouse of 1708, Daniel 399, Diana 397, Elnathan 396, Hannah 150, Hannah 155, Huldah 398, John 153, Mary 158, Phebe 401, Robert 154, Sarah 157, Thomas spouse of 75, Thomas 151

STEVENSON: Emily M. spouse of 1242

STEWART: Cynthia spouse of 622, Fielding W. spouse of 941, John parent of spouse of 464, Mary "Polly" spouse of 464, Mary "Polly" parent of spouse of 627, Sarah "Sally" parent of spouse of 933, Thomas H. spouse of 650

STILSON: Cornelia Luella "Nellie" spouse of 1662

STINEHAGEN: Rebecca parent of spouse of 1222

STIVERS: Arthur S. spouse of 1279, Elizabeth Jeannie 1731

STOCKSDALE: Annie 861, Annie Howard 910, Annie Ida 903, Arthur Lee 914, Catherine spouse of 165, Clara May 909, Dolly Maud 908, Edmund Howard parent of spouse of 454, Edmund Howard parent of spouse of 455, Edmund Howard 614, Edward parent of spouse of 165, Elias Cockey 609, Elias Cockey 919, Elizabeth Jane 1314, Emma R. 902, Florence 860, George Tevis 907, Georgia Virginia 900, Gertrude 913, Harry Cockey 906, Harry Cockey 899, Howard Hewett 915, John Hitchens 1312, John Thomas Cockey 608, John Thomas Cockey 911, Lewis Henry 605, Lillie Eliza 912, Louisianna 904, Mordecai Bramwell 901, Mordecai Cockey spouse of 566, Mordecai Cockey 604, Rebecca 603, Rebecca Jane 917, Rebecca Jane 920, Ruth Ann Elizabeth 613, Solomon spouse of 455, Solomon parent of spouse of 601, Solomon Tevis 611, Stephen Brown spouse of 601, Stephen Brown 612, Stephen Thomas 607, Susannah 918, Thomas Edward spouse of 454, Thomas Edward parent of spouse of 566, Thomas Franklin 606, William G. 905, William Jackson 610, William Vinton 916

STOW: Phebe spouse of 228, Phebe spouse of 320, Samuel spouse of 290

STROEBEL: George spouse of 1089

STUMP: Leroy L. spouse of 920

STURGILL: Francis Harvey spouse of 661

SYBIL: see 5

SULLIVAN: Hannah R. spouse of 727, Richard parent of spouse of 727

TALBOTT: Alice parent of spouse of 93

TATE: Catherine Curtis 1631, Curtis L. spouse of 1106, Garnet Zelma 1630, Orlia Arthur 1632, Ruby Thelma 1629

TAYLOR: Alton Edward child of 1589, Aubrey Brown child of 1589, Faith child of 1589, Francis Edward spouse of 1589, Grace Belle child of 1589, Harry S. spouse of 829, Harry S. spouse of 1274, John spouse of 760, Louise E. spouse of 1206, Sarah Eloise child of 1589

TERRY: Belle parent of spouse of 1461

TEVIS: Naomi spouse of 164, Robert parent of spouse of 164

THOMPSON: Bertha Alice spouse of 1603, Charles spouse of 1212, Dovie spouse of 1023, Susie E. spouse of 822, Thomas spouse of 732

THOMSON: Cora A. 1529, Ethel 1530, James F. spouse of 1056, John C. 1531, Kate A. 1534, Mary Edna 1533, Maud 1535, Susan E. 1532

THURSTON: Ida M. spouse of 1564

TILDEN: Emily S. spouse of 724

TILLSON: Mollie spouse of 1039

TILYARD: Alfred A. spouse of 559, Charles H. 846, Dorothy 1300, Florence Patterson 858, Irene 857, John S. 845, Mattie 847, Mattie Virginia 855, Phillip H. spouse of 561, Tyson 854, Walter 856, Walter Robert 1301

TINKER: Harry spouse of 1346

TODD: --- spouse of 184, --- 1055, Adie 1543, Alexander spouse of 183, Alexander 505, Alexander 709, Alexander 722, Anna 712, Anna M. 1552, Anna R. 1559, Basil 503, Ben Ive 1564, Benjamin 502,

Benjamin 1061, Benjamin Warfield 1058, Cachel 1060, Charles 1563, Charles W. 1550, Charles Warfield 723, David Withrow 1049, Edna 711, Elizabeth 504, Elizabeth 707, Ellen M. 1549, Ellen Warfield 1064, Emma 1562, Frank B. 1551, George W. 717, Henrietta 1069, Henrietta Jackson 1066, Henry Barramore spouse of 1278, Howard 720, Ira A. 1052, James F. 1553, JamesForrest 1065, Janet 704, Janet 1054, Jennie 1561, Jesse Lee 1544, John 1557, John H. 705, John W. 1554, Josefa Frye 1555, Joshua 506, Joshua 719, Lucy 715, Margaret A. 1056, Martha Alice 1059, Mary Ann 703, Mary Elizabeth 1063, Mary Ellen 1051, Nancy 708, Nancy PEARCE 1730, Nellie 1560, Rachel 508, Rachel 714, Rachel Ruth 1053, Samuel 507, Samuel 710, Samuel 721, Sarah 1070, Sarah A. 706, Susan 716, Susan 1558, Susanah Cevelah 1057, Susannah 510, Sydney Jane 1062, Upton B. 1565, Vachel 713, Vachel B. 724, Vachel H. 1068, Warfield 509, Warfield Benjamin 1067, William 718, Wilson 1566

TORMAS: --- spouse of 1653
TOWNER: Nathaniel H. spouse of 951
TRAYLOR: Edith spouse of 1611
TREADWAY: Margaret parent of spouse of 164
TREAT: John spouse of 206, Mary spouse of 199, Mary spouse of 217, Stephen spouse of 225
TREGALLAS: Samuel spouse of 844, Samuel Staley 1285
TRIMM: Charles W. spouse of 953
TRIPLETT: Blanche spouse of 1721
TROTT: Blanche spouse of 1259
TROWBRIDGE: Ebenezer spouse of 110, Ebenezer 234, Hannah 233, Mary 236, Sarah 235
TUCKER: Arthur B. 1523, Dewit 1528, Effie Kate 1525, Hannah spouse of 28, Henry parent of spouse of 41, Jepthah Entler spouse of 1053, Jesse 1526, John parent of spouse of 28, Lee Forest 1524, Margaret 1527, Mary spouse of 41, Sarah spouse of 43
TURNER: Abraham spouse of 139, Elizabeth 373, Ezra 371, Martha 372, Ollie May spouse of 1647, Viola Ruth parent of spouse of 1825
TURNIDGE: William J. spouse of 1789
TWIST: Ann 428, Charlotte 427, Eliza E. 801, Elizabeth 424, Elizabeth companion of 167, Hillary 543, James 800, John 799, Margaret 544, Mary Ann 426, Norbury G. 802, Rachel 430, Rebecca 429, Rebecca 797, Samuel 803, Sarah 804, William 425, William H. 798
VANCE: David parent of spouse of 586, Zebulon Baird spouse of 586
VEASY: Minnie Mae spouse of 1437
VERMILLION: Sarah A. spouse of 1356
VOGT: --- spouse of 1755
WADE: M.C. spouse of 463
WADSWORTH: William spouse of 219
WAITMAN: Solomon parent of spouse of 1100
WAITMAN JARRETT: Bertha Etta spouse of 1100
WAKEFIELD: Almeda 967, Dianna 969, George Washington 971, George Washington spouse of 632, John Allen 965, Martha Adeline 968, Ruth Emma 970, Susan 966, William 964
WALKER: Frances child of 1646, William spouse of 1646
WAMPLER: Sarah parent of spouse of 1102
WARFIELD: Azel parent of spouse of 175, Dinah parent of spouse of 495, Elizabeth Ann 463, Dr. Evan parent of spouse of 850, Dr. George F. 458, George Frazier spouse of 175, Lewis 457, Mary E. parent of spouse of 439, Mary Thomas "Mamie" spouse of 850, Rebecca 462, Susannah 461, Warner W. 459, William H. 460
WARNER: Ruth spouse of 231
WARREN: James spouse of 671
WATERS: Agnes 1736, Delilah Elizabeth parent of spouse of 434, Eleanor Mildred 1734, Robert O. spouse of 1282, Robert O. 1735
WATKINS: William Chamberlain spouse of 855
WATTS: Ellinor spouse of 24, Mary A. spouse of 1364, Richard parent of spouse of 24
WEBB: John spouse of 1332, John S. spouse of 1344
WEBBER: Emma Amelia spouse of 1703
WEBSTER: Joshua spouse of 214, Permelia spouse of 1804
WEEKS: Aaron W. spouse of 677, Lula 1486, Samuel 1028
WELLER: Zaccheus spouse of 251
WERTH: Sally Ann 1746, Virginia Lee 1745, William Maury spouse of 1294
WESTIN: --- spouse of 1764
WHALEN: Marian Louise spouse of 1724, Martha spouse of 609, William parent of spouse of 609
WHISLER: Mary Ann parent of spouse of 1100
WHITE: Archibald spouse of 974, Cora B. spouse of 1155, Malissa Ellen spouse of 737
WHITMORE: Isabel spouse of 57
WHITTAKER: Mary parent of spouse of 474
WICHTERMAN: David child of 1710, Denny child of 1710, Ernest spouse of 1710, Richard child of 1710
WILCOX: Rebecca spouse of 304
WILFONG: Frances Rosetta spouse of 1774
WILHEIMS: Samuel P. spouse of 1336
WILKERSON: Samuel spouse of 1826, Tabitha spouse of 647
WILKINSON: Darlene child of 1608, Earl spouse of 1608, Helen Delmaya child of 1608, Margaret spouse of 1108
WILLCOCK WILCOX: Mary E. spouse of 538
WILLIAM I THE LION: see 5
WILLIAMS: Anderson spouse of 662, Ida 1777, Jacob spouse of 1083, James O. spouse of 983, James William spouse of 577, John Samuel 1775, Minnie 1779, Prudence spouse of 136, Samuel H. spouse of 1336, Samuel Kingston 1776, William Mead 1778

WILLOUGHBY: Eleanor see 5, Hugh see 5
WILLSON: Sarah spouse of 194
WILSON: Anna Catherine spouse of 1793, Eliza Jane spouse of 1027, John G. spouse of 1146, P.M. spouse of 1029, William spouse of 651
WINKLER: Fred parent of spouse of 1616, Marjorie Elizabeth spouse of 1616
WINN: William spouse of 664
WITHROW: Elizabeth spouse of 709
WOODRUFF: John spouse of 266
WOODWARD: Geneva L. spouse of 1597
WORF: Rev. William spouse of 1496
WORTHINGTON: Comfort parent of spouse of 440
WRIGHT: Albert W. spouse of 1175, Chester 1666, Christina spouse of 630, J. Taylor spouse of 1150, Joseph spouse of 944, LaVern 1668, Lorene 1669, Mabel 1667, Mary spouse of 631, Samuel spouse of 208, Susan Elizabeth spouse of 1081
WYSONG: Sarah spouse of 736
YORK: Henry A. spouse of 1628
YOST: Phoebe Alberta Bertha spouse of 1149
YOUNG: Loney spouse of 1582
YOX: Annie spouse of 907, Rosse spouse of 926
ZENZ: Matilda Ann spouse of 540

www.ingramcontent.com/pod-product-compliance
Lightning Source LLC
Chambersburg PA
CBHW080409300426
44113CB00015B/2451